McMahon Line: Then and Now

McMahon Line
Then and Now

Dr. Amitabh Bhatt

PRASHANT PUBLISHING HOUSE
DELHI-110094

Published by :
PRASHANT PUBLISHING HOUSE
C-34, 28 Foota Road, Gali-3,
West Karwal Nagar, Delhi-110094
Phone : 011-22963970, Mob. : 9810396373, 8826258746
e-mail.: prashantpublishinghouse@gmail.com

McMahon Line: Then and Now

First Published 2020

ISBN : 978-93-88526-26-5

PRINTED IN INDIA
Published by Mr. R.K. Jha M/s Prashant Publishing House and Published at H.S. Offset House Press, Delhi.

Preface

The McMahon Line is the demarcation line between the Tibetan region of China and the North-east region of India proposed by British colonial administrator Henry McMahon at the 1914 Simla Convention signed between British and Tibetan representatives. It is currently the effective boundary between China and India, although its legal status is disputed by the Chinese government.

In 1826, British India gained a common border with China after the British wrested control of Manipur and Assam from the Burmese, following the First Anglo-Burmese War of 1824–1826. In 1847, Major J. Jenkins, agent for the North East Frontier, reported that the Tawang was part of Tibet. In 1872, four monastic officials from Tibet arrived in Tawang and supervised a boundary settlement with Major R. Graham, NEFA official, which included the Tawang Tract as part of Tibet.

Thus, in the last half of the 19th century, it was clear that the British treated the Tawang Tract as part of Tibet. This boundary was confirmed in a 1 June 1912 note from the British General Staff in India, stating that the "present boundary (demarcated) is south of Tawang, running westwards along the foothills from near Ugalguri to the southern Bhutanese border." A 1908 map of The Province of Eastern Bengal and Assam prepared for the Foreign Department of the Government of India, showed the international boundary from Bhutan continuing to the Baroi River, following the Himalayas foothill alignment.

India and China, both amongst the largest and most populous nations of the world, share over two thousand miles of common border; the exact figure is difficult to ascertain because of border disputes. India, the seventh largest and second most populous nation in the world, lays at the southern extension of Asia. China, the third largest and most populous nation of the world, occupies central and western Asia. The length of the China-India border increased dramatically following the 1950-51 annexation of Tibet into the People's Republic of China. The roots of the disputed border between the two nations extend back into the 19th Century. Two general areas were in contention: the northeast border areas of Kashmir (including Aksai Chin), the northern section of India on China's south-western border; and the North East Frontier Agency (NEFA), the northeastern portion of India, on China's southern border.

The Sino-Indian War also known as the Sino-Indian Border Conflict was a war between China and India that occurred in 1962. A disputed Himalayan border was the main pretext for war, but other issues played a role. There had been a series of violent border incidents after the 1959 Tibetan uprising, when India had granted asylum to the Dalai Lama. India initiated a Forward Policy in which it placed outposts along the border, including several north of the McMahon Line, the eastern portion of a Line of Actual Control proclaimed by Chinese Premier Zhou Enlai in 1959.

The McMahon Line is regarded by India as the legal national border, but China rejects the Simla Accord and the McMahon Line, contending that Tibet was not a sovereign state and therefore did not have the power to conclude treaties. Chinese maps show some 65,000 square kilometres (25,000 sq mi) of the territory south of the line as part of the Tibet Autonomous Region, known as South Tibet in China. Chinese forces briefly occupied this area during the Sino-Indian War of 1962. China does recognise a Line of Actual Control which closely approximates most of the "so called McMahon line" in the eastern part of its border with India, according to a 1959 diplomatic note by Prime Minister Zhou Enlai.

This is a reference book. All the matter is just compiled and edited in nature, taken from the various sources which are in public domain.

It is hoped that the book will serve the purpose of students and scholars on the subject and can be useful to them in allied fields.

—Editor

Contents

	Preface	(*v*)
1.	Introduction	1
2.	The McMahon Line	23
3.	The Collision of the Sino-Indian War	51
4.	Sino-Indian Border Dispute and Their Competitive Symbiotic Relationship	93
5.	The McMahon Line: India-China and Tibet Policy	127
6.	Aksai Chin : The Sino-Indian Boundary Partition	187
7.	Line of Actual Control	222
8.	Facts Behind China-India Border Dispute and McMahon Line	240
	Bibliography	271
	Index	275

1

Introduction

The cause of the war was a dispute over the sovereignty of the widely separated Aksai Chin and Arunachal Pradesh border regions. Aksai Chin, claimed by India to belong to Kashmir and by China to be part of Xinjiang, contains an important road link that connects the Chinese regions of Tibet and Xinjiang. China's construction of this road was one of the triggers of the conflict.

THE MCMAHON LINE

British India and China gained a common border in 1826, with British annexation of Assam in the Treaty of Yandabo at the conclusion of the First Anglo-Burmese War (1824–1826). Subsequent annexations in further Anglo-Burmese Wars expanded China's borders with British India eastwards, to include the border with what is now Myanmar.

In 1913–14, representatives of Britain, China, and Tibet attended a conference in Simla, India and drew up an agreement concerning Tibet's status and borders. The McMahon Line, a proposed boundary between Tibet and India for the eastern sector, was drawn by British negotiator Henry McMahon on a map attached to the agreement. All three representatives initiated the agreement, but Beijing soon objected to the proposed Sino-Tibet boundary and repudiated the agreement, refusing to sign the final, more detailed map. After approving a note which stated that China could not enjoy rights under the agreement unless she ratified it, the British and Tibetan negotiators signed the Simla Convention and more detailed map as a bilateral accord. Neville Maxwell states that McMahon had been instructed not to sign bilaterally with Tibetans if China refused, but he did so without the Chinese representative present and then kept the declaration secret.

V.K. Singh argues that the basis of these boundaries, accepted by British India and Tibet, were that the historical boundaries of India were the Himalayas and the areas south of the Himalayas were traditionally Indian and associated with India. The high watershed of the Himalayas was proposed as the border between India and its northern neighbours. India's government held the view that the Himalayas were the ancient boundaries of the Indian subcontinent and thus should be the modern boundaries of British India and later the Republic of India.

Chinese boundary markers, including one set up by the newly created Chinese Republic, stood near Walong until January 1914, when T. O'Callaghan, an assistant administrator of North East Frontier Agency (NEFA)'s eastern sector, relocated them north to locations closer to the McMahon Line (albeit still South of the Line). He then went to Rima, met with Tibetan officials, and saw no Chinese influence in the area.

By signing the Simla Agreement with Tibet, the British had violated the Anglo-Russian Convention of 1907, in which both parties were not to negotiate with Tibet, "except through the intermediary of the Chinese Government", as well as the Anglo-Chinese Convention of 1906, which bound the British government "not to annex Tibetan territory." Because of doubts concerning the legal status of the accord, the British did not put the McMahon Line on their maps until 1937, nor did they publish the Simla Convention in the treaty record until 1938.

Rejecting Tibet's 1913 declaration of independence, China argued that the Simla Convention and McMahon Line were illegal and that Tibetan government was merely a local government without treaty-making powers. In 1947, Tibet requested that India recognise Tibetan authority in the trading town of Tawang, south of the McMahon Line. Tibet did not object to any other portion of the McMahon line. In reply, the Indians asked Tibet to continue the relationship on the basis of the previous British Government. Tibetan officials continued to administer Tawang and refused to concede territory during negotiations in 1938. The governor of Assam asserted that Tawang was "undoubtedly British" but noted that it was "controlled by Tibet, and none of its inhabitants have any idea that they are not Tibetan." During World War II, with India's east threatened by Japanese troops and with the threat of Chinese expansionism, British troops secured Tawang for extra defence.

China's claim on areas south of the McMahon Line, encompassed in the NEFA, were based on the traditional boundaries. India believes that the boundaries China proposed in Ladakh and Arunachal Pradesh have no written basis and no documentation of acceptance by anyone apart from China. Indians argue that China claims the territory on the basis that it was under Chinese imperial control in the past, while Chinese argue that India claims the territory on the basis that it was under British imperial control in the past. The last Qing emperor's 1912 edict of abdication authorised its succeeding republican government to form a union of "five peoples, namely, Manchus, Han Chinese, Mongols, Muslims, and Tibetans *together with their territory in its integrity*" However, V.K. Singh cites the presence of the Mauryan Empire and Chola Dynasty in regions India does not place a claim to but which were heavily influenced by Indian culture.

India's claim line in the eastern sector follows the McMahon Line. The line drawn by McMahon on the detailed 24–25 March 1914 Simla Treaty maps clearly starts at 27°45′40"N, a trijunction between Bhutan, China, and India, and from there, extends eastwards.

Most of the fighting in the eastern sector before the start of the war would take place immediately north of this line. However, India claimed that the *intent* of the treaty was to follow the main watershed ridge divide of the Himalayas based on memos from McMahon and the fact that over 90 per cent of the McMahon Line does in fact follow the main watershed ridge divide of the Himalayas.

They claimed that territory south of the high ridges here near Bhutan (as elsewhere along most of the McMahon Line) should be Indian territory and north of the high ridges should be Chinese territory. In the Indian claim, the two armies would be separated from each other by the highest mountains in the world.

During and after the 1950s, when India began patrolling this area and mapping in greater detail, they confirmed what the 1914 Simla agreement map depicted: six river crossings that interrupted the main Himalayan watershed ridge. At the westernmost location near Bhutan north of Tawang, they modified their maps to extend their claim line northwards to include features such as Thag La ridge, Longju, and Khinzemane as Indian territory.

Thus, the Indian version of the McMahon Line moves the Bhutan-China-India trijunction north to 27°51′30"N. India would claim that the treaty map ran along features such as Thag La ridge, though the actual treaty map itself is topographically vague (as the treaty was not accompanied with demarcation) in places, shows a straight line (not a watershed ridge) near Bhutan and near Thag La, and the treaty includes no verbal description of geographic features nor description of the highest ridges.

HISTORIC ROOTS - EARLY BORDER CLAIMS

India and China, both amongst the largest and most populous nations of the world, share over two thousand miles of common border; the exact figure is difficult to ascertain because of border disputes. India, the seventh largest and second most populous nation in the world, lays at the southern extension of Asia. China, the third largest and most populous nation of the world, occupies central and western Asia. The length of the China-India border increased dramatically following the 1950-51 annexation of Tibet into the People's Republic of China. The roots of the disputed border between the two nations extend back into the 19th Century. Two general areas were in contention: the northeast border areas of Kashmir (including Aksai Chin), the northern section of India on China's south-western border; and the North East Frontier Agency (NEFA), the northeastern portion of India, on China's southern border.

At the western extremity of the Himalayan Range lies Kashmir, composed of mountains, watersheds and valleys; large sections of this area are uninhabited. Yet in this region, three international disputes have raged in recent decades: the China-India conflict we now examine, the India-Pakistan conflict which resulted in a brief but bloody war in 1965, and the China-Soviet conflict which has smothered since the 1960s. The history of the border claims in Kashmir is complex, and has been thoroughly examined by British historian Alastair Lamb1. However, a brief review of Kashmir's history and of various border claims in Kashmir is relevant in establishing the roots of the 1962 China-India border War. * Propulation and area figures are 1965 figures: India -1,227,180 square miles and 479,000,000 population; China - 3,691,500 square miles and 700,000,000 population.

Because of its strategic location between India, China, Russia and Afghanistan, Kashmir and neighboring Tibet have been the focus of international events in Asia for centuries. In 1720, the Chinese Emperor K'ang Hsi invaded Lhasa, Tibet. Later Mongol invasions into Tibet made China aware of the vulnerability of its border lands. In the late 18th Century, the British East India Company began to explore Tibet as a commercial market; the Chinese reaction thwarted British interests.

In the 19th Century, the expansion of Imperial Russia eastward collided with Manchu expansion westward; this started the Sino-Soviet disputes which continue into the current time. While Imperial Russia tended to prevail in the early disputes, the Chinese people continued to strive for Chinese occupation of all lands which they consider "traditionally Chinese." As Kashmir gained in geographic importance, numerous surveys and border claims arose in the late 19th and early 20th Centuries. In 1904, the British invaded Tibet to thwart what Lord Curzon described as the "Russian Domination of Asia." In 1907, Britain and Russia agreed to a neutral buffer zone, extending from Persia to Tibet, to separate the two empires. Chinese suzerainty over Tibet suited both Russia and England. Soon, Britain pressed for a secondary buffer zone between

Tibet and China—"Inner Tibet"— but China would continue to insist for sovereignty over Tibet. Even as a weakened China approached the Japanese occupation and World War II, she maintained her legal claim to territories she considered art of China.

The post-World War II era saw dramatic change in the area. India acquired independence from Britain and became a sovereign state. However, this process of decolonization saw two new states emerge on the subcontinent: India and Pakistan, and both clashed over Kashmir. At the same time, the Chinese Communists came to power in China. Both India and China were conscious of their new status and of past history. The stage was thus set for India and China to come to conflict over the Aksai Chin area in the Karakoram Mountains of Kashmir. As noted above, the various border claims within the Aksai Chin area are complex. And while China and India disputed the border on two fronts (east in NEFA and west in Aksai Chin, this western border was especially significant, for China had built a military highway—to link Sinkiang and Tibet—here in 1956-57; Peking was adamant in retaining her right to this land. However, China would eventually readily surrender her claims in North East Frontier Agency.

Until the 19th Century, the desolate highlands of Aksai Chin were rarely visited or explored; no major migrations or invasions crossed the Karakoram Range. Until the middle of that century, there was a general understanding that the Karakoram Range separated areas traditionally Indian and Chinese, although no specific attempt was made to Denmark a boundary.

But in 1864, the Kashmir Survey set out to define the boundary; this Survey included both surveying and inquiries to local mountain residents as to the location of the "traditional" boundary. A surveyor, W. H. Johnson, was responsible for the Ladakh-Tibet border in the entire Aksai Chin area. Johnson's work has been severely criticized for gross inaccuracies, with description of his boundary as "patently absurd"; he even extended it eighty miles further north than the Indian claim when she and China came to conflict over the border. Johnson was reprimanded by the British Government for crossing into Khotan without permission, and resigned from the Survey. Despite the criticisms of Johnson, his boundary still appeared on some maps in the late 1860'.

A great watershed range divides the two territories (Turkestan and hashmir). But it will be observed that from the Karakoram Pass eastward to past the meridian of 80o, the line is more finely dotted. This has been done to denote that the boundary is not defined. There has been no authoritative demarcation of it at all; and as the country is quite uninhabited for more than a hundred miles east and west and north and south we cannot apply the principles of representing the state of actual occupation.

We have by the dotted boundary only represented my own opinion of what would be defined were the powers interested to attempt to agree to a boundary.... I can vouch that the boundary marked accurately represents the present state. For this part my information dates from 1871, when I was the Governor of Ladakh. This applies also to the rest of the boundary between the Maharaja's and the Chinese territories. Generally published by governments, usually represent official demarcations of boundaries. Drew's lines were simply his best estimate of an unofficial boundary in this remote mountainous area of Aksai Chin.

Thus, by the late 1870s, there were two Aksai Chin boundaries. One, the Johnson line, was published in Atlases but was clearly inaccurate and may have had some British political pretences. The other—essentially the Drew boundary—was better documented, an alignment based on history, tradition, and surveys in Ladakh. For London, the exact border did not matter, for British interests in Aksai Chin were simply strategic: a buffer between India and Tibet, China, and Russia to the north. Under these circumstances, the specific boundary line was flexible, the key intent only to maintain Britain's buffer zone.

By 1890, the Chinese began to assert their claim to the Karakoram Range as their southern boundary in Sinkiang. In 1892, they placed a pillar of stone and wooden boundary notice on the summit of the harakoram Pass. The Indian Government, in 1907, learned of the Chinese border marker and expressed themselves in favour of the Chinese filling up the "no-man's-land" beyond the Karakoram.... and as seeing no reason to remonstrate with the Chinese over the erection of these boundary marks, though they could not regard them as having any international value, the demarcation not having been undertaken by (Britain and China) jointly.

The British then asked the Chinese to clarify their intentions and ambitions in the Karakoram area, showing the Chinese a Russian map which showed the boundary considerably north of the Karakoram Range—probably the Johnson line—and placing Aksai Chin in Kashmir territory. The Chinese responded with a survey team sent to Aksai Chin; this survey team produced a map showing the karakoram Range as the Sino-Indian boundary, with Aksai Chin as part of China. But the Chinese survey, too, was of poor quality, and did nothing to clarify or to make official the boundary in the Aksai Chin area.

Perhaps the best attempt to resolve the Aksai Chin boundary occurred in 1896; George Macartney, the British representative in Kashgar, brought the issue of the disputed border to the leading Chinese official in Kashgar. Macartney was half-Chinese and spoke fluent Chinese; his father had been advisor to the Chinese Legation in London.

Macartney was loyal to Britain, yet he had a deep understanding of the Chinese. Macartney agreed that the British claims (the Johnson line) were inappropriate, and that if this deserted area were to be divided, then it should be half British and half Chinese. He felt that Aksai Chin proper, north of the Lokzhung Range, was Chinese; south of the Range, British. In the summer of 1898, Lord Elgin's Indian Government incorporated Macartney's ideas into a definite proposal. The proposal asked the Chinese to accept a verbal description of the Kashmir boundary, and that physical demarcation on the ground did not seem necessary in this remote area. The relevant portion of the proposal was as follows:

From the Karakoram Pass the crests of the range run nearly east for about half a degree, and then turn south to a little below the 35th parallel.... Rounding... the source of the Karakash, the line of hills to be followed runs northeast to a point east of Kizil Jilga and from there, in a south-easterly direction, follows the Lak Tsung (Lokzhung) Range until that meets a spur... which has hitherto been shown on our maps as the eastern boundary of Ladakh.

Lord Elgin's proposal was fortunate not only as an attempt to resolve the boundary, but also to stem the growing number of lines demarking the Kashmir border in Aksai Chin. The variety of claims which had evolved by the turn of the century.

On March 14, 1899, Sir Claude MacDonald, the British minister to China, submitted the description of this alignment of the proposed border (in writing, but regretably without any maps) to the Chinese Department of External Affairs in Peking. The MacDonald proposal included the boundary suggested by Macartney, and further added: It will not be necessary to mark out the frontier. The natural frontier is the crest of a range of mighty mountains, a great part of which is inaccessible. It will be sufficient if the two Governments (of Great Britain and China)... enter into an agreement to recognize the frontier as laid down by its clearly marked geographical features.

The Department of External Affairs in Peking communicated the proposal to the Sinkiang Provincial Government. The Sinkiang Government had no objections to the boundary alignment, and the British Legation was informally notified that there were no objections; however, no formal acceptance was forwarded from Peking. By the time the Chinese had responded, the British were beginning to reconsider the proposed boundary; hence, the British made no efforts to secure a formal response to MacDonald's proposal. The Chinese

Communist government of the mid-20th Century would regret that the 1899 Chinese government did not convey a formal acceptance of the MacDonald boundary proposal, the controversial Chinese military road—the key issue which eventually led the two nations to war—lies to the north (the Chinese side) of the 1899 MacDonald line.

The rising British interests which called for a more northern (Johnson line) boundary in Kashmir were clearly not the issue of whether India or China would lay claim to the barren Aksai Chin area; rather, Great Britain simply wanted her border as far north as possible to maximize the buffer zone between British India and Imperial Russia. The Elgin Government, which had rejected the Johnson line and had submitted the 1899 MacDonald proposal, was replaced by Lord Curzon's ministry that year. Lord Curzon, and Lords Minto and Hardinge who followed him, advocated the northern (Johnson) boundary. For the next decade, the British made no attempt to secure either a Chinese definition of the Kashmir boundary or an official boundary agreement with China. From the turn of the century, the Johnson* boundary became accepted British policy. The Chinese Revolution erupted in 1911, toppling the imperial dynasty. In the disorder which followed, the central government's power collapsed in Central Asia. Great Britain and Russia began negotiations regarding the status and boundaries of Kashmir; however, the Bolshevik Revolution of 1917 ended attempts to resolve boundaries in Central Asis. At the end of World War I, British India emerged with the Johnson-Ardagh boundary as its more-or-less official border in Aksai Chin.

In 1927, the Indian Government appears to have decided to adjust their version of the Kashmir frontier border. From *Also known as the Ardagh or Johnson-Ardagh boundary Afghanistan to Karakoram Pass, the Indian Government abandoned the northern Johnson-Ardagh line in favor of a boundary along the Karakoram Range (up to Karakoram Pass); while this would indicate an abandonment of the Ardagh line, the old (Ardagh) line remained on British and Indian maps until about 1950! These maps also continued to show the Johnson-Ardagh line as the Indian boundary around the north of Aksai Chin, even though the border was still never openly discussed with China or Tibet.

By 1940, Britain still had never attempted to establish outposts or exert authority in Aksai Chin; China still considered the territory theirs, as was reflected on Chinese maps. World War II distracted the governments from minor border claims. The bleak and empty reaches of Aksai Chin thus remained without an official boundary between India and China/Tibet. In 1947, the new Indian government took as its boundaries those claimed by Britain for decades; thus, India considered Aksai Chin as part of her state of Kashmir. But the rulers in Peking had other ideas about this. The new regimes, in India and in China, thus would soon find disagreement and conflict over the Ladakh frontier.

Between Aksai Chin and the North East Frontier Agency, there were minor border disputes. In the Spiti, Niti Pass, and Nilang regions—about 200 miles south of Aksai Chin and 100 miles northwest of Nepal—laid several disputed borders.

But the total contested area here was small, about 200 square miles (compared to over 15,000 square miles contested in Aksai Chin). These small areas had practicied dual allegiance to British India and to Tibet for decades. So long as Britain felt that she had enough influence to exclude rival powers in these regions, she was content with an informal boundary on the plains beneath the foothills in the Nilang region. When the Chinese and Indian border disputes arose, the aggression in this middle section was minimal. The western (Aksai Chin) and eastern (NEFA) disputes were far more grave; thus, this disputed middle section came to have only minimal importance in the Border War.

The eastern element of dispute centers around the North East Frontier Agency (NEFA), with a 700 mile border and about 32,000 square miles disputed between India and China. The North East Frontier Agency is a sparsely populated mountainous area in the extreme northeast of India. Britain acquired the territory in 1826 as a result of victory in the First Burmese War; the Treaty of Yandaboo gave all of Assam to the British. The northern section of Assam was to become the North East Frontier Agency. The Tawang Tract, in the western end of NEFA and adjoining east Bhutan, had been heavily influenced by Tibetan culture, religion and government for centuries. Through the 19th Century, the Tawang Tract was an important trade route between India and Tibet; it was this trade route that first attracted British attention here. In the middle of the 19th Century, however, Britain was surprised to learn that Tawang was part of Tibet.

Major J. Jenkins, Agent for the North East Frontier, filed a report in 1847 noting that the Tawang Raja "is a fuedatory of the Raja or Governor of Lassa."* The Tawang Tract boundary was the only one in NEFA to be demarked in the 19th Century. In 1872, four monastic officials from Tibet arrived in Tawang and supervised a boundary settlement with Major R. Graham, NEFA official, which included the Tawang Tract as part of Tibet. Thus, in the last half of the 19th Century, it was clear that the British treated the Tawang Tract as part of Tibet. This boundary was confirmed in a June 1, 1912 note from the British General Staff in India, stating that the "present boundary (demarcated) is south of Tawang, running westwards along the foothills from near Ugalguri to the southern Bhutanese border."

The Bengal Eastern Frontier Regulation of 1873 created the "Inner Line" and the "Outer Line." The Inner Line was an administrative line, in the Assam triba areas, to keep hunters and traders out of the Assam tribal areas; no taxes were collected beyond the Inner Line. The Outer Line was the international boundary of British India. Part of the Outer Line was demarcated, from the Bhutanese border to the Baroi River at latitude 27°, longitude 93° 20'. East of the Baroi, no demarked Outer Line existed; the line was verbally defined as a readily recognizable line along the foot of the hills as far as Nizamghat. However, little publicity was given to the demarcation of the Outer Line. In the 20th Century, the British would attempt to deny that the international border ever followed the foothill alignment. However, a 1908 map of The Province of Eastern Bengal and Assam (32 miles to the inch), prepared for the Foreign Department of the Government of India, showed the international boundary from Bhutan continuing to the Baroi River.

In 1905, Noel Williamson, Assistant Political Officer in Sadiya, argued that British officers should venture further into tribal areas, establish posts, and make the tribes aware of the benefits of British rule in India. Lord Morley, Secretary of State for India, rebuffed this notion because establishment of British posts would be... followed by further progressive annexation to which it would be difficult to set a limit.... At the back of the Abor hills lies foreign territory, Tibet, and between the Abors and Tibet proper there may be tribes which are more or less under Tibetan influence.

Williamson was formally warned not to cross the Outer Line without expressed permission. In 1908, 1909, 1910, and 1911, Williamson made four trips into the Tawang Tract, well north of the Outer Line, against Government prohibitions. Then on March 30, 1911, Williamson and a tea estate doctor were attacked and killed by Abor tribesmen in Kebang, well north of the Outer Line. Williamson's death provided for the revision of the tribal policy for which Williamson himself had argued for years.

In 1904, the British had sent an army to Lhasa, ostensibly because of Tibetan refusal to communicate with the Government of India; the real reason for the expedition was Lord Curzon's fear of Russian influence in Tibet. As a result of the British occupation of Lhasa, Chinese influence in Tibet grew; the British refused to deal with Tibet except through China. Tibet was soon incorporated into the Chinese provincial structure. Between 1905 and 1910, the Chinese attempted to assert their influence in Nepal and Bhutan, regions adjoining British Assam. The British became alarmed as Chinese activity and influence penetrated into the Tawang Tract. In 1910, Chinese troops planted boundary flags just below Walong; the British could not protest, as they regarded Walong as marking the Tibetan border. Yet, they felt that they could not stand by and let China assert influence into the Tawang Tract.

The British had to do something. Sir Lancelot Hare, the Lieutenant Governor of Eastern Bengal and Assam stated that "in view of the Chinese pushing forward, that it would be a mistake not to put ourselves in a position to take up strategic points of defense." The British Government in both India and London rejected moving the Outer Line northward to meet the present limits of Chinese influence; they feared Russian reaction to any advance. The 1911 murder of Williamson appears to have provided the solution.

A British expedition, headed by Major General Hamilton Bower, was mounted in late 1911; the mission continued until 1913. The alleged purpose of the expedition was punitive; indeed, the Abors were punished for slaying Williamson. However, much of the expedition's time and manpower was spent in determining the extent of Chinese penetration, and in establishing a new boundary which would keep the Chinese as far as possible from the Assam tea plantations. The ultimate objective of the expedition was to define a new border along the mountain crests and watersheds, to exercise British control up to that boundary, and to inform the Chinese of the new limits of British sovereignty. By the end of 1913, the British had explored much of the Assam Himalayas. The British had inspected the Chinese boundary markers near Walong and put up British markers beside them. The British surveys were to provide a good map of the Himalayas in Assam and in the Tawang Tract—all as an indirect result of Williamson's murder. These surveys and maps would soon form the basis for the McMahon Line.

While the British were exploring Assam, the 1911 Chinese Revolution erupted. By 1912, Chinese influence in Tibet had fallen drastically. As Chinese power in Tibet waned, Chinese pressure on the Assam border ceased to exist. The British now endeavored to secure the Assam Himalayas from any future Chinese intervention.

The fall of Chinese power in Tibet led to negotiations between British Indian, Chinese, and Tibetan delegates to the Simla Conference of 1913-14. The British had decided to make Tibet a genuine buffer state. The British chief delegate, Sir Henry McMahon, introduced the idea of a second buffer into the long Sino-Tibetan debates over the boundary between Chinese control and the Tibetan buffer. McMahon wanted to divide Tibet, just as Mongolia had been divided. Outer Tibet would be the buffer between China and the British Indian frontier. Inner Tibet would be part of China. However, the complexity of this concept provided severe problems for the Conference. The Chinese could not accept the definition of the Outer Tibet-Inner Tibet boundary which was agreeable to the Tibetans. In April, 1914, McMahon pressured the Chinese delegate into initialing a text based on the Tibetan-approved line. The Chinese government immediately repudiated the agreement. The Chinese rejection was a blow to McMahon's buffer scheme. However, McMahon had meanwhile negotiated another buffer and zone of defense for the Himalayas. He had made a separate agreement with the chief Tibetan delegate; this agreement defined the frontier line along the crest of the Assam Himalayas, based on the 1911-13 Abor Expedition. The line was marked on a large-scale (eight miles to the inch); however, the McMahon-Tibetan agreement were not communicated to the Chinese. The discussions of the Inner Tibet-Outer Tibet boundary, the McMahon-Tibetan boundary (which would become the McMahon Line) was shown as a sort of appendix to the boundary between Inner Tibet and China proper. The McMahon Line was never discussed with the Chinese at the Conference. The Chinese (both Koumintang and Communist) have maintained that the negotiating of the McMahon Line was a British trick, and have prefixed the word "illegal" to any mention of the McMahon Line or the boundary it represents. Lamb asserts that, in a sense, it was a British trick, since McMahon realized that the Chinese were capable of arguing the border for years without resolution, and McMahon wanted to get the Assam border settled with a minimum of fuss. It is likely, though, that the Chinese were somewhat aware of what McMahon was doing; in any case, the Chinese Government had rejected the April 1914 text.

In July, 1914, after McMahon had failed to acquire Chinese agreement to the April text, he again negotiated directly with the Tibetan delegate. McMahon and the Tibetans initialed a new Convention with a text only slightly modified from the April text. At the same time they signed a declaration pronouncing the Convention binding, and denied to the Chinese any rights under it until they too agreed. Thus, the Simla Convention would become the basis for much controversy, and the question of a boundary along the Himalayas was essentially left unresolved.

The old Outer Line had protruded east from Bhutan just south of the 27th line of latitude. The new McMahon Line extended from Bhutan at latitude 27o 45', to 92o of east longitude, and thence northeasterly. All of Tawang was now within the British Indian Empire. In the eastern Lohit Valley, the boundary retreated northwards from Walong (where both Chinese and british markers had been placed) to Kahao, 20 miles north. It simply appeared that the British wanted the boundary alignment northward to permit good defensive points in ranges far enough north to eliminate any Chinese influence into Assam.

It is possible that the British simply wanted to take over Tawang, for a better strategic border alignment.

The Tibetans apparently had no qualms with the McMahon Line, and continued to conduct traditional Tibetan administration in those areas where it extended across the new boun- dary. The Chinese, on the other hand, denied that the Conference had any validity. Not only had the Chinese failed to validate the McMahon Line, but the Chinese also repudiated Tibet's authority to negotiate any treaty or boundary independent of Chinese influence or sovereignty. Chinese maps of the 1930s showed the border with Assam to follow the old Outer Line, with the Himalayas shown as part of Tibet and hence as part of China. It is interesting that the 1929 Encyclopaedia Britannica showed the disputed area as part of China, with the boundary following the alignment shown on Chinese maps!

In January, 1914, T. O'Callaghan, assistant administrator of the Eastern Sector of the North East Frontier, was sent up the Lohit Valley. Just below Walong, he found both old Chinese boundary markers and a new marker placed in 1912 by the Chinese Republic. O'Callaghan removed all the markers, took them upstream, and simply replaced them near Kahao, just below the McMahon boundary! He then went to Rima, conferred with Tibetan officials, and found no Chinese influence in the area. O'Callaghan proposed a road to, and a post in, Walong; but his superiors showed no interest in his proposal.

As late as 1936, the Tibetans were still administering and taxing the Tawang Tract. The Governor of Assam noted that Tawang was " undoubtedly British, (but)... controlled by Tibet, and none of its inhabitants have any idea that they are not Tibetan."13 The Governor instructed Captain G. S. Lightfoot of the Western Sector to go up to Tawang in 1938 and demonstrate British sovereignty. The Tibetan Government protested Lightfoot's arrival, and demanded that he withdraw. Upon his return, Lightfoot proposed that the Tibetans be forced to withdraw all their officials in Tawang to the north of the McMahon Line. The Government of India rejected this proposal, not wanting any permanent occupation and further expenditure

When World War II erupted, there was still no decision about Tawang, and the Tibetans continued to administer it. But the war showed the Government of India the vulnerability (this time from the Japanese) of the eastern frontier of India. British policy in the eastern Himalayas again gained momentum, and Britain resolved to make the Simla Convention boundary good. Official Chinese maps still showed the pre-1914 Outer Line as the boundary in Assam; with Allied victory coming in the Far East, the British feared an expansionistic China. The British placed armed posts up the Lohit

Valley to the McMahon border. In the Dihang Valley, British military patrols were sent to turn back Tibetan tax collectors. In the Tawang Tract, British armed posts were established up to Se La.

By late 1947, the British had thus laid the groundwork for control up to the McMahon Line. But Tawang was still essentially under Tibetan administration; the loyalties of the tribes were still with Tibet. This was the situation which the new Indian republic inherited from Britain.

The Indian republic, threatened by the Communist take-over in China and then the Chinese occupation of Tibet, formed the North East Frontier Agency to administer the Assam frontier. It is of interest that NEFA came under the Ministry of External Affairs—despite British and Indian claims that this area had been claimed as Indian for years. In 1951, an Indian NEFA official was stationed in Tawang, ending any Tibetan control south of the McMahon Line.

Thus, as new regimes came to power in India and in China, the new governments inherited the border disputes in NEFA and in Aksai Chin. Just as strategic interests—India's desire for a buffer zone between her and China, and Chin'a claims to areas "always traditionally Chinese"—had created minor disputes for decades, similar strategic objectives would create problems for the two new governments. The NEFA and Aksai Chin regions were question marks. India occupied NEFA and believed it to be hers. But, as in Aksai Chin, China firmly and honestly believed that the areas in question were Chinese (or Tibetan, and therefore Chinese after the takeover of Tibet).

The stage was set—in Aksai Chin and in the NEFA—for controversy, frunstrating negotiations, and eventual conflict and war.

THE INDIA-CHINA DIVIDE

The Chinese Communist Party's (CCP) dislike for the 'hardline Hindu nationalist' Bharatiya Janata Party (BJP) is no secret. The shifts in India's China policy since May 1998, as evidenced in the nuclear and missile arena, military spending, and pro-Tibet and pro-Taiwan views expressed by some ministers, are said to have undermined the key assumptions underlying China's India policy. Conversations with officials and strategic analysts reveal that the Chinese are concerned over the rise of BJP as a major political force in Indian politics and its implications for China's strategic objective of supremacy in Asia. Before Pokhran II, China's India-watchers had convinced themselves that there would be 'no significant or fundamental changes' in the BJP-led Government's nuclear policy and that BJP-led India would not take any major strategic initiative (such as overt nuclearisation, strategic alliance with the United States, or support to Tibetan independence).

Although the aspirations for major power status are held by almost all Indian political parties (barring the Communists who fear provoking their Chinese masters), the BJP covets that status most ardently and is the most willing to assert it through military policy. Beijing would prefer a non-BJP weak government like the left-dominated United Front (UF) government before Pokhran II, and the successive Congress governments that preceded it, which had fine-tuned Sino-Indian bilateral relations by playing second fiddle to an assertive China. A policy paper prepared for the Chinese leadership has recommended 'targeting the BJP' as its policies have eroded Beijing's leverage against New Delhi. One analyst compared India with Nazi Germany and Iraq arguing that since the end of the Cold War, India had become too powerful and ambitious (for example, demanding a permanent seat on the UN Security Council) and warned that if India does not wish to suffer the fate of Japan in the 1940s or Iraq in the 1990s, it should give up its ambition for regional hegemony and take concrete steps to improve relations with China.

The main objective of China's Asia policy has always been to prevent the rise of an Asian rival or peer competitor to challenge its status as the Asia-Pacific's sole 'Middle Kingdom'. As an old Chinese saying goes, 'one mountain cannot accommodate two tigers'. That China does not want India to emerge as an equal is evident from its staunch opposition to India's membership of the P-5 (UN Security Council), N-5 (Nuclear Club), ASEM (Asia-Europe Summit), and APEC (Asia-Pacific Economic Cooperation). (India was made the ARF (ASEAN Regional Forum) member in December 1995 despite Beijing's opposition to it.) Speaking at the Munich Security Conference in February 1999, India's National Security Advisor, Brajesh Mishra, hinted at the BJP government's much broader political ambition by predicting that 'in the 21st century a new security order is likely to arise in the Asia-Pacific region in which India should be granted as much respect and deference by the United States and others as is China today.' Beijing's India-watchers believe that only a firm policy based on absolute strength and proactive containment of India will force the BJP-led government to act soberly towards China. Beijing knows that while China's emergence as a great power has been accepted by Western and Asian nations, India's claim to great power is yet to be accepted. So it is in the CCP's interests to keep the BJP out of power. Beijing has been blamed by India's intelligence agencies, media and some politicians for the overthrow of the BJP-led government in April 1999.

Strange as it may seem, the CCP has more in common with its bete noire, BJP, than its counterpart in India, the Communist Party of India-Marxist (CPM). In the BJP, the CCP has met its match, the latter's 'communist' pretensions notwithstanding. Contrary to the popular conception of the CCP and the BJP occupying opposite ends of the political spectrum, the BJP is the CCP's mirror image. Just as the CCP believes in the superiority of the Han race, Han civilisation and the Han culture while displaying patronising and condescending attitude towards minorities such as Tibetans, Mongols and Muslims and downplaying the repeated colonisation of the Han race first by Inner Asian tribes such as Mongols, Manchus and Hsingnus and then by the Europeans, the BJP believes in the superiority of the Hindu race, Hindu civilisation and Hindu culture while downplaying the repeated colonisation of India by Greek, Muslim and European invaders as a result of Hindu disunity and their contributions to Indian culture. What is more, the CCP's goal of a unified 'Greater China' is not much different from the RSS/BJP's dream of 'Akhand Bharat' (United India). Just as the Chinese Communists lay claim to territories annexed by non-Chinese Mongol and Manchu empires (such as Tibet, Eastern Turkestan, Mongolia), the 'Akhand Bharat' concept includes territories (such as Burma and Sri Lanka) brought under control by the British. Much like the CCP, the BJP wants India to be an economic and military superpower in order to 'stand up' to great powers' bullying and coercion. Both have long nurtured the belief that as the two oldest civilisations and once great powers which were subjected to centuries of foreign domination, they must acquire the full spectrum of economic, technological and military (conventional, nuclear and information warfare) capabilities in order to be dominant regionally and influential globally.

Furthermore, the BJP's slogan of 'prosperous and powerful country' bears remarkable resemblance to the CCP's national goal: 'rich country, strong military' (fuguo qiangbing). Interestingly, both are courting the United States to help balance their relationships with each other until they are strong enough to do so on their own. Both want a new international status that is commensurate with their size, strength and potential. Historically and civilisationally, while China was the 'Middle Kingdom' of eastern Asia, India was the 'Middle Kingdom' of southern Asia.

The two parties are thus manifestation of the growing nationalism in India and China. Both also share remarkable similarity in economic outlooks and rhetorical excess. The BJP-led government is as aggressive in the pursuit of national interests as the CCP. Nor is it shy of flexing muscles and warning neighbours with 'serious consequences' if they don't behave-just as the Chinese Communists have always done! Although both the CCP and BJP have been labelled 'fascist', 'militarist' and 'ultra-natonalist' parties by their critics, the reality is that both are nationalist parties deeply conscious of their countries' history, culture and civilisational heritage to humankind and committed to restoring their countries' great power status. Both China after a century and India after a millenium of decline are keen to assume the great power roles they believe to be their historical and civilisational right.

Both remain suspicious of each other's long-term agenda and intentions, and are attempting to fill any perceived power vacuum or block the other from doing so. At the heart of Sino-Indian antagonism is the familiar Indian suspicion, which has now matured into a certainty, that China is seeking to deny India its proper stakes in the game of international politics. Both see themselves as newly rising great Asian powers whose time has finally come. This means that BJP's resurgent India will face CCP's rising China which will ensure a conflict of interests between the two giants unless their power competition is managed carefully. Their underlying power rivalry and their self-images as natural great powers and centres of civilisation and culture will continue to drive them to support different countries and causes. India versus China, not India versus Pakistan, has always been the main game in Asia. However, post-colonial Asia has not experienced both a strong China and a strong India at the same time. The BJP-CCP clash is borne not out of conflicting, but complementary, visions for their respective countries.

THE MYSTERY OF THE MCMAHAN LINE

After Russia successfully divided Mongolia into Outer and Inner Mogolia with the Outer Mongolia as a buffer zone between China and Russia, the British- Indian authorities dreamed the same dream and tried to divideTibet into Outer Tibet and Inner Tibet and made the Outer Tibet as a buffer zone between British India andChina. To achieve such a objective, the Simla conference was held in 1914,with British Henry McMahon, Chinese Chen Ivan, and Tibetan Lonchen shatra as representatives.

There were actually two parallel conferences at Simla, the tripartite conference focusing on the division ofTibet, and the other was the secret one, keeping Chen Ivan out of their negotiations on the Indian-Tibetan boundary. In early 1914, Henry McMahon and Lonchen Shatra secretly negotiated on thc division of Tibet and the boundary between Assam and Tibet as a package deal. An agreement was reached through a secret exchange of notes in Delhi on March 24 and 25, 1914. This boundary line, later known as the McMahon line, was shown on a map in two sheets.

The tripartite conference focused on McMahon's proposal referring to China's suzerainty over Tibet and the outer-inner division of Tibet. On the map attached to the draft convention of the conference, two lines were drawn, one red and the other blue. The red line showed Tibet as a geographical and political unit, and the blue line divided Inner from Outer Tibet. In its southern extension, the red line curves around along the crest of theHimalayas, roughly conforming to the McMahon Line except in the Tawang tract where the McMahon Line reached short of the Tawang tract , implying that the Tawang tract remained part of Tibetan territory. On this map, the Tawang tract was not put within the British-Indian territory.

Without the consent of the Chinese government, Chen Ivan, under McMahon's threat and pressure, initiated the draft convention on April 27, 1914, but with the clear understanding that "to initial and to sign are two different actions," and that his initials would not bind his government, whose views he would immediately seek. The next day, the Chinese government instructed Chen Ivan that "The Chinese representative was forced to initial the draft convention. The Chinese government cannot accept it. You should declare it invalid." Since Chen Ivan refused to sign the draft convention, it was then amended and initialed by McMahon and Lonchen Shatra on July 3, 1914. On the map attached to the draft convention, the McMahon Line was marked just across the town of Tawang, indicating that the area to the north of Tawang would fall within the Tibetan territory.

The British-Indian government did not accept the Simla convention. Viceroy Hardinge forwarded McMahon's report on the Simla conference to London on July 23, 1914, stating that the Indian government recognized that a consideration of the northeastern frontier did not form part of the functions of the conference, and the views and proposal put forward might be regarded as personal to Henry McMahon, not carrying the endorsement of the Government of India. Chen was also instructed to declare that the Chinese government "would not recognize any treaty or similar document that might now or hereafter be signed between Great Britain andTibet." The Tibetan authorities understood that without securing the Sino-Tibetan boundary, they could not accept the Indo-Tibetan boundary.

The Dalai Lama even recognized the logic relationship between the status of Tibet and the legality of the McMahon Line. In his 1959 address to the Indian Council of World Affairs, he contended that if Tibet had no sovereignty when the Simla convention laid down the McMahon Line, that line was invalid. He challenged Nehru that if you deny the sovereign status to Tibet, you deny the validity of the McMahon Line."

Three maps are related to the Simla conference. One is attached to the March 24 notes; one to the April 27 convention, and the third to the July 3 convention. As far as the Tawang Tract is concerned, the three maps show the McMahon line quite differently. On the first map, the McMahon Line was shown running alng south of the Thagla range far north of Tawang; on the second map, it is not shown in the Tawang tract; and on the third one, it is superimposed on the word " Tawang".

In 1936, Basil Gould, Political Officer in Sikkim, was dispatched to Lhasa and discussed the Tawang issue with the Tibetan government. The Tibetan attitude was Tawang had been Tibetan up to 1914 and they regarded the adjustment of the Tibet-Indian boundary as part and parcel of the general adjustment and determination of boundaries contemplated in the 1914 convention. If they could, with British help, secure a definite Sino-Tibetan boundary, they would observe the Indo-Tibetan border as defined in 1914.

In 1944, just before the British quit from India, basil Gould informed the Tibetan authorities that the Bitish-Indian government was willing to modify the McMahon Line soas to exclude Tawang from the territory it claimed. He also proposed that the Se La range should be a new boundary line. However, The Tibetan authorities did not accepted it and continued to collect revenues in the Tawang tract and remained administrative control over the Tawang tract.

It was in February1951 that the Indian government took over the Tawang tract by force before the PLA entered and liberated Tibet. The Tibetan authorities organized protest demonstrations in Tawang and Lhasaagainst India's occupation of the Tawang tract, but no avail.

As far as the objective of the Simla conference was concerned, it certainly aborted. The McMahon Line was not even accepted by the British-Indian government.

After the Simla conference, from 1914 to 1935, on the official maps published by the Survey of India, the McMahon Line was not shown, but instead the Outer Line along the foothills of the Himalayas was shown. The Tibetan authorities continued to exercise administrative jurisdiction in the tribal areas as they did before. The Simla conference went down in history as an unaccomplished cause.

As to the Simla conference, the first official record appeared in Volume XIV of the 1929 edition of Aichison'sTreaties. It did not refer to the McMahon Line, but to the discussion on the Sino-Tibetan frontier. It was stated that a tripartite convention was drawn up and initialed in 1914, but the Chinese government refused to permit its representative to proceed to full signature.

In 1935, Olaf Caroe, deputy secretary of the Foreign and Political Department of the British-Indian Government discovered the secret documents of the Simla conference in dealing with a case involving the illegal entry into Tibet through the Tawang tract. He realized that the northeastern frontier might be a matter of dispute with the Chinese in the future. He proposed to revise the official record of the Simla conference in the Aichison's Treaties and show the McMahon Line on the official maps. The British government approved his proposal.

This original 1929 edition was soon withdrawn from circulation and replaced by a spurious edition, actually printed in 1938, but with an imprint of 1929. However, at least three copies of the original 1929 edition survived, one in Peking Library, one in Harvard University library, and one in the India Office. In the revised edition, it was stated that the Simla conference negotiated an agreement on the status of Tibet and the boundary of Tibet with both China and India. Such a revision was nothing but scandalous diplomatic forgery. Then the McMahon Line began to appear o the Indian official maps. However, it was still marked as "Undemarcated Boundary."

TERRITORIAL PROBLEMS BETWEEN SINO-INDIA

In terms of "the rise of China" and its "implications for India", the title of this book, the Sino-Indian territorial dispute represents an immediate arena in which India is having to face the uncomfortable implications from having an increasingly stronger neighbour. For India, the ability of China to deny India's hopes of territorial settlement on India's terms has become ever clearer in the wake of China's rise in military power in and around their disputed territory, which remains the biggest amount of land still in dispute in Asia.

As such, "the 4,056—kilometre (2,520 miles) frontier between India and China, one of the longest inter-state borders in the world, remains ... not defined, let alone demarcated, on maps or delineated on the ground". Here, the judgement over a century ago of Lord Curzon, British Viceroy of India 1898-1905 still seems relevant; the most urgent work of Foreign Ministers and Ambassadors ... is now the conclusion of Frontier Conventions in which sources of discord are removed by the adjustment of rival interests or ambitions at points where the territorial borders adjoin", for "frontiers are indeed the razor's edge on which hang suspended the modern issues of war or peace, of life or death to nations".

Admittedly, the territorial issue has been officially decoupled from the wider Sino-Indian relationship; as with the PRC rhetoric that "China and India have already reached consensus on the border issue. Before it is completely resolved, both countries will endeavour to maintain peace and stability in the border areas and will not let the border issue affect the general picture of China and India's cooperation". However, in reality their territorial issues do affect their wider relationship, in PRC terms "the existence of immense territorial disputes between China and India".

In dispute terms, this chapter argues that, in International Relations (IR) theory terms, the territorial disputes between India and China involve *classical geopolitics* entwined with *critical geopolitics*. Each strand of geopolitics, in their different ways, both involve the respective "position" that India and China hold for themselves and for each other in their immediate and extended neighbourhood.

Whilst each side argues from history, the chapter argues that in reality the evidence from history is rather ambiguous and inconclusive for both sides' territorial claims. Indeed, history is a sterile area to argue from, as one Indian commentator put it, "can we go beyond history to look at solutions which do not hark back to the past?"

The chapter argues that, from the outside, resolution of the issue seems feasible enough in terms of simple seeming territorial trade offs involving Arunachal Pradesh and Aksai Chin; but is complicated by smaller geographic issues surrounding Tawang, and wider geopolitical issues surrounding Tibet and indeed the balance of power in Asia between India and China.

The two main areas of dispute along this Himalayan frontier are the *Western Sector* (Aksai Chin, around 37,250 square kilometres/ 14,380 square miles); and the *Eastern Sector* (Arunachal Pradesh, around 83,740 square kilometres/ 32,330 square miles). On the one hand, Arunachal Pradesh is inhabited by over a million people, Indian citizens, and includes important Buddhist centres like Tawang. On the other hand, Aksai Chin is a virtually uninhabited bleak barren plateau with no permanent settlements. It is the place "where not a blade of grass grows" as Jawaharlal Nehru once dismissively said; but where China's National Highway 219 runs through Aksai Chin as a key geopolitical infrastructure link for the PRC between its provinces of Tibet and Xinjiang.

One further complication is China's occupation of the Shaksgam valley; around 5,180 sq kilometres/1,930 square miles, to which Pakistan relinquished its Baltistan-related claims in 1963, but over which India maintains its own Kashmir-derived claims. Smaller pockets of disputed territory are found, the *Middle Sector* fringes of Himachal Pradesh and Uttar Pradesh. Elsewhere along the Himalayas, lingering uncertainty over China's recognition of Sikkim's incorporation into India in 1975 is entwined with continuing PRC claims to the "Finger Area" in the north of Sikkim, with 71 supposed incidents reported of Chinese troop "incursions" in 2008.

Nearby territorial disputes between China and Bhutan around the Chumbi Valley triangulation point with India are of further concern to New Delhi, given the Chumbi Valley's location looking down onto the India's sensitive Siliguri corridor which links India's northeastern states with the rest of India.

Wider nuances arise with India's Foreign Secretary (2004—2006) Shyam Saran, and his comments about *the logic of geography*. In front of one audience, it was a question for Saran of "geopolitical reality" in which "I would like to focus particularly on Asia, where the interests of both India and China intersect. It is said that the logic of geography is unrelenting. Proximity is the most difficult and testing among diplomatic challenges a country faces", where "to those who harbour any skepticism about this fact, it would suffice to remind that we share one of the longest [and disputed] land borders in the world with China.

In front of another audience, it was again a question that "it is said that the logic of geography is unrelenting and proximity is the most difficult and testing among diplomatic challenges a country faces"; with the following gloss that "frontiers with neighbours are where domestic concerns intersect with external relationships. This is where domestic and foreign policies become inextricable and demand sensitive handling", and in which "it is important for us to look at the [disputed] boundary question from the long-term and strategic perspective of India-China relations, rather than as a mere territorial issue.

The territorial issues between India and China form one of the biggest land disputes in Asia, and are of significance not only for the size of area under dispute, but also because the two disputants are the big countries most evidently on the rise in Asia. Alongside this *logic of geography*, there is then what Neville Maxwell called "the logic of power"; a *logic of power* whereby powerful states "in their expansive phases push out their frontiers until they meet the resistance of a strong neighbour or reach a physical barrier which makes a natural point of rest". In geopolitical terms, the current point of rest is along the Himalayas/Karakoram range, but in the long term where exactly is the "natural" point of rest between them? Amidst talk of mutual IR *security dilemma* dynamics, China's strengthening of military forces and related infrastructure in Aksai Chin and Arunachal Pradesh zones is now a spur to India's own more halting augmentation of military forces and related infrastructure. Meanwhile, both countries are seeking to expand their wider strategic space at a time when their immediate mountain borders remain unresolved.

2

The McMahon Line

In 1826, British India gained a common border with China after the British wrested control of Manipur and Assam from the Burmese, following the First Anglo-Burmese War of 1824–1826. In 1847, Major J. Jenkins, agent for the North East Frontier, reported that the Tawang was part of Tibet. In 1872, four monastic officials from Tibet arrived in Tawang and supervised a boundary settlement with Major R. Graham, NEFA official, which included the Tawang Tract as part of Tibet.

Thus, in the last half of the 19th century, it was clear that the British treated the Tawang Tract as part of Tibet. This boundary was confirmed in a 1 June 1912 note from the British General Staff in India, stating that the "present boundary (demarcated) is south of Tawang, running westwards along the foothills from near Ugalguri to the southern Bhutanese border." A 1908 map of The Province of Eastern Bengal and Assam prepared for the Foreign Department of the Government of India, showed the international boundary from Bhutan continuing to the Baroi River, following the Himalayas foothill alignment.

In 1913, representatives of Great Britain, China and Tibet attended a conference in Simla regarding the borders between Tibet, China and British India. Whilst all three representatives initialed the agreement, Beijing later objected to the proposed boundary between the regions of Outer Tibet and Inner Tibet, and did not ratify it. The details of the Indo-Tibetan boundary was not revealed to China at the time. The foreign secretary of the British Indian government, Henry McMahon, who had drawn up the proposal, decided to bypass the Chinese (although instructed not to by his superiors) and settle the border bilaterally by negotiating directly with Tibet.

According to later Indian claims, this border was intended to run through the highest ridges of the Himalayas, as the areas south of the Himalayas were traditionally Indian. However, the McMahon Line lay south of the boundary India claims. India's government held the view that the Himalayas were the ancient boundaries of the Indian subcontinent, and thus should be the modern boundaries of India, while it is the position of the Chinese government that the disputed area in the Himalayas have been geographically and culturally part of Tibet since ancient times.

Months after the Simla agreement, China set up boundary markers south of the McMahon Line. T. O'Callaghan, an official in the Eastern Sector of the North East Frontier, relocated all these markers to a location slightly south of the McMahon Line, and then visited Rima to confirm with Tibetan officials that there was no Chinese influence in the area. The British-run Government of India initially rejected the Simla Agreement as incompatible with the Anglo-Russian Convention of 1907, which stipulated that neither party was to negotiate with Tibet "except through the intermediary of the Chinese government". The British and Russians cancelled the 1907 agreement by joint consent in 1921. It was not until the late 1930s that the British started to use the McMahon Line on official maps of the region. China took the position that the Tibetan government should not have been allowed to make a such a treaty, rejecting Tibet's claims of independent rule. For its part, Tibet did not object to any section of the McMahon Line excepting the demarcation of the trading town of Tawang, which the Line placed under British-Indian jurisdiction. However, up until World War II, Tibetan officials were allowed to administer Tawang with complete authority. Due to the increased threat of Japanese and Chinese expansion during this period, British Indian troops secured the town as part of the defence of India's eastern border.

In the 1950s, India began actively patrolling the region. It found that, at multiple locations, the highest ridges actually fell north of the McMahon Line. Given India's historic position that the original intent of the line was to separate the two nations by the highest mountains in the world, in these locations India extended its forward posts northward to the ridges, regarding this move as compliant with the original border proposal, although the Simla Convention did not explicitly state this intention.

MCMAHON LINE BORDER

The McMahon Line is a line agreed to by Britain and Tibet as part of the Simla Accord, a treaty signed in 1914. It is the effective boundary between China and India, although its legal status is disputed by the Chinese government.

The line is named after Sir Henry McMahon, foreign secretary of the British-run Government of India and the chief negotiator of the convention at Simla. It extends for 550 miles (890 km) from Bhutan in the west to 160 miles (260 km) east of the great bend of theBrahmaputra River in the east, largely along the crest of the Himalayas. Simla (along with the McMahon Line) was initially rejected by the Government of India as incompatible with the 1907 Anglo-Russian Convention. This convention was denounced in 1921. After Simla, the McMahon Line was forgotten until 1935, when British civil service officer Olaf Caroe convinced the government to publish the Simla Convention and use the McMahon Line on official maps.

The McMahon Line is regarded by India as the legal national border. It is disputed by China. As recently as 2003, the Dalai Lama said that the disputed region was part of Tibet, but he reversed his position in 2008, acknowledging the legitimacy of the McMahon Line and the Indian claim to the region.

China rejects the Simla Accord, contending that the Tibetan government was not sovereign and therefore did not have the power to conclude treaties. Chinese maps show some 65,000 square kilometres (25,000 sq mi) of the territory south of the line as part of theTibet Autonomous Region, known as South Tibet in China. Chinese forces briefly occupied this area during the Sino-Indian War of 1962. China does recognise a Line of Actual Control which closely approximates most of the "so called McMahon line" in the eastern part of its border with India, according to a 1959 diplomatic note by Prime Minister Zhou Enlai.

History

Drawing the Line

Early British efforts to create a boundary in this sector were triggered by their discovery in the mid-19th century that Tawang, an important trading town, was Tibetan territory. In 1873, the British-run Government of India drew an "Outer Line," intended as an international boundary. This line follows the alignment of the Himalayan foothills, now roughly the southern boundary of Arunachal Pradesh. Britain concluded treaties with Beijing concerning Tibet's boundaries with Burma and Sikkim. However, Tibet refused to recognise the boundaries drawn by these treaties. British forces led by Sir Francis Younghusband invaded Tibet in 1904 and imposed a treaty on the Tibetans. In 1907, Britain and Russia acknowledged Chinese "suzerainty" over Tibet and both nations "engage not to enter into negotiations with Tibet except through the intermediary of the Chinese Government."

British interest in the borderlands was renewed when the Qing government sent military forces to establish Chinese administration in Tibet (1910–12). A British military expedition was sent into what is now Arunachal Pradesh and the North East Frontier Tracts was created to administer the area (1912). In 1912–13, this agency reached agreements with the tribal leaders who ruled the bulk of the region. The Outer Line was moved north, but Tawang was left as Tibetan territory. After the fall of the Qing dynasty in China, Tibet expelled all Chinese officials and troops, and declared itself independent (1913).

In 1913, British officials conferred at Simla, India to discuss Tibet's status. The conference was attended by representatives of Britain, China, and Tibet. "Outer Tibet," covering approximately the same area as the modern "Tibet Autonomous Region," would be under the administration of the Dalai Lama's government as well as the "suzerainty" of China. Suzerainty is an Asian political concept indicating limited authority over a dependent state. The final 3 July 1914 accord lacked any textual boundary delimitations or descriptions. It made reference to a small scale map with very little detail, one that primarily showed lines separating China from "Inner Tibet" and "Inner Tibet" from "Outer Tibet." This map lacked any initials or signatures from the Chinese plenipotentiary Ivan Chen; however Chen had signed an earlier, similar draft of it from 27 April 1914.

Both drafts of this small scale map extend the identical red line symbol between "Inner Tibet" and China further to the southwest, approximating the entire route of the McMahon Line, and thus dead ending near Tawang at the Bhutan tripoint. However, neither draft labels "British India" or anything similar in the area that now constitutes Arunachal Pradesh.

The far more detailed eight miles to the inch McMahon Line map of 24–25 March 1914 is signed only by the Tibetan and British representatives. This map and McMahon Line negotiations were both done without Chinese participation. After Beijing repudiated Simla, the British and Tibetan delegates attached a note denying China any privileges under the agreement and signed it as a bilateral accord.

Britain Attempts to Enforce Line

Simla was initially rejected by the Government of India as incompatible with the 1907 Anglo-Russian Convention. C.U. Aitchison's *A Collection of Treaties*, was published with a note stating that no binding agreement had been reached at Simla. The Anglo-Russian Convention was renounced by Russia and Britain jointly in 1921, but the McMahon Line was forgotten until 1935, when interest was revived by civil service officer Olaf Caroe. The Survey of India published a map showing the McMahon Line as the official boundary in 1937. In 1938, the British published the Simla Accord in Aitchison's *Treaties.* A volume published earlier was recalled from libraries and replaced with a volume that includes the Simla Accord together with an editor's note stating that Tibet and Britain, but not China, accepted the agreement as binding. The replacement volume has a false 1929 publication date.

In April 1938, a small British force led by Captain GS Lightfoot arrived in Tawang and informed the monastery the district was now Indian territory.

The Tibetan government protested and its authority was restored after Lightfoot's brief stay. The district remained in Tibetan hands until 1951. However, Lhasa raised no objection to British activity in other sectors of the McMahon Line. In 1944, NEFT established direct administrative control for the entire area it was assigned, although Tibet soon regained authority in Tawang. In 1947, the Tibetan government wrote a note presented to the Indian Ministry of External Affairs laying claim to Tibetan districts south of the McMahon Line. In Beijing, the Communist Party came to power in 1949 and declared its intention to "liberate" Tibet. India, which had become independent in 1947, responded by declaring the McMahon Line to be its boundary and by decisively asserting control of the Tawang area (1950–51).

India and China Dispute Boundary

In the 1950s, India-China relations were cordial and the boundary dispute quiet. The Indian government under Prime Minister Jawaharlal Nehru promoted the slogan *Hindi-Chini bhai-bhai.* (India and China are brothers). Nehru maintained his 1950 statement that he would not accept negotiations if China brought the boundary dispute up, hoping that "China would accept the *fait accompli.* In 1954, India renamed the disputed area the North East Frontier Agency.

India acknowledged that Tibet was a part of China and gave up its extraterritorial rights in Tibet inherited from the British in a treaty concluded in April 1954. Nehru later claimed that because China did not bring up the border issue at the 1954 conference, the issue was settled. But the only border India had delineated before the conference was the McMahon Line. Several months after the conference, Nehru ordered maps of India published that showed expansive Indian territorial claims as definite boundaries, notably inAksai Chin. In the NEFA sector, the new maps gave the hill crest as the boundary, although in some places this line is slightly north of the McMahon Line.

The failure of the 1959 Tibetan uprising and the 14th Dalai Lama's arrival in India in March led Indian parliamentarians to censure Nehru for not securing a commitment from China to respect the McMahon Line. Additionally, the Indian press started openly advocating Tibetan independence. Nehru, seeking to quickly assert sovereignty in response, established "as many military posts along the frontier as possible", unannounced and against the advice of his staff. On discovering the posts, and already suspicious from the ruminations of the Indian press, Chinese leaders began to suspect that Nehru had designs on the region. In August 1959, Chinese troops captured a new Indian military outpost at Longju on the Tsari Chu (the main tributary, from the north, of the Subansiri River in Arunachal Pradesh.) Longju was and is just north of the McMahon Line according the inside back cover map in Maxwell and according to notable Indian mountaineer Harish Kapadia who explored the area in 2005. His published map and text locate Longju a kilometer or two on the China side of the McMahon Line "near the Chinese garrison town of Migyitun" (which is now quite sizable, at 28-39-40 north latitude, over four kilometers north of the line.) (The rarely reliable coordinates in the Geonames database (National Geospatial-Intelligence Agency) incorrectly place "Longju" in snow and ice 10 kilometers away from the river at over 12,000 feet in elevation.) In a letter to Nehru dated 24 October 1959, Zhou Enlai proposed that India and China each withdraw their forces 20 kilometers from the line of actual control. Shortly afterward, Zhou defined this line as "the so-called McMahon Line in the east and the line up to which each side exercises actual control in the west".

In November 1961, Nehru formally adopted the "Forward Policy" of setting up military outposts in disputed areas, including 43 outposts north of Zhou's LAC. Chinese leaderMao Zedong, at this time weakened by the failure of the Great Leap Forward, saw war as a means of reasserting his authority. On 8 September 1962, a Chinese unit attacked an Indian post at Dhola in the Namka Chu valley immediately south of the Thag La Ridge, seven kilometres north of the McMahon Line according to the map on page 360 of Maxwell. On 20 October China launched a major attack across the McMahon Line as well as another attack further north. The Sino-Indian War which followed was a national humiliation for India, with China quickly advancing 90 km (56 mi) from the McMahon Line to Rupa and then Chaku (65 km southeast of Tawang) in NEPA's extreme western portion, and in the NEFA's extreme eastern tip advancing 30 km (19 mi) to Walong. The Soviet Union, United States, and Great Britain pledged military aid to India. China then withdrew to the McMahon Line and repatriated the Indian prisoners of war (1963).

NEFA was renamed Arunachal Pradesh in 1972—Chinese maps refer to the area as South Tibet. In 1981, Chinese leader Deng Xiaoping offered India a "package settlement" of the border issue. Eight rounds of talks followed, but there was no agreement. In 1984, India Intelligence Bureau personnel in the Tawang region set up an observation post in the Şumdorong Chu Valley just south of the highest hill crest, but three kilometres north of the McMahon Line (the straight line portion extending east from Bhutan for 30 miles). The IB left the area before winter. In 1986, China deployed troops in the valley before an Indian team arrived. This information created a national uproar when it was revealed to the Indian public. In October 1986, Deng threatened to "teach India a lesson". The Indian Army airlifted a task force to the valley. The confrontation was defused in May 1987 though, as clearly visible on Google Earth, both armies have remained and recent construction of roads and facilities are visible.

The Indian Prime Minister Rajiv Gandhi visited China in 1988 and agreed to a joint working group on boundary issues which has made little apparent positive progress. A 1993 Sino-Indian agreement set up a group to define the LAC; this group has likewise made no progress. A 1996 Sino-Indian agreement set up "confidence-building measures" to avoid border clashes. Although there have been frequent incidents where one state has charged the other with incursions, causing tense encounters along the McMahon Line following India's nuclear test in 1998 and continuing to the present, both sides generally attribute these to disagreements of less than a kilometre as to the exact location of the LAC.

THE SINO/INDIAN DISPUTE

Ever since its establishment in 1949, the attitude of the Communist Chinese Government towards India has been bound up with the Tibetan issue. India had, on gaining independence in 1947, inherited the British "special position" in Tibet, along with the Mission in Lhasa and trade agencies in larger towns. It had retained the services of British officials stationed in Tibet. When, in 1949, Tibetan leaders made their bid to contact foreign Governments, they first contacted these officials, and it was only a short step for the suspicious minded Chinese to regard this as evidence of Indian collusion with the British.

The Communist Chinese also had ideological reasons for believing that such collusion existed. At the time of their coming to power, Moscow was propagating the line of a world divided into two camps, with the Indian Government depicted as a tool of British imperialism and firmly situated in the opposing camp. The Communist Chinese leaders, who previously had little contact with the outside world, faithfully repeated these accusations against Nehru and his Government. The Chinese occupation of Tibet in late 1950, Peking's suspicions of the Indians were further aroused when Nehru, in notes to the Chinese Government, expressed the "surprise and regret" of his Government at the Chinese action. He described as "deplorable" the Chinese use of force in Tibet.

Standard diplomatic practice stipulates that a state does not criticise the behaviour of another state acting within its own territorial boundaries unless there are special reasons for so doing. The Indians justified their criticism of the Chinese on the ground of their special interest in Tibet, from which the Chinese inferred that the Indians were implying some restriction on Chinese sovereignty. A sharp reply was received from the Chinese accusing the Indians of unwarranted interference and claiming that the policy of the Indian Government was "affected by foreign influences hostile to China in Tibet".

Nevertheless, whatever suspicions the Chinese may have felt about the Indians in 1949-50 must to some extent have been allayed by subsequent developments. India opposed the 1950 Tibetan appeal to the United Nations; it was one of the few non-communist countries not to condemn China's intervention in the Korean War; it sought to have China seated an the United Nations. The culmination of these moves to improve relations with China was the signing, in April 1954, of an agreement by which India recognised without qualification China's sovereignty over Tibet and conceded many of India's former rights there. A few months later the Chinese Premier, Chou En-lai, paid a successful visit to India, and in October of the same year Nehru visited Peking.

The very considerable improvement in Sino/Indian relations from 1950 to 1954 was on the Indian side almost entirely the result of efforts by Nehru, who saw friendship between China and India as the starting point of a new order in world affairs. It must have been obvious to the Chinese that considerable opposition to Nehru's pro-China policies, at least as far as Tibet was concerned, existed both within and outside the Indian Government. It should also have been clear that problems were going to arise over wide discrepancies in the claimed Sino/Indian border, as shown in maps published by both sides. However, as long as Nehru's China policy appeared to produce results, his opposition in India remained silent. It was important for both Nehru and the Chinese that this policy continued to appear to give results, and hence the efforts made by both sides to keep intact the edifice of good relations. The Chinese, under the 1954 agreement, allowed India to maintain certain trade and pilgrimage rights in Tibet. They sought to play down the significance of border differences, stating that they had simply inherited their claimed Sino/Indian frontier from the pre-1949 Nationalist Government and that it would be "revised" in due course. Nehru, for his part, avoided public mention of the reality and extent of border differences, and it seemed that both sides were moving towards a compromise settlement of the question.

What were these differences, and what evidence was there that both sides were in fact prepared to compromise? The Sino/Indian border can be divided into three sectors: (i) an eastern sector where 99,000 square kilometres of territory described by the Indians as the Northeast Frontier Agency, or N.E.F.A is in dispute: (ii) a middle sector where some 2.000 square kilometres of territory on either side of the main Himalayan passes is disputed: and (iii) a western sector where the Indian province of Ladakh borders on Tibet and Sinkiang and where both the Indian/Tibet and Indian/Sinkiang borders are disputed, in particular the ownership of some 30,000 square kilometres of high plateau country known as the Aksai Chin.

To an outside observer looking at the frontier as it stands, an apparent basis for a compromise settlement would be for China to drop its claim to the N.E.F.A. in exchange for India dropping its claim to the Aksai Chin, with both sides making concessions over the middle sector and the Ladakh/Tibetan border. Such a settlement accords with the realities of both geography and administrative control two important criteria in the settlement of border disputes. The N.E.F.A. lies to the south of the Himalayan watershed and is controlled by India. The Aksai Chin, for the most part, lies to the north of the main range, and the Chinese claim to have controlled the area since 1950. In 1956-7, they built a strategic road across the Aksai Chin, linking Sinkiang with Tibet. That the Indians learnt about the road only from a map published by the Chinese in 1958 is substantial evidence that India was not in control of the area.

The historical basis of the border is more confused. The Indian claim to the N.E.F.A. rests almost entirely on acceptance of the McMahon Line, a line agreed to by the Tibetans and British in 1914 as the border in this area. In the Aksai Chin area no agreement has ever been reached on the alignment of the border. Nevertheless, if both sides were to take a generous view of the historical data, a basis for a N.E.F.A./Aksai Chin exchange could be found. During the post-1954 honeymoon period of Sino/Indian relations, both sides did in fact seem prepared to take a generous view of the situation and to move towards a compromise settlement.

In 1956, Chou En-lai admitted privately to Nehru that, although lie thought the McMahon line "was not fair", nevertheless China would accept the line as the border with India after they had "consulted with the Tibetan authorities". Chinese recognition of the McMahon Line was also implied when its eastern extension was accepted as a basis for border negotiations with Burma, and by Chinese de facto acceptance of the line as the dividing line between Chinese and Indian forces in the area.

Nehru, for his part, appeared willing to play down the Indian claims to the Aksai Chin. He tried to delay disclosure if the news that the Chinese had built a road in the area. After the news had been revealed, he sought to play down the economic significance of the area, describing it as a "barren tundra". He even went so far as to cast doubt on the validity of the Indian claim to the area. In statements to the Indian Parliament during early 1959, Nehru pointed out that "during British rule, this area was neither inhabited: nor were there any outposts", adding that "this place, Aksai Chin area, is distinguish completely from other areas. It is a matter for argument which part belongs to us and which part belongs to somebody else. It is not clear".

Nehru's efforts to take the heat out of the Aksai Chin question were not entirely successful. (One of his critics even suggested building an atomic reactor in the area to promote its economic development.) News of the Chinese road in the area appeared to trigger off long-suppressed Indian sensitivity over the border issue, and, in August 1958, the Indian Government made a formal claim to the disputed territory in all three sectors.

In a letter to Nehru of January 1959, Chou En-lai claimed that the Aksai Chin was Chinese territory and added that the McMahon Line was a "product of British aggression", illegal, and had "never been recognised by the Chinese Central Government". He proposed that the existing status quo he maintained, however, pending a negotiated settlement of the dispute, and added that China would take a "realistic attitude" over the McMahon Line.*

The Tibetan uprising of March 1959 upset the delicate balance of Sino/Indian relations. Reports of Chinese military action to suppress the uprising, together with the sight of thousands of Tibetan refugees crossing into Indian territory, quickly aroused feelings of alarm and anger in India, particularly among those who believed their country had an historic interest in Tibet.

Nehru's Right-Wing critics charged that India should never have allowed the Chinese into Tibet in the first place. Nehru, influenced possibly both by Indian public opinion and his own feelings on the question, came out in open condemnation of Chinese behaviour in Tibet. The Chinese reacted even more strongly than they had in 1950. Nehru, in addition to condemning the Chinese, had spoken of his sympathy with "the aspirations of the Tibetans for autonomy". He had given asylum to the Dalai Lama, who was also allowed facilities to make his 1959 appeal for U. N. action over Tibet. And finally, the Chinese had reason to believe that the Tibetan guerrillas were receiving arms from across the Indian border.

In May 1959 the Chinese published a long article urging, almost begging, Nehru not to be swayed by his reactionary Right-Wing critics and to return to the path of Sino/Indian friendship. With a frankness and detail probably unmatched by any other Chinese statement on foreign policy, the article set out the Chinese case over Tibet, and accused the Indians of unjustified interference. Indian trade with Tibet was greatly restricted. Clashes involving casualties occurred at several points along the disputed border as the Chinese Army extended its control over border areas in an effort to restrict the move-court of Tibetans across the frontier.

These border clashes, following in the wake of the Tibetan uprising, appeared to put an end to Nehru's willingness to compromise over the border dispute. Having earlier in 1959 cast doubt on the Indian claim to the Aksai Chin, in September he stated before the Indian Parliament that the Chinese claims were "absurd" and would mean "handing over the Himalayas to them as a gift". A Chinese call in November 1959 for negotiations and a twenty-kilometre military withdrawal from the McMahon Line in the east and the "line of actual control" in the west to prevent a recurrence of border clashes was met with an Indian demand for a prior Chinese withdrawal from the Aksai Chin. A Chinese reply pointing out that this should also be paralleled by an Indian withdrawal from the NE.F.A. was ignored. In the end the Chinese appeared to settle for a freezing of the existing status quo - without negotiations or a twenty-kilometre withdrawal.

However, if the Chinese were happy to keep things as they were (keeping also their road across the Aksai Chin), Nehru and his Government were not. Throughout 1960-61 Indian opinion progressively hardened, and demands for the Government to do something about Tibet and the disputed border increased. The army was given full control over the frontier districts and it proceeded to build up its strength in these areas. During the summer (northern) of 1962, Indian military patrols repeatedly crossed the Chinese-claimed line of actual control in the western sector of the frontier. Posts were established well behind the Chinese forward positions in territory claimed and occupied by the Chinese. Frequent and insistent Chinese protests were met with the bald statement that the Indians were merely operating in Indian territory. By August 14, Nehru was able to announce that India had three times as many posts in the western sector as the Chinese. He asked for a free hand to continue the build-up of Indian strength in the area.

The Chinese had repeatedly warned that a continuation of such activity would end in hostilities. On July 9, they had warned the Indians "to rein in on the brink of the precipice". On August 4, they called for immediate negotiations on the border. The Indians replied that negotiations could not be held until the Chinese had ceased their occupation of "every square inch of sacred Indian territory", and that the Chinese must first "vacate their aggression" in the Aksai Chin. The Chinese replied on September 13 proposing talks to begin on October 15 "without preconditions", that is, without a Chinese withdrawal from the Aksai Chin. The Indians refused the offer.

While Indian military pressure was building up along the Chinese-claimed border in the western sector, a curious situation was developing along the McMahon Line in the eastern sector. The Indians claim that at its western end the McMahon Line was not accurately drawn: that it was meant to have followed the crest of a line of hills known as the Thag La ridge. The Chinese claim, and have produced the original McMahon Line from the Tibetan archives to prove their point, that the line as originally drawn lies approximately twelve miles south of this ridge along the southern side of a small river valley. (Western maps show the McMahon Line in conformity with the Chinese claim.) The area between the Indian and Chinese versions of the McMahon Line is described by the Indians as the Dho La strip. This was not the only unilateral revision of the McMahon Line carried out by the Indians. In his letter to Chou En-lai of September 29, 1959, Nehru admitted that in the Migyitun area (to the east of the Dho La strip) the border shown on Indian maps "differs slightly from the boundary shown in the Treaty map". He claimed that when the McMahon line was drawn, "the exact topographical features in this area were not known". The Indians have also now come to admit that "blind adherence" to the original McMahon Line would leave the Dho La strip on the Chinese side at the border.

It is not clear who first occupied the Dho La strip. The Chinese claim that the area had always been under their control and that Indian troops moved in during 1962. The Indians claim they had long occupied the area and that the Chinese began a to establish posts in the area after September 8, 1962. What is clear is that on October 12, 1962, Nehru announced in the Indian Parliament that he had given the order to drive the Chinese out of the Dho La strip.

Eight days later, on October 20, the Chinese attacked in force across the Thagla La ridge and into the disputed strip, while advancing their troops into the Chinese-claimed territory in the western sector where the Indians had earlier established posts. Four days later, the Chinese called for a ceasefire to be followed by a withdrawal of both sides from the line that separated them at that moment (the so-called October 24 line of actual control). Failing to get a satisfactory response from the Indians, they advanced troops south of the Dho La strip into the N.E.F.A., defeating Indian military forces in the area. Two weeks later, they withdrew to the positions occupied on October 24. The main point of contention between the Chinese and Indians ever since has been whether the Chinese should maintain their October 24 positions or withdraw further to the positions they occupied before fighting broke out.

The Chinese attack of October 1962 has led to an almost complete breakdown in relations between China and India. The level of each country's diplomatic representation in the other has been greatly reduced. Many thousands of Chinese nationals have been expelled from India. The few Indian nationals living in China have, in one way or another, been forced to leave. Border incidents have continued. Both sides have launched extreme propaganda campaigns against each other, the Chinese denouncing Nehru as a representative of the "big bourgeoisie" and a tool for U. S. aggressive designs against Tibet, while the Indians denounce the Chinese for having aggressive, imperialist designs against Indian territory. Both sides have gone to great lengths to discredit each other inter- nationally. Both sides have increased their military preparedness along the Himalayan frontier, particularly India, which has doubled its military budget to a level it cannot afford.

The question thus arises: Who is primarily to blame for the hostility in Sino/Indian relations? From the account already given, the primary cause of the hostility was the post-1959 dispute over the Sino/Indian border leading to the Chinese attack of October 20. But why the sudden emergence of such a dispute between two countries previously enjoying good relations? Reverting to the terminology of our previous discussion on hostility between states, both sides see the breakdown in relations as being caused by the active hostility of the other side. This hostility, they claim, is both ideologically and national-interest based. The Chinese are accused of having acted in a hostile manner out of a desire to acquire territory and out of strong ideological dislike for the Indian Government. The Chinese claim the Indians have designs against Chinese territory and that their Government is under the influence of anti-Chinese and pro-U. S. reactionary elements.

Both sides realise that they have somehow or other to explain why the other side suddenly, in 1959, decided that its interests were no longer served by the maintenance of normal relations. The Indian explanation is that Chinese pre-1959 policy was designed to lull India into a false sense of security and so facilitate Chinese ambitions. The Chinese explanation was that reactionary elements began to gain the upper hand in the Indian Government in 1959, and point to the post-1959 increase in U. S. aid to India as evidence.

In fact there is good reason to believe that the hostility shown by each side towards the other was reactive rather than active: that each side was reacting to the believed hostility of the other. To take the Chinese side of things first. In terms of the account already given, it seems likely that the Chinese attack of October 20, 1962, was primarily a reaction to Indian military pressure along the disputed frontier during preceding months. It could be argued, however. that the behaviour of the Chinese before October 20, and in particular their propaganda attacks against the Indians from 1960 onwards, cannot be explained simply as a reaction to previous events: that overall Chinese behaviour must therefore include some aggressive component.

The Chinese had in fact made their first hostile move against the Indians back in 1959 when they restricted Indian trading and other rights in Tibet. The Chinese had also, according to the Indians, extended somewhat the area they claimed in the western sector. And they had, according to the Indians, been responsible for the 1959 border clashes already mentioned. The Indian charge is based on alleged differences between the frontier claimed by the Chinese to 1956 and that shown on a map of the claimed Sino/Indian frontier handed to the Indians by the Chinese in 1960. The Chinese deny any difference between the two lines.

Unless these apparently hostile acts of the Chinese can be explained in reactive terms., in terms of their reacting to previous Indian actions, then it would seem that the Chinese had taken the initiative in hostility towards India and were largely responsible for the eventual breakdown in relations.

The hardening of the Chinese attitude towards India in 1959 was clearly related to Tibetan developments in that year. In judging the behaviour of the Chinese, we need, in effect, to ask whether their sensitivity over Tibet was sufficient to explain this hardening of attitude. To accept that the Communist Chinese are, in fact extremely sensitive toward Tibet does not necessarily imply a simple acceptance of Chinese propaganda. What we know of Chinese thinking and behaviour, strongly suggests that this sensitivity does exist. If all non-communist Chinese believe that China has the right to consider Tibet as an integral part of her territory, we should accept that Communist Chinese are equally convinced. If many non-communist Chinese believe (as they do) that Britain had designs against Tibet, we should accept that Communist Chinese, educated to believe in the evils of US Western imperialism, will be at least equally fearful. We do not need accept that these views are correct; we may even consider they are absurd. But if we are going to get anywhere in trying to understand China's behaviour, we should start from the assumption that these views may be sincerely hold in Peking.

Nor may it be so absurd for the Communist Chinese to think along these lines. The Chinese legal claim to Tibet, it has been argued, appears difficult to refute. As for fears of foreign designs, if the British had earlier convinced themselves that the activities of one Russian agent in Lhasa could lead the politically unstable Tibetans to ally themselves with Tsarist Russia, the Chinese could be excused for thinking that the presence of a British Mission in Lhasa dealing directly with the independent-minded Tibetans and arranging on occasion for the supply of arms from India was evidence of British ambitions eventually to detach Tibet from China, and that India may have inherited these ambitions. Similarly, it would not be entirely surprising if the Chinese viewed the supply of foreign arms to Tibetan guerrillas from northern India in 1959 as confirmation that such ambitions existed. Finally, the Chinese were hound to be impressed by the demands of the Indian Right Wing for action against the Chinese in Tibet.

For example: some weight could be attached to the fact that the then Chief of the Indian Army Staff wrote a not unenthusiastic foreword for a book published in 1961 entitled The Chinese Aggression. The author of the hook, a Dr. Satyanarayan Sinha, predicted that the "clash of the Indochinese weapons for the possession of the Himalayas will lead to making Tibet an independent country again", and suggested ways in which this could be done.

These, then, are the reasons for believing the Chinese may he sensitive about Tibet. Chinese behaviour provides further confirmation. British officials captured in Tibet in 1950 were subjected to long imprisonment and continual interrogation - treatment far more severe than that meted out to British nationals who fell into communist hands elsewhere in China. And there was Nehru's sad admission to the Indian Parliament in 1959 after talks with Chou En-Iai, of the Chinese having "some sort of kink in their minds... of foreign countries, United Kingdom or America, somehow making incursions into Tibet".

In sum, therefore, it does not seem unreasonable to conclude that the Communist Chinese sincerely believed they had a right to Tibet and that their position in the area was threatened from the direction of India. In which case they would have interpreted Indian behaviour in 1959 as an indication of hostility to which they felt compelled, or entitled, to react. However, if Chinese behaviour in 1959 can be explained in reactive terms, can the same be said about the Chinese attack of October 1962? Even if the Indian claim to the Dho La strip was doubtful, does not the violence and intensity of the 1962 attack suggest that China was doing more than retaliate for any wrongs she may have believed the Indians to base committed?

By 1962, the Chinese were confronted not only by Indian agitation over Tibet, but also by two further aspects of Indian behaviour which would even more easily have been misunderstood. They were: (i) the Indian military build-up along the Sino/Indian border in 1961-2 and (ii) rigid Indian insistence that, as a precondition to border negotiations, the Chinese must first evacuate the whole of the Aksai Chin.

At the time, the Indians justified their position on negotiations and their military build up in terms of the correctness of their border claims. Indeed, the official Indian position was that the line claimed by India as a border had already been defined historically, and that the only purpose of negotiations was to demarcate on the ground the exact alignment of this border. From this it followed that they were justified (a) in regarding rival Chinese claims, and the occupation of the Aksai Chin, as evidence of Chinese hostility, and (b) in insisting that occupied territory had to be vacated before there could be negotiations. In the meantime the Indians had no alternative but to use military means to counter the Chinese "aggression".

If India was in fact the injured party in the territorial dispute, the Indian attitude over the disputed border would have been explicable at least to an impartial observer, and possibly even to the less impartial Chinese. There would be less justification for the Chinese reacting in the way they did. But was this the case? To answer this question we need to take a closer look at the historical background to the Sino /Indian frontier, and shall begin with the eastern sector, or N.E.F.A.

Until the 1920's, the region now known as the N.E.F.A. was largely unexplored. It was, and still is, inhabited by tribes of Tibeto-Burmese origin, some of which enjoyed trade and tributary relations with Tibet. Certain areas in the north of the region, the Tawang district for example, were inhabited by Tibetans and were under administrative control from Tibet.

The McMahon Line was negotiated with the Tibetans in 1914 at the time of the Simla Conference. It was drawn as far to the north as possible, since the British at the time sought to forestall a feared Chinese expansion into the foothills bordering the Assam plains. The McMahon Line as part of a bargain whereby the British would press the Chinese to concede territory elsewhere to Tibet.

Even so, the Tibetans were not entirely happy about losing territory south of the McMahon Line, the Tawang district in particular. Their acceptance of the line was conditional on possible future adjustments in their favour. No such adjustments, were ever made. The British also failed to extract the promised concessions from the Chinese, since the latter refused to accept the Convention produced at the Simla Conference. Thus, even as a Tibetan/British frontier, the McMahon Line does not have full validity, particularly as the Tibetans subsequently, in 1936, made a formal request to the British for revision of the line in their favour a request which the British ignored. As late as 1946, the Tibetans were still collecting taxes in the Tawang area. And, in 1947, the Tibetans approached the newly established Indian Government, seeking the "return" of "Tibetan territories" from Assam to Ladakh.

The Indian reply to this approach may be of interest in the light of complaints to be voiced later by the Indians over the manner in which the Chinese spoke of their border claims being inherited from previous Chinese Governments "The Government of India should be glad to have an assurance that it is the intention of the Tibetan Government to continue relations an the existing basis until new Agreements are any reached... This is the procedure adopted by all other countries with which India has inherited Treaty relations from His Majesty's Government".

The validity of the McMahon Line as a Chinese/Indian frontier is considerably more doubtful. True, in rejecting the draft Simla Contention, the Chinese did not specifically object to the McMahon Line as drawn on the map of Tibet attached to the Convention. But, as the Chinese point out, the then Chinese Government had no way of knowing what this line was supposed to represent, since the terms of the McMahon Line agreement were for some reason kept secret by the British and Tibetans until 1929. It could, in theory, have been a border between Tibet and a Chinese-owned N.E.F.A. Moreover, Chiang Kaishek's Government was later to make it clear to the British (and the Indians after 1947) that it did not accept the McMahon Line. The Chinese have also pointed out that, since neither the British nor the Chinese regarded Tibet as a sovereign entity, the Tibetans were obliged to obtain Chinese approval for any frontier negotiated with a foreign power. * Failure to obtain this approval, both at the Simla Conference and later, meant that the McMahon Line never at any stage enjoyed international legality. And finally, as the Chinese never tire of pointing out, many Western and Indian maps, including one reproduced in a book by Nehru himself, Discovery of India, have, even in recent years., shown the Sino/Indian border as running along the edge of the Assam plain in conformity with the traditional Chinese claim.

The 1906 Convention between Britain and China had required China to accept responsibility for Tibet's foreign relations. "The 1907 Anglo/Russian Convention required Britain 'not to enter into negotiations with Tibet except through the intermediary of the Chinese Government". Negotiations with the Tibetans over the McMahon Line were thus a breach of both conventions - a possible reason why the terms of the McMahon Line agreement were kept secret.

For the Communist Chinese to appear to be willing to drop their N.E.F.A. claim is no small concession in view of the very considerable doubts as to the validity of the McMahon Line. Indeed, the Nationalist Government in Taiwan feels so strongly shout the justice of the Chinese clams that its official newspapers have accused Peking of being willing to abandon "sacred" Chinese territory. They have predicted that the present Communist Chinese leaders will be condemned by future generations of Chinese for their betrayal of China's interests. Nevertheless, the Indian position was that the Chinese should not only drop their claim to the N.E.F.A. but to the Aksai Chin also. How strong is the Indian claim in the western sector of the disputed frontier?

The province of Ladakh, which lies on the Indian side of the disputed western sector, was originally a semi-independent state with a complex tributary relationship with Tibet. It was far from being clearly defined Indian territory. These links with Tibet were severed as a result of the 1841 invasion of Tibet from Kashmir, and Ladakh was incorporated into India. In the agreement which followed the invasion, the Ladakh/Tibet border was defined simply as following "the old established frontier", and it was only subsequently that British cartographers decided where this frontier should lie. A small area lying between the Chinese-claimed and Indian-claimed frontiers is in dispute.

By far the larger area in dispute, the Aksai Chin, lies for the most part north of the Ladakh/Tibet frontier, and its ownership depends on a definition of the Ladakh/Sinkiang border. At the end of the nineteenth century, the British decided an effort should be made to define this border, and in 1899 a note was delivered to the Chinese suggesting a possible alignment. This alignment is shown on the map above, and it will be seen that it leaves with China much of the territory at present in dispute. The Chinese never replied to the note. Shortly afterwards, the British attitude changed.

Alarmed by growing Chinese weakness in Central Asia, and fearing Russian expansion into the area (fears similar to those being entertained in connection with Tibet), the British felt they should establish the border as far north as possible to forestall any southward advance by the Russians. British maps began to show the border as lying far to the north along the Kun Lun mountains. Chinese agreement was never sought for this claimed border (despite the fact that the British recognised Chinese sovereignty in Sinkiang) ; presumably it was only being put forward as an emergency measure in case the Russians attempted to seize Sinkiang. By the 1920's the Russian threat had disappeared, and it was deemed safe to drop this particular claim.

In subsequent years, British and Indian maps showed a variety of claim lines some coinciding with the present Chinese claim line, some the claim line along the Kun Lun mountains, and some an in-between claim line which ran south of the Kun Lun mountains but which included the Aksai Chin as Indian territory.

Maps showing this last claim line were in general use at the time of the 1947 transfer of power, and appear to constitute the basis of the present Indian claim to the Aksai Chin. However, the only border to have ever been officially proposed to the Chinese by the British in this area was that of 1899, and, as already mentioned, this border left most of the Aksai Chin with China. Whatever the merits of rival Chinese and Indian claims to the Aksai Chin area, it does seem clear that the Indians can hardly speak of the frontier they claim in this area as being already defined by history and therefore subject only to demarcation.

In this connection a rather curious aspect of the Indian position should be mentioned - an aspect which has been overlooked by most students of the Sino/Indian dispute.

Numerous Indian authorities, including Nehru himself, have claimed historical validity for their version of the Indian! Sinkiang frontier on the ground that the line proposed by the British in 1899 "ran along the Kun Lun range to a point east of 80° longitude, where it met the eastern boundary of Ladakh". In fact, the 1899 line ran well to the south of the Kun Lun mountains, and the text of the proposal speaks only of the tine meeting "the spur running south from the Kun Lun range, which [the spur] has hitherto been shown on our maps as the eastern boundary of Ladakh. This is a little east of 80° east longitude".* A misquotation of these dimensions is rather serious, particularly when it is used to justify an official claim to some 30,000 square kilometres of territory, and when, on the basis of this claim, negotiations are refused in favour of a military solution of a complex border dispute.

The only observer who appears to have noted this misquotation is Alastair Lamb. In his book, *The China-India Border*, he gives the full text of the British note of 1899 and lists some of the Indian authorities who have misquoted the 1899 proposal. Distribution of his book within India has been banned.

It would seem, therefore, that an impartial observer who takes into account not only the historical background of the border dispute, but also the equally relevant criteria of geography and administrative control, would agree that the Chinese are not being unreasonable when they call for border negotiations on the basis of the present status quo.

If, as seems to be the case, the Chinese are prepared to do a N.E.F.A./ Aksai Chin exchange leaving India in control of far the largest and most valuable of the territories in dispute, he may even feel that the Chinese are being quite generous. And if our impartial observer were to reach such a conclusion, it seems highly likely that the Chinese would be convinced of the reasonableness of their position and the unreasonableness of the Indian demand for a unilateral Chinese withdrawal from the Aksai Chin.

If the Chinese were in fact convinced that they were in the right over the border dispute, they would in all probability have interpreted the Indian military build-up along the disputed border in 1961-2 as evidence of active hostility. Striking confirmation that this was the case is contained in the "Tibetan Documents" - official Chinese documents which were captured by Tibetan rebels in 1961 and which subsequently found their way to the U.S., where they have been translated and published.

These documents were intended as background briefing to senior Chinese military commanders stationed along the Sino/ Indian border. As such, their contents cannot be dismissed simply as propaganda. The documents warned of U.S./Indian collusion to build up pressure along the Tibetan frontier as a prelude to a joint attack against Tibet. Military commanders were instructed to observe strictly the twenty-kilometre troop withdrawal from the line of actual control and to avoid clashes with advancing Indian patrols since this would provide the "imperialists" with the pretext they needed to justify their planned attack.

INNOVATIVE TENSIONS, OLD TROUBLES ON THE INDO-SINO BORDER

As China deepens its economic and strategic relations with Pakistan, and makes diplomatic in-roads with Nepal and Myanmar, it is worth examining an issue that continues to mar Sino-Indian relations. The China-India border conflict has long stirred tensions between Beijing and New Delhi, in spite of regular attempts to put the border issue on the backburner. However, provocative incidents continue to occur between Chinese and Indian forces along the vaguely demarcated and often disputed Line of Actual Control (LAC). The latest major such incident between the two sides took place on September 11 near Burtse, situated on the far western end of the roughly 3488 kilometer (3,4883,488km) long LAC, between the Ladakh neighborhood of the Indian state of Jammu and Kashmir and Xinjiang province. After receiving information that the Chinese were constructing a hut with a camera, Indian soldiers and border police demolished the structure, in spite of Chinese attempts to push them back. This resulted in a stand-off between the two sides.

As it often chances with incidents on the border, the stand-off provoked a small storm of attention from the Indian media, but was downplayed by the Indian government and completely ignored by the Chinese one. Unusually, however, a week after the stand-off had ended a Chinese military spokesperson knocked India for not following border agreements. Eventually, the two sides called two "flag meetings" between senior officers, a mechanism for addressing border incidents at five meeting points along the LAC, and resolved the incident. Both sides agreed to pull out their soldiers and, in what was seen as success for India, abstain from building structures on the disputed LAC.

What made the incident significant was its place and timing. The Chinese incitement took place just before the Indian Home Minster, Rajnath Singh, seen as a hawk on the territorial dispute, was scheduled to make a highly-symbolic visit to the disputed border close to the location of the incident. The minister subsequently postponed his visit to later in September. The location of the incident was also concerning because the area around Burtse is of great strategic significance. It is close to both the G219 and G314 highways. The latter of these is better known as the Chinese part of the Karakorum highway, one of the major arteries through which Chinese aid and personnel come to Pakistan. Burtse is also close to India's small but strategic Daulat Beg Oldi airbase, which New Delhi activated in 2008 to Beijing's displeasure, and not far from the site of a severe border standoff in 2013.

The Border Argument

The Burtse stand-off is just one of a long string of incidents which mark the decades-long border dispute. The conflict concerns three areas around the border 1) the western sector, known as Aksai Chin, which is mostly occupied by China; 2) a middle sector where there are relatively small disagreements on where the border should run; 3) and the fiercely disputed Eastern sector, which is occupied by India and largely covers the Indian state of Arunachal Pradesh. In the middle sector the dispute also concerns Sikkim, a strategically located Indian state which Beijing has not recognized, unequivocally, as part of India.

With roots stretching back to the 19th and betimes 20th century, this dispute was inherited in the 1950s by the recently established People's Republic of China and a newly independent India. China's subsequent consolidation of control in Tibet resulted in the gradual souring of the Sino-Indian relationship. The nadir came in 1962, when, in response to India's seizure of territory, China attacked India and inflicted a heavy, albeit limited, defeat on Indian forces. The brief war has adversely shaped mutual perceptions to this day, and has turned the dispute into a highly sensitive issue, especially for India. Several advertises have been made to resolve the dispute since the 1980s, most notably in 2003, when the two sides initiated the Special Representatives Talks headed by India's National Security Advisor and China's State Counsellor responsible for foreign policy, and in 2005, when the two parties agreed on a set of guidelines for resolving the dispute. Nevertheless, in spite of eighteen rounds of such talks, regular declarations that both sides seek to settle the dispute, and years of work of a Joint Working Group on the boundary dispute, there has been little progress toward a final settlement. Instead, focus has progressively shifted to managing the frequent border tensions.

A quick review of the borders would suggest that China and India can easily accept the status quo and swap their claims over Aksai Chin and Arunachal Pradesh. Nevertheless, a key obstacle is the nexus between the dispute and the issue of Tibet. Beijing's territorial claims are based on the logic that Tibet has been part of China, and India's case is founded on agreements signed by a Tibetan government and British India without Beijing's consent, particularly the 1914 Simla Accord determining the McMahon Line which delineates the eastern sector of the border. Hence, accepting a territorial swap or the legitimacy of some parts of the LAC, which is partly based on the McMahon Line, will bring up the issue of the historical status of Tibet. The Tibet question also involves another great impediment to resolving the dispute, Tawang, a border town with a Tibetan Buddhist monastery that had historically been a part of Tibet and where the next Dalai Lama could reincarnate in the future. Predictably, these characteristics have made the Indian-controlled Tawang a requirement for Beijing in any border closure. Some analysts have additionally noted domestic constraints on both sides, strategic concerns and the potential that the two sides deliberately want to keep the dispute unresolved.

Incursions and Dispute

While the border dispute cannot be resolved, it cannot be put on the backburner, either. The reason are the incidents, usually incursions, which regularly take place on the border. On average, about 400 such incidents occur every year, starting in 2012, although the number might be somewhat on the decline this year. Most incidents are the result of Chinese patrolling beyond the LAC or the building of small structures, such as huts, bunkers or surveillance installations, by either side. The last years have witnessed several major incidents. The largest was a three-week stand-off at Daulat Beg Oldi in April and May 2013 which witnessed Chinese soldiers set up tents 19 km inside India-controlled district in the run-up to the visit of India's foreign minister to Beijing and the visit to India of Chinese Premier Li Keqiang.

When incident was resolved, in a deal about which little is known to this day, India destroyed a number of bunkers that its troops had recently built on the LAC. Another standoff took place in September 2014, just before President Xi Jinping's trip to India when, in response to Indian construction of a hut with a surveillance camera about the border and the digging of a canal, Chinese soldiers moved to disputed territory in Ladakh to build a road.

An incident also took place in November when a PLA light-armored vehicle went patrolling beyond the LAC during the Indian home minister's visit to Beijing and just days before a meeting between President Xi and Prime Minister Modi at the G-20 summit in Turkey.

Three features characterize border incidents. First, the incidents have grown since 2007, a development which has led some analysts to connect China's behavior with the U.S.-India nuclear deal and the Tibet uprising from 2008. Second, there has been a particular increase in incidents in the western sector, usually around Ladakh. Third, larger incidents tend to precede high-ranking bilateral meetings, which might suggest that Beijing is using incursions to gain advantage in negotiations or signal its position. The last point leads to the fundamental question why China seeks to provoke border tensions. Explanations have varied from a strategy to keep India on the defensive or punish it for its closer ties with Washington, to a form of coercion on the dispute, to the provocative behavior of local Chinese commanders. Beijing, itself, often excuses the incidents with the undetermined LAC, an explanation supported by some independent analysts, although Chinese observers have also sometimes suggested that Indian media deliberately exaggerates the incidents.

Repeated attempts have been made to manage border tensions, starting with the 1993 agreement in which both sides state "No activities of either side shall overstep the line of actual control". In 2013, China and India signed the Border Defense Cooperation Agreement, which adopts measures to reduce tensions, such as flag meetings between officers at designated points, the proposed establishment of a hotline between the two regional military headquarters, on the two sides of the LAC, and prohibitions against tailing the other side's patrols. In 2012, the two countries' ministries of foreign affairs also established a Working Mechanism because Consultation and Coordination on India-China Border Affairs between senior diplomats. Most recently during a visit to Beijing by India's home minister and during the visit of a Chinese military delegation led by Fan Changlong, Vice Chairman of the Central Military Commission, to New Delhi. Nevertheless, neither agreements nor bilateral diplomacy have succeeded in decisively reducing tensions.

Border Infrastructure Structure

Beside border incidents, which receive most media attention, border tensions are fueled by an infrastructure building race. This infrastructure building, which has accelerated dramatically in the last ten years, serves three goals: 1) integration of the disputed territories under control; 2) establishment of sovereignty through facts on the ground; and 3) setting up the necessary infrastructure since moving troops and equipment to the LAC fast, in case of armed conflict.

On the Chinese side, as part of a huge project for developing Tibet, Beijing has built a network of roads that reaches every county in Tibet and connects with four main highways, the Central Highway, the Eastern Highway, the Yunnan-Tibet Highway and the Western Highway which eventually extends into the China-Pakistan Karakoram Highway and passes through India-claimed Aksai Chin. Many of the roads of this network run identical close to the LAC and even beyond it, such as the Chip Chat Heights road in the western sector, which is four kilometers inside Indian occupied territory. China plans to extend this highway network from about 70,000 km in 2013 to 110,000 km by 2020. China has also been extending its rail lines up to or close to the border. One line between Lhasa and Xigaze, next to Sikkim, comprised completed in 2014 (with plans for extension to the border), and work has been going on lines to Yatung, next to Sikkim and the strategic Nathula Pass, and Nyingchi, on the border with Chinese-claimed Arunachal Pradesh. Beijing has also built five airbases in the area around the borders, numerous landing strips and oil depots.

Indian infrastructure building has also progressed, although at a much slower pace and from a lower starting point, due to decades-old fears that China could use infrastructure to its advantage in case of attack. Since 2006, New Delhi has initiated a major program of building 73 all-weather roads and 14 rail lines on the border. However, as of 2014, only 18 roads and none of the rail lines have been completed. In terms of Advanced Landing Grounds, India has fared better with five airstrips operational by the end of 2014 and two more projected. The slow progress on the Indian side has been attributed to bureaucratic inertia, the complex politics between the central government and the states in which the infrastructure is to be built and the fact that several different agencies work on these projects. On his visit to the border at Ladakh after the Burtse incident, Home Minister Rajnath Singh anticipated the prompt construction of three strategic new roads in the increasingly contested Ladakh region. This comes on top of a Home Ministry plan of building 27 new roads, a proposed $6 billion new highway in Arunachal Pradesh and suggestions that India might inaugurate a program of population settling in the disputed territories.

China is far ahead of India in terms of building strategic infrastructure. In case of military conflict, it is estimated that China can presently transport up to 32 divisions in six weeks, along with heavy equipment, all year round and sustain them, from a previous limit of 22 divisions mobilized in six months and not during all times of the year. Such a mobilization would leave

Indian forces outnumbered 3:1. However, India has been increasingly worried by this disparity and has assayed to accelerate its infrastructure building, especially as it discusses plans to raise up to two new divisions on the border, three artillery brigades and three armored brigades.

The Burtse incursion in September is one of a long string of incidents on the Sino-Indian border which often coincide with major bilateral meetings. These incidents, and the race between China and India in building border infrastructure, regularly generate tensions on the LAC and trouble Sino-Indian relations. Efforts to manage such stresses have been consistently unsuccessful. Hence, a more stable relationship between Beijing and New Delhi will require either a real breakthrough in managing border tensions or a resolution of the dispute which underlines them. Neither seems likely in foreseeable future.

THE TIBETAN QUESTION AND THE CAUSE OF THE DISPUTE

The fact is that a large part of the border dispute hinges on the uncomfortable question of Tibet's sovereignty. If Tibet was sovereign at the time of the Simla conference, then the treaty is legal and it serves India's cause. If Tibet was not sovereign at that time, then the treaty is illegal and serves China's cause.

Some activists campaigning for a free Tibet often bring up the Simla conference as proof of Tibet's independence. Their arguments are mainly two fold -

a) The Tibetan representative signed the treaty even though he was instructed by the Chinese representative not to sign, a clear indication undermining (Tibetan acceptance of) Chinese suzerainty over Tibet.

b) More importantly, since Tibet concluded a treaty with a foreign power on its own,*it was an independent country on that day.*

At the time of the Simla conference, although the Tibetan government had driven out all Chinese officials from Tibet after the collapse of the Qing dynasty and declared independence, the Nationalist government did not accept this and neither has the PRC nor any other government.

India had enjoyed certain privileges with regard to Tibet under the Simla Agreement, including those regarding trade and commerce. However, when China 'annexed' Tibet in 1951, India under Nehru recognized it as Chinese territory, thus giving up those privileges and undermining Tibet's sovereignty (which it may have momentarily enjoyed during the time of the Simla agreement). Thus in a sense the Indian government tacitly admitted that the Simla agreement was effectively illegal, which to this day remains China's official position. In doing so, India weakened its own position with respect to the border dispute. The Simla agreement was signed between Britain, Tibet and China. Now, from this information, two questions present themselves -

1) If Tibet *was* sovereign, why was China invited at the conference at all? Why didn't the British negotiate directly with Tibet?
2) If Tibet was *not* sovereign, why was *it* invited at the conference? Why didn't the British negotiate directly with China? (In other words, why did China accept to attend a conference where Tibet was represented as a separate party?)

The answer to (1) is that, as stated above, Britain recognised Tibet to be under Chinese suzerainty. Hence, any *bilateral* agreement that Britain signed with Tibet (without Chinese agreement) would be illegal. (But ironically, that is exactly what the British did)

(2) is a bit more complicated. There are indications that the British had blackmailed the Chinese into attending by threatening to -

a) withdraw their recognition of the new nationalist government, and,
b) sign the treaty with Tibet alone if China didn't participate, thus acknowledging that Tibet was in fact sovereign. (But later the British did exactly the same thing when China didn't agree to its terms during the conference).

Hence, it is clear that Britain's imperial designs and its policy of 'divide and rule' and double crossing everyone was in effect the cause of the entire dispute.

RESOLVING THE BOUNDARY DISPUTE: CHINA'S REASONS AND INDIA'S CHOICES

The final settlement of the Sino-Indian territorial and boundary dispute is not a question of 'if' but 'when'. Four pertinent reasons suggest that China can be ultimately trusted to settle the dispute. On its part, India can take certain steps to ensure that China's reasons do not alter and that 'compromise' is seen as mutually beneficial.

One, China has steadily resolved its territorial disputes with almost all of its 15 land neighbours. Negotiations with the Soviet Union and Vietnam began in 1964 and 1977 respectively. However, it was not until much later that the negotiation processes fructified; it was only in October 2004 that the eastern sector of the Sino-Russian border was finally resolved with the signing of the Supplementary Agreement. With Vietnam, China signed a land boundary agreement in 1999, although they continue to meet regularly at the governmental level to thrash out details pertaining to the Beibu Gulf and the placement of border markers. Therefore, boundary negotiations between China and its other neighbours have been long and arduous affairs. The slowness of the boundary negotiations between India and China needs to be seen in this context.

Two, China has settled 17 of its 23 territorial disputes since 1949, according to M. Taylor Fravel, Assistant Professor of Political Science at MIT. Fravel suggests that regime insecurity and legitimacy crises in peripheral border regions best explain why China not only made concessions but also favoured the peaceful resolution of its territorial disputes. Despite a significant rise in China's economic and military strength vis-a-vis weaker neighbours, China received less than 50 per cent of the contested land. China's 'peaceful development' and 'new security concept' are directly responsible for the gradual stabilization of its borders-both concepts demand peaceful and stable borders for sustained economic growth.

Three, the absence of territorial disputes on China's western flank is a consequence of its 'western development' strategy. Starting with Myanmar and Nepal in the 1960s, a flurry of diplomatic activity saw the resolution of China's borders with Tajikistan and Kazakhstan (in 2002), Kyrgyzstan (in September 2004), Russia (in October 2004), and Mongolia (in November 2005). The pacification of China's western border is driven by the need to build cross-border linkages for economic development as well as the suppression of the three evils-separatism, extremism and terrorism. China's two westernmost provinces that border India, Xinjiang and Tibet, are important to China not least due to the fear that an economic imbalance can potentially fuel secessionist sentiments amongst the Uighurs and Tibetans.

Four, China is likely to reserve the use of force to settle heartland disputes. The hard component of China's comprehensive national strength will continue to dictate an inflexible stance on Taiwan's reunification as well as territorial conflicts of strategic value. Therefore, China is unlikely to make concessions on approximately 30,000 square kilometres of Aksai Chin, not least due to the fact that the Karakoram highway that traverses it provides a strategic link between Pakistan, and China and a shorter route between Tibet and Xinjiang. However, even in the case of disputes over territory of great economic value, such as the South China Sea, China has emphasized the joint development and exploitation of resources, albeit without making any concessions.

As emerging powers, India and China will continue to be pitted against each other. The sheer size and altitude of the disputed area is likely to make demarcation a difficult and lengthy process. However, India can take certain steps to ensure it remains in China's interest to settle the dispute. India must do its utmost to convince China that it is not the target of the newly sealed Indo-US strategic relationship. India must clarify that the support for Tibetans in India is humanitarian and cultural and not a challenge to China's sovereign territoriality. China's friendship with Pakistan cannot be wished away; however, India can make itself important to China by promising trade and joint border development projects that make good business sense. India's inclusion into the Shanghai Cooperation Organisation as an observer in July 2005 was an important recognition of India's commitment to curbing cross-border terrorism.

Even though there are reasons to believe that China is not a revisionist state determined to use force to uphold its territorial claims, proactive steps to create lobbies with vested interests in resolving the dispute must be taken. The seventh round of Sino-Indian border talks in March 2006 helped provide a 'constructive and friendly' atmosphere. It is time for India and China to carry that forward and focus on opening Nathu La for trade, reviving the Stilwell Road for trade across India's northeast, building border free trade zones similar to the Sino-Kazakh one and establishing independent inter-linkages between border regions through transport linkages akin to the Kashgar (Xinjiang, China)-Gilgit (Northern Areas, Pakistan) bus service. Discussion on the Sino-Indian boundary talks must therefore go beyond the rhetoric on China's 'concirclement' of India; it must emphasize the domestic constraints and foreign policy concerns of the Chinese government and the resolution of territorial disputes that such a study reveals.

3

The Collision of the Sino-Indian War

In many ways, how China and India relate to each other indicates where they see themselves in the international system. Firstly, however, it is necessary to have an understanding of the events leading up to and following the 1962 Sino-Indian War, as this continues to affect the contemporary Sino-Indian relationship. The major causes of conflict between China and India – namely, the disputed border and the issue of Tibet, including the fourteenth Dalai Lama's ongoing residency in India – have their roots in the political dealings that went on in the late 1800s and early 1900s between British India, pre-Communist China and feudal Tibet. The major question was whether treaties signed by British India and Tibet demarcating the border – known as the McMahon Line – were valid, given that, according to the Chinese, Tibet was part of China and had no authority to act unilaterally. Disagreements of this nature and the exact location of the border persisted throughout the early twentieth century, further complicated by Indian independence in 1947 (which removed British backing and so altered the balance of power in the region in favour of China) and the Chinese 'liberation' of Tibet in 1950.

1954, marked with a visit to India Chinese by Premier Zhou Enlai in June, and a reciprocal visit by Indian Prime Minister Jawaharlal Nehru to China in October, was a high point in the relationship; it was during the latter visit that the term 'Hindi-Chini bhai-bhai' (Indians and Chinese are brothers) was coined, and denoted a period of rapprochement after decades of strife over the disputed India-Tibet border.

This new-found friendship in theory forged a renewed basis for discussions over the disputed border, though this was tested only two years later. There were (and still are) two contested areas: the north-eastern stretch, which was known under the British as the North-East Frontier Agency (NEFA) and since 1986 has been the Indian state of Arunachal Pradesh (claimed by the Chinese as Southern Tibet), and the western region of Aksai Chin (claimed by the Indians and currently administered by the Chinese), which borders the Indian state of Jammu and Kashmir. Although up until the mid-50s most of the border tensions had existed over the eastern stretch – and specifically the disputed border known as the McMahon Line – the western region became the focus when in 1956 the Chinese constructed a highway from Xinjiang province to Tibet through the Aksai Chin to allow the rapid movement of troops between the two restive provinces. In spite of disputing the occupation of the territory, India did not actually administer the Aksai Chin in any way, and consequently after the building of the road the region effectively passed into Chinese hands. Nevertheless, the Aksai Chin continued to be a volatile area – not helped by the fact that the rest of Jammu and Kashmir was the subject of an ongoing and often violent dispute between India and Pakistan – and subsequently provided one of the flashpoints for the 1962 Sino-Indian war.

Matters were further complicated with the Lhasa Revolt of March 1959, an uprising of Tibetans which culminated in the fleeing of the fourteenth Dalai Lama (and subsequently thousands of Tibetan refugees) to India and the systematic crushing of the resistance by Chinese forces. In the northern autumn Chinese and Indian troops clashed along the McMahon Line border. An attempt at resolving the border issue was made during a visit by Premier Zhou Enlai to Delhi from19-25 April 1960, but "the talks...did not resolve the differences that had arisen and the two Prime Ministers decided that officials of the two Governments should examine the factual material in the possession of the two Governments in support of their stands" (Ministry of External Affairs, 1961:1). The committee met three times throughout 1960, with both sides producing reports of the discussions for their respective governments.

The contents of these reports illustrate how intractable the border problem was and indeed still is, with the two sides unable to agree even on the basic tenor of the talks, such as whether the border had ever been officially delimited (no, according to China; yes, according to India). Consequently no resolution was reached at the 1960 talks which, with hindsight, were really the last opportunity to effect an agreement before relations broke down completely.

The Sino-Indian War began on 8 September 1962 when the Chinese crossed into NEFA (now Arunachal Pradesh) and attacked an Indian border post, alleging that the Indians had already violated the McMahon Line. This was the first time the conflict flared along the McMahon Line, though there had been some fighting around the Aksai Chin region, inflamed by Sino-Pakistani border talks which the Indians alleged were aimed at undermining their position in Kashmir. These skirmishes continued throughout September and into October.

On 20 October the Chinese launched a full-scale offensive all along the frontier, from Ladakh to NEFA, arguing that it was a pre-emptive strike against Indian aggression. This was significant because it moved the conflict beyond the disputed areas and into Indian territory, essentially becoming an invasion of India. The Indian force was fatally under-prepared and crumbled before the Chinese onslaught.

The fighting lasted for just over a month, with the Chinese declaring a unilateral ceasefire on 21 November. Statistics released by the Indian government on 29 October had between 2000 and 2500 Indian soldiers killed during the first week of fighting, with 1102 held prisoner, 291 wounded and 5174 missing and presumed dead. On 8 November the Chinese proposed a ceasefire agreement whereby both parties would withdraw twenty kilometres behind the positions held on 7 November, 1959. This meant that the Chinese would withdraw back behind the McMahon Line, but they would maintain control of Indian-claimed territory in Ladakh, including the strategically important Aksai Chin road linking Xinjiang and Tibet. This was initially rejected by the Indians, but after another fortnight of fierce fighting the Chinese surprised everyone by announcing a unilateral ceasefire and the withdrawal of troops from 1 December to the 7 November 1959 positions. The Chinese also added that, provided the Indian government took corresponding measures, the two parties could meet to discuss troop withdrawal and an end to hostilities. Militarily weakened, and with the rest of the world supporting all measures to solve the conflict, India was in no position to argue.

In December 1962 six non-aligned nations (Ceylon, Burma, Cambodia, Indonesia, the United Arab Republic and Ghana) met in Colombo to try to broker a formal peace deal, but their lack of condemnation of the Chinese invasion incensed India. India nevertheless accepted the Colombo proposals, but China rejected them, insisting on a "unilateral implementation" of its 21 November 1962 statement; consequently the talks broke down and nothing was resolved, even in subsequent bilateral meetings.

Sino-Indian relations did not begin to normalise until the mid-1970s; a turning point was the resumption of ambassadorial relations in 1976. Although the two countries retained non-official diplomatic relations throughout the 1960s (with missions headed by a *charge d'affairs* rather than an ambassador), interaction was minimal. In fact, Gautam Das describes the period between 1962-76 as a period of "cold peace" rather than cold war, and notes that "Sino-

Indian relations after 1962 are, in substance if not chronology, Sino-Indian relations after 1976 [because very little of note happened in the intervening period]".

Rapprochement continued after the resumption of diplomatic relations, albeit with a few hiccups, but it wasn't until 1988 that the turning point came with Indian Prime Minister Rajiv Gandhi's visit to Beijing. This made him the first Indian Prime Minister to visit China since Nehru in 1954 and marked the end of the impasse on the border issue which had lasted for most of the 1980s; the two sides agreed to maintain peace and stability along the Line of Actual Control (LAC) in Arunachal Pradesh (roughly equivalent to the McMahon Line), and they also agreed to set up a Joint Working Group (JWG) to help defuse the border issue.

In addition, India agreed to curtail the anti-China actions of Tibetans in India. According to Das, "the decade that followed the Rajiv Gandhi visit up to the 1998 Indian nuclear explosions (Pokhran-II) has been the most cordial phase of Sino-Indian relations after 1962".

These warm relations continued during the mid-1990s, and were further consolidated by Chinese President Jiang Zemin's visit to India in 1996, where four mutual cooperation agreements were signed, and it appeared that a breakthrough in the tensions had finally occurred.

Unfortunately, this series of small steps forward was followed by a giant leap backwards in 1998. During a visit of the People's Liberation Army (PLA) Senior General Fu Quanyou to New Delhi, the Indian Defence Minister, George Fernandes, publicly stated that he believed China was continuing to carry out border incursions into Indian territory , and later accused China of being India's number one security threat, greater even than Pakistan. This was immediately followed by India's second ever nuclear tests, known as Pokhran II (ibid). The fact that the tests occurred before Fu had even arrived back in Beijing caused a huge loss of face for the Chinese, because they felt that after a decade of overtures to the Indians they had been callously rebuffed and humiliated.

Nevertheless, the overall Chinese reaction to the tests was initially quite controlled, and might have remained so, had India not justified the tests by claiming they were in response to the 'China threat'. This was articulated in a letter from Indian Prime Minister Vajpayee to US President Bill Clinton, which was printed in the *New York Times* on 13 May (ibid). This was seen as "unwarranted and provocative", and the fact that the issue was given such a public airing caused another immense loss of face for the Chinese; consequently they reacted angrily, cancelling the next meeting of the Joint

Working Group on the border issue. This issue of the 'China threat' still permeates relations today, with more than one Chinese interviewee claiming that the Indian military deliberately promotes China as a threat in order to get increased defence spending, and that 1998 was one of the clearest examples of this (Author interviews with Wang Dehua and anonymous interviewee, 2010).

After the low point of the 1998 tests, relations began once again to normalise, in spite of a brief hiccup over Tibet when 14-year-old Ugyen Thinley Dorje, the 17th Karmapa Lama of the Kagyupa sect of Tibetan Buddhism, fled China for Dharamsala in January 2000.

Nevertheless, in February 2000 India and China concluded an agreement for China's accession to the World Trade Organisation ; in March India participated in the first ever Sino-Indian security dialogue in Beijing, and the Joint Working Group sessions resumed in April of the same year. In 2003 an incursion by Chinese troops into Indian territory occurred in Arunachal Pradesh, shortly after Indian Prime Minister Vajpayee's visit to Beijing; Vajpayee put this down to "differences in perceptions" regarding the Line of Actual Control, but some politicians and analysts took it much more seriously.

This incident shows that in spite of another gradual thawing of relations, the border question still remains a highly contentious issue in the Sino-Indian relationship. Furthermore, in addition to ongoing Indian concerns about the Sino-Pakistani relationship, China is also disturbed about the growing relationship between India and the USA, fearing that such an alliance will upset the balance of power in the region.

Seen in the light of history, the most recent incidents to affect the Sino-Indian relationship – the 2008 Tibet protests and the subsequent disruption of the Olympic torch relay (including in Delhi); and the border skirmishes and associated negative media coverage throughout 2009 – are unlikely to cause permanent damage to the relationship.

They do, however, highlight the fact that the border issue is still unresolved, and most analysts agree that the Sino-Indian relationship will not be able to move forward in any meaningful way until this question is answered. As well as being rooted in political reality, however, a large element of the Sino-Indian conflict also stems from misplaced perceptions, both of each other's motives and of their own place in the world order.

The concept of 'Chindia' is popular at present but it is based on flawed logic. Although the geo-civilisational aspects, where cultural practices flowed freely across what is now Central Asia to India and China and back again, cannot be denied, China and India are also distinct civilisations with their own histories and cultures and to conflate them is to understate the importance of this in shaping their distinctive governments and policies.

It also minimises the very real animosity which remains between them and deeply influences not only the Sino-Indian relationship but also how they see themselves and how they relate to the wider international community. On a political and strategic front, India and China have followed extremely different developmental trajectories with different outcomes and they also have different aims for their status in the international system.

These differences in aims, policy and strategic thought can be seen to be playing out in Central Asia at present.

The 'Chindia' concept is for the most part a Western construct developed as a response to the 'China threat' perception and tied into the former US and ASEAN policy of containment, in which India would play an important role. This idea of a mutual rise or equating China and India was seized upon by some in India who were attracted by the idea that India has or will soon have the same type of international economic and political clout as China, even when the present reality suggests otherwise. In fact, India should not seek to emulate China because it is unlikely that such a course of action would succeed; in any case the two countries' systems are extremely different. Rather, India must forge its own path and decide what kind of a role it wants to play internationally, and how it will achieve this. It must also in the immediate-term concentrate on domestic development and remember that 'national security' cannot just be about the military but must also include human, food, environmental and other types of security as well as poverty reduction. This seems to be the path which the Indian government is beginning to take and it is likely to be far more successful than any which frames the question of India's development in relation to China. Regarding China, we need to rethink the way we examine it in terms of international relations theory in order to avoid overlooking the real issues in Chinese strategic thought because of a desire to fit Chinese development into an established international relations model.

Finally, scholarship – both in China and India and further afield – needs to be developed so that more scholars are educated in the practices and policies of both countries, and communication is facilitated between China and India scholars the world over, rather than operating simply in closed 'China studies' or 'India studies' spheres. This would not only prove beneficial to promoting stability in the Sino-Indian relationship, but would also go some way to ensuring that the two countries can be viewed as separate but parallel entities rather than as 'Chindia'.

THE BORDER WAR

The serious fighting of the 1962 China-India Border War extended from October 10, 1962, until November 20, 1962. While the entire border was the issue, the actual fighting occurred in three widely separated areas: Walong, Tawang, and Aksai Chin.

It is significant that while over 47,000 square miles of frontier were in contention between China and India, that the fighting was confined to areas where the Chinese felt that they had legitimate claims. In Walong, the British (O'Callaghan, in 1914) had moved the previously agreed British and Chinese border markers northward. In Tawang, portions of India's forward policy extended even north of their claim, the McMahon Line. And in Aksai Chin, the Chinese firmly believed that the (1899) MacDonald-Macartney Line had been the accepted boundary for decades. In any case, no official boundary, over the 2,500 miles frontier, had ever been negotiated and established between the two countries.

An Indian patrol of fifty Rajputs had moved to Yumtso La without incident on the evening of October 9th. At daybreak on October 10th, they began to move toward the Yumtso La bridges. Outnumbering the Indians by about 20:1, a full battalion of Chinese emerged from their positions and quickly moved down the ridge, to form for attack. The Indian positions came under fire from heavy mortars. The Indians were able to hold off the first Chinese assault; the Chinese were apparently unaware of the Indian positions covering Tseng Jong village from the flank, and enfilade fire caused heavy Chinese casualties. The Indian commander at Tseng Jong asked for covering fire while he withdrew from what he felt was a hopeless position; but the covering fires were refused. As the Chinese pressed their attack, the Indian force of fifty was ordered to disengage and retreat to the river; engagement at Tseng Jong would have meant disaster for the Indians. The Chinese allowed them to withdraw, and held their fire as the survivors crossed the bridge to the south. Chinese casualties were 33 killed or wounded. Indian casualties were seven killed, seven missing, and eleven wounded—50% casualties. The Chinese buried the Indian dead with full military honors, in plain view of the retreating Indian comrades withdrawing south of the river.

The brief battle at Tseng Jong would have grave implications. The Chinese had attacked the Indians with force and determination. Most important, Chinese forces had not retired as General Kaul and Prime Minister Nehru had assumed when they formulated their forward policy. It was now clear to Kaul that capturing Thag La Ridge was out of the question. The Seventh Brigade remained on the Namka Chu, and was even ordered to extend its posts to the western end of the ridge. On October 12th, Nehru confirmed that he had ordered the army to clear the Chinese from Indian territory. But by October 18th, it was evident that the Chinese were making preparations for an attack; their troop and supply buildups provided ample indication of pending assault.

Meanwhile, on October 18th, the Indians were concerned about Tsang Le; Tsang Le was no more than a positon marked by a herdsman's hut at the sourse of the Namka Chu, but it was tactically important as a possible flank approach to the Chinese positions below Thag La Ridge.

One Indian company had occupied Tsang Le since early October; the Chinese had promptly dispatched troops to protect against a flank attack. On October 18th, General Kaul ordered two companies to Tsang Le. Tsang Le, though, was not only north of the McMahon Line, but also was inside Bhutan; the Indian companies were told to ignore the Line and the boundary.1 On the 19th, the two companies prepared to move toward Tsang Le.

On the night of October 19-20, three regiments of Chinese troops prepared and deployed for their assault on the (Indian) Seventh Brigade in the Namka Chu River area. The Indians had expected the Chinese to cross the Namka Chu by one or more of the five bridges, and hence were defending these crossings. But the Namka Chu, running easterly 1 - 2 miles north of the McMahon Line, was fordable; the Chinese generally forded rather than use the bridges. the Chinese struck near Hathung La and at Tsangdhar; but the weight of the Chinese attack was in the center of the river line. Gurkhas on their way to Tsang Le were victims of Chinese artillery. The Indian units fought fiercely against overwhelming odds, but their positions were overrun one by one. By 9 a.m. the Chinese had secured the riverline. Not only had the Chinese readily taken Indian positions, but they also cut Indian telephone lines. The Seventh Brigade quickly lost cohesion as a fighting force, and was granted permission to withdraw.

The Chinese plan was to sieze Tsangdhar and Hathung La, to cut off both escape and possible resupply. The plan had worded perfectly, especially with the massive Chinese advantage in both troops and firepower. The survivors and remnants of Indian troops withdrew back to Tawang, and the Seventh Brigade effectively ceased to exist as a fighting force by October 22nd. And Tsang Le, so important to General Kaul, was ignored by the Chinese, probably because the Chinese maps (like the Indians') showed Tsang Le in Bhutan.

General L. P. Sen, Commander-in-Chief of Eastern Command, flew to Tawang on October 22nd by helicopter. He ordered the remnants of the Indian troops—two infantry battalions and some artillery—to "hold Tawang at all costs." Sen flew back to Tezpur on October 23rd.

Immediately following the Thag La Ridge-Namka Chu River victory, the Chinese developed a three-prong attack. On October 23rd, the three regiments which had defeated the Seventh Brigade had come throug Shakti and were poised ten miles north of Tawang. A second prong had come through Khinezemane and joined with the first force. A third line of advance came dwon through Bum La. Tawang was poorly suited for the defense, and the Indians decided to withdraw. Tawang was evacuated on October 23rd, and the Chinese occupied it—essentially unopposed—on the next day. Indian forces had now withdrawn to Se La, which they planned to reinforce and defend in strength. There were attacks against Indian posts elsewhere along the McMahon Line in the Tawang Tract; these had fallen under varying degrees of pressure.

In the eastern end of NEFA, the Chinese made some probing attacks against Walong on October 24th and 25th. But after October 25th, NEFA fell into a lull, with the majority of Chinese forces paused in Tawang, about ten miles south of the McMahon Line.

Meanwhile, there had been significant fighting in the western sector, in Aksai Chin. On October 20th, simultaneous with the Thag La Ridge attack, the Chinese assaulted Indian posts in Chip Chap Valley, Galwan Valley, and Pangong Lake. The Galwn post had been surrounded by the Chinese in August, and had thence been sup- polied by air. Galwan post was finally attacked and overrun on October 20th; after reporting that the Chinese had begun to shell the post, it was not heard from again. Numerous small posts were soon overwhelmed and the scant garrisons were either captured or killed. The Western Command then recognized the magnitude of the Chinese attack, and many of the small, isolated posts withdrew to the southwest. On October 21st, after heavy fighting, the Chinese took the posts at the north side of Pangong Lake. More posts, including Daulet Beg Oldi, were evacuated; but the Chinese did not approach Daulet Beg Oldi, for it laid south of their claim line. By pulling troops back, General Daulat Singh of the Western Command had methodically and rapidly built up strength to prepare for any further Chinese attacks. By the first week of November, three brigades—each with four infantry battalions—were organizing under Singh in Leh.

In late October, the Eastern Command made numerous changes—in both command and organization—in the Indian forces after the October defeats. Much of the energies of the Eastern Command were absorbed with these personnel moves; instead of organizing forces, these changes only resulted in confusion amongst the Indian troops on the eastern front.

After the Chinese victories in mid- to late-October, there was a two week lull in Chinese military activity. But it was replaced by a flurry of diplomatic activity. On October 24th, four days after the outbreak of heavy fighting in NEFA and Aksai Chin, Chou sent a letter to Nehru, proposing: 1) a negotiated settlement of the boundary, 2) that both sides disengage and withdraw twenty kilometers from present lines of actual control, 3) a Chinese withdrawal north in NEFA, and 4) that China and India not cross lines of present control in Aksai Chin.

Nehru's reply of October 27th appeared eager to restore peace and friendly relations, but questioned a mutual twenty kilometer withdrawl after "40 or 60 kilometers of blatant military aggression." Nehru proposed, instead, a return to the "boundary prior to 8 September 1962" before any Chinese attacks; only then would India be interested in talks.

Chou's reply came on November 4th, and clarified his intent of "line of actural control." Chou's "line"—the same that he had repeatedly offered since 1959—was simply the Indian-claimed McMahon Line in NEFA and the traditionally claimed MacDonald Line in Aksai Chin.

Simultaneously, external forces began to influence the Border War situation. Russia, India's supporter through the 1950s, was endorsing the Chinese peace proposal. But in early November, Russia was preoccupied with the Cuban Missile Crisis, and paid little attention to the Border War. Without Soviet support, India had courted support from both England and the United States; military supplies from both countries began arriving in early November. The Americans seemed eager to help India against the perceived menace of Communism; Washington also made plans to send a carrier task force to the Bay of Bengal. The political activities continued. On November 8th, the Indian Parliament proclaimed a state of national emergency and adopted a resolution to "drive out the aggressors from the sacred soil of India." Through the first two weeks of November, China had refrained from any further assaults; Peking obviously wanted a diplomatic resolution. On November 14th, Nehru wrote another letter to Chou, again rejecting Chou's October 24th proposal, and again refuting any Chinese border claims. But the exchanges between the two countries and the external military support to India had produced no movement toward settlement or compromise. On November 14th, the fighting resumed again.

The Indians had withdrawn from Tawang on October 23rd. The initial withdrawls plan was to draw back to Bomdi La, the northermost point which would allow for a logistic buildup. But the withdrawl orders were almost immediately modified to a withdrawal only to, and defense of, Se La. Se La did appear to be a good defensible position: the only road to Bomdi La ran through Se La, Se La Pass dominated the road from Tawang, and there were dominating peaks on both sides of the Pass. At 14,000+ feet altitude, Se La was definitely "high ground." The problem, however, was the altitude: the weather was harsh, Se La was far from supplies in Bomdi La, and the altitude made air drop of supplies quite difficult. Even if Se La was strongly defended, the Indians knew that they must simultaneously prepare to defend Bomdi La, for they now realized that the Chinese were not a road-bound fighting force. The decision to hold Se La committed the Indians to an extended area, from Se La to Bomdi La, over sixty miles of high-altitude, difficult road.

Over the next several days, the Se La-Bomdi La defense began to form. Se La was sporadically supplied by air. The Indian Government had considered tactical air operations against Chinese positions, but ruled out air strikes because of fear of Chinese retaliation. A supply and manpower buildup began in NEFA. But there was no Chinese attack during the first two weeks of November; and when the first new assault came, it was far from Se La.

The Eleventh Brigade of the Second Division took over the Walong sector on October 31st; the Eleventh was the third unit in ten days to be assigned responsibility for Walong (because of the numerous changes in command). The Walong detachment of three infantry battalions was not, however, preparing for a defense. Even though Chinese strength at Rima was estimated at a Division, the Walong force was planning to attack the Chinese on November 14th, Nehru's birthday. General Kaul had planned a "first major success against the enemy" as a birthday present to Nahru.

On November 14th, two companies of the Kumaon battalion, supported by mortars and artillery, launched an assault against a strategic hill held by company of Chinese fire, then stopped fifty yards from the crest, exhausted. A Chinese night counter-attack cleared the Indians off the hill. The survivors—less than half the attacking force—returned to Walong. The Chinese followed the retreating Indians and penetrated the main Indian defences. Indian artillery could not assist the defense; all rounds had been used in the attack on the Chinese hill. Key defensive points were overrun, and a withdrawal was ordered at 10 a.m. on November 16th. But many of the Indian troops did not receive the order, and fought to the death at their positions. The remnants of the Walong brigade withdrew down Lohit Valley; even in withdraw, many died either from amushes or from privation. The Chinese did not pursue the retreating troops further. The withdrawing General Kaul sent a rather frantic message to New Delhi:

The enemy strength is now so great and his overall strength so superior that you should ask the highest authorities to get such foreign armed forces to come to our aid as are willing to do so.... it seems beyond the capability of our armed forces to stem the tide of the superior Chinese forces which he has and will continue to concentrate against us to our disadvantage. This is not a counsel of fear, but facing stark realities. Only hours after the Walong defeat, fighting would resume in both Aksai Chin and Se La.

In Ladakh, the Western Command continued a steady buildup of forces. By mid-November, a brigade was in place at Chushul (Chusul). Some of the forces were at Chushul village and airport, west of the Chinese claim line. Some of the Indian defences were to the east of the claim line; in fact, the forces east of Chushul were the only Indian forces left in Chinese-clamed territory in Aksai Chin; all other Indian posts in Chinese-claimed territory had been either withdrawn or wiped out. Western Command had made Chushul key terrain as a blocking point between the Chinese and the city of Leh. It is notable that the positions around Chushul were at 14,000-16,000 feet altitude: there was no wood for fires or for constructing bunkers, frozen ground had to be blasted for entrenchments, and even acclimatized troops could work only for short periods. Yet, some strong Indian positions were in place by November 17th.

Chinese reconnaissance patrols were visible east of Chushul in mid-November, but no fire was exchanged. On November 17th, a strong Chinese force moved westward toward Chushul. And in the early hours of November 18th, Chinese artillery opened fire on Indian outposts. Mortars and rockets also softened the Indian entrenchments. The Chinese attempted a frontal infantry attack, but it was repelled. Soon, though, the Chinese moved to envelop the Indian positions. In heavy fighting, the Chinese rear and flank attacks were successful. The casualties were heavy for the Indians; one company had only three survivors—the remainder was found fronzen as they died weapons in hand. The Chinese suffered heavy casualties, too. Five hours into the attack, the Chinese had overrun, or forced the evacuation of, every Indian position east of the claim line. The withdrawing Indians regrouped as best they could in the village (and heights behind) Chushul. But the Chinese attack on Chushul village never came; the Chinese stopped at their claim line and did not assault Chushul itself. The War in the western sector was over. Not a single Indian force remained within the Chinese-claimed territory. By the end of November 18th, all of Aksai Chin was in Chinese hands.

In the Se La-Bomdi La sector of NEFA, a steady Indian buildup continued. By November 17th, Fouth Division had ten infantry battalions and some supporting arms—mortars, artillery, and twelve tanks. Concentrated, it could have been a formidable defense; but the force was spread out over the 60 twisty miles of road between Se La and Bomdi La, with the commander and main defences at Se La. Five battalions were at Se La; three, at Bomdi La; and two were at Dirange Dzong*, halfway between. The commander, Brigadier

Hosair Singh, soon established his headquarters at the Dzong. Dirang Dzong was poorly suited for defences; but the Indians intended strong defences at Se la and Bomdi La, both of which were well surrounded by hill masses. The defense might have been more successful—if the Chinese had been limited to the road. But there were trails—most notably the Bailey Trail.

Captain F. M. Bailey had explored into Tibet in 1913; his work helped McMahon to draw his boundary line. Bailey had made his way from Tulung La to Lap, and thence through Tse La Pass and southward. The 1962 Indian forces soon came to realize that the Chinese could use the Trail that Bailey had used half a century before. If the Chinese did come down Bailey Trail, they would emerge at Thembang, between Dirang Dzong and Bomdi La. Such a Chinese move would cut off Dirang Dzong and Se La. Yet, despite this, there remained the underlying Indian faith that the Chinese would not attack.

A few blocking forces were sent out in early November: a company to Phutang and a platoon sent up the Bailey Trail to Poshing La. As November advanced, more attention was given to Bailey Trail. Three more platoos—now making a company—were dispatched to Poshing La.

On November 15th, the Chinese—probably a battalion—at- tacked the company at Poshing La. Radio reports indicated that the Chinese had wiped out the Indian force. But Headquarters could not believe that the Chinese could bring a full battalion down the mountain trail, and a second company from Bomdi La was sent up Bailey Trail. A third company was brought from Bomdi La to Dirang Dzong. By November 16th, the three battalions stationed at Bomdi La was cut to half strenght.

The second company sent to Bailey Trail dug in at Tembang (Thembang) on the morning of November 17th. A Chinese force of about 1500 attacked the company soon after midday. The Indians resisted for three hours, inflicting heavy Chinese casualties.

But logistics problems struck again: the Indians began to run out of ammunition. With darkness falling, the Indian company began to withdraw. But in the darkness and in thick vegetation, and orderly withdrawal soon turned into chaotic flight. None of the company returned to Bomdi La; weeks later, stragglers began appearing on the plains to the south. Again the superior strength of the Chinese and the logistic problems of the Indians had lead to another Indian defeat. But now, the Chinese had cut the road between Bomdi La and Dirang Dzong; about 10,000 Indian troops were northwest of the Chinese road block.

There was a brief (and almost the only) bright moment for the Indians on November 17th. Simultaneous with the Bailey Trail action, the Chinese had launched an attack on Se La. But Se La was well defended; between dawn and midafternoon, the Chinese launched five assaults on Se La, and five times they were repulsed. With five battalions plus artillery, the Se La force was strong—until its main supply route was cut off when the Chinese took Thembang.

Were the Indians at Se La to hold and continue defending, supplied by air? Or should the force withdraw, and if so could it break through the Chinese roadblock? Meanwhile, the Headquarters position at Dirang Dzong, pooly defended, was in jeapordy. Brigadier Singh, commander at Se La, requested guidance from General Kaul.

But General Kaul was still flying around the lost battle at Walong. General P. N. Thapar, Chief of Army Staff, and General Sen, Commander in Chief of Eastern Command, were both at Kaul's headquarters. They both declined to give orders or guidance, deferring instead to General Kaul. An urgent operational decision was needed, but it waited until 7:30 p.m. when Kaul returned.

By the time General Kaul returned that evening (November 17th), there were reports that the Chinese had begun an enveloping movement at Se La and threatened to cut the road between Se La and Dirang Dzong. After a half hour meeting of the three highest ranking officers of the Indian Army, General Kaul issued his order: all units were to pull back from Se La and Dirang Dzong to Bomdi La.

But immediate further discussions amongst the generals resulted in a modification to Kaul's order. The highlights of the new order were as follows:

You will hold on to your present positions to the best of your ability. When the position becomes untenable I delegate the authority to you to withdraw to any alternative position you can hold.... You may be cut off by the enemy.... Your only course is to fight it out as best you can.

The wording of this order hardly constituted clear guidance.

General A. S. Pathania, commander of 65 Brigade at Dirang Dzong, ordered a withdraw to the plains to the south. Going through Phutang, he himself withdrew. He had hurriedly ordered his tanks to try to fight through to Bomdi La; if the crews could not, they were to abandon their tanks and head for the plains.

But no one took command of the force—two infantry battalions, some tanks, some artillery, and headquarters personnel—left at Dirang Dzong. A few field grade officers (who did not know that withdrawal was ordered) attempted to organize the forces and fight toward Bomdi La. But Chinese forces and ambushes quickly ended the attempt. The survivors straggled southward to the plains. General Pathania would resign soon after the ceasefire.

Good control was maintained over the initial withdrawal from Se La; the Indians cleared the first Chinese found behind Se La. But ahead, the Indian column came under heavy machine gun fire. Attempts to knock out Chinese gun positions failed; the road was impassable. Under heavy Chinese fire, the retreating troops headed chaotically south for the plains. In their retreat, many were killed or captured.

By mid-morning of November 18th, the 48 Brigade—six rifle companies at Bomdi La—was the only Indian Army force left in NEFA. The six companies were dug into defensive positions that had been designed for three battalions. They had artillery and mortars, and were expecting reinforcements.

But poor command/control/communications again struck the Indians. At 11 a.m., General Kaul—not knowing that Dirang Dzong was now abandoned—ordered a mobile column (at Bomdi La) to move out to reinforce Dirang Dzong. Brigadier Singh protested that such a move would weaken Bomdi La. But Kaul angrily ordered tow infantry companies, with tanks and artillery, to move out onto the winding road to Dirang Dzong. Support personnel—cooks and clerks—were ordered to aid in the defense of Bomdi La.

The Chinese attacked about ten minutes after the column left. The first attack was beaten off. The infantry in the column was quickly ordered back to their defensive positions; but these were already occupied by the Chinese, and the Indians were caught in the open. A second, stronger Chinese assault followed. Many Indian positions were overrun, and the Chinese brought fire onto the Brigade headquarters; attempts to counterattack failed. By 4 p.m., Singh ordered a withdrawal to Rupa, eight miles to the south.

The Brigade began to organize a defense around Rupa on the night of Novemeber 18th. Then, Singh received orders from IV Corps to withdraw to Foothills, just above the plains. As he began his withdrawal, he received orders from General Kaul to defend Rupa! Turning back, he found that the Chinese were already taking up positions around Rupa; thus, defense of Rupa was impossible. His 48 Brigade was then ordered to Chaku, the next defensible position down the road. The Chinese harrassed the withdrawing troops, and then broke contact. The Brigade, now only one battalion in size, reached Chaku on the evening of November 19th. The Chinese struck at midnight, on three sides. The Chinese had attacked an ammunition supply train, and burning vehicles illuminated the Indian defensive positions. The Brigade broken, scattered groups made their way southward to the plains. Remaining Indian command elements were headed far to the south.

With the disintegration of 48 Brigade at 3 a.m. on November 20th, no organized Indian military force was left in NEFA (nor in Aksai Chin). Militarily, the Chinese victory was complete, and the Indian defeat absolute. Late on the evening of November 20th, prime Minister Nehru made an urgent and open appeal to the United States for armed intervention against the Chinese; he asked for bomber and fighter squadrons to begin air strikes on Chinese troops in Indian territory "if they continued to advance" and cover for Indian cities "in case the Chinese air force tried to raid them." An American carrier was dispatched toward the Bay of Bengal; but the aircraft carrier was ordered back on November 21st. The victorious Chinese had ordered a ceasefire effective midnight, November 21, 1962.

1962: THE VIEW FROM BEIJING

In 1985, the Chinese side formally reinterpreted the package proposal saying that we had misunderstood Deng's words. The fresh Chinese position was that since the area of largest dispute was in the eastern sector, India had to make meaningful concessions in that sector and the Chinese side would then make appropriate and corresponding concessions in the western sector. Additionally, an explicit demand was now advanced for ceding Tawang, which the Indian side was accused of occupying at a much later date after its independence. It was pointed out to us that since the fifth Dalai Lama had been born in Tawang, the place was of special significance for the Chinese people, in particular for China's Tibetan nationality. This remains the current Chinese position on the border dispute and the Indian side, of course, rejects it.

In 1992, an informal suggestion was made to the Chinese side that India gives free access to Chinese pilgrims to Tawang, while China reciprocally gives similar access to Indian pilgrims to Kailash Mansarovar. The Chinese never responded. One reason for the insistence on Tawang being conceded may be the fear that if the next Dalai Lama were to be "discovered" in Tawang , a Chinese rival may not enjoy the same legitimacy. As will be apparent, the issue of Tibet continues to be embedded in any consideration of the border.

In 2005, during Chinese Premier Wen Jiabao's visit, India and China announced a set of Guiding Principles and Political Parameters for resolving the border issue. From India's standpoint, these principles and parameters are welcome as they include those that are extremely relevant, such as the need to consider the interests of "settled populations". This would have a direct bearing on the status of Tawang. However, in typical Chinese fashion, there is a continuous attempt to reinterpret these principles to suit Chinese positions. In the series of talks between the Special Representatives of the two prime ministers, now in their 11th year, little progress has been recorded on settling the border issue, though the talks have been useful in managing the border and in advancing confidence-building measures.

Given this chequered history, what are the prospects of an India-China border settlement and what are its likely contours? One cannot see a solution that diverges significantly from the existing alignment of the Line of Actual Control (LAC), and the longer the status quo continues the more likely is the LAC to eventually morph into a settled boundary. At a recent track-II interaction, a senior Chinese army official remarked that India was unlikely to go to war to recover Aksai Chin just as China was unlikely to go to war to recover southern Tibet, or what India refers to as Arunachal Pradesh. In the meantime, he went on to add, the LAC needed to be clarified so that incidents such as the recent one at Depsang could be avoided.

Given the experience of 1962, however, one should never base one's actions on the basis of perceptions of the other side's intentions. It was the entrenched belief that China would never attack that caught Indian forces totally unprepared and virtually defenceless. Our border defences including logistics, must take into account the rapidly growing capabilities on the Chinese side. Although the size of our forces deployed at the border and its vicinity is substantial, our transport infrastructure and logistical capabilities have fallen steadily behind that of China. These shortcomings are being addressed but we need to consider ways in which we can cope with the growing asymmetry. The use of air capabilities may be one answer. There is also an urgent need to improve and extend our reconnaissance capabilities, so that there is sufficient warning time in case of an attack. Intelligence failure was one of the major causes of our failure to anticipate and respond to the 1962 crisis. The point one is making is that any prospect of sustaining the status quo at the border is dependent upon our ability to make any attempt to change it costly and risky to the other side.

It is also clear that the evolution of the Tibet issue will have a significant influence on both the prospects of an eventual border settlement with China and, in the meantime, maintaining peace and tranquility along the LAC. A successful reconciliation process between the Dalai Lama and the Chinese side would be to India's advantage. There were some signs earlier last year that the new Chinese leadership was reaching out to the Dalai Lama but these seem to have lost momentum. If there are ways in which India could encourage this, it would help in managing India-China relations. A worsening of the situation inside Tibet or greater militancy among Tibetan youth in India could make the job of keeping India-China relations on an even keel more difficult.

China is likely to show restraint in dealing with India, including on the border issue, the more diversified and stronger India's relations are with other countries. China was more amenable and sensitive to India's interests in 2005 because of India's growing relationship with the US, Japan and the countries of South East Asia. The fewer options India is seen to have in its external relations, the more likely Chinese pressures on it will increase. This will be particularly relevant if the capability gap between the two countries continues to widen. Alternatively, if the forthcoming elections throw up a political leadership that enables India to resume accelerated economic growth and pursue a more coherent foreign policy, the prospects for India-China relations will improve. One should watch carefully the changing dynamics among major powers as a result of the Ukraine crisis and the worsening of relations between Russia and the West. On balance, China appears to be a net gainer with both Russia and the West seeking its neutrality, if not support. For India, the choices are more difficult.

Much will be determined by what the Indian electorate delivers in terms of a new political dispensation later this year. In 2005, India was riding high. New Delhi was the indispensable destination for leaders from across the world and the Indian growth story was putting India in the same league as China. Permanent membership of the UN Security Council seemed to be within reach. One could feel that one had more cards to play with in dealing with the world. That is no longer the case. The impending political renewal nevertheless gives one hope that India will get another chance to get back into reckoning.

COPING WITH ASYMMETRY

A reading of the document, now widely available on the internet, does not reveal any fresh, earth-shaking revelations or insights. Much of the report has been leaked in bits and pieces over the years and supplemented by considerable details supplied by other actors involved in this unfortunate saga. The main conclusions of earlier analyses remain valid:

* Right up to the point when China launched a major offensive, both the political *and* the Indian Army top brass were convinced that military engagement at the contested border would never go beyond small-scale skirmishes and limited operations. There was no expectation and hence preparation for dealing with a large-scale assault, despite mounting evidence to the contrary

* The so-called Forward Policy was a political initiative and not a military operation, designed to strengthen Indian territorial claims and forestall further Chinese ingress. China had been putting in place its own version of a forward policy through the relentless advance into the unoccupied border zones separating the two countries. This had intensified after the Tibet revolt and the Dalai Lama's escape to India in 1959. That same year, the first serious incidents of Chinese aggression took place, one in Longju in the eastern sector

and the other at Galwan in the western sector. Chinese territorial assertiveness continued thereafter, accompanied by a significant build-up of both logistics and forces. It was only in November 1961 that the Forward Policy was adopted in response but without corresponding means in men and material to respond to a serious military attack, the capabilities for which were being steadily built up on the Chinese side. The ill-considered probing missions and the setting up of additional and mostly isolated and indefensible posts were, therefore, more in the nature of "showing the flag" operations rather than military manoeuvres.

The revelations in the Henderson Brooks Report should be examined in the light of considerable archival material that is now available on Chinese perceptions and decision-making on India-China relations leading up to the breakout of hostilities on October 20, 1962.

The first important point to note is that the India-China border dispute took on an altogether different dimension in Chinese perceptions as a result of the Tibet revolt of 1959 and the subsequent grant of refuge by India to the Dalai Lama and a large number of Tibetans, who were escaping a violent Chinese crackdown. Indian statements and actions on the border were increasingly interpreted as aimed at undermining Chinese control over Tibet. Even contemporary Chinese studies of the 1962 conflict, such as those by Xu Yan and Wang Hongwei, make this point repeatedly, accusing Nehru of trying to "convert Tibet into a buffer zone" and to "instigate Tibet to leave China". In 1964, while speaking to a visiting Nepali delegation, Mao Zedong said the major problem between India and China was not the McMahon Line but Tibet, which Indians considered to be theirs.

A second conclusion to emerge from the archives is the key role played by Mao himself in the events leading up to the war. The failure of the Great Leap Forward and three years of economic distress and famine between 1959 and 1961 had forced Mao to retreat to the "second line of leadership", yielding place to pragmatists such as Liu Shaoqi, Deng Xiaoping and Peng Zhen. By the summer of 1962, however, Mao was already in the process of regaining his control over the levers of power, using the People's Liberation Army under a new commander, Marshal Lin Piao, as his ally. From the summer of 1962, it was Mao who was personally issuing directives on the evolving military situation on the India-China border. It was his decision in August 1962, to launch a full-scale military assault on Indian forces and to "liquidate the invading Indian army".

Interestingly, it now transpires that this decision was a contested one. A Chinese TV feature on the 1962 war, broadcast in January 2005, reveals that there were differences of opinion among the leadership with some arguing that it would be unwise to make an enemy out of India just when China was confronting both domestic and external challenges. However, according to the broadcast, these elements were denounced as "right opportunists" and the military offensive went ahead.

It is also clear now that China made a careful assessment of the regional and international situation before undertaking these military operations. There were fears in China that the US may help the Chiang Kai-shek regime in Taiwan launch attacks on China across the Taiwan Straits. These were laid to rest when China's ambassador to Warsaw, Wang Bingnan, was able to get a categorical assurance from his American counterpart that the US had no intention of supporting any Taiwanese offensive against China by taking advantage of Sino-Indian tensions. In his memoirs, Wang claims that this assurance played an important part in enabling the decision to attack India later in the year.

Similarly, fears that the Soviet Union would play a negative role on the Sino-India dispute were laid to rest as Moscow sought to obtain Chinese support in the looming Cuban missile crisis, which would burst into the open around the same time as the India-China war. This also distracted the major powers from taking full cognisance of what was happening on a remote border somewhere in Asia.

Just as the Chinese military offensive came as a rude surprise, so did the subsequent Chinese decision to withdraw from the territories it occupied as a result of the 1962 operations with some exceptions particularly in the Western sector. The Indian leadership fully believed that the withdrawal was probably due to approaching winter and extended supply lines and that a renewed offensive was likely during the summer the following year. This explains the sense of panic that prevailed in those days evident in Jawaharlal Nehru's desperate letter to US President John F Kennedy, which surfaced recently. Chinese archives, however, suggest that it was always Mao's plan that Chinese forces should withdraw after delivering a knockout blow on the Indians. The objective was not territorial. It was to forestall any threat to Chinese consolidation in Tibet, while bringing a chastened India to the negotiating table to acquiesce in a Chinese package proposal for settling the border. Neither objective was achieved in any real sense.

In 1980, the two countries resumed a bilateral dialogue on the border after a gap of two decades. In the initial phase the Chinese terms for settlement were the same as in 1960, i.e. that China would retain Aksai Chin in the West but would generally settle along the alignment corresponding to the McMahon

Line, though it would never accept the legitimacy of that line. In his interview to the editor of *Vikrant* in 1982, Deng Xiaoping explicitly put forward the "package proposal" as the basis for a border settlement, arguing that in keeping the area currently in its occupation in the east, India was getting a very good deal. After all, he suggested, Nehru himself had described Aksai Chin as a desert where "not a blade of grass grows".

BORDER NEGOTIATIONS

China's 1958 maps showed the large strip of land between Ladakh and Bhutan (the Aksai Chin) as Chinese. In 1960, Zhou Enlai proposed that India drop its claim to Aksai Chin and China would withdraw its claims from NEFA. According to John W. Garver, Zhou's propositions were unofficial and subtle. Zhou consistently refused to accept the legitimacy of India's territorial claims; he proposed that the any negotiations had to take into account the facts on the ground. Zhou tried many times to get Nehru to accept conceding Aksai Chin, he visited India four times in 1960. However, Nehru believed that China did not have a legitimate claim over both of those territories and was not ready to give away any one of them. However, they had different opinions as to the legality of the Simla agreement which eventually led to the inability to reach a decision. Nehru's adamance was seen within China as Indian opposition to Chinese rule in Tibet, as China needed the highway through Aksai Chin to maintain an effective control over the Tibetan plateau.

According to Neville Maxwell, Nehru wasn't ready to simply concede the territory and leave negotiations at that. He was open to continued negotiations, but did not accept the idea of Indian troops withdrawing from their claimed regions. Nehru stated "*We will negotiate and negotiate and negotiate to the bitter end. I absolutely reject the approach of stopping negotiations at any state.*" He remained firm that there would be no boundary negotiations until Chinese troops withdrew from Aksai Chin and areas south of the British McMahon Line. This was unacceptable to the Chinese, which never recognized the legal validity of the McMahon Line. Nehru stated "*We will never compromise on our boundaries, but we are prepared to consider minor adjustments to them and to talk to the other side about them.*" In light of these comments, the international community rallied behind Nehru in claiming that China was at fault in failing to conduct proper negotiations. Maxwell argues that Nehru's words were ambiguous.

According to the official Indian history: "Nehru did not agree to barter away the Aksai Chin area, under illegal occupation of China, in return for China giving up its unreasonable claim to Indian territory south of the McMahon Line."

After the talks, India produced its official reports on the talks and translated the Chinese report into English. India believed it would improve a feeling of understanding between the nations. China saw it as an unreasonable attempt by India to secure its claim lines. Nehru's adamance that China withdraw from Aksai Chin and thus abandon the highway was seen as further Indian attempts to undermine China's presence in Tibet. According to John W. Garver, China reached the incorrect conclusion that Nehru was continuing his "grand plans in Tibet".

Forward Policy

At the beginning of 1961, Nehru appointed General B.M. Kaul QMG but he was influential in all army decisions. Kaul reorganized the general staff and removed the officers who had resisted the idea of patrolling in disputed areas, although Nehru still refused to increase military spending or otherwise prepare for war. In the summer of 1961, China began patrolling along the McMahon Line. They entered parts of Indian administered regions and much angered the Indians in doing so. After May 1961 Chinese troops occupied Dehra Compass and established a post on the Chip Chap River. The Chinese, however, did not believe they were intruding upon Indian territory. In response the Indians launched a policy of creating outposts behind the Chinese troops so as to cut off their supplies and force their return to China.

According to the Home Minister in Delhi on February 4, 1962: "If the Chinese will not vacate the areas occupied by her, India will have to repeat what she did in Goa. She will certainly drive out the Chinese forces." This has been referred to as the "Forward Policy". There were eventually 60 such outposts, including 43 north of the McMahon Line. Kaul was confident through previous diplomacy that the Chinese would not react with force. According to the Indian Official History, Indian posts and Chinese posts were separated by a narrow stretch of land. China had been steadily spreading into those lands and India reacted with the Forward Policy to demonstrate that those lands were not unoccupied. India, of course, did not believe she was intruding on Chinese territory. British author Neville Maxwell traces this confidence to Mullik, who was in regular contact with the CIA station chief in New Delhi. Mullik may therefore have been aware of Mao's sensitivity concerning U-2 flights.

The initial reaction of the Chinese forces was to withdraw when Indian outposts advanced towards them. However, this appeared to encourage the Indian forces to accelerate their Forward Policy even further. In response, the Central Military Commission adopted a policy of "armed coexistence". In response to Indian outposts encircling Chinese positions, Chinese forces would build more outposts to counter-encircle these Indian positions. This pattern of encirclement and counter-encirclement resulted in an interlocking, chessboard-like deployment of Chinese and Indian forces. Despite the leapfrogging encirclements by both sides, no hostile fire occurred from either side as troops from both sides were under orders to fire only in defence.

On the situation, Mao Zedong commented, Nehru wants to move forward and we won't let him. Originally, we tried to guard against this, but now it seems we cannot prevent it. If he wants to advance, we might as well adopt armed coexistence. You wave a gun, and I'll wave a gun. We'll stand face to face and can each practice our courage.

Other developments

At a Communist Party conference in Beijing in January 1962, Chinese President Liu Shaoqi denounced the Great Leap Forward as responsible for widespread famine. The overwhelming majority of delegates expressed agreement, but Defence Minister Lin Biao staunchly defended Mao. A brief period of liberalization followed while Mao and Lin plotted a comeback. Jung Chang writes that China was prepared for war with India after the border clashes in May and June, but were concerned about the Nationalists, which had been making active preparations for invasion from Taiwan, and had moved large forces to the south-east coast.

Transcripts from the decision for war was not made by China's leaders until early October 6, 1962, and only then were war plans drawn by China's Central Military Commission. Roderik McFarquhar states, "In May–June 1962, the main concern in Beijing was over the threat of an invasion from Taiwan... Chinese leaders would have been reluctant to provoke hostilities in the Himalayas, which might have meant diverting military resources from the main danger point along the Fujian coast."

The Indian military was not ready for full-scale combat. India had just annexed the Portuguese State of India or, Goa and was facing border disputes with Pakistan in Kashmir. The Indian National Congress proposed non-violent means to solving India's problems, and Indian military leaders, who proposed that India should prepare for a full scale attack, were ignored or dismissed.

Early incidents

Various border conflicts and "military incidents" between India and China flared up throughout the summer and fall of 1962. According to Chinese sources, in June 1962, a minor skirmish broke out between the two sides, and dozens of members of the People's Liberation Army killed and wounded. Units of the Indian and Chinese militaries maintained close contact throughout

September 1962; however, hostile fire occurred only infrequently. On May 2, 1962 the Directorate of Military Operations in India had suggested that the air force should be readied for use in NEFA and Ladakh. The Air Force was considered a feasible way to repel the unbalanced ratio of Chinese troops to Indian troops and the Chinese air force was assessed as only capable of limited strategic raids which could be countered by the Indian air force. Indian Air Force soon started reconnaissance flights over the NEFA border. On May 7, 1962 Chinese troops shot down an Indian Dakota plane in which young officer B. P. Tiwari was lost. Following this incident, the Indian Air Force was told not to plan for close air support.

In June, 1962, the Indian Intelligence Bureau said it received information about a Chinese military buildup along the border which could result in a war. Information was also received that Pakistan was considering to attack simultaneously in the west. Chinese airfields in Tibet and Yunnan were addressed as a threat to Indian cities, as the PLAAF could conduct heavy bombings through their use of Soviet aeroplanes.

On July 8, the Chinese initiated another diplomatic communication, to protest against an alleged Indian incursion into the Galwan Valley. According to China Quarterly, the Government of India released press reports to the public indicating that Indian had gained 2,000 mi^2 of territory from the Chinese. However, in their diplomatic reply to the Chinese, India denied that any incident had taken place.

On July 10, 1962, 350 Chinese troops surrounded an Indian post at Chushul, in the Galwan Valley, north of the MacMahon Line. They used loudspeakers to obtain contact with the Gurkha forces stationed there. The Chinese troops attempted to convince the Gurkhas that they should not be fighting for India, to cause an abandonment of the post. After a fiery argument the 350 Chinese withdrew from the area.

July 22, 1962 saw a change in the Forward Policy, according to the official Indian history of the war. While the Forward Policy was initially intended to prevent the Chinese from advancing into empty areas (by occupying them first), "it was now decided to push back the Chinese from posts they already occupied." Whereas Indian troops were previously ordered to fire only in self-defence, all post commanders were now given discretion to open fire upon Chinese forces if threatened.

In August, 1962, the Chinese military improved its combat readiness along the McMahon Line, particularly in the North East Frontier Agency, Tibet and Xinjiang. In Tibet, there were constructions of ammunition dumps and stockpiling of ammunition, weapons and gasoline, though there were no indications of a manpower buildup. China's preparedness for war strongly contrasted with India's, which had largely neglected its military throughout the 1950s. Nehru believed that the Himalayas were a large enough defence against China, however, the Korean war had provided China with practice in mountain combat. This neglect on behalf of India would decide numerous pivotal battles where logistical inadequacy and lack of leadership led to defeat after strong starts.

Confrontation at Thag La

In June 1962, Indian forces had established an outpost at Dhola, on the southern slopes of Thag La Ridge, overlooking the village of Le in Tibet. Based on the treaty map of the 1914 Simla Convention, the McMahon Line lay at 27°44'30''N. However, Dhola post lay about one mile (1.6 km) north of the McMahon Line The Indian government maintained that the *intention* of the McMahon Line was to set the border along the highest ridges, and that the international border fell on the highest ridges of Thag La, about 3 to 4 miles (4.8 to 6.4 km) north of the line drawn by Henry McMahon on the treaty map. Brigadier John Dalvi would later write of this claim: "The Chinese had raised a dispute about the exact alignment of the McMahon Line in the Thag La Ridge area. Therefore the Thag La-Dhola area was not strictly territory that 'we should have been convinced was ours' as directed by the Prime Minister, Mr. Nehru, and someone is guilty of exceeding the limits prescribed by him." In August, China issued diplomatic protests which accused India of violating even the McMahon Line, and Chinese soldiers began occupying positions at the top of Thag La, north of Indian positions. On September 8, 1962, a 60-strong PLA unit descended from the heights and occupied positions which dominated one of the Indian posts at Dhola. Neither side opened fire for 12 days. Nehru had gone to London to attend a Commonwealth Prime Ministers' Conference and, when told of the act, said to the media that the Indian Army had instructions to "free our territory".

According to the official Indian history, a decision was made on September 9 to evict the Chinese from the southern part of the Thag La Ridge, by force, if necessary. Two days later, it was decided that "all forward posts and patrols were given permission to fire on any armed Chinese who entered Indian territory".

According to author Neville Maxwell, officers at the Indian Defence Ministry had expressed the concern that Indian maps showed Thag La as Chinese territory; they were told to ignore the maps. However, Nehru's directives to Defence Minister V.K. Krishna Menon were unclear, and the response, code named Operation LEGHORN, got underway only slowly. As the Chinese numbers were exaggerated to 600 instead of about 50 or 60, the 9 Punjab battalion, numbering 400 riflemen, was sent to Dhola.

By the time the Indian battalion reached the Thag La Ridge in the Chedong region on September 16, north of the McMahon Line, Chinese units controlled both banks of the Namka Chu River. The day after, India's Chief of the Army Staff Gen P N Thapar ordered his men to re-take the Thag La Ridge. According to the official Indian history, on September 20, Indian eastern command ordered all Indian posts and patrols to engage any Chinese patrols within range of their weapons. On September 20, at one of the bridges on the river a firefight developed, killing nine Chinese and Indian soldiers. Skirmishes continued throughout September. On 3 October, Zhou Enlai visited Nehru in New Delhi, promising there would be no war between the nations and reiterating his wishes to solve the dispute diplomatically. On October 4, a new corp was created 4 corp, under Lt. Gen. B.M. Kaul, tasked with evicting the Chinese from Dhola-Thag La October 10 was the planned date for Operation Leghorn. Because of the difficulties involved in directly assaulting and taking Thag La, Kaul made the decision instead to occupy nearby Yumtso La to the west, to position his troops behind and dominate the Chinese positions.

Brigadier John Dalvi, tasked with taking Yumtso La, argued that he lacked necessary supplies and resources to take the pass. On October 9, Kaul and Brigadier Dalvi agreed to send a patrol of 50 soldiers to Tseng Jong, the approach to Yumtso La, to occupy the position and provide cover before the rest of the battalion would move forward for the occupation of Yumtso La.

On October 10, these 50 Indian troops were met by an emplaced Chinese position of some 1,000 soldiers. The Chinese troops opened fire on the Indians believing that the Indians had intruded upon Chinese land. The Indians were surrounded by a Chinese positions which used mortar fire. However, they managed to hold off the first Chinese assault, inflicting heavy casualties. In the second assault, the Indians began their retreat, realising the situation was hopeless. The Indian patrol suffered 25 casualties, with the Chinese suffering 33. The Chinese troops held their fire as the Indians retreated, and then buried the Indian dead with military honours, as witnessed by the retreating soldiers. This was the first occurrence of heavy fighting in the war.

This attack had grave implications for India and Nehru tried to solve the issue, but by 18 October it was clear that the Chinese were preparing for an attack on India, with massive troop buildups on the border.

CEASEFIRE

On November 20, 1962, India and the world speculated about the nature and aims of the Chinese attack. They had rapidly eliminated all Indian military in all disputed frontier territories (Aksai Chin and NEFA). Would China continue attacking toward India proper? A worried India's November 20th request for an American aircraft carrier had been approved. Dramatically, on November 20th, Chou Enlai publically announced a ceasefire. Actually, Chou had given the details of the ceasefire to the Indian charge d'affaires in Peking on the evening of November 19th (before India's request for United States air strikes), but New Delhi did not receive the report for over 24 hours. The ceasefire proclaimed that

Beginning from....0000 on November 21, 1962, the Chinese frontier guards will cease fire along the entire Sino-Indian border. Beginning from December 1st, 1962, the Chinese frontier guards will withdraw to positions 20 kilometers behind the line of actual control which existed between China and India on November 7th, 1959. In the eastern sector, although the Chinese frontier guards have so far been fighting on Chinese territory north of the traditional customary line*, they are prepared to withdraw from their present positions to the north of the illegal McMahon Line, and to withdraw twenty kilometers back from that line. In the middle and western sectors, the Chinese frontier guards will withdraw twenty kilometers from the line of actual control.

Chou had simply restated the compromise that he had been offering for over three years: India could keep the disputed territory north to the McMahon Line in NEFA, but China would keep the disputed territory in Aksai Chin. Of the 47,000 square miles of disputed border land, Chou's ceasefire gave a full 68% (the 32,000 square miles of NEFA) to India, and kept only 32% (the 15,000 miles of Aksai Chin) for China! Rather than the "victor keeping the spoils," Peking kept only what was strategically vital: the area surrounding her critical military road in Aksai Chin. Chou's ceasefire dictum made it clear that the Indians would keep their troops twenty kilometers back from the ceasefire line, and that China "reserved the right to strike back" if India did not do so.

On the NEFA front, the November 21st ceasefire was a formality. Organized fighting had ended two days before with the breakup of 48 Brigade at Chaku. The two sides had generally ceased to be in contact anywhere in the eastern sector, and there had been no Chinese followup after either Chaku or Walong.

Some Indian troops who had been outflanked by the Chinese had skirmishes, with casualties, as they withdrew to the south; these retreating soldiers had no knowledge of the ceasefire, and the Chinese may have ignored the ceasefire when retreating Indians fired on them.

In Aksai Chin, the ceasefire was more definitive. The Chinese had not advanced on Chushul, and all firing ceased at the given time. The Indian force at Chushul was still in a fighting posture, ready to defend if the Chinese advanced. The Indians even sent out some patrols. But there was no more fighting in Aksai Chin.

Indian troops in Ladakh remained in defensive posture. But on the plains below NEFA, the Indian Army was cautions. A new brigade there was ordered to keep back from the hills, to make no provocations, and to avoid patrol clashes. Indian survivors of NEFA battles emerged onto the plains for several weeks; the trek back was very arduous, and many died from exposure on the way back. China clearly expected India to keep her forces twenty kilometers south of the lines of control specified in the ceasefire. Nehru could not admit defeat, and publicly would continue to refuse China's terms. But privately, Nehru told Chou that Indian forces would conform with the ceasefire.

The Chinese started withdrawing on December 1st, as per the ceasefire. In NEFA, they withdrew north of the McMahon Line. In Aksai Chin, they withdrew as agreed, but set up strong check points and posts to ensure their position.

The Chinese then began repatriating Indians through Bomdi La. The sick and wounded were returned during December, 1962. Other prisoners of war were returned over the next six months. At one point, Nehru had announced that 6,277 Indian soldiers were captured or missing. India's casualties for the Border War were finally reported as follows:

Killed	1,383
Captured	3,968
Missing	1,696

India released no figures for Wounded, but casualties were high.

FACTORS RESPONSIBLE FOR WAR

Tibet Controversy

The 1940s saw huge change in South Asia with the Partition of India in 1947 (resulting in the establishment of the two new states of India and Pakistan), and the establishment of the People's Republic of China in 1949. One of the most basic policies for the new Indian government was that of maintaining cordial relations with China, reviving its ancient friendly ties. India was among the first nations to grant diplomatic recognition to the newly-created PRC. At the time, Chinese officials issued no condemnation of Nehru's claims or made any opposition to Nehru's open declarations of control over Aksai Chin.

In 1956, Chinese Premier Zhou Enlai stated that he had no claims over Indian controlled territory. He later argued that Aksai Chin was already under

Chinese jurisdiction, implying that there was therefore no contradiction with his earlier statement since China did not regard the region as "Indian controlled", and that since the British hand-over China had regarded the McCartney MacDonald Line as the relevant border. Zhou later argued that as the boundary was undemarcated and had never been defined by treaty between any Chinese or Indian government, the Indian government could not unilaterally define Aksai Chin's borders. However, within a short time the PRC announced its intention to reclaim Tibet from the British, and later extended its influence by placing border posts within the Indian-claimed territory of Aksai Chin. India protested against these moves and decided to look for a diplomatic solution to ensure a stable Sino-Indian border.

To resolve any doubts about the Indian position, Prime Minister Jawaharlal Nehru declared in parliament that India regarded the McMahon Line as its official border. The Chinese expressed no concern at this statement, and in 1951 and 52, the government of China asserted that there were no frontier issues to be taken up with India. In 1954, Prime Minister Nehru wrote a memo calling for India's borders to be clearly defined and demarcated: in line with previous Indian philosophy, Indian maps showed a border that, in some places, lay north of the McMahon Line. Chinese Premier Zhou Enlai, in November 1956, again repeated Chinese assurances that the People's Republic had no claims on Indian territory, although official Chinese maps showed 120,000 square kilometres of territory claimed by India as Chinese.

CIA documents created at the time revealed that Nehru had ignored Burmese premier Ba Swe when he warned Nehru to be cautious when dealing with Zhou. They also allege that Zhou purposefully told Nehru that there were no border issues with India. In 1950 the Chinese People's Liberation Army invaded Tibet. Four years later, in 1954, China and India negotiated the Five Principles of Peaceful Coexistence by which the two nations agreed to abide in settling their disputes. India presented a frontier map which was accepted by China, and the Indian government under Prime Minister Nehru promoted the slogan *Hindi-Chini bhai-bhai* (Indians and Chinese are brothers).

According to Georgia Tech political analyst John W Garver, Nehru's policy on Tibet was to create a strong Sino-Indian partnership which would be catalyzed through agreement and compromise on Tibet. Garver believes that Nehru's previous actions had given him confidence that China would be ready to form an "Asian Axis" with India. This apparent progress in relations suffered a major setback when, in 1959, Nehru accommodated the Tibetan religious leader, the Dalai Lama, who was fleeing Lhasa after a failed Tibetan uprising against Chinese rule.

The Chairman of the Chinese Communist Party, Mao Zedong, was enraged and asked the Xinhua News Agency to produce reports on Indian expansionists operating in Tibet. Border incidents continued through this period. In August 1959, the PLA took an Indian prisoner at Longju, which had an ambiguous position in the McMahon Line, and two months later in Aksai Chin a clash led to the death of nine Indian frontier policemen. On 2 October, Soviet Premier Nikita Khrushchev defended Nehru in a meeting with Mao.

This action reinforced China's impression that the Soviet Union, the United States and India all had expansionist designs over China. The PLA (People's Liberation Army) went so far as to prepare a self-defensive counterattack plan. Negotiations were restarted between the nations, but no progress was made. As a consequence of their non-recognition of the McMahon Line, China's maps showed both the North East Frontier Area (NEFA) and Aksai Chin to be Chinese territory.

In 1960, Zhou Enlai unofficially suggested that India drop its claims to Aksai Chin in return for a Chinese withdrawal of claims over NEFA. Adhering to his stated position, Nehru believed that China did not have a legitimate claim over either of these territories, and thus was not ready to concede them. This adamance was perceived in China as Indian opposition to Chinese rule in Tibet. Nehru declined to conduct any negotiations on the boundary until Chinese troops withdrew from Aksai Chin; a position supported by the international community. India produced numerous reports on the negotiations, and translated Chinese reports into English to help inform the international debate.

China believed that India was simply securing its claim lines in order to continue its "grand plans in Tibet". India's stance that China withdraw from Aksai Chin caused continual deterioration of the diplomatic situation to the point at which internal forces were pressurizing Nehru to take a military stance against China.

The Forward Policy

At the beginning of 1961, Nehru appointed General B M Kaul as army Chief of General Staff, but he refused to increase military spending and prepare for a possible war. That summer, China's continuing patrols south of the McMahon Line provoked an Indian response known as the "Forward Policy". According to James Barnard Calvin of the U.S. Navy, in 1959, India started sending Indian troops and border patrols into disputed areas. This program created both skirmishes and deteriorating relations between India and China. The aim of this policy was to create outposts behind advancing Chinese troops to interdict their supplies, forcing their return to China. There were eventually 60 such outposts, including 43 north of the McMahon Line. China viewed this as further confirmation of Indian expansionist plans directed towards Tibet. According to the Indian official history, implementation of the Forward Policy was intended to provide evidence of Indian occupation in the previously unoccupied region through which Chinese troops had been patrolling. Kaul was confident, through contact with Indian Intelligence and CIA information, that China would not react with force. Indeed at first the PLA simply withdrew, but eventually Chinese forces began to counter-encircle the Indian positions. This led to a tit-for-tat Indian reaction, with both forces attempting to outmanoeuver each other. However, despite the escalating nature of the dispute, the two forces withheld from engaging each other directly.

Chinese attention was diverted for a time by the military activity of the Nationalists on Taiwan, but on 23 June the U.S. assured China that a Nationalist invasion would not be permitted. China's heavy artillery facing Taiwan could then be moved to Tibet. It took China six to eight months to gather the resources needed for the war, according to Anil Athale, author of the official Indian history. The Chinese sent a large quantity of non-military supplies to Tibet through the Indian port of Calcutta.

Early Incidents

Various border conflicts and "military incidents" between India and China flared up throughout the summer and autumn of 1962. In May, the Indian Air Force was told not to plan for close air support, although it was assessed as being a feasible way to repel the unbalanced ratio of Chinese to Indian troops. In June, a skirmish caused the deaths of dozens of Chinese troops. The Indian Intelligence Bureau received information about a Chinese buildup along the border which could be a precursor to war.

During the period of June–July 1962, the Indian military planners began advocating "probing actions" against the Chinese, and accordingly, moved mountain troops forward to cut off Chinese supply lines. According to Patterson, the Indian motives were threefold:

1. Test Chinese resolve and intentions regarding India.
2. Test whether India would enjoy Soviet backing in the event of a Sino-Indian war.
3. Create sympathy for India within the US, with whom relations had deteriorated after the Indian annexation of Goa.

On 10 July 1962, 350 Chinese troops surrounded an Indian post in Chushul but withdrew after a heated argument via loudspeaker. On 22 July, the Forward Policy was extended to allow Indian troops to push back Chinese troops already established in disputed territory. Whereas Indian troops were previously ordered to fire only in self-defence, all post commanders were now given discretion to open fire upon Chinese forces if threatened. In August, the Chinese military improved its combat readiness along the McMahon Line and began stockpiling ammunition, weapons and gasoline.

Confrontation at Thag La

In June 1962, Indian forces established an outpost at Dhola, on the southern slopes of the Thag La Ridge. Dhola lay north of the McMahon Line but south of the ridges India maintains the McMahon Line was supposed to represent. In August, China issued diplomatic protests and began occupying positions at the top of Thag La. On 8 September, a 60-strong PLA unit descended to the south side of the ridge and occupied positions that dominated one of the Indian posts at Dhola. Fire was not exchanged but Nehru said to the media that the Indian Army had instructions to "free our territory" and the troops had been given discretion to use force. On 11 September, it was decided that "all forward posts and patrols were given permission to fire on any armed Chinese who entered Indian territory".

However, the operation to occupy Thagla was flawed in that Nehru's directives were unclear and it got underway very slowly because of this. In addition to this, each man had to carry 35 kg of luggage over the long trek and this severely slowed down the reaction. By the time the Indian battalion reached the point of conflict, Chinese units controlled both banks of the Namka Chu River. On 20 September, Chinese troops threw grenades at Indian troops and a firefight developed, triggering a long series of skirmishes for the rest of September.

Some Indian troops, including Brigadier Dalvi who commanded the forces at Thag La, were also concerned that the territory they were fighting for was not strictly territory that "we should have been convinced was ours". According to Neville Maxwell, even members of the Indian defence ministry were categorically concerned with the validity of the fighting in Thag La.

On 3 October, a week before the triggering of the war, Zhou Enlai visited Nehru in New Delhi promising there would be no war. On 4 October, Kaul assigned some troops with securing regions south of the Thagla Ridge. Kaul decided to first secure Yumtso La, a strategically important position, before re-entering the lost Dhola post. Kaul had then realised that the attack would be desperate and the Indian government tried to stop escalation into an all-out war. Indian troops travelling to Thagla had suffered in the previously unexperienced conditions, two Gurkha troops died of pulmonary edema. On 10 October, an Indian Punjabi patrol of 50 troops to Yumtso La were met by an emplaced Chinese position of some 1,000 soldiers. Indian troops were in no position for battle, as Yumtso La was 16,000 feet (4,900 m) above sea level and Kaul did not plan on having artillery support for the troops. The Chinese troops opened fire on the Indians under their belief that they were north of the McMahon Line. The Indians were surrounded by Chinese positions which used mortar fire. However, they managed to hold off the first Chinese assault, inflicting heavy casualties.

At this point, the Indian troops were in a position to push the Chinese back with mortar and machine gun fire. However, Brigadier Dalvi opted not to fire, as it would mean decimating the Rajput who were still in the area of the Chinese regrouping. They helplessly watched the Chinese ready themselves for a second assault. In the second Chinese assault, the Indians began their retreat, realising the situation was hopeless. The Indian patrol suffered 25 casualties, with the Chinese suffering 33. The Chinese troops held their fire as the Indians retreated, and then buried the Indian dead with military honours, as witnessed by the retreating soldiers. This was the first occurrence of heavy fighting in the war.

This attack had grave implications for India and Nehru tried to solve the issue, but by 18 October it was clear that the Chinese were preparing for an attack on India, with massive troop buildups on the border. A long line of mules and porters had also been observed supporting the buildup and reinforcement of positions south of the Thagla ridge.

THE AFTERMATH

The 1962 Debacle, as it is remembered in India, was the inexorable ramification of a century-old British border dispute, thrust upon a newly independent India. When China reached a juncture whence it could act proactively to the sense of injustice about colonial actions against them, the result was an eruption of a xenophobic, aggressive imperialism.

There is a Chinese phrase oft quoted within the Chinese government: "If he strikes me once, it is his fault. If he strikes me again, it is my fault." The People's Republic of China seemed to have taken this mentality to heart, and in the effort to exorcise the demons of colonialism, have become imperialists themselves. Subverting various indigenous countries and areas in affirmation of vague "historical" citings had become a fundamental cornerstone of China's geo-strategic maneuvering in the '50s and '60s.

The Chinese claims to Aksai Chin and large areas of Arunachal are a mix of an expression of this neo-colonial sentiment and the desire to acquire a dominant status in Asia by keeping rival India in a weaker bargaining position.

This is not saying that the PRC is necessarily "evil" in this respect, as many Indian journalists are prone to claim; it is simply geopolitics. What is unusual, however, is the rather unscrupulous means, even among the big-power nations, that the PRC has taken to reach this position. When China sought recognition of its claim on Tibet after its occupation, the Chinese leadership avidly cultivated India, and won the heart of a high-minded but naïve Prime Minister Nehru. "Hindi-Chini Bhai-Bhai" (India and China are brothers) became the soundbyte of the day - and the Chinese cannot be faulted in their execution of this deception. While the shells fell and the bullets flew around the Jawans in the snow-capped hell of the Himalayan battlefield, the Indian leaders in Delhi were romancing the fluffy pull of empathy with a fraternal Asian nation that, too, had suffered exploitation by the Western colonial powers.

Added to the chaos and the mounting of tensions after the border clashes and failed settlement talks in 1960, and arguably a prime factor in making the dispute a mutual national prestige issue, was the internal political flux within both India and China. India was democratic and, therefore, more sensitive to its public and parliamentary opinion, and highly politicized debates about the Chinese question raged across the Parliament floor and in stratified governmental agencies. In particular, the elected representatives of the various Communist parties in India were indignant by the notion that their fraternal socialist brethren would be capable of starting such a conflict, and laid the blame solely on the "capitalist-lackey" Nehru's shoulders. At the opposite end of the political spectrum, the right-leaning parties blamed the crisis on a "socialist" Nehru's ignorance and non-recognition of the reality of situation. On the other side, a communist Peking did not have this intra-political problem, but it was engaged in intense ideological remolding and suffered from a sense of political isolation, aggravated by its increasing ideological differences with Russia since 1958, when the latter, for example, refused to give it a sample atom bomb.

The '62 war highlighted several critical failures in India's warmaking abilities. First, and perhaps most significantly, the conflict highlighted political naïveté and ignorance toward the strategies of warfare and international relations. During the entire conflict, Indian diplomatic actions remained flaccid, and fluctuated between being confrontational to being manhandled. For example, intel told that the Chinese were building a road through Aksai Chin, yet the Government, apart from a few angry condemnations, chose to ignore the strategic significance of it for almost a decade, instead repeating to itself the mantra of Hindi-Chini bhai-bhai. Even upon discovery of this transgression, India's protests were weak-kneed. Later, in the middle of 1962, Indian leaders suddenly woke up to the presence of Chinese soldiers, to the exasperation of much of the army, on the Thagla Ridge. Nehru, advised by Krishna Menon and a coterie of sycophantic generals, ordered a reckless operation on the attacking Chinese. In the adoption of a forward policy, against the clamoring of sound tacticians, India deployed on ground chosen for its political significance, rather than tactical defensibility. The leadership's untenable demands on the Army were the root cause of the '62 debacle.

The war also highlighted the fact that the army was acutely under-equipped, out-dated, and ill-trained to deal with sustained conflict in the Himalaya. The acclimatization of troops was of critical import in this mountain war. Though Indian kill ratios were vary favorable, the damage caused by non-acclimatization of troops, particularly in the eastern sector, compared to the troops in Ladakh, who were better equipped and acclimatized, is very evident.

The psychological and political effects of the '62 war were far-reaching. Because of the war, India's image, especially among the "Third World", the nations remaining non-aligned during the Cold War, suffered. But internally, the shock galvanized the people into one united nation. Krishna Menon resigned and Nehru's dream of Sino-Indian friendship was shattered, but India did not relinquish its independent policy of Non-Alignment, though a shadow was shed on India's position as the leader of the Non-Aligned Movement (NAM). However, statements by the PRC promoting the Chinese revolution as a model and Beijing's actions in the Taiwan Strait in 1958 and the 1962 Sino-Indian War alarmed many Third World nations. During the 1960s China cultivated ties with Third World countries and insurgent groups in an attempt to encourage "wars of national liberation" and revolution to forge an international united front against both the superpowers. Third World appreciation for Chinese assistance coexisted, consequently, with growing suspicions of China's militancy. These increasingly militant tendencies, contradictory to the much lauded "Principles of Peaceful Coexistence" soundbyte, destroyed what active influence the PRC had on the NAM. Discord between China and many Third World countries continued to grow, while relations India and the Soviet Union warmed to counter the decision by Pakistan to cavort to the Western Camp in an effort to counter Indian superiority and influence. The two most powerful nonaligned nations strayed further from their NAM policies, and thus the weakened NAM did not wield as much influence during the later part of the Cold War as it did during the beginning, and thus the era of a strictly bi-polar Cold War world was ushered in.

The Indian Army's defeat by the Chinese in the border war of 1962 was a national humiliation, but the nation reacted to the '62 war with an unprecedented surge of patriotism. The main lesson India learned was that right does not make might in the world of geopolitics, and that India must strengthen its defenses and stand on its own feet to be of consequence in the world. India's policy of weaponization via indigenous sources and self-sufficiency was thus cemented. National sovereignty, it would affirmed, could not come at the expense of becoming a client state of any superpower or by joining any military alliance with or under them.

In the early '80s, following a new paradigm shift in the Indian military, it was decided that the Army was to actively patrol the Line of Actual Control. Friction began to ensue over the Chinese occupation of the Sumdorong Chu pasturage, lying north of Tawang. The media, catching wind of the situation, gave it national prominence, and an angry exchange of official protests between the Indian and Chinese governments followed. Adding to the bickering, a bill was passed creating the state of Arunachal Pradesh, a territory that China claims in its entirety.

The military re-occupied Hathung La ridge, across Namka Chu, twenty-five years after vacating it. Army chief K. Sundarji airlifted an entire brigade to nearby Ximithang, alarming the panicked Chinese. The Indian government collectively flinched against the tough talk from Beijing, but stood firm at the insistence of the army. The result paradoxically was a thaw. In 1993 and 1996, the two sides signed the Sino-Indian bilateral Peace and Tranquillity Accords, an agreement on maintaining peace and tranquillity along the LAC. Ten meetings of a Sino-Indian Joint Working Group (SIJWG) and five of an expert group to determine where the LAC lies have taken place but the pace of progress has been tardy to say the least.

THE COMBATANTS: THE CHINESE AND INDIAN ARMIES IN 1962

The Chinese People's Liberation Army (PLA) is the unified organization, under a single command, of all Chinese land, sea, and air forces. The estimated strength of the PLA in 1962 was approximately three million officers and men. The 1962 ground combat forces consisted of about 130 divisions, mostly infantry. China is divided into eleven military regions, including the Sinkiang Military Region—responsible for Aksai China—and Chengtu Military Region—responsible for the northeast Indian border.

Chinese combat power was organized around an Army, with a strength of approximately 4,500 officers and 38,400 soldiers. Each Army has three Infantry Divisions, with a strength of approximately 1,300 officers and 11,300 soldiers in each Division. Major equipment of the Infantry Division included the Light Machine Gun, Antitank Grenade Launcher, and Mortars. Infantry Divisions included three Infantry Regiments, a Tank Regiment and an Artillery Regiment. An Infantry Regiment had three Infantry Battalions, equipped with

7.62mm Assault Rifles and Carbines. Even with China's massive combat manpower available, the nature of the 1962 Border War—mountain and cold weather operations—dictated tactics generally limited to the battalion and company level.

The PLA had both strengths and weakness in its readiness for mountain warfare against India. Perhaps China's biggest weakness was the economic and budgetary constraints on the Army. The Soviets has willingly supplied the PLA in the 1950's. But deteriorating relations—including border disputes—with Russia led to the end of Soviet military aid in 1960. Further, China faced national economic difficulties in the late 1950s and early 1960s. This resulted in progressive cutbacks and constraints from 1960 to 1962 for the PLA: ".... so serious was the shortage of military equipment and materials that it caused trouble in the training program.... The Ground Force is also facing the difficulties of obtaining fuel, ammunition, and batteries for the use of their vehicles and in training."

The 1962 Taiwan Strait Crisis put further strains on the PLA's resources. Clearly, the watchword for the PLA was self-reliance—making due with the supplies and equipment that were available. Finally, while there has often been political control of the PLA, there was especially tight central control regarding border incidents; official orders in all border regions stated that ".... under no circumstance should an officer upon his own personal responsibility take steps to carry out an unauthorized decision" regarding any border/international incident; officers were directed to report incidents, and then await decisions and orders.

On the positive side, the PLA was well prepared for mountain warfare in the Himalayas. China had gained extensive experience in both mountain and cold weather warfare in Korea; many Korea verterans were still in the PLA in the early 1960s. Not only had China gained further experience in alpine warfare over the past twelve years in Tibet, but she was fighting in the same area (the Himalayas being the southern frontier of Tibet). The Chinese were acclimitized to the weather and the altitudes. They had outposts, patrols, and military construction (e.g. the two Aksai Chin roads) in the frontier. Further, the Chinese augmented their strength and mobility by using local Tibetan guides.

Finally, the PLA was well prepared for this type of warfare. The troops had warm, padded uniforms. They carried only what rations they needed to complete a particular mission. And they trained and practiced mobility, moving through mountain passes or over ridges at night, encircling the enemy. Even their mortars and small artillery was mobile. The Indian soldiers would report that the Chinese burp gun and human wave assaults were "demoralizing."

Despite its defense budget problems, the People's Liberation Army appeared to be prepared and ready for military operations in the Himalayas. The Indian Army's readiness for alpine warfare was quite a different story.

The Indian Ministry of Defense was the central agency for formulating and implementing the government's policy decisions on defense matters. There were three branches of service: army, navy, and air force. The Army was organized into three Commands - Western, Eastern, and Southern. Units from the Eastern and Western Commands would be organized into Corpslevel Border Commands. XXIII Corps was responsible for all of NEFA; within XXXIII Corps, 4 Division was responsible for the McMahon Line. The IV Corps would be formed in September, 1962, to assume portions of the NEFA defense. In the west, XV Corps had responsibility for Aksai Chin.

When India gained her independence in 1947, the Indian components of the British Indian Army were divided between Indian and Pakistan on a ratio of 2:1. The first years of the Indian republic were marked with a generally anti-military attitude; many Indian leaders remembered the role of the army in the bloody civil war that preceeded independence; this helped contribute to pacifistic attitudes. Further, Nehru (and others) minimized foreign threats; in regard to China, Nehru stated that the Himalayas "made an effective barrier." Thus, the 1950s was generally a decade of neglect for the Indian Army.

Because India believed that there was no external threat to her—with the exception of Pakistan—the national defense budget was minimal. In the mid-1950s, the Army numbered about 350,000, and there was only minimal growth in manpower over the next several years; after India's 1962 defeat, the Army's numbers would leap to 827,000!

The Indian Army had significant personnel problems. The Army had only eight divisions—seven infantry and one armour. Only three battalions were available to the Western Command in the early 1960s. The budget constraints on the army and India's pacifistic attitude aggravated another problem: the British had provided much of the leadership of the British Indian army; without the British, there was a shortage of experienced officers and NCOs. It was thus difficult to build up military strength, especially when the advice of experienced senior officers was often ignored.

Apparently, Indian intelligence was also lacking. Their lack of preparedness for warfare in the Himalayas would indicate a very poor concept of the topography and weather in the area, resulting in very poor mobility across the mountains. Indian intelligence and reconnaissence seemed ignorant of Chinese strength, mobility and tactics, especially night movements and human wave attacks which the Indians called the "Red Ant Swarm."

The Indians had problems with fire power. Because of limited budget, they had minimal artillery and difficulty keeping it adequately supplied with ammunition. The artillery they did have was often immobile in the mountains.

Another area affected by the budget was training. Technical training was lacking, and there were simply not enough supplies and munitions for adequate training. Worse, there was little training for mountain warfare.

Perhaps the major problem—another result of the limited defense budget—was the logistic one. Even with foreign aid (primarily from Russia), the Indian army was lacking in virtually every area of equipment and supplies. The logistic shortfalls had many serious consequences. India lacked the engineering equipment for alpine operations. They had tentage, but not enought to house even half the soldiers. Rations were often in short supply, resulting in many hungry days for the Indian soldiers. Their communications equipment was minimal. And, almost unbelievably, the Indian army came to the Himalayas (to altitudes above 15,000 feet) in cotton, summer uniforms! Finally, transportation of supplies was a serious problem. Roads into the mountains were few; often, supplies came on long final legs by pack animal. The Indians resorted to supply by air drop, but even this had problems. Aging parachutes were used with supplies, and supplies crashed to the ground often when the parachutes failed. To make matters worse, many of the air drops landed on Chinese, rather than Indian, encampments (and to add insult to injury, the Chinese would throw out the "inedible" Indian rations)!

In summary, the Indian army was in a poor state, especially in their readiness for alpine warfare. Their fire power, supply system, training, and readiness for mountain operations were all quite lacking. They had significant personnel shortages, and would often be outnumbered by the Chinese by 5:1.[2] To pit troops in such circumstances against an enemy superior in every detail of military strength would be absurd; to leave them in an early winter of heavy snow and freezing temperatures would be to condemn them to steady and severe attrition from exposure and illness and, before long, starvation. But this is what India did.

Under these circumstances, India's forward policy was militarily nonsensical. But some politicians and leaders simply believe what they want to believe. Nehru was still convinced that his army would be almost invincible against the Chinese. He would soon learn how wrong he was.

CONCLUSIONS

The Border War and the ceasefire brought many changes and many implications to both India and the world. The political and military climate in southern Asia was dramatically changed in the last three months of 1962.

India recognized many of the weaknesses in her Army; and many lessons—still relevant today—emerged from the 1962 Border War.

Nations continue to go to war, especially if negotiations yield no compromise, over issues that are strategically important to them. India had long been concerned about maintaining a buffer zone between her and her powerful neighbours—Russia and China—to the north.

China not only felt that Aksai Chin was legitimately hers (especially with little or no Indian presence in the area to indicate otherwise), but she was also adamant about the area because of the strategically important military highway which bisected it. There may well have been room for compromise over these issues, but stuubornness and India's aggressive forward policy resulted in armed conflict. World leaders must heed other nations' stated vital strategic objectives. Assumptions are dangerous. Nehru's assumption that China would not confront Indian troops and would passively retreat caused Nehru to pursue a very assertive forward policy of thrusting troops and border patrols into-and sometimes even beyond—disputed frontier areas. His assumptions and resulting policy eventually brought retaliation frown China. Assumptions are still dangerous; hypotheses about one's enemy must be validated by accurate intelligence.

Ignoring the advice of senior, experienced army officers was disasterous for India. Many officers had warned Nehru that India was poorly prepared for war with China: they were relieved or replaced, their advice ignored. Leaders may believe what they want to believe, but foolishly discounting the counsel of experts may lead them to disaster.

Intelligence and appropriate interpretation of intelligence is vital; only valid information—not assumptions—is important to military planning. India seemed almost totally unaware that she was heavily outnumbered along the border and that China (unlike India) was well prepared logistically and well versed in alpine warfare tactics. Both sides used reconnaissance patrols, but battle results would indicate that China had good intelligence and used it to good advantage. One must "know your enemy."

Logistic readiness is vital to any military operation. India was very poorly prepared logistically, especially for cold weather and mountain operations. On several occasions, India ran out of ammunition or was otherwise unable to sustain herself. The Chinese had stockpiled supplies in Tibet, and had the manpower to keep the front well supplied. The Border War's mountain operations were relatively slow moving. Today, high mobility will make proper logistic support even more crucial.

Similarly, India was neither trained nor prepared for alpine warfare. Until Nehru's assertive forward policy was initiated, few Indian soldiers had operated in mountain areas. Altitudes above 14,000 feet can be frigid even in summer. In October and November, many Indian soldiers had only summer uniforms and jackets to warm them. Many Indians died not from combat, but from exposure. Today's military forces must be prepared for operations in any locale or climate, from hot arid deserts to frozen mountain slopes.

Generalship, leadership, command and control are always important. Even though defeated in Aksai Chin, the Indian forces in Western Command always deemed well organized and led. But in NEFA, there was often confusion; numerous command changes resulted in disorganization and poor combat readiness. Poor communications and control resulted in troop movements which were totally inappropriate, such as sending out forces to positions which had already been overrun. General Kaul often ignored or disputed the advice of his junior generals; further, he was often indecisive, changing orders minutes after they had been issued. Immediately after the ceasefire, General Kaul was relieved; days later, he would resign from the army. Today's lethal firepower and high mobility make command, control and communications more vital than ever.

Hopefully, future military and political leaders will study the causes and the lessons learned from this Border War. And hopefully, they will learn.

The 1962 China-India Border War was a major dispute between two third world states that went to war over strategic frontier and border issues. The War would have significant implications for politics, strategy, and military power in southern Aisa.

India was decisively defeated in the Border War. But in many ways, India gained benefits from the 1962 conflict. The war united the country as never before. The communist party in India lost what little strength it had. India did get 32,000 square miles of disputed territory—even if she felt that NEFA was hers all along. The new Indian republic had avoided international alignments; by asking for during the war, India demonstrated her willingness to accept military aid from several sectors. And, finally, India recognized the serious weaknesses in her Army. She would more than double her military manpower in the next two years; and she would work hard to resolve the military's training and logistic problems. India's efforts to improve her military posture significantly enhanced her army's capabilities and preparedness.

The War would also have significant impacy on India's relationship with Pakistan (which then bordered India on two sides, east and west). Seeing that India was militarily weak after the Border War, Pakistan felt that she was in a favorable position to reslove lingering border disputes in Kashmir. China was friendly toward Pakistan, and Pakistani leaders believed that China might support them in a dispute with India. When India reorganized and built up her Army, Pakistan became quite alarmed. In 1965, India and Pakistan would fight a border war in Kashmir.

China had easily won a military victory on the ground. But Peking may have lost in terms of its international image. Western nations, especially the United States, were already suspicious of Chinese attitudes, motives and actions; after all, People's Republic leader Mao had stated that "The way to world conquest lies through Havana, Accra, and Calcutta."1 These western nations, including a suspicious United States, appeared to minimize, or not fully to understand, the China-India dispute background: that China believed that Aksai Chin had been legally Chinese since 1899 or before, that no official boundary had been agreed upon between the two nations, and that Nehru's "forward policy" had thrusted troops even beyond India's claim line into Tibetan/Chinese territory. These same nations saw China's goals as monolithic intent on world conquest, and clearly viewed China as the aggressor in the Border War. China's first nuclear weapon test in October, 1964, and her support of Pakistan in the 1965 India-Pakistan Bordr War tended ot confirm the American view of monolithic communist world objectives, including Chinese influence (if not expansionism) over Pakistan. Yet, an examination of China's international objectives, since the Communists came to power in 1949, shows a pattern of conservative aims and limited objectives, rather than expansionism. China's role in the Korea Conflict was not simply to assist North Korea, but also to protect herself again assault from anti-Communist western forces. China's actions in Tibet in 1950 were viewed by India as blatant aggression; but China saw her move into Tibet as simply reuniting what is "traditionally Chinese" territory. The 1962 Border War, again, had only the objective of keeping what was "traditionally Chinese"; otherwise, why would have China given all of NEFA back to India? In 1979, China feared increasing anti-Chinese attitude in Viet Nam. When Viet Nam invaded Kampuchea—and after much preplanning and thought—China launched a limited objective assault, to punish Viet Nam. Thus, the People's Republic of China has been historically non-expansionistic.

But we should not, on the other hand, be totally lulled into a false sense of security about China's non-expansionism. Remembering that nations will go to war over strategically (including economically) important issues, we must remain alert to China's rapidly expanding population and accompanying need for food to feed her hungry. Where will China get rice to give to her billion-plus numbers? To answer this, we must not forget another lesson of this Border War: China intends— eventually—to reclaim what is "traditionally Chinese."

4

Sino-Indian Border Dispute and Their Competitive Symbiotic Relationship

ANALYSIS

Recently, the Sino-Indian border dispute once again became a focus of for the world's mass media. A "tent confrontation" between the Chinese and Indian armies took place and continued near the Line of Actual Control (LAC) for several days. From the Indian point of view, the Chinese army invaded Indian territory, and this incident was "the most serious one in the past 25 years". Level-headed analysis will indicate, however, that China would not wish to provoke simultaneous conflicts with Japan and India, two major Asian powers. In fact, the Indian mass media's reports about Chinese incursions have been heard continually in recent years. Some reports that the Chinese have invaded India for more than 600 times in the past three years are ridiculous.

The Sino-Indian border issue is very complicated. It was left over from the time of British rule in India and has never been resolved. In the 1960s, a military conflict broke out between China and India over territorial boundaries. That conflict became the excuse for India to develop its armed forces vigorously, to get ready for battle, and to make nuclear weapons. The root reason cause of many of the "incursion" incidents reported by India is that the two sides have never reached a consensus on the position of the LAC since the boundary conflict in 1962. They have never delimited the LAC, let alone a formal border. It is therefore debatable to say the Chinese army invaded Indian territory.

Since 1993, however, China and India have signed two agreements and one protocol on the maintenance of peace and tranquillity and the establishment of confidence-building measures in the border areas. They have set up a working mechanism for consultation and coordination on border affairs. These efforts have helped ensure a durable peace and stability in the border areas. The possibility that China and India will come to serious conflict is very small.

Bilateral relations between China and India are very subtle; apart from the boundary problem, the issues of China-Pakistan relations, the Dalai Lama and water resources also hinder the promotion of China-India relations. These problems have given India a deep-seated distrust of China. Some Indians are gradually losing self-confidence as they observe the growing economic gap between China and India.

The Indian mass media and some Indian strategic scholars frequently refer to a "Chinese incursion" and the "China threat" and propagate an attitude of no confidence in China's intentions. This situation provides opportunities for some Western countries to undermine Sino-India relations. With the US "rebalancing" toward the Asia-Pacific, the Sino-Indian relationship is undergoing subtle changes these days.

Some Indian scholars promote an alliance under the US leadership to counterbalance China. For example, Harsh V. Pant, a professor of defence studies at King's College London, argues that India's strategic interests can only be realised by an Asia-Pacific arrangement in which the US retains its predominant status. The Indian Express columnist C. Raja Mohan similarly urges India to shift its policy of strategic autonomy and strategically cooperate with the US.

So far, India has concentrated on strengthening its "Look East" Policy to enhance strategic and security cooperation with countries such as Japan, South Korea, Malaysia and Vietnam.

It has also taken a high profile in the South China Sea disputes. In December 2011, the first trilateral dialogue between the US, Japan and India was presided over by the US. One of the discussion topics was China's growing military and political global position. It is no wonder that many think that India may abandon strategic autonomy to ally itself with the US and contain China.

Currently, Indian policymakers have a relatively clear view of Sino-Indian and India-US relations. India doesn't yet have the ability to directly confront China, and, as a country prioritising economic development, it is in need of a peaceful neighbouring environment. History shows that the US is not a reliable ally for India. Because of the effect of the economic crisis, the US is heavily burdened by its domestic economic problems, and there are doubts about how much money can be invested in counterbalancing China. The US anchors its hope on the strategy of "offshore balancing" to achieve balance with, or even contain, China by stirring up tensions between it and its Asian strategic partners. It is just taking advantage of India's strength to balance China, which, in effect, should kill two birds with one stone.

So, at present, we have the ironic spectacle of articles in both the US and Indian media trying to provoke each other into tensions with China. The Indian media highlights the idea that Uncle Sam is well-prepared to battle China, while the US media points out that India is engaging in military expansion in preparation for possible Sino-Indian boundary conflicts.

India still maintains its status as a "swing state" in the international system. Although it has recently become more pro-US, since the US recognised India as a nuclear power despite it not being a signatory to the Nuclear Non-Proliferation Treaty (NPT), India will not abandon its strategic autonomy to ally with the US.

I have published articles that arguing that the Sino-Indian relationship is, in essence, a competitive symbiotic relationship. I say that for the following reasons: First of all, there really are some areas of competitions between China and India, mainly in geopolitics, trade and energy, etc. But that competition is not necessarily cutthroat and zero sum. China and India can cooperate if they have mutual trust. In fact, they do cooperate in fields such as energy and anti-terrorism.

In addition to the aspect of competition, the Sino-Indian symbiotic relationship can be divided into four areas: First, as two big powers that are rising simultaneously, China and India are in similar positions in the current international system. They are beneficiaries of that system, but at the same time, they are constrained by it and also suppressed by the dominant power in the system.

They want to gradually advance the reform of this system. So, China and India have common interests on many global issues, such as the reform of the international financial system, climate change, and the WTO negotiations. China, India, Brazil and South Africa have organised the BRICS and BASIC groups, which promote the reform of the international order. If China, India and other countries cannot consolidate their views on these global issues, they could be crushed one by one by the dominant power in the system and lose forever the chance to rise again.

Secondly, in the trilateral relations between China, India and the United States, India's status will benefit from China's rise. China's growth is a prerequisite for India's rise. If India really becomes embroiled in conflicts with China, it's hard to say whether the US will stretch out a hand to help it. But if India surpasses China, it will definitely replace its neighbour as the target of the US.

Thirdly, as two neighbouring powers in Asia, both China and India need a peaceful and stable periphery to develop their economies. Statesmen in both countries know clearly that development is their primary task, and that development needs stable circumstances. So, China and India have a common task to maintain the stability of the region. This is the determining factor that encourages China and India to keep their border areas stable for at least 10 years.

At least, the Chinese and Indian economies are complementary. Since they are in symbiosis, they could, theoretically, nourish and assist each other's survival and development. Sino-Indian bilateral trade has developed quickly in the past ten years, and the trade volume has risen 20 fold.

Although India complains that there are some problems in the bilateral trade structure, and the Indian trade deficit is too large, it is evident that Chinese goods, which are of good quality and cheap, raise Indian people's living standards. China and India have ample room to cooperate, especially in infrastructure construction. China has large amounts of capital and extensive experience in the construction of infrastructure; India on the other hand needs to improve its infrastructure facilities, but lacks finance. Sino-Indian cooperation in this field will benefit both sides.

Within India, the so-called "China threat" is a trick of Indian political figures to pull the wool over the eyes of their people and Western countries. From the aspect of domestic politics, by making waves in relations with China, Indian politicians can obscure domestic contradictions, bolster up national morale, pull votes, and the military can get an increasing budget. From the aspect of international politics, India can obtain advanced weaponry and technologies from Western countries.

In fact, the major direction of Indian military expansion is the Indian Ocean - the Navy received the largest part of India's rapidly growing defence budget. India's military strategy on land is defensive in nature but in the Indian Ocean, India has another competitor that is much stronger than China. The so-called "China threat" is just a cover.

The direction of Sino-Indian relations is determined for the medium-term at least, but the border issue is still a hindrance to bilateral relations. India did undertake some domestic reflection on the Sino-Indian conflict of 1962 and Nehru's policy towards China at that time, but no consensus was achieved.

The Indian government never released publicly the Henderson-Brooks report that summarised the reasons why India was defeated.

Taking a coherent view of this history will play a decisive role in the peaceful resolution of the Sino-Indian border problem. We should not neglect the negative role of the Indian multiparty system, in which foreign policy is often hijacked by domestic affairs. The role of the opposition parties and mass media in the Sino-Indian border conflict of 1962 is a case in point. It is necessary for the Indian government to reveal the truth about the Sino-Indian boundary conflict to the Indian people, and for Chinese and Indian scholars to conduct joint research projects on some historical problems, to alter the longstanding misconceptions held by both sides.

SINO-INDIAN RELATIONS 1950-1959

The Sino-Indian relationship from 1950 to 1959 was particularly warm, and several reasons for these cordial relations existed. Arguably the most important was the hasty diplomatic recognition of the PRC in December 1949 by India, making them the second nation in the world after Burma to do so. This conferment of legitimacy was helpful in establishing a cooperative environment with China, as many nations chose instead to recognize the Republic of China (ROC) in Taiwan. Furthermore, India's existence as a socialist and not a capitalist state, allowed for greater cooperation with the PRC since they did not come into direct conflict with Maoist ideology like the U.S. This basis of diplomatic and ideological congruency led Prime Minister Nehru to attempt to revolutionize international affairs by producing the Panchsheel Agreement between China and India in 1954. The Panchsheel Agreement stressed five points; (1) mutual respect for each other's territorial integrity and sovereignty; (2) mutual non-aggression; (3) non-interference in each other's domestic affairs; (4) equality and mutual benefit, and finally; (5) peaceful coexistence. This agreement originates from Nehru's optimism that post-colonial nations could invalidate the precepts of a bipolar world, and that the regional powers of Asia can contradict the validity of traditional balance of power politics.

The diplomatic and ideological reasons for Sino-Indian cooperation are bolstered by shared historical experiences. Both China and India share a long and uninterrupted cultural and historical tradition. Both nations at one time were great powers. Most importantly though, both nations were invaded by Western imperialists and consummately humiliated and exploited. This occupation and exploitation by the West caused the growth of significant nationalist forces within India and China, and the desire to gain independence. The ROC received its independence in 1912, and the later consolidation of the

PRC in 1949 ushered in a new era of Chinese sovereignty and independence from imperialism. Likewise, India achieved its independence from Britain in 1947.

Due to their history of Western occupation, China and India had additionally failed to develop independent industries. Their occupations meant that the Chinese and Indian economies were still largely agrarian, and dependent on the import of finished goods. This led the Indian government to implement a form of democratic socialism, while the PRC engaged in agrarian based communism, or Maoism. Regardless of their system's differences, both nations abhorred capitalism creating an ideological common ground. Their common historical experience produced a familiar perspective upon which Indian and Chinese policymakers could relate to one another.

This environment of common history and diplomatic cooperation producing positive relations would be challenged by the Chinese policy of taking back historical possessions. The 1950 invasion and takeover of Tibet by the PRC would begin to show strains in the relationship. Trepidation over Tibet's seizure by the PRC was based in the idea of a historical Indian-Tibetan relationship, but the Seventeen Points Agreement of May 1951 ironed out their differences with India recognizing China's historical sovereignty over Tibet while still preserving Indian economic and social interests in Tibet. The agreement appeared to settle a possible dispute over Tibet between the two powers, but right-wing elements in the Indian parliament expressed this viewpoint of the PRC invasion, "the final action of the Chinese, in my judgment, is a little short of perfidy". This underlying opinion of the Tibet invasion by the PRC would bring forward another issue heightening tension in the relationship.

This issue was the definition of China's border with India in the Northeast and Northwest. Maxwell argues that one of China's diplomatic priorities was defining diplomatically agreed boundaries, as "boundaries are one of the first expressions of a modern state" and the PRC sought this validation of modernity. However, to not endanger Sino-Indian relations over the border question, Nehru and Zhou Enlai agreed to leave the border issue between mid-level bureaucrats to be mediated at a later date paving the way for the 1954 Panchsheel Agreement. Thus, this issue remained on the back-burner of Indian foreign policy until the PRC began to make moves towards its historical conception of Sino-Indian boundaries south of the McMahon Line in 1957. Two years later Tibet rose up in a massive revolt against Chinese authority. China's People's Liberation Army (PLA) moved in to put down the rebellion by breaking popular will in the capital of Lhasa. March 31, 1959 the Dalai Lama fled from Tibet into India where he was granted political asylum. This course of events angered the Indian public as they saw it as a renunciation of Indian trade and cultural access to Tibet guaranteed in the Seventeen Points Agreement. PRC officials chaffed at India's meddling in their domestic affairs by granting asylum to the Dalai Lama and thereby violating the 1954 Panchsheel agreement. The Tibetan revolt combined with gradual Chinese assertion of borders in 1957 due to diplomatic impasse, are the primary factors contributing to a hostile Sino-Indian diplomatic relationship from 1959 to the outbreak of hostilities.

SINO-INDIAN RELATIONS IN CHANGING CIRCUMSTANCES

Having gone through a decade of exploratory efforts by the two sides in the new century, Sino-India relations at present display the following outstanding features:

Top leaders of both countries define Sino-Indian relations as one of the most important sets of bilateral relationships in their foreign relations and an increasing higher priority in their diplomatic agenda. As the two largest countries in Asia and the developing world as well as countries with an ancient civilization and major emerging market economies, China and India have great potentials for bilateral cooperation and more and more common interests and carry growing strategic weight in the restructuring of regional forces in Asia. Clearly, Sino-Indian relations have an increased impact on the international trading system, the international financial order, the global development agenda and regional cooperation in Asia and the Pacific. If one used to observe Sino-Indian relations by gradually shifting one's perspective from South Asia to the Asia and the Pacific at large five or six years ago. One should now shift one's focus from Asia and the Pacific to the world at large in analyzing Sino-Indian relations. Just as Indian Prime Minister Singh points out, "Today, both India and China are in the midst of rapid transformation. The development agenda has taken centre-stage in both our societies. Our systems are different, but people in both countries are united in their aspiration for a better future. When countries of the size of China and India, together accounting for 2.5 billion people begin to unshackle their creative energies, it impacts on the whole world."

Pragmatically and Rationally

Due to the lack of strategic mutual assurance in the past several decades, anything in the offing or any contingency might easily stir emotions on both sides. This has always been a major deficiency in the bilateral relations. In recent years, however, under the guidance of top leaders of both countries, Sino-Indian relations have again become more practical and rational. The manifestation of this are: 1) Leaders of the two countries have reiterated that the earth is a vast planet which allows for the rise of China and India as new emerging powers; 2) in 2012, the year that marks the fiftieth year after the border conflict, the mainstream view in the media and public opinion in both countries was that the two sides should reflect on and learn lessons from the past with a conclusion that the two countries should never fight again and work together for a better future; 3) Each side is more keen on discovering and learning from the strong points of the other, refraining from treating it emotionally or with preconceived ideas, and drawing on good experiences and valuable assets of the other side to the good of its own development. This is particularly the case in the areas of trade, economic cooperation and the mutual investment. Such changes have markedly highlighted the importance of cooperative Sino-Indian relations and facilitated the growth of friendship mass organizations and associations as a valuable asset in Sino-Indian relations.

Reserving or Solving Differences

In the past fifty years and more, an important principle governing Sino-Indian relations has always been to bear longer interests of bilateral relations in mind and seeking common ground while reserving differences. While "freezing", controlling and shelving major differences, the two sides taking store by the overall interests of bilateral relations, have been working hard for cooperation and common development in other areas so as to prepare conditions for resolving such differences and contradictions in the future. In recent years, both sides have realized that an important way of enhancing strategic mutual reassurance and future promoting bilateral relations as well as freezing Sino-Indian relations from interference of third parties is to iron out their disputes through better communication, dialogue and consultation. While continuing to find out and expand the convergence of interests, the two sides should proactively try to narrow down or resolve the differences. Despite the fact that the two sides are yet to prepare all necessary conditions for the resolution of the boundary dispute and that one has not seen a marked increase of favorable factors, they wish to talk and settle this issue and act accordingly with a deeper understanding of the importance of maintaining peace and stability in the border areas. With this in mind, China and India have made progress on some "theory issues" in their relationship. They have launched, or are ready to launch, talks on establishing new mechanisms for the border issue, strategic and economic dialogue, maritime security dialogue, dialogue on the Tibetan questions in addition to steady progress in the consultations on trans-border water resources, combating terrorism and mil-to-mil relations.

Bilateral Relationship

In the past ten years, China and India have gradually found out how to keep on good terms through properly handling their differences and disputes and making cooperative efforts for common development and better bilateral relations.

First, new ideas and suggestions for enhancing Sino-Indian relations have kept emerging, such as "new concept of China-India relationships", "2.0 edition of China-India relations", "Five Principles of Peaceful Coexistence", "How emerging powers should treat one another", etc. Of late, Mr. Sanjaya Baruÿformer Press Consultant of Prime Minister Singh has made a comparative analysis of President Xi Jinping's recent "Five –Point proposal" on Sino-Indian relations and Prime Minister Singh's five principles governing Indo-China relations. The fact that leaders of both countries are thinking of putting bilateral relations more on a theoretical basis indicates that Sino-Indian relations are becoming more and more important and that the bilateral relationship now stands at a critical juncture of reaching a new height.

Second, each side tends to take a more pragmatic and forbearing approach to the presence and activities of the other side in the region of its pivotal interests. The joint "China-Indo-Japan ship escorts" in the Gulf of Aiden and China-Indian consultation and collaboration at East Asia Summits point to the fact that the two countries have less "zero-sum mentality" and more cooperation and win-win in mind.

Third, the two sides are less on the alert and more accommodating towards each other in exchanges of views in multilateral fora. Cases in points are their collaboration in G20 events, BRIC meetings and UN conferences on climate change.

SINO-INDIAN RELATIONS: A GROWING UNEASE

The dramatic rise of two Asian giants set against the backdrop of a troubled diplomatic history has propelled India and China into a trajectory that will likely prove difficult to navigate in the coming years. With the world riveted by Chinese aggression against Japan and Southeast Asian states in recent months, one country was not surprised: India. After all, New Delhi has been grappling with the challenge of China's rapid rise for some time. Bilateral ties between China and India nosedived so dramatically last year that Indian strategists were even predicting'the year of the Chinese attack on India'; it was suggested that China would attack India by 2012 primarily to divert attention from its growing domestic troubles. This suggestion received widespread coverage in the Indian media, which was more interested in sensationalizing the issue than interrogating the claims.

Meanwhile, the official Chinese media picked up the story and gave it another spin. It argued that while a Chinese attack on India is highly unlikely, a conflict between the two neighbours could occur in one scenario: an aggressive Indian policy toward China about their border dispute, forcing China to take military action. The Chinese media went on to speculate that the'China will attack India' line might just be a pretext for India to deploy more troops to the border areas.

A Growing Unease

This curious exchange reflects an uneasiness that exists between the two Asian giants as they continue their ascent in the global inter-state hierarchy. Even as they sign loftily worded documents year after year, the distrust between the two is actually growing at an alarming rate. True, economic cooperation and bilateral political, as well as socio-cultural exchanges are at an all time high; China is India's largest trading partner. Yet this cooperation has done little to assuage each country's concerns about the other's intentions. The two sides are locked in a classic security dilemma, where any action taken by one is immediately interpreted by the other as a threat to its interests. At the global level, the rhetoric is all about cooperation, and indeed the two sides have worked together on climate change, global trade negotiations and demanding a restructuring of global financial institutions in view of the global economy's shifting centre of gravity. At the bilateral level, however, mounting tensions reached an impasse last year, when China took its territorial dispute with India all the way to the Asian Development Bank. There China blocked India's application for a loan that included money for development projects in the Indian state of Arunachal Pradesh, which China continues to claim as part of its own territory. Also, the suggestion by the Chinese to the US Pacific fleet commander last year that the Indian Ocean should be recognized as a Chinese sphere of influence has raised hackles in New Delhi. China's lack of support for the US-India civilian nuclear energy cooperation pact, which it tried to block at the Nuclear Suppliers Group (NSG), and its pro-Pakistan position on anti-India terrorist groups operating on Pakistani soil, including the orchestrators of the November 2008 Mumbai attacks, have further strained ties.

Sino-Indian frictions are growing, and the potential for conflict remains high. Alarm is rising in India because of frequent and strident Chinese claims about the Line of Actual Control in Arunachal Pradesh and Sikkim, where Indians have complained of a dramatic rise in Chinese intrusions into Indian territory over the last few years, most along the border in Arunachal Pradesh, which China refers to as "Southern Tibet". China has recently upped the ante on the border issue. It has been regularly protesting against the Indian prime minister's visit to Arunachal Pradesh, asserting its claims over the territory. What has caught most observers of Sino-Indian ties by surprise, however, is the vehemence with which Beijing has contested recent Indian administrative and political actions in the state, even denying visas to Indian citizens of Arunachal Pradesh.

The recent rounds of boundary negotiations have been a disappointing failure, with a growing perception in India that China is less willing to adhere to earlier political understandings about how to address the boundary dispute. Even the rhetoric has degenerated to such an extent that a Chinese analyst connected to China's Ministry of National Defence claimed in an article last year that China could "dismember the so-called 'Indian Union' with one little move" into as many as 30 states. Pakistan, of course, has always been a crucial foreign policy asset for China, but with India's rise and US-India rapprochement, its role in China's grand strategy is bound to grow even further. Not surprisingly, recent revelations about China's shift away from a three-decades' old cautious approach on Jammu and Kashmir, its increasing military presence in Pakistan, planned infrastructure linking Xinjiang and Gwadar, issuing stapled visas to residents of Jammu and Kashmir and supplying nuclear reactors to Pakistan, all confirm a new intensity behind China's old strategy of using Pakistan to secure its interests in the region.

India's Formidable Challenge

While it has not yet achieved the economic and political profile that China enjoys regionally and globally, India is increasingly bracketed with China as a rising or emerging power-or even a global superpower. Indian elites who have been obsessed with Pakistan for more than 60 years suddenly have found a new object of fascination. India's main security concern now is not the increasingly decrepit state of Pakistan but an ever more assertive China, a shift that is widely viewed inside India as one that can facilitate better strategic planning.

India's defeat at Chinese hands in 1962 shaped the Indian elite's perceptions of China, and they are unlikely to alter them anytime soon.

China is thus viewed by India as a growing, aggressive nationalistic power whose ambitions are likely to reshape the contours of the regional and global balance of power with deleterious consequences for Indian interests. Indian policymakers, however, continue to believe that Beijing is not a short-term threat to India but needs to be watched over the long-term. However, Indian defence officials are increasingly warning in rather blunt terms about the disparity between the two Asian powers. The Indian naval chief has warned that India neither has "the capability nor the intention to match China force for force" in military terms, while the former Indian air chief has suggested that China posed more of a threat to India than Pakistan.

China's recent hardening toward India could well be a function of its own internal vulnerabilities, but that is hardly a consolation to Indian policymakers who have to respond to an Indian public that increasingly wants the country to assert itself in the region and beyond. India is rather belatedly gearing up to respond with its own diplomatic and military overtures, setting the stage for a Sino-Indian strategic rivalry. Both India and China have a vested interest in stabilizing their relationship by seeking out issues on which their interests converge, but pursuing mutually desirable interests does not inevitably produce satisfactory solutions to strategic problems. A troubled history coupled with the structural uncertainties engendered by their simultaneous rise is propelling the two Asian giants into a trajectory that they might find rather difficult to navigate in the coming years. Sino-Indian ties have entered turbulent times, and they are likely to remain there for the foreseeable future.

The Indian and Chinese Experience

One of the cruel ironies of today's world is that India which is applauded as the world's largest democracy has the largest number of poor and destitute in any country, and China which has achieved, a steady rise in people's living standards and has also acquired the status of a world power has failed to develop democratic institutions and practices. It is also interesting to note that despite the absence of liberal democratic freedoms the West has a deep fascination with China which is reflected not only in the tourist inflow to China but also in the flow of foreign investment and government good will. Operation of democratic institutions such as free and fair elections, existence of competitive politics and dissent do not particularly attract either Western tourists or Western capital to India. On the contrary the geopolitics of South Asia has been governed by the US and other Western countries as compared by India's pre-eminent position and therefore they have followed by an large a policy of containment of India vis-a-vis its neighbours. The functioning democratic system of India has had little effect on their policy. The experience of India and China have put the theory of democracy to a severe test. Two old questions need to be asked again about democracy. In addition, two new questions have to be raised. Do formal political institutions and practices constitute democracy or does it involve appropriate socio-economic conditions which enable citizens to exercise their political rights. On this issue India scores poorly with nearly forty per cent of its people below what is statistically called a "poverty line". China has asserted that it is engaged in creating better living conditions for its people after overthrowing semicolonial and semifeudal domination. Today, however, this dichotomy between economic and political conditions of democracy is seriously questioned. Their mutual dependence is emphasised. Therefore both India and China have to achieve yet more conditions of democracy.

The other familiar question relates to equality and freedom. Western liberal democratic theory asserts the priority of freedom over equality even though the radical stream in liberalism stresses that gross inequalities are detrimental to the exercise of freedom. On this criterion pre-Reform China scored higher marks than India. Social inequalities were reduced in China to a very large extent with the abolition of landlordism and formation of cooperatives and Communes and also takeover of the bourgeoisie owned industries by the state. The wage system was directed towards promoting equality and limiting income differences within the six point grade system. In India too there were a number of measures taken in the early decades following independence to curb monopoly in industry, abolish zamindari system and carry out land reforms.

In both the countries the stress on equality declined in the 1980s and almost disappeared in the 1990s. In the past decade or so equality has been a low priority in both China and India. The "equalitarianism", "theory of eating from the iron rice bowl" and such ideas of the Cultural Revolution were severely criticised by the Chinese reformers as being obstacles to the development of the productive forces. The perspective of the present day leadership in China is to "allow some people to get rich first" so that the general level of growth is raised steadily. In India the introduction of the Structural Adjustment Programme promoted the ideology of profit and the egalitarian programmes of social transformation took the back seat.

The two new issues arise from the great democratic upsurges of the past few decades, namely the social movements such as the women's movements, the environmental movement, the autonomy movement and the human rights movements. One question posed by them is to concretise freedom as freedom from multiple forms of domination so that freedom to realise the potentialities of the human being is advanced. Patriarchal domination continues substantially in all the countries of the world as evident from the deliberations at the Fourth World Congress of Women in Beijing and as documents in the 1995 *Human Development Report*. China and India have only marginal difference among them. As to ethnic self-determination there has not yet been a scientific measurement. But both the countries have fairly centralised regimes and both have regions manifesting popular discontent. The caste hierarchy and disabilities in India are targets of public attention and social action. There is no comparable social problem in China though new forms of social stratification have emerged in the recent years.

The other issue is response of the modern state to these expanding democratic demands. All ruling elites would like to have an appearance of being popular and responsive to the demands of the various unprivileged groups. And they engage in innumerable measures of legitimation to create a climate of acceptability among the people. Thus the modern state is coercive, responsive and legitimative at the same time. For this purpose it has developed sophisticated systems of management of society, complex methods of propaganda and innovative techniques of manipulation.

PROSPECTS FOR SINO-INDIAN RELATIONS

As the need to enhance cooperation and dialogue is the consensus of decision makers in both countries, Sino-Indian Strategic partnership is entering a new phase of development. This general orientation would not be affected by changing domestic political circumstances in both countries. Looking ahead, one needs to take note of the following developments in Sino-Indian relations:

Near-term Uncertainties and Variables

As the General Election is approaching in the coming year, rivalry among all political forces in India will be in full swing. Current top leaders and policy makers, such as Prime Minister Singh, National Security Advisor Menon, and Minister of External Affairs Salman Khurshid, might leave their posts in addition to other personnel changes. This might affect China-Indian relations. There are not many "China hands" among Young Turks in the National Congress Party and their position and views on India's China policy are not quite clear. If "Right-deviant" party as represented by Bharatiya Janata Party (BJP) comes into power, Sino-Indian relations may proceed in a "learning curve". Of course, whichever political force assumes power in the coming election in India, India's fundamental policy toward China would not change dramatically, but one would definitely see some "fine-tuning" of the strategic tendency and certain specific issues in India's China policy.

Sino-Indian relations

Though years of concerted efforts, China and India have learned hot to treat each other in good terms and properly handling their differences while working for peaceful development. The two countries will gradually rid themselves of the negative impact of old scores and historical disputes and construct a normal relationship as between two close neighbors, a cooperative relationship as between two major powers and a new-type relationship as between two emerging powers sharing weal and woe. Sino-Indian relations will have a more salient and stronger impact on regional and international patterns of relationship. As it rises, India will be more and more confident and poised in its relations with China. The growth of India's own strategic deterrent and increasingly close ties with the United States and other western powers have somewhat alleviated its feeling of insecurity and mentality of being encircled. As India is more confident and is deporting itself in a calmer manner in handling its relations with China, it will more firmly believe that the two countries will mutually benefit from cooperation and friendly exchanges. India has realized that as rapidly rising power, China has a pivotal impact on India's development and security. The mainstream view in India is that maintaining a stable, cooperative and mutually beneficial relationship with China is in India's national interests. Even those strategic analysts and politicians in India who still stubbornly cling to their view that China is "a long-term threat to and a rival of India" tend to think that India can keep such threat and rivalry under control by way of economic engagement, military preparation, diplomatic skill and a balancing strategy of maneuvering among big powers, thus making the bilateral relationship less vulnerable to contingencies.

China and India should not Fight Again

In the foreseeable future, the outbreak of a planned, long-scale military conflict in the border areas between China and India is virtually impossible. A major constraint is the fundamental national interests of both countries for which the top priority is to grasp strategic opportunities in the coming years and shape a secure and stable domestic and international environment for national rejuvenation. This is also the primary concern in formulating their military and security policies. Moreover, the military strength of both countries has grown markedly in the past several decades. Both countries possess large quantities of conventional arms and a significant nuclear deterrent force, each side having a greater capability to deter and defend against the other. With all these factors at play, war would mean an unbearable disaster fraught with danger ever afterwards for both sides.

Focus of Sino-Indian Relations Shifting

In future, bilateral trade, economic ties and mutual investment will be an increasingly important factor that will affect the evolution of Sino-Indian relations. In other words, more "low politics" issues will affect bilateral relations. Some issues and matters which seemed to be less important or less sensitive in the past may now have major impact on bilateral relations.

While economic cooperation, trade and investment are favorable assets for strengthening and promoting Sino-India relations trade and economic frictions will likewise affect the vital interests of the peoples of the two countries, thereby upsetting the overall bilateral cooperation. National sentiments in the two countries, individual cases of economic disputes and different lobby groups and interest groups would exert more influence on bilateral relations. "High politics" issues such as the border dispute, the Tibetan question and military issues would undoubtedly continue to affect bilateral relations, but they would be less and less important and sensitive. This objectively will be conducive to the solution of such issues.

IMPORTANT THE SYSTEMS THEORY

Now that a historical context for Sino-Indian relations during the 20th Century has been established, it is necessary to define the systemic level theory from which the case will be analyzed. A systemic level of analysis eschews the individualities of states and the impact of individual leaders on foreign policy outcomes. Instead it focuses on the structure of the international system, and how this structure forces states to conform to a set of probable responses regardless of their individual differences.

In Kenneth Waltz's seminal work, *Man the State and War*, he lays down the foundation for a levels-of-analysis framework for studying international relations. Waltz does not contend to have created this framework, but instead argues that different theories of international relations promote one or another level of analysis over the other. The basis of this assertion is in Waltz's take on how is politics best to be studied, "Can man in society best be understood by studying man or by studying society" ? If one believes that man in society can best be understood by studying man then you will focus on individuals and reject the influence of society on them, and vice versa. This idea is then refocused from the question of man and politics to the question of why states go to war.

Classical realists like Hans Morgenthau believe that war is driven essentially by the natural evilness of man. Essentially the "ubiquity of evil in human action arising from man's ineradicable lust for power and transforming churches into political organizations ...revolutions into dictatorships... love for country into imperialism". From this perspective, society and government are not influential forces in history, but instead magnifiers of mans collective malevolence when grouped into nations. From a classical model states cannot cooperate because "passion often obscures the true interests of states as of men," and not because "states are never honorable and peaceful". Waltzian neo-realism departs from these ideas by exploring the other half of the question. Believing that "Man is born and in his natural condition remains neither good nor bad," but is influenced by society to one extreme or the other, as states are influenced by a society of states (the international arena) to engage in war or not.

Neorealist systems theory is driven by one primary characteristic: in no matter what form the system is structured, the system is driven by the essential existence of anarchy. The source of this anarchy is the absence of an overarching international body with the power to force the conformity of the units of the structure (the states). As such the United Nations and other international organizations are not important and have no bearing on the system since they lack the capability of shaping the unit actors decisions. Acknowledging this, states are the only relevant actors, and the anarchic system leaves them with two realities. The first is that states are responsible for their own security, and secondly that threats to this security are unending.

Additionally, neo-realism departs from classical realism in that classical realists view power itself as the ultimate goal of the state, whereas neorealists view power as a means with the end being security. Peace in an anarchic system is fragile, and therefore each state must provide for its own security. However, providing for one's own security through military power or alliances often times undermines the security of neighboring states. This paradox where increasing a states security undermines the perception of security in another state is known as the "security dilemma," and is a major structural explanation for the outbreak of war. This is due to the fact that one can never be certain if additional security measures are defensive or offensive in the anarchic system. Another cause on the systemic level for the outbreak of war is the failure of deterrence. Deterrence strategy implies a buildup of military force adequate enough in perception or reality to prevent a state from threatening another states security. If any state misperceives the deterrent capability of another, or believes it has a greater offensive capability war is likely to break out.

In addition to these universal characteristics of the systemic structure is the variable concept of how power in the international system is actually divided. In the period of the Sino-Indian war the world was locked in a bipolar balance of power led by the U.S. and the Soviet Union. In a bipolar system states are rigidly aligned to either pole, but states in each camp have great flexibility of strategy. This was caused by the zero-sum nature of a bipolar system, in that the gain of one side is the loss of the other. As such, the leader of either faction is unwilling to allow client members to fail in policy endeavors. Finally, in a bipolar system states that refuse to join either faction drastically increase their security dilemma unless they have the power to challenge the international structure towards a multi-polar balance. Now that the neorealist systemic level theory is defined it shall be applied to explain the variables causing the outbreak of the Sino-Indian war.

Derivation and Events Leading to Border Dispute

The 1914 Simla Convention between Britain and Tibet established the McMahon Line as the official border between British India and China, denying the right of Chinese suzerainty over Tibet. However, the line's namesake McMahon, was ordered back to London in disgrace over the "chicanery" he exercised in border negotiations in which he presented a different map to the Chinese envoy, thus distancing Britain from the legitimacy of the negotiated border. Thirty years later British cartographers began drawing the McMahon Line as the border between British India and China, thus reviving the lines legal legitimacy.

When India gained its independence from Britain in 1947 it inherited all of the British territorial agreements, and as such inherited the McMahon Line as the border between it and China. Indian belief in the legitimacy of the McMahon line dated back to the Simla Convention of 1914, as well as to the numerous maps of British India with the line delineating its northern border. As such Nehru shrugged off Chinese insistence in border negotiation during the 1954 agreement stating that "the McMahon line marked their border with China, where was the need" ? Despite India's view of the McMahon Line's legitimacy, China had not signed the Simla Convention and under no circumstances consented to any bilateral agreement between Tibet and Britain because it violated their sovereignty.

Indian intransigence on negotiating a border acceptable to both parties led the PRC to act independently in areas south of the McMahon line. The justification for this was that in the absence of mutually negotiated borders, the true national boundary was a line of actual control represented by the extent of either nation's ability to administrate the territory.

Practical assertion of this idea was first revealed to India in 1957 when an Indian patrol discovered an all-weather road which had been constructed in the Aksai-Chin Plain connecting Xinjiang and Tibet. The Indian government launched diplomatic protests asserting a violation of their territorial integrity; however the PRC "considered [Aksai-Chin] to have long been Chinese territory". This issue was not resolved as the Indian government refused to engage in territorial negotiations until Chinese forces completely withdrew from the Aksai-Chin Plain. The PRC refused to do so, and instead of a diplomatic solution India began to pursue a more confrontational approach to assert their territorial claims.

The rebellion in Tibet helped to drastically sour relations between the PRC and India, but the border dispute widened due to a change in Indian military strategy. This change in military strategy was to create forward-posts behind the Chinese claim line, and in strategic locations to flank Chinese military positions.

These posts were constructed to assert Indian territorial claims in the Ladakh region and to threaten the Xinjian-Tibet road in Aksai-Chin. By September, 1962 a similar series of forward posts had been built beyond the Chinese claim line in Tibet, and four such posts were built even beyond the McMahon Line. This resulted in an inability to claim that these posts were simply to defend Indian territorial integrity. The territorial dispute from India's perspective, coupled with the building of forward military posts by the Indian military caused the 1954 Panchsheel Agreement to not be renewed in 1961. Crossing both the claim and McMahon lines, both nations were in violation of each other's territorial conception, and India was now physically challenging Chinese sovereignty in Tibet.

BORDER DISPUTE AN OBSTACLE TO BUILDING TRUST BETWEEN CHINA AND INDIA

The then Indian chargé d'affaires Brajesh Mishra couldn't believe his ears at Chairman Mao Zedong's cue as they shook hands at a May Day parade on the Tiananmen rostrum in 1970. The wounds of the 1962 border war, in which India suffered a humiliating defeat, were still raw. Pointedly, Mishra was placed at the end of the line-up of diplomats arranged in order of precedence to meet Mao - after the British chargé d'affaires - making the gesture all the more dramatic.

Mishra immediately saw the opening Mao was creating for ties to resume, and was relieved it meshed with his own brief. Before he left for Beijing, then prime minister Indira Gandhi had laid it out for him in one sentence: "I am in a box so far as relations with China are concerned, and I want us to get out of that box." Despite this common yearning for détente, China and India would soon drift further apart - this time over the Bangladesh liberation war in 1971. While India backed the Bengali freedom fighters, Beijing threw its lot behind its "all-weather friend" Islamabad - a relationship that would dog Sino-Indian relations for decades.

It wasn't until the 1990s that China and India would finally start a structured process of normalising ties. Economic relations have since gone from strength to strength, with China now India's largest trading partner. But as the recent three-week Himalayan stand-off brought home, the undercurrent of animosity still runs deep, and the possibility of unfriending each other all over again is never far away. Arcing a curious trajectory, India and China's modern history would easily qualify for an "it's complicated" relationship status: active courting, followed by demonstrative friendship, violent break-up and now cautious reconciliation. It is this pull of a volatile past and the prospect of profitable cohabitation that Premier Li Keqiang will negotiate as he starts his India visit on Sunday. Li has already had a foretaste of the job at hand. His goodwill gesture of picking India as his first foreign destination on assuming power almost came undone with last month's border crisis. Even though both sides agreed to stand down, the episode will continue to hang heavy when Li lands in New Delhi.

According to Neville Maxwell, author of the seminal *India's China War*, such run-ins are natural as history shows an undefined border acts as a running sore between even the least bellicose of neighbours and can quickly turn malignant. "However much the neighbours may try to develop cordial relations in other aspects, the territorial dispute lurks in the background, making full trust unattainable," he says.

Not that the "other aspects", notably economic engagement, are insignificant. Chinese goods have flooded Indian markets and Indian companies routinely raise yuan debt from Chinese banks. As the two sides have set a goal of US$100 billion trade by 2015, Li's visit is likely to see a raft of billion-dollar deals, with the attendant fanfare and boilerplate diplomatese on "strategic partnership".

But Professor Ma Jiali, executive deputy director of the Strategy Study Centre at the Beijing think tank China Reform Forum, points out: "The border dispute is the biggest obstacle to building strategic trust between China and India. It is directly related to the territorial sovereignty, core interests and national sentiment of the people of both countries." The dispute is over two separate territories, one in the western sector of the border and the other in the east. In the west, both China and India lay claim to 38,000 square kilometres of snowy wastelands known as Aksai Chin.

There is no demarcated border there, only a Line of Actual Control that fuzzily separates the territories controlled by them. And, each side has its own perception of where that line lies. It was in these icy heights that the recent stand-off took place. In the eastern sector, China claims some 90,000 square kilometres to the south of the McMahon Line, which was agreed to by Britain and Tibet in a secret deal in 1914 and not recognised by China. While China calls the region South Tibet, for India it is its Arunachal Pradesh state. The McMahon Line is the de facto border in this sector.

Although China never accepted the McMahon Line, it was open to a land swap, under which India could keep what it claims on the eastern border while China would keep Aksai Chin in the west. Providing the best route into Tibet from the rest of China, Aksai Chin was non-negotiable for Beijing. For Delhi, both territories were off the table as inviolable flanks of national identity.

India and China have held 15 rounds of border talks at the special representative level since the mid-1990s but the gains have been limited. The border is remarkably well managed, with not a shot fired across it in over 20 years, but it's far from being settled, meaning the pre-1962 claims still hold for both sides. Half a century later, the border war today is seen largely as a dispute over land in the high mountains. But for a long time, India's first prime minister, Jawaharlal Nehru, who invested, and lost, substantial political capital in a policy of friendship with China (embodied in the early 1950s Indian slogan of*Hindi-Chini bhai bhai*, or India and China are brothers), would describe Aksai Chin as a place "where not a blade of grass grows".

And, in the course of the 1962 war, Chinese troops swept towards the plains as Indian forces retreated. Rather than holding on to their gains, China called a ceasefire and the troops returned to their old positions. Land was not the only thing the war was about. Far deeper factors were at play. The war coincided with the Sino-Soviet split. Declassified documents show Soviet leader Nikita Krushchev's irritation with China's handling of the border tension, and the Chinese leadership's anger at the Soviet backing of Nehru. For China, showing India its place was also a loaded message for the Soviet Union.

In India, Nehru was being squeezed between a rising left movement and the ascent of the right. In China, Mao was trying to reassert power within the party as the voices against the Great Leap Forward grew louder.

And then there was Tibet. Nehru, while accepting China's sovereignty over Tibet, sought greater autonomy for it to act as a buffer between the two Asian giants. For him, Sino-Indian friendship was the cornerstone of Asia's rise, and for the relationship to work, China and India needed some space. Tibet would give them that space and guarantee the two armies would never come face to face. But for China, as Ma puts it, Tibet is a "core national interest". It is just as central to China's national pride as the border lands are for India's, with or without grass.

Dibyesh Anand, an associate professor at London's Westminster University, says: "There is a nationalist-security dissonance at the heart of how China and India approach Tibet and the border dispute. For China, Tibet is a nationalist issue and the border is a strategic issue, while for India, Tibet is a strategic issue and the border is a nationalist issue. The difference is, you can bargain over a strategic issue but not over a nationalist one." In *Protracted Contest: Sino-Indian Rivalry in the Twentieth Century*, sinologist John Garver notes the "brief period of Sino-India friendship from 1954 to 1958 coincided with a limited but genuine degree of Tibetan autonomy". India interpreted a 1954 pact signed with China on Tibetan border trade as an implicit guarantee of Tibet's relative autonomy while China read it as India's promise to keep its hands off Tibet. The honeymoon ended when they started blaming each other for breaking the deal.

Things came to a head when the Dalai Lama fled to India following the Lhasa revolt of March 1959. China was furious that India provided him refuge and allowed him to set up a government-in-exile. Nehru was peeved that China wasn't cutting him any slack on Tibet, weakening his position at home. Mao was convinced India was colluding with the Americans to incite Tibetan refugees and India started patrolling the far-flung borders more aggressively under a "forward policy". From there on, war was but a matter of time.

Many of the anxieties of 1962 linger. China still feels encircled by hostile powers and is as insecure over Tibet. "India uses the special status of Dalai to allow Tibetan refugees to launch separatist activities for creating trouble to resolve the border problem in the future. Indian politicians also interact with officials of the government-in-exile and Dalai," complains Ma. But Professor Susan Shirk, author of *China: Fragile Superpower,* believes that for the Chinese, it should be possible to shelve the territorial dispute. "This is because the media and the nationalist public don't pay much attention to it," says Shirk.

China sees India as one of the possible sources of trouble. For India, China*is* the trouble. India's sense of betrayal, at what it sees as a sudden and unwarranted land grab by a trusted friend, has festered with time, with China's rise and its proximity to Pakistan only fuelling its own fears of encirclement.

"Tibet and the border dispute can take them back to a 1962-like situation. Economic interdependence should not be seen as replacing political negotiation," warns Anand. Unless, of course, they find a way to live with their differences and yet profit from each other.

Mishra, the chargé d'affaires in Beijing who went on to become India's national security adviser, would later recall in *Across the Himalayan Gap* that during his stint in China, he would attend the regulation diplomatic banquets but never actually got to eat anything. This was because the speeches would start during the second course and since the Chinese hosts would invariably lay into India and praise Pakistan, Mishra and his wife would have to walk out in protest. This went on for a while until Mishra noticed the speeches weren't starting until after the cakes and ice cream came out. A Pakistani diplomat told him the Chinese had noticed the Mishras were missing out on the food and decided to hold the speeches until after dessert.

THEORETICAL FRAMEWORK OF THE CBMS

At the outset of this section it is desirable to define CBMs. Confidence Building Measures (CBMs) are regarded as "diverse arrangements that can help reduce tensions and promote good neighborly relations.

Traditionally they are designed to make the behaviour of states more predictable by facilitating communication among or between states and establishing rules or patterns of behaviour for state's military forces." Succinctly CBMs can be defined as broader concept to defuse tension and increase the possibilities of peace among the hostile nations by concerted efforts. It has been fashionable in much of the English literature on the subject to visualize confidence building measures (CBMs) essentially in their Western framework. However, the CBMs in the Asian context have preceded all these Western models, most of which owe their origins to the Final Act of the Helsinki process of the Conference on Security and Cooperation in Europe (CSCE) that was concluded in 1975. Besides, the Asian CBMs have also been far more broad based than even those Western mechanisms that were launched later under the Document of the Conference on Disarmament in Europe held in 1986 at Stockholm (Sweden). Similar arrangements had been for long experimented amongst various Asian nations, including both China and India. There are propositions saying that India-China CBMs were borrowed from the western literature which is not true. The truth of the matter is that the CBMs had been institutionalized in Asia much earlier the Helsinki Accord of 1975. The peace process consists of three stages namely Conflict Avoidance Measures (CAMs), Confidence Building Measures (CBMs) and Peace Building Measures (PBMs).

Conflict Avoidance Measures (CAMs)

It means the avoidance of unwanted and unintended conflicts or wars arising particularly from miscalculations or misinterpretations. To start the peace process, we need here a minimum political will to stop wars. This is workable especially in the nuclear era. These initial steps like the establishment of hotlines between two countries' military, or even between Prime Ministers or Presidents but cannot solve underlying political and territorial disputes. Nevertheless, it has enormous worth in the context of nuclearisation of both India and China. CBMs have been particularly ineffective, if not absent, during times of conflict, because despite declarations to the effect, neither country has moved beyond the point of 'conflict avoidance', towards actual confidence building measures, and finally, towards strengthening peace. One thing you have to keep in the mind that to start negotiations between adversaries especially one whom you consider as someone stabbed in the back is very very difficult. Whereas which is not so in the case of parties where no prior enmities exist. Of course if you see Henderson Brooks Report it says it is India which started war than the normal perception in India looking at China as aggressor.

Confidence Building Measures (CBMs)

The second stage of this process is far more difficult as it requires far more political capital to resolve the deep-seated grievances or core issues. In the case of Sino-Indian conflict, the transition phase from conflict avoidance to confidence building is extremely difficult, because of the persistence of irritants between India and China. Probably this transition might be easier if there are no core issues blocking the way. The 1954 Sino-Indian Agreement on Trade and Intercourse between India and the Tibet Region, the 1962 Colombo Power Proposals, various Border Talks, the 1993 Agreement on Maintaining Peace and Stability in the Region in the Vicinity of the Actual Control Line were some of the examples of confidence building measures. Probably this transition might be easier if there are no core issues blocking the way. However, following the June 1989 Tiananmen Square incident, while most world powers had imposed sanctions, thus, completely isolating China, the relations between China and India not only continued to be smooth but experienced a greater momentum: the period between the second half of 1989 and 1990 saw ten high-level visits between the two countries that included visits to New Delhi by Vice Premier Wu Xueguian in October 1989 and Foreign Minister Qian Qichen in March 1990. This bonhomie can be attributed to the mutual goodwill of India and China which is essential for the success of CBMs.

Peace-Building Measures (PBMs)

This last stage requires enormous amount of political will for conflict reconciliation and resolution, where the peace process have to encounter with vested interests, hardliners. It is here the role of leadership is put to test as leaders must be able to take risk taking efforts for peace against their own constituencies. If formidable hurdles like the 1962 aggression, sporadic border skirmishes can be crossed to avoid war and to negotiate a fragile peace, national leaders can go ahead with further broadening and deepening existing patterns of co-operation and making positive developments as irreversible as possible. It is here the role of people to people contacts must also be emphasized. Perhaps if we all made a conscious effort to ignore our preconceptions and be more optimistic, the road to peace would be smoother.

MAIN DEVELOPMENTS: SINO-INDIAN CBMS PROCESS

In this chapter we will be seeing the various CBMs between India and China and will be delved the most important agreements among them. There was no improvement in bilateral relations until the reestablishment of full diplomatic ties in 1976. In 1986-87 India and China were involved in a crisis in the Sumdorong Chu area of Arunachal Pradesh where a Chinese incursion had taken place. This led to the mobilization of both Indian and Chinese forces and something of a stand-off ensued. This tension lasted over twelve to eighteen months.

At least one lesson relevant to CBMs was that even in a period of relative calm things can veer out of control to the detriment of both sides. Relations began to improve after the then Indian Prime Minister Rajiv Gandhi, visited China in December 1988. The border question still remains unresolved. However, even in the absence of a formal settlement, both countries have been willing to negotiate CBMs to avoid conflict and to provide the basis for increased cooperation. In 1981 for example, China unilaterally allowed Indian pilgrims access to pilgrimage sites in Tibet. Between 1981 and 1988 a series of eight official discussions on the border issues and Sino-Indian relations took place. Following Rajiv Gandhi's visit, an India –China joint working Group (JWG) was established to go into the boundary dispute. Relations improved markedly with the visit of the then Indian Prime Minister Narasimha Rao, to Beijing in September 1993.

The mandate of the JWG is to settle the border issue and to promote peace and tranquility along the frontier. Some of the measures negotiated by the JWG include:

1) Military-to-military meetings to be held twice a year, in June and October, along both the eastern and western sectors of the border at Bum La Pass and Spanggur Gap.
2) Military-to-military communication links to be installed at key points along both the eastern and western sectors of the border.
3) An agreement was reached on the establishment of dedicated communication links, or "hotlines," between military headquarters.
4) Local commanders are to be encouraged to conduct meetings, as needed, using color-coded flags to initiate contact.
5) Exchanges between defence educational institutions and between Strategic Studies Research Institutes were to be arranged.
6) An agreement was reached regarding prior notification of military maneuvers and troop movements along the border.
7) An agreement on the prevention of airspace violations was arrived at.

8) Exchanges between defence educational institutions and between strategic studies research institutes wee to be arranged.
9) Exchanges between high-level defence officials began with Sharad Pawar, the then Indian Defence Minister, who visited Beijing in July 1992.
10) Another working group was established in 1988 to cover issues relating to economic cooperation, trade, science and technology.

In addition to progress on border issues through the JWG, India and China have begun to explore other areas of cooperation. The Sino-Indian rapprochement that began with the Narasimha Rao–Li Peng Summit in Beijing in September 1993 led to what has been an epoch-making agreement on the Maintenance of peace and Tranquility along the Line of Actual Control in the India-China border Areas. This agreement begins by reiterating the five principles of peaceful coexistence mutually agreed upon by the two countries in the April 1954 agreement on trade between India and the Tibet Region of China. This Sino-Indian rapprochement culminated in a historic visit by the then Chinese President Jiang Zemin to New Delhi in December 1996. During his visit, the two countries signed the agreement on CBMs in the military field along the line of actual control in the china-India border Areas.

Thanks to the joint efforts, China and India have established following CBMs:

1) In 1990, China and India decided to establish the meetings between the soldiers on both sides of the actual control lines on an unfixed basis.
2) In 1992, the two countries established a hotline between the meeting stations on both sides of the actual control line.
3) In September 1993, China and India signed the Agreement on Maintaining Peace and Stability in the Region in the Vicinity of the Actual Control Line. The agreement stipulates that the two sides should seek solutions to the border disputes through peaceful means: the two sides do not use force or threaten to use force; before the final solution to the border issue, two sides strictly respect and obey the actual control line; the military strength of reach side in the respective area of actual control line should be kept at minimum size, which serves to match the relationship of friendly neighbourhood between the two countries; the two sides should reduce the armed forces to the limit reached between them in the areas along the actual control line etc.
4) In 1993, for the implementation of the afore-mentioned agreement, a special working group composed of diplomats and military experts was established.

5) In 1995, China and India agreed to withdraw from the two confronting outposts near the actual control line and agreed that they would never enter them.
6) Also in 1995, China and India agreed to carry out mutual visits by the personnel from the military agencies, organize joint expeditionary part for exploration of ventures; the two sides also agreed to forbid hunting, firing guns and explosion in the area near the actual control line.
7) In 2005, an agreement on 'political parameters and guiding principles for settlement of the boundary dispute' was signed when the then Chinese Premier Wen Jiabao was in Delhi.
8) Hand-in-Hand 2008: The India-China Joint Military Exercise
9) In 2010, India and China signed an agreement to establish a hotline between the Prime Ministers or heads of the two countries.
10) In 2013, India and China signed set of CBMs called Border Defence Cooperation Agreement (BDCA).

Of all these agreements, the author thinks that only two agreements are significant.

They are the 1993 and the 1995 agreements because these agreements were actually responsible for paving the way for the institutionalization of the subsequent CBMs.

SINO-INDIAN CONVERGENCE: BILATERAL AND GLOBAL

Bilateral relations between India and the People's Republic of China (PRC) have indeed come a long way after they touched their nadir in the immediate aftermath of India 's nuclear tests in May 1998. China had been singled out as the "number one" security threat for India by India's Defence Minister just before the nuclear tests. After the tests, the Indian Prime Minister wrote to the US President justifying Indian nuclear tests as a response to the threat posed by China. Unsurprisingly, China reacted strongly and diplomatic relations between the two countries plummeted to an all time low.

However, some six years later, the relations between the two countries seem to be on an upswing. The visit of the Indian External Affairs Minister to China in 1999 marked the resumption of high-level dialogue and the two sides declared that they were not threats to each other. A bilateral security dialogue was also initiated that has helped the two countries in openly expressing and sharing their security concerns with each other. India and China also decided to expedite the process of demarcation of the Line of Actual Control (LAC) and the Joint Working Group (JWG) on the boundary question, set up in 1988, has been meeting regularly. As a first step in this direction, the two countries exchanged border maps on the least controversial middle sector of the LAC.

The Indian Prime Minster visited China in June 2003, the first such visit in a decade. The joint declaration signed during the visit stated that China was not a threat to India. The two states appointed special representatives in order to impart momentum to border negotiations that have lasted twenty two years, with the Prime Minister's principal secretary becoming India's political-level negotiator, replacing the India-China JWG. India and China also decided to hold their first joint naval exercise later in the year and discussions on joint air exercise continue. India also acknowledged China 's sovereignty over Tibet and pledged not to allow "anti-China" political activities in India. On its part, China has acknowledged India 's 1975 annexation of the former monarchy of Sikkim by agreeing to open a trading post along the border with the former kingdom and later rectified official maps to include Sikkim as part of India.

India and China have found substantial convergence of interests at the international level. Both share similar concerns about the growing international dominance of the US, the threat of terrorism disguised as religious and ethnic movements and the need to accord primacy to economic development. India and China have both expressed concern about the US ' use of military power around the world and publicly opposed the war in Iraq. This was merely a continuation of the desire of both states to oppose the US *hyperpuissance* ever since the end of the Cold War.

Like other major powers in the international system, India and China favour a multipolar world order where US unipolarity remains constrained by the other "poles" in the system. China and India zealously guard their national sovereignty and have been wary of US attempts to interfere in what they see as domestic affairs of other stares, be it Serbia, Kosovo or Iraq. Both took strong exception to the US air strikes on Iraq in 1998, the US-led air campaign against Yugoslavia in 1999, and more recently the US campaign against Saddam Hussein arguing that these violated the national sovereignty and undermined the authority of the United Nations system.

Both nations also favour more democratic international economic regimes. They have strongly resisted efforts by the US and other developed nations to link global trade to labour and environmental standards, realizing clearly that this would put them at a huge disadvantage vis-à-vis the developed world, thereby hampering their drive towards economic development, a top priority. Both have committed themselves to crafting joint Sino-Indian positions in the World Trade Organization (WTO) and global trade negotiations in the hope that this might provide them greater negotiating leverage over the developed states. They would like to see further liberalization of agricultural trade in the developed countries, tightening of the rules on anti-dumping measures and ensuring that non-trade related issues such as labour and environment are not allowed to come to the WTO.

In recent years, India and China have attempted to build their bilateral relationship on the basis of their larger worldview of international politics. As they have found a distinct convergence of their interests on world stage, they have used it to strengthen their bilateral relations. They have established and maintained regular reciprocal high-level visits between political leaders. There has been a sincere attempt to improve trade relations and to compartmentalize intractable issues that make it difficult for their bilateral relationship to move forward.

India and China have strengthened their bilateral relationship in areas as distinct as cultural and educational exchanges, military exchanges, and science and technology cooperation. Bilateral trade has recorded rapid growth from a trade volume of US $265 million in 1991 to US $3596 million in 2001. In 2001, bilateral trade saw an increase of 23.4 percent over 2000. It is expected to rise to $10 billion this year. The two nations are even evaluating the possibility of signing a comprehensive economic cooperation agreement and a free trade agreement by the end of this year, thereby building on strong complementarities between the two.

Both states are also taking steps to upgrade their military-related cooperation, leading to greater understanding on the bilateral military front, something that would have been unthinkable just a few years ago.As a first step in this direction, the Chinese and Indian navies carried out joint search and rescue operations off the Shanghai coast in November 2003. Both states are also seeking to cooperate on the nuclear front with China planning to import heavy water from India to be utilized in the pressurized heavy water reactors near Shanghai.

Many observers have also pointed out a subtle shift in Beijing 's stance on Pakistan vis à vis India. China 's "neutral" position during the Kargil conflict and the intense Indo-Pak crisis following the terrorist attack on the India 's Parliament is seen by many as a reflection of China 's sincerity in its attempts to improve ties. In keeping with China's attempts to project itself as a responsible regional player, China is seen by some as supporting peace and anti-terrorist efforts in South Asia by cooperating with the US and India. China is also seen as playing a central role in encouraging Pakistan to negotiate with India by using its leverage over Pakistan.

After assuming office Prime Minister Manmohan Singh's government made it clear that it favoured closer ties with China and would continue to work towards improving bilateral relations with China. In his first address to the nation, the Prime Minister, Manmohan Singh, also emphasized the carrying forward of the process of further development and diversification of Sino-Indian relations. The late J.N. Dixit, National Security Advisor in the current government, wrote that "the Congress will continue the process of normalizing, strengthening and expanding India's relations with China, which is the most important factor affecting Asian security and stability". One of the first foreign visits of the new Indian foreign minister, Natwar Singh, was to China to attend the Asia Cooperation Dialogue in Qingdao, in East China's Shandong province and apparently had "substantive discussions" with his Chinese counterpart.

All this reflects on India continuing to build its relations with China on the convergence of interests that the two nations have achieved in recent years. Aside from the positive developments, one should not ignore the enormous obstacles that confront this bilateral relationship. There has been a dominant tendency in the Indian foreign policy establishment to focus on the strengths of its bilateral relations with China while pretending that problems confronting the relationship would somehow take care of themselves. The challenges in the Sino-Indian relationship are by no means insignificant nor will China take care of Indian interests. It is for India to recognize them for what they are and evolve a coherent strategy to tackle them.

Divergences and Challenges

The number one priority for China's leadership today is economic growth and social stability. China soon underwent one of the most peaceful and orderly political transformations in its recent history, even though its exact ramifications remain far from clear.

Hu Jintao became Communist Party chief in 2002 and President of China in 2003 replacing Jiang Zemin. He also finally ceded the effective control of the armed forces to Hu Jintao in September 2004. Hu Jintao is now formally in command of the vast party, government, and military bureaucracies that rule China.

This shift, although important for the smooth working of the Chinese government, is unlikely to produce any radical change in China 's foreign policy. China 's focus is going to be on maintaining its high rate of economic growth in the coming years.

It should be remembered that Hu Jintao is a product of the "evolutionary policies" of Deng Xiao Peng that emphasize economic growth and orderly governance. President Hu Jintao has made it amply clear that Western-style multiparty democracy is something that would not serve the Chinese people well, terming it a "blind alley" for China. Therefore, one can expect China to continue on its current economic trajectory and shaping its foreign policy accordingly.

China has enjoyed average annual rates of real income growth of around 10 percent in the last two decades of the twentieth century, something unprecedented historically. China accounts for about 5 percent of world trade and foreign direct investment (FDI) to China is predicted to reach an annual utilized rate of 100 billion in 2005. After its accession to the WTO, China 's already-high global economic profile is set to rise manifold. China will continue to focus on maintaining its high rates of economic growth in the coming years, even as some of the economic challenges China faces will become more acute.

The burgeoning income disparities, restructuring of its states owned enterprises and the problem of non-performing loans in its banks are just a few of the economic problems China 's economy is likely to face in the coming years. So far China has managed remarkably even though the future remains uncertain.

Broadly speaking, Indians either view China 's economic growth as a façade or envy it. While India has achieved some remarkable growth rates in the last few years enjoying average annual rates of real income growth of six percent in the last two decades of the twentieth century, it still lags behind China.

India accounts for less than one percent of world trade in goods and services. Currently, China outperforms India in terms of levels of growth, education, health, and living standards of its population, and global integration of its economy. China outpaces India, in sectors where the two compete for third country markets. Sino-Indian competition for these markets is bound to further intensify in the coming years.

Though some argue that the long term economic prospects of India are much better than China 's, China remains the undisputed economic powerhouse of the moment driving the Asian and global economy with India somewhere far behind. The fact of the matter is so long as India does not place its own economic house in order; it will remain a second-rate power even in Asia. And China will remain the Asian power that the world will look up to when trying to manage problems in Asia.

What should be equally, if not more, significant for India is the fact that it is China's economic transformation that has given it the capability to become a military power with China spending as much as $65 billion a year on its military. China's military may or may not be able to challenge US supremacy in the next few years but it will surely become the most dominant force in Asia. According to authoritative sources, China is set to overtake Japan in the next decade to become Asia 's major regional military power. The US involvement in the global war on terror has put the "containment" of China on the backburner and China has seized on this opportunity to strengthen its armed forces further.

China imbibed the lessons of US military undertakings such as the 1991 Gulf War, war in Afghanistan and the recent operation Iraqi Freedom. These have spurred China's pursuit of the latest Revolution in Military affairs (RMA) manifested in the buying, adopting of latest technologies and weapons systems (particularly from Russia) along with concomitant changes in doctrine and organizational structures.

The People's Liberation Army (PLA) has been shedding its manpower since late 1990s to save funds so as to be able to focus on high tech. Despite a western embargo on China preventing transfer of military technologies, China has been able to deftly use US corporations to garner and apply dual-use technologies. China is simultaneously pursuing a qualitative and quantitative transformation of its nuclear infrastructure. China plans to deploy new road-mobile, solid-fuelled, long-range missiles over the next several years possibly to counter US ballistic missile defence.

Overtime, China 's enhanced military prowess will lead it to assert its interests more forcefully, thereby, adversely affecting Indian interests. As China becomes more reliant on imported oil for its rapidly growing industrial economy, China will develop and exercise military power projection capabilities to protect the shipping that transports oil from the Persian Gulf to China.

The capability to project power would require access to advanced naval bases along the sea lines of communication and forces capable of gaining and sustaining naval and air superiority.

China 's assistance to Myanmar in constructing and improving port facilities on two islands in the Bay of Bengal and the Andaman Sea is the first step to securing military base privileges in the Indian Ocean. This can be used as a listening post to gather intelligence on Indian naval operations and a potential forward base for future Chinese naval operations in the Indian Ocean. India 's traditional geographic advantages in the Indian Ocean are also increasingly at risk with deepening Chinese involvement in Myanmar. China 's increasing naval presence in the Indian Ocean is of tremendous strategic consequence for India. There are also suggestions that the balance of air power in the China-India theatre has shifted in China 's favour with it acquiring an inventory of about 1500 modern combat aircraft for deployment in the theatre. China remains the only major power in the world that refuses to discuss nuclear issues with India for fear that this might imply a de facto recognition of India 's status as a nuclear power. It continues to insist on the sanctity of the UN resolution 1172 which calls for India (and Pakistan) to give up its nuclear weapons program and join the Nuclear Non-Proliferation Treaty (NPT) as a non-nuclear weapon state.

This was reflected in China 's lack of response to the Indian Foreign Minister's proposal of a common nuclear doctrine for China, India, and Pakistan. China would not like to get into any sort of nuclear dialogue with India that might give the impression of China recognizing India as a nuclear power. Moreover, while both India and China have a "no first use" nuclear doctrine, China 's doctrine is not applicable to India as it is not a party to the NPT.

China has done its best to maintain a rough balance of power in Indian Subcontinent by preventing India from gaining an upper hand over Pakistan. It has consistently assisted Pakistan 's nuclear weapons and ballistic missile programs to counterbalance India 's development of new weapons systems. India 's preoccupation with Pakistan reduces India to the level of a regional power while China can claim the status of an Asian and world power. China signed a charter to step up bilateral defence cooperation with Pakistan "to help maintain peace and stability in South Asia " even as it professes to improve its relations with India. Moreover, even as India and China share similar concerns regarding Islamic terrorism in Kashmir and Xinjiang respectively, China has been rather unwilling to make a common cause with India against Pakistan. China 's use of India 's neighbours to curtail Indian influence has not been restricted to Pakistan. China has actively sought to contain India all around its periphery by engaging Nepal, Bangladesh and Myanmar.

Despite resolving most of its border disputes with other countries, China is reluctant to move ahead with India on border issues. India 's discussion of border issues with China is seen as a concession. India remains satisfied with the "positive" and "satisfactory" Joint Working.Group negotiations on the boundary issue. Despite the need for an expeditious demarcation of the Line of Actual Control, the talks seem to be continuing endlessly and the momentum of the talks itself seems to have flagged.

The momentum of the issue of Tibet seems to have been lost. Tibet has become a platform for the projection of Chinese military power. India 's tacit support to Dalai Lama's government-in-exile has failed to have much of an impact either on China or on the international community. Today even Dalai

Lama seems ready to talk to the Chinese as he realizes that in a few years Tibet might get overwhelmed with the Han population and Tibetans themselves might become a minority. The proposed opening up of the Nathula trade route that connects Tibet and Sikkim has been much trumpeted by the Indian government as a major achievement of Indian diplomacy. However, this step is fraught with dangers as there is no certainty that internal security threat posed by Chinese infiltration would not get worse with the opening of Nathula. This has probably led to some rethinking in India on this issue.

There were disturbing reports during the Indian Prime Minister's visit to China, that Chinese troops had intruded into the Indian territory along a stretch of the unfenced border with Arunachal Pradesh. China refuses to recognize Arunachal Pradesh as part of the Indian territory, laying claim to 90, 000 sq. km. of its land. If recent reports are to be believed after a two-decade gap, China has resumed the supply of weapons to various insurgent groups fighting in northeastern India. China seems to be getting successful in hemming India in from both, the eastern and the western flanks.

5

The McMahon Line: India-China and Tibet Policy

HISTORY OF TIBET BEFORE THE CHINESE INVASION OF 1949

Tibet has a history dating back over 2,000 years. A good starting point in analyzing the country's status is the period referred to as Tibet's "imperial age", when the entire country was first united under one ruler. There is no serious dispute over the existence of Tibet as an independent state during this period. Even China's own historical records and the treaties Tibet and China concluded during that period refer to Tibet as a strong state with whom China was forced to deal on a footing of equality.

At what point in history, then, did Tibet cease to exist as a state to become an integral part of China? Tibet's history is not unlike that of other states. At times, Tibet extended its influence over neighboring countries and peoples and, in other periods, came itself under the influence of powerful foreign rulers-the Mongol Khans, the Gorkhas of Nepal, the Manchu emperors and the British rulers of India.

It should be noted, before examining the relevant history, that international law is a system of law created by states primarily for their own protection. As a result, international law protects the independence of states from attempts to destroy it and, therefore, the presumption is in favor of the continuation of statehood. This means that, whereas an independent state that has existed for centuries, such as Tibet, does not need to prove its continued independence when challenged, a foreign state claiming sovereign rights over it needs to prove those rights by showing at what precise moment and by what legal means they were acquired.

China's present claim to Tibet is based entirely on the influence that Mongol and Manchuk emperors exercised over Tibet in the thirteenth and eighteenth centuries, respectively.

As Genghis Khan's Mongol Empire expanded toward Europe in the west and China in the east in the thirteenth century, the Tibetan leaders of the Sakya school of Tibetan Buddhism concluded an agreement with the Mongol rulers in order to avoid the otherwise inevitable conquest of Tibet. They promised political allegiance and religious blessings and teachings in exchange for patronage and protection. The religious relationship became so important that when Kublai Khan conquered China and established the Yuan dynasty, he invited the Sakya Lama to become the Imperial Preceptor and supreme pontiff of his empire.

The relationship that developed and still exists today between the Mongols and Tibetans is a reflection of the close racial, cultural and especially religious affinity between the two Central Asian peoples.

To claim that Tibet became a part of China because both countries were independently subjected to varying degrees of Mongol control, as the PRC does, is absurd.

The Mongol Empire was a world empire; no evidence exists to indicate that the Mongols integrated the administration of China and Tibet or appended Tibet to China in any manner. It is like claiming that France should belong to England because both came under Roman domination, or that Burma became a part of India when the British Empire extended its authority over both territories. This relatively brief period of foreign domination over Tibet occurred 700 years ago. Tibet broke away from the Yuan emperor before China regained its independence from the Mongols with the establishment of the native Ming dynasty. Not until the eighteenth century did Tibet once again come under a degree of foreign influence.

The Ming dynasty, which ruled China from I368 to I644, had few ties to and no authority over Tibet. On the other hand, the Manchus, who conquered China and established the Qing dynasty in the seventeenth century, embraced Tibetan Buddhism as the Mongols had and developed close ties with the Tibetans. The Dalai Lama, who had by then become the spiritual and temporal ruler of Tibet, agreed to become the spiritual guide of the Manchu emperor. He accepted patronage and protection in exchange. This "priest-patron" relationship, which the Dalai Lama also maintained with numerous Mongol Khans and Tibetan nobles, was the only formal tie that existed between the Tibetans and Manchus during the Qing dynasty. It did not, in itself, affect Tibet`s independence.

1911-1950

From 1911 to 1950, Tibet successfully avoided undue foreign influence and behaved, in every respect, as a fully independent state. The 13th Dalai Lama emphasized his country's independent status externally, in formal communications to foreign rulers, and internally, by issuing a proclamation reaffirming Tibet's independence and by strengthening the country's defenses. Tibet remained neutral during the Second World War, despite strong pressure from China and its allies, Britain and the U.S.A. The Tibetan government maintained independent international relations with all neighboring countries, most of whom had diplomatic representatives in Lhasa.

The attitude of most foreign governments with whom Tibet maintained relations implied their recognition of Tibet's independent status. The British government bound itself not to recognize Chinese suzerainty or any other rights over Tibet unless China signed the draft Simla Convention of 1914 with Britain and Tibet, which China never did. Nepal's recognition was confirmed by the Nepalese government in 1949, in documents presented to the United Nations in support of that governments application for membership.

The turning point in Tibet's history came in 1949, when the People's Liberation Army of the PRC first crossed into Tibet. After defeating the small Tibetan army, the Chinese government imposed the so-called "I7-Point Agreement for the Peaceful Liberation of Tibet" on the Tibetan government in May 1951. Because it was signed under duress, the agreement was void under international law. The presence of 40,000 troops in Tibet, the threat of an immediate occupation of Lhasa and the prospect of the total obliteration of the Tibetan state left Tibetans little choice. It should be noted that numerous countries made statements in the course of UN General Assembly debates following the invasion of Tibet that reflected their recognition of Tibet's independent status. Thus, for example, the delegate from the Philippines declared: "It is clear that on the eve of the invasion 1950, Tibet was not under the rule of any foreign country." The delegate from Thailand reminded the assembly that the majority of states "refute the contention that Tibet is part of China." The US joined most other UN members in condemning the Chinese "aggression" and "invasion" of Tibet.

In the course of Tibet's 2,000-year history, the country came under a degree of foreign influence only for short periods of time in the thirteenth and eighteenth centuries. Few independent countries today can claim as impressive a record. As the ambassador for Ireland at the UN remarked during the General Assembly debates on the question of Tibet,"[f]or thousands of years, or for a couple of thousand years at any rate, [Tibet] was as free and as fully in control of its own affairs as any nation in this Assembly, and a thousand times more free to look after its own affairs than many of the nations here." From a legal standpoint, Tibet has to this day not lost its statehood. It is an independent state under illegal occupation.

Neither China's military invasion nor the continuing occupation has transferred the sovereignty of Tibet to China. As pointed out earlier, the Chinese government has never claimed to have acquired sovereignty over Tibet by conquest.

Indeed, China recognizes that the use or threat of force (outside the exceptional circumstances provided for in the UN Charter), the imposition of an unequal treaty or the continued illegal occupation of a country can never grant an invader legal title to territory. Its claims are based solely on the alleged subjection of Tibet to a few of China's strongest foreign rulers in the thirteenth and eighteenth centuries. If other countries were to make such tenuous claims based on their imperial past, how seriously would they be taken? Are we not, in even considering the merits of China's arguments, accepting the right of powerful modern rulers to invade foreign countries in order to recreate lost empires of their ancestors?

TIBETAN RESISTANCE AGAINST THE CHINESE INVASION

According to an Asian historian, Melvyn Goldstein, political contact between Tibet and China was established in the seventh century A.D. when Tibet was unified under the rule of King Songtsen Gampo, whose strong dynasty managed to expand Tibetan borders over the course of two centuries. Much of these northern and eastern territories conquered by Tibet were kingdoms subordinate to the Tang Dynasty (618-907 A.D.), and thus China was well aware of the emergence of this new dominant kingdom. Gampo married a Chinese princess and as a result a tributary relationship was established between powerful Tang China and the emerging Tibetan kingdom on the frontier.

This alliance was formed because the Chinese were aware of the strategic importance of the location of Tibet at its frontier. At that point Tibet developed its own form of sophisticated language and adopted Buddhism as the official religion. "Tibet was in no way subordinate to China during the imperial era," Goldstein comments, "[E]ach was a distinct and independent political entity." However, internal conflict of different religious sects during the ninth century in Tibet brought an end to its unity and autonomy and several principalities emerged. At the same time China's Tang dynasty collapsed and, like Tibet, the country was divided and fragmented. For three centuries there were no political relations of any kind between Tibet and China, as Tibet was barely mentioned in Chinese historical records of the time.

In the thirteenth century a new power swept through East Asia, the Mongols. In 1207 Tibet cooperated with the Mongols, and submitted to Genghis Khan without bloodshed. The contemporary Chinese considered this to be the period during which Tibet first became part of China, while Tibetans "by contrast, accepted only that they, like China, were subjugated by the Mongols and incorporated into a Mongol empire centered in China, In fact, an interesting ideological relationship formed between the Mongols and Tibetans. The relationship was called "priest-patron" (in Tibetan *mchod yon*) and it almost equated the Tibetan lama (priest) and the Mongol khan (emperor) due to each one's position within the religious and political hierarchy respectively. The Tibetan lama provided religious instruction, performed ceremonial rites, and bestowed titles upon the khan, such as "religious king" and "protector of religion."

This placed the khan in the position of the student, or subordinate, while the lama was the teacher, therefore occupying a more dominant religious position. In terms of government, the khan occupied a dominant position mainly due to the protection he offered from external and internal conflicts. The Tibetans hence believed there was a balance of power as well as an ideological relationship between the two cultures, instead of hostile takeover.

Also, the Mongol khan reserved the right to appoint regents from an array of Tibetan elite, understanding that Tibetans more readily obeyed their own leaders, even if said leaders had Mongol interests in mind. Later, the Chinese used a similar strategy when they wished to occupy Tibet. After this period, Chinese control over Tibet varied according to the status of inner stability of China. The Ming emperors (1368-1644), for example exerted no political authority over Tibet, simply sending representatives of the Ming government to the capital city of Lhasa. As the Ming was loosing power and was eventually overthrown by the Qing Dynasty (1644-1911), China reestablished its jurisdiction in Tibet. In the early 1700s China conquered some Tibetan territories, mainly eastern borderlands which were previously a part of Kham and Amdo. Large parts of Tibetan land were placed under Chinese jurisdiction due to revolts against the Qing rule. Evidently, as history suggests, the eastern regions of Kham and Amdo were a source of rebellion and thus the Chinese Sichuan, Yunan, and Xining provinces incorporated previously Tibetan territories. The Qing Empire also sent troops to instill law and order in the disorganized country. For the most part, this action was successful, and Tibet was internally peaceful for some time. Accordingly, this set a precedent of the Chinese intervention into Tibetan affairs.

With the fall of the Qing Dynasty in 1911, and the Republican Revolution which brought about the dynastic decline, the Thirteenth Dalai Lama was looking forward to the return of his power as a "temporal and ecclesiastic rule[r]." However this was not granted by the newly established government; instead the Dalai Lama was reinstated as "Loyal and Submissive Vice-Regent," a title given to him towards the end of the Qing Dynasty, but with the addition of the title of the "Great Good and Self-Existent Buddha... [who would] support...and help the Republic." The Dalai Lama officially rejected this title, and by doing this unofficially declared Tibetan independence.

For the following forty years China was politically unstable and there was little change in the Tibetan question. Both World Wars as well as China's Civil War diverted attention away from Tibet. However, the founding of the People's Republic of China in the 1949 and the government that was established as a result meant a much more dominating regime, armed with the notion of saving or "liberating" Tibet, as well as the goal of a united China, At least such was the pretext of the Chinese Liberation Army's invasion of Tibet. The Chinese claim to suzerainty over Tibet throughout the centuries became a secondary argument at this point.

China had other reasons to reestablish itself in Tibet. One of the reasons was that the Chinese believed they were doing Tibet a favor, because the Chinese Communist Party (CCP) was aiming to introduce modernization into a country held back by a traditional way of life. It all started in the early twentieth century when Great Britain showed interest in Tibet due to the proximity of its borders with British Colonial India. Seeing the disparity between Tibet and China (which was then already a substantial trading partner for Great Britain) the British wished to serve as a mediator. In 1914 representatives of Tibet, China and Great Britain met in Simla, India in order to come to an agreement regarding the status of Tibet. Alas, no agreement was reached as Tibet and China quarreled over where borders should be drawn between the two countries. Although nothing politically useful came of the Simla Convention, Great Britain attempted to persuade Tibet to take first steps toward modernization (i.e. building an army, organizing a postal service, establishing English schools, etc.) however the Tibetan elite were reluctant to accept this innovation. The monastic elite saw this modernization as a threat to the unique religious way of life, and the aristocratic elite did not wish to pay high taxes. Consequently, conservatives appealed to the Dalai Lama that Buddhism and the fundamental way of life, not technology, was at the core of Tibet's strength against China. In the 1920's the Dalai Lama demoted all officials in charge of reform and closed the English schools. Goldstein points out that, "[O]vernight Tibet lost its best chance to create a modern polity capable of coordinating international support for its independent status and defending its territory."

Years later, Communist China saw this lack of modernity as an excellent reason to lay claim to Tibet. According to the CCP, not only was Tibet to be incorporated into China, but it was also in dire need of industrialization and modernity. This nearly inaccessible mountainous region was in desperate need of modern modes of communication and transportation. Also, the very way of life that Tibetans were used to was considered "backward" and unacceptable to the Communist Chinese. Pre-1950's Tibet was a feudalist state, in a sense it was very similar to medieval Europe. A small elite class of Tibetan nobility, which made up about five percent of the population, controlled most of the wealth and political power. Serfs, who were essentially attached to the land owned by their master and were required to perform labor in return for housing and food, made up nearly sixty percent of the population of Tibet. 15 Essentially slaves, serfs were trapped within a lower stratum of a rigid class-based society. The rest of the population consisted of clergy, who made up fifteen percent, and herdsmen (nomads), who made up another twenty percent of the population. Serfs, however, were the main concern for the Chinese Communists, whose main objective was to narrow the gap between the elite and the peasant class within their own society. The Tibetans nevertheless viewed the serfs as a happy and simple people who were content with their place in society. On the one hand, serf labor was seen as a form of slavery, on the other a serf was seen as a part of the family or household. Gompo Tashi Andrugtsang, one of the main leaders of the Tibetan rebellion, commented on this in his memoirs by saying, Critics of the Tibetan agrarian and social system are apt to overlook some very relevant factors which countered its apparent faults. Inspite of differences of status or material possessions, there was no great gulf between the rich and the poor. The landowner was more a patriarchal head of household than an exacting or oppressive master. The universal belief in the principles and teachings of Buddhism encouraged, on the one hand, generosity and desire to improve the lot of the less fortunate and, on the other, the absence of envy or resentment on the part of the poor. Of course, Andrugtsang himself grew up as a son in a relatively wealthy family, thus his vision of class division could have been slanted. Since serfs themselves left no written records of their affairs, we must assume the truth lies somewhere between the two extremes. Nevertheless, the negative aspect of serfdom was gladly used to the Chinese as a reason for their "liberation" campaigns.

It is important to note that for centuries Tibetan political matters were handled by the elite of Lhasa, including the Dalai Lama himself. Thus, Chinese political influence over Lhasa and the central government there had little effect on the eastern border regions in question; particularly Kham and Amdo.

And Tibet was a feudalist state. More importantly however, was its unusual form of theocratic feudal government. Grunfeld explains that Tibetan theocracy was both *centralized*—in a government in Lhasa headed by…the Dalai Lama—and also *decentralized*, giving local control to the countless monastic and aristocratic estates. The central government maintained a military force, issued currency and postage stamps, negotiated with other governments and acted as a final court of appeal. The heads of the feudal estates maintained monopoly of power over all local matters; the central government normally intervened only when the flow of taxes was disrupted. All officials in Tibet, both lay and ecclesiastic, in Lhasa and on the estates, came from the same small pool of noble families.

Evidently, this type of government allowed for much independence for the local governing bodies, especially in isolated regions like Kham and Amdo. The political decisions of either Lhasa or Beijing barely affected these eastern frontiers. The tribal and monastic networks were the only modes of government there. Land was the only real measure of wealth, and when land possession was threatened the Khampas and Amdowas were quick to fight back. Grunfeld comments on their way of life by saying, [T]he nomads…living mostly in Kham and Amdo, were divided into rigid social classes in either tribes or principalities led by hereditary chiefs or monastic lords…They are fiercely independent, with a long-established history of rejecting rule from either Beijing or Lhasa. This independence makes them feel superior to the sedentary population, an in return the nomads are held in some awe by other Tibetans.

This puts the Khampas and Amdowas in a different position than the elite of Lhasa with regards to Chinese political authority and demands. While the Lhasa elite were pushing the Dalai Lama toward collaboration, due to their fear of losing their property and socioeconomic power, the peasants and nomads of the eastern frontier were not afraid to stand up to the Chinese People's Liberation Army, because the basis for their very way of life was being threatened: their land. The Khampas and Amdowas' fearlessness and toughness proved to be a dangerous combination. In order to really understand the nature of Tibetan people, it is imperative to picture Tibet. Tibetan climate had much to do with the disparity between the residents of Lhasa and those of Kham and Amdo. These differences thus created the inconsistency in the perception of the Chinese claim to Tibet, and negativity of the residents of Tibet towards the incoming Chinese People's Liberation Army. Tibet is mainly a high plateau surrounded by mountains. The capital city of Lhasa is situated within the plateau region where it receives little snow, with temperatures ranging from 10 to 20 C (14-74 F) This was not the case in Kham and Amdo, however, since "Tibetans live between 1,200m (4,000 ft.) and 5,100m (17,000ft.) above sea level"; the higher mountainous regions were much harsher and more extreme. Also, Kham and Amdo regions were directly on the Chinese border and were the first to come in contact with Chinese hostility. Lhasa was weeks behind on the events that occurred on the Tibetan border due to lack of modern communication and the distance between the capital city and eastern Tibet. Nor did the Khampas necessarily wish for the Tibetan authorities to know of the situation.

John Knaus, a CIA operations officer in charge of American covert operations in Tibet, speaks from personal experience about the Khampas' feelings towards Lhasa, "[T]hey were fervently devoted to the Dalai Lama, but paid only nominal allegiance to the distant Tibetan political establishment and its lay and clerical aristocrats, whom they generally held in contempt. They were Khampas first and then Tibetans."

Because of the differences between the Lhasa's elites, who had the political control over Tibet for centuries, and the Khampas and Amdowas the reactions to the Chinese invasion differed by region in Tibet. As mentioned previously, the elite had little concern for, or power over, the easternmost regions of Tibet all throughout Tibet's long history. According to Melvyn Goldstein, [I]t was also the view of the Tibetan Government in 1949, which did not consider the Chinese Communist conquest of... [Amdo and Kham] as an invasion of its territory.

As a result, in 1949 it neither sent its troops to defend any of these areas nor issued any protests, appeals or charges that its territory had been invaded. As mentioned earlier, the elites were simply afraid to lose their status, stability, and established socioeconomic power; accordingly, they pushed the Dalai Lama to cooperate with the Chinese instead of resisting their invasion. Therefore, any rebellious guerilla activity along the eastern borders was never officially supported by Lhasa authorities.

Religious feeling was also extraordinarily strong among the people of the eastern region. Due to the distance and detachment between Lhasa and Kham and Amdo, the Dalai Lama himself was viewed more as a religious figurehead, as a god or Buddha rather then a ruler, since his jurisdiction rarely affected the everyday life of the people in this region. Buddhism and the worship of the Dalai Lama was, and still is, imperative to the residents of Kham and Amdo. Andrugtsang wrote in his memoirs, [R]eligion deeply permeated Tibetan society and a sizable proportion of the population consisted of monks and nuns. The laymen were exceptionally scrupulous about observing the...ritual of prayers and offerings. Great importance was attached to religious studies and monasteries were the main repositories of what was deemed the profoundest scholarship and knowledge. The entire educational system had its basis in religion...

Because religion was such a central part of everyday life, monasteries were everywhere. In addition to providing education and religious worship, monasteries later became a major source of local organization. During the Khampa Uprising monastic networks came to be used by guerilla forces to relay messages, hide rebels and guns, and organize riots. In a way, these networks became just as important as the local tribal networks in the role of organization and mobilization of guerilla troops.

Such were the conditions and earlier history of this region when on October 7, 1950 Chinese forces invaded Tibet. The People's Liberation Army marched into Tibet through Kham and settled there. Interestingly, even though the PLA was extraordinarily more modern that the comparatively small Tibetan Government Army, they were completely unprepared for the cold and thin air of the Himalayas. The PLA was desperately short on food and was forced to rely on the villagers for food and shelter. This caused a major burden for the native Tibetans and thus led to unrest and resentment. Shakya asserts, [the] unprecedented number of soldiers in the area caused severe shortages of food. The Khampas attacked the exhausted [army], causing them great hardship. Passing into the Tibetan territories, the [soldiers] for the first time faced a populace united in its hostility to them, and their suffering on this part of the trek exceeded anything of the past. This hostility and small skirmishes did not grew into a full fledged rebellion until the signing, and then the constant violations of, The Seventeen Point Agreement. All throughout the year of 1950, Tibetan officials attempted to negotiate with the Chinese to end the violence and allow Tibet to retain political rights over its own land and people. Tibetans appealed to India for help, later even involving the United Nations. Unfortunately, the United Nations postponed this matter on the pretext that Tibet was officially an "autonomous nationality region belonging to territorial China, and on those grounds could not be considered by the United Nations. Desperate for a resolution, the Dalai Lama sent a delegation headed by Ngabo Ngawang Jigme, a governor of the Kham region, to Beijing to negotiate an agreement to stop further violence. These discussions turned out to be more of threatening ultimatum, rather than a negotiation. The Dalai Lama wrote about this troubling time in his autobiography, "[O]ur delegates were not allowed to make any alterations or suggestion. They were insulted an abused and threatened with personal violence, and with further military action against the people of Tibet. Thus on May 23, 1951 the Seventeen Point Agreement was signed by the delegation, without any approval by the

Dalai Lama. The Agreement took away an incredible amount of rights from the people and government of Tibet, placing them instead in the hands of the CCP and the PLA. In essence, the Agreement stipulated that the Dalai Lama would retain his function and powers and the Buddhism was to be protected; however, Tibetan army, education, commerce, agriculture, industry and foreign relations with other countries were put in the hands of the CCP.

Nonetheless, even the little freedom this agreement entailed was not respected in Tibet. The PLA army was stationed in every major city. The CCP made constant demands of change within the simple way of life of the Tibetans. The Chinese attempted to diplomatically persuade the Dalai Lama and the high officials of Lhasa that change was good for their country. A show of friendliness was maintained by the Chinese for several years, while the Dalai Lama attempted to peacefully, and unsuccessfully, renegotiate the Seventeen Point Agreement. At this point Mao Zedong did not want to conquer Tibet, "he wanted China's claim to Tibet legitimized by having the Dalai Lama accept Chinese suzerainty and work with the [People's Republic of China] to gradually reform Tibet's feudal economy." Mao saw the Dalai Lama as a spiritual leader who would guide Tibetans to gradually accept their place in the "new Multiethnic Communist State." However, this was impossible on the local level, due to the growing resistance to the Chinese occupation. Again, the Khampas emerged as both the first victims and the first to fight back. "Most people in Lhasa were not yet aware of the drastic changes which the Chinese were carrying out with much ruthlessness in eastern Tibet," writes Andrugtsang, "the Chinese begun experimenting with their program of so-called reforms and the 'Liberation' of the countryside, as early as 1953." Andrugtsang further claims that the Chinese collected large sums of money for taxes, that locals were selectively arrested and publicly executed to arouse terror, monasteries were destroyed, and monks were imprisoned or executed without reason. Therefore, Andrugtsang explained, "Tibet was invaded and the Tibetans were forced to resist the Chinese by violence. Despite the awareness that China was a big and powerful nation possessing an awesome armed might, the Tibetans struck back, fired by the patriotic conviction that theirs was a just cause."

The Chinese army was now facing a serious problem. Dunham comments, "[T]he peasantry, the so-called downtrodden masses—the very group who were supposed to naturally embrace communism—were the Tibetans who were now most willing to kill Chinese." In fact, leaders emerged from the ranks of merchants in Kham and Amdo, who were willing to spend their own wealth to arm the village people who were ready to stand up to the PLA. Norbu points out that out of twenty three leaders of the Khampas, a majority were merchants who made money after the "liberation." However, "instead of making more money or running away to India safely with their silver fortunes, the Kham[pas] spent the Chinese money for the purchase of arms and ammunition for the revolt."

One of these unlikely leaders was a Gompo Tashi Andrugtsang, a man who, despite his acquired wealth and status, could not watch as his homeland was torn apart and the very way of life of his ancestors was being destroyed. A need for organized resistance was becoming vital to the Khampas. In December 1956, Andrugtsang decided that the various nationalist elements in Kham needed to be united as to form a stronger, more unified resistance movement. Andrugtsang sent out the following message to the various leaders in this vast and scattered area. The message read:

For some time you people have been rebelling against the Red Chinese. The time has now arrived to muster all your courage and put your bravery to the test. I know you are prepared to risk your lives and exert all your strength to defend Tibet. I also know that the tremendous task that you have undertaken is a noble cause and that you will have no regrets despite the ghastly atrocities committed by the enemy. In this hour of peril, I appeal to all people, including government servants, who value their freedom and religion, to unite in the common struggle against the Chinese. Messages are being sent to people in other parts of Tibet and the neighboring countries, such as India, to explain that the Tibetans now have to alternative but to take up arms against the Chinese.

Such was the general feeling of throughout Tibet at the time, and thousands of Khampas began organizing guerilla bands in the mountains of Kham and Amdo. In Early 1956, Chinese outposts were brazenly attacked, communications were cut off, and Chinese garrisons stationed in several provinces in Kham were completely wiped out by the Khampa guerillas. Due to the lack of modern communication within Tibet, the people of Kham organized through a series of tribal and familial networks. With the help of the monks from the numerous monasteries they were able to move from place to place unnoticed. The average lama had a very clear picture of the enemy's strength and was in a great position to plan effective tactics, mainly due to the amazing communication network between monasteries. The familiarity with the terrain, as well as the physical vigor that came from living at a high altitude in a harsh climate, meant that the Khampas were at a clear advantage. Their guerilla tactics were effective even though they were severely outnumbered by PLA troops.

The Dalai Lama had only heard the stories of the Khampa resistance and the Chinese misdoings there due to his isolation in Lhasa. He was a boy of fifteen when he was instated as the Dalai Lama the year after the Communists took control of Chinese government. This young man not only had no prior knowledge of government, but he was also easily intimidated by the much older and more politically skilled Mao Ze-dong. As a supreme ruler he was also carefully protected by the government officials of Lhasa, and thus he did not possess a broad understanding of the situation in Tibet, especially the country's the eastern region. In the mid-1950s, the Dalai Lama traveled to Kham and this visit "was a real eyeopener... Either his Lhasan advisors hadn't known of these events, or simply hadn't cared enough about the plight of the Eastern Tibetan tribes to inform His Holiness. Now he was learning first hand." The Dalai Lama was most shocked by the disparity between what was promised to him by Mao during his 1955 visit to Beijing, and what was really going on within Tibet. During this visit Mao introduced a new program: Preparatory Committee for the Eventual Establishment of the Autonomous Region of Tibet (PCART). The hopeful Dalai Lama was invited to the unveiling of PCART in Beijing. The program promised an avoidance of excessive reforms and an expansion of Dalai Lama's authority by increasing the number of Tibetans in the Chinese government. This was far from the truth and upon his visit to Kham and Amdo the Dalai Lama became aware of this deception. Furthermore, he was inspired by the growing spirit of revolt and claim for independence circulating in Kham and Amdo. "There was a very strong anti-Chinese feeling...[the Khampas] spoke about the independence of Tibet," exclaimed the Dalai Lama in his interview with Michael Dunham, At the time, my mind was going in a different direction. Because of my meetings with Mao in Beijing, I was quite hopeful [about PCART]. But then the Khampa leader mentioned independence—openly!—and his intentions of independence for Tibet—including all of Kham and Amdo—I was quite surprised! What I saw, among the Khampas, was not only their negative feelings about China, but also that they were nurturing an idea of an independent Tibet. Even though the Dalai Lama was now aware of the struggle in Eastern Tibet and even admired the Khampas, he could not support them openly because doing so would only give the Chinese further reason for ruthless military actions toward the Tibetan people and complete occupation of Tibet. Due to the dire situation in Tibet, the delicate nature of the Sino-Tibetan relationship, as well as the brute force of the PLA and Mao Ze-dong, the Dalai Lama had to take on not only the role of a religious leader, but as a political one as well. He had to mature fast and learn to represent his country in front of a powerful nation and a Chinese ruler who saw the Dalai Lama as a malleable teenager.

Nevertheless, the movement was definitely increasing in numbers. Andrugtsang himself bought guns for his units, and more and more people joined the fight. In 1958, a meeting was held which was attended by many supporters of the guerillas from all over Tibet. At this meeting an official flag was unfurled and the organization was named the Volunteer Freedom Fighters (VFF). The VFF leaders spoke to the masses encouraging them to fight hard against the oppression by the Chinese. The fighters were also encouraged to befriend the Tibetan villagers, so that the VFF would be provided food and shelter by the residents of the villages. This was another clear demonstration of the importance of tribal networks. The freedom fighters were motivated, and ready, Andrugtsang commented,

...[S]lowly building in size and strength, as they became a howling storm; it was like a gigantic storm one could see forming on the distant horizon in the east that would gradually come closer and closer until its full fury was felt...And in the meantime, the tribal leaders were organizing and communicating.

Overall, Andrugtsang proved to be a charismatic leader. In the beginning of he resistance, the Khampas attacked the PLA as small tribal bands but they were now becoming well-organized and numerous due to monastic and inter-tribal communication, as well as keen knowledge of the climate and terrain. However the PLA army did not lack resources or weaponry, and thus was a formidable enemy. By 1957, Eastern Tibet was in a chaotic state; persecutions of accused rebels, as well as civilians, became more and more brutal. Men and women were beat and starved, and prisoners' wives were repeatedly raped by Chinese soldiers in front of their husbands if the prisoners refused to 'confess' to the crime. Monks and nuns were made to have sex with each other and forcefully denounce the vows of celibacy. After being tortured, these men and women were often killed.

One of the main problems Andrugtsang and the Freedom Fighters faced was an uncooperative Central Government which feared upsetting the Chinese. As mentioned above, the Lhasa elite had a lot to lose from an economic and political standpoint. They were afraid to support the VFF because they were afraid to lose their lives as the farmers and nomads of Kham and Amdo were already losing their lives upon the mere suspicion that they were part of the resistance movement. The situation in Lhasa was also calm at the time, so calm in fact, that many refugees from Kham and Amdo filled the city. Therefore, it was understandable that the Dalai Lama's second in command, Lord Chamberlain's answer to Andrugtsang's request for support was always the same: "[T]his is not the time. This is not the course of action that we should be taking. We need patience." However this repeated answer did not diminish the freedom fighters' desperate need for help.

The Tibetan struggle for independence attracted the attention of several countries for different reasons. Britain, India and the United States often meandered for decades regarding their respective foreign policies toward Tibet. For Great Britain, and thus for India before its 1947 Declaration of Independence, Tibet was a strategic outpost and buffer zone on the northern border of India. As it was mentioned previously in this paper, Great Britain even attempted to rectify the situation between China and Tibet in the early twentieth century with the Simla Convention. After the loss of India as a colony in 1947, Great Britain lost interest in Tibet. India, however, attempted to help in whatever way possible, providing weapons, writing notes to the Chinese government, and even offering a safe refuge for the Dalai Lama and the Tibetan people.

In the early 1950s, Tibet appealed to the United Nations for help with the Chinese occupation; yet the claim was quickly dismissed due to the ambiguous political status of the Tibetan region. Largely, this was due to the fact that none of the countries concerned was willing to openly discuss the issue. The British called Tibet's status ambiguous, the Soviet Union condemned U.N. intervention in a Chinese internal matter, India voiced their hopes for a peaceful resolution, and the Americans said it was largely an Indian concern.

For the United States, however, it was actually World War II that sparked significant interest in Tibet for the first time. Immediately, there was a division in U.S. opinions regarding foreign policy toward Tibet. The Office of Strategic Services (OSS), a wartime spy agency, had interest in the Tibetan region due it is central strategic location in East Asia. The State Department officials, on the other hand, did not want to dismantle the good relationship with the Republican Chinese Government by questioning its jurisdiction. During the Second World War, and for nearly a decade thereafter, both of these agencies pursued their own agendas. After the Allied Powers' victory, however, the pro-China attitude prevailed in American politics, at least until the Communist uprising in 1949. Conboy comments, "[A]lthough Washington might not have liked the idea of losing Tibet to communism, it appeared loath to do anything to stop it."

Officially the United States knew of the unrest and Tibetan resistance to Chinese suzerainty even before the Communists came to power. A 1944 OSS Research and Analysis Report claimed, "the Tibetans are basically hostile to the Chinese...The Chinese minority is pushing the Sino-Tibetan ethnic frontier westward, and the Tibetan theocratic state is attempting to maintain independence for Tibet...On the whole...they desire strict isolation for their country." Other official intelligence reports further documented the abuse of Tibet by the Chinese authorities. In a 1951 Office of Intelligence Research report, it was clear that the United States realized the problems with the so called "Peaceful Liberation" of Tibet and with the Seventeen Point Agreement. The report stated, "A brief analysis of the terms of the agreement, however, reveals that the intention of the Pei-'ing [Beijing] regime is to replace China's former nominal suzerainty over Tibet by an absolute Chinese Communist control of the government and the territory," The report further upholds that, Such powers as are implicit in the terms would effectively destroy the actual autonomy that amounted to *de facto* independence enjoyed by the Tibetans in the past, despite the provision of point 3, which accords the Tibetans "the right of exercising national regional autonomy under the unified leadership of the Central People's Government."

Thus the U.S. State Department expressed concern, but did not officially wish to get involved. For the same reasons, India wished not to officially support Tibet: both nations desired stable foreign relations with China. The CIA however, was another matter entirely. The Dalai Lama's brothers Gyalo Thondup and Thubten Norbu were "talking to Americans from an early point on. Gyalo...instigated fist contact in Calcutta in either '51 or '52", claimed Roger E. McCarthy, the creator of the CIA Tibetan Task Force, in an interview with Michael Dunham, "...the least America could do was to give [the Khampas] the assistance...to do as much as they...could do on their own. To simply abandon them at that point, in [President] Eisenhower's estimation, would have been unconscionable." Along with Gyalo, Andrugtsang selected the first six Khampas to be trained by the CIA Task Force. Later these six were trained in Saipan for five months by CIA operatives in warfare and communications, and then air dropped in Kham to rejoin the ranks of Andrugtsang, and to train others. In 1958, more Tibetans were flown to Camp Hale in the Colorado Rockies for training. According to Roy Starke, a communications instructor who trained the Tibetans there, "[the Tibetans] really enjoyed blowing things up during demolition class, but when they caught a fly in their mess hall, they would hold it in their cupped palms and let it loose outside."

These were people peaceful by nature, but were pushed into warfare against their better judgment, due to the hate they felt toward their oppressors. In 1959, the situation has become worse, but the guerilla struggles continued. Using similar networks of tribal and monastic communication, the ranks of the freedom fighters swelled to the hundreds of thousands. In March of 1959, things began to completely fall apart. According to the International Commission of Jurists, on March 11, 1959, a meeting of Governmental officials was called at the Potala Palace and a proclamation was issued in the name of the Cabinet, declaring that Tibet was independent. The next day a meeting concerning the declaration of independence was and the action necessary for its implementation was held at the Palace. On March 17 Chinese troops fired two shells at the Potala Palace, which caused the Dalai Lama to secretly flee to India. A day later, the serious bombardment of Lhasa began and the Tibetans bravely faught back. This uprising made the international news as the Lhasa uprising. For the Chinese this was the last straw, now it was an all out war. According to the International Committee of Jurists, on March 28, 1959 Beijing reported that the rebellion was crushed by March 22 and that some 20,000 rebels were involved. The Tibetan Local Government was then dissolved, and now only the Preparatory Committee for the proposed Tibetan Autonomous Region now exercised the functions and powers of government. 58 CIA officers who worked with and trained the Tibetans wished to continue supporting their cause. However, this would not be possible due to the politics of the cold war era. According to Dunham, [O]n May 1, 1960, an American U2 spy plane...hauled itself up over the Himalaya en route to the Soviet Union. The Soviets shot it down.... And East-West diplomatic relations took an ugly U2-like nose-dive. Eisenhower's dream of conducting an international peace conference was shattered [after]...the summit meeting between Eisenhower and Soviet Premier Nikita Khrushchev...was canceled.

Such were the politics of the Cold War era, and this turn of events had serious ramifications for the Tibetan resistance. Air drops were to be cancelled, thus no weapons or supplies were dropped in Tibet by the CIA. Eisenhower was also advised do discontinue "any potentially dangerous covert action, lest they backfire and affect election results."60 Thus American politics were the cause of the cessation of support for the rebellion. The Khampas and Amdowas still struggled to maintain their movement, even without American support; even after the death of their great leader, Gompo Tashi Andrugtsang, they stayed strong. Other leaders emerged, and the Tibetans were unstoppable in their quest. Unfortunately, the freedom fighters' supplies were running low without the air drops and financial support from the CIA. And their ranks were dwindling due to constant battles with the PLA. The last bloody fight between the Khampas and the Chinese occurred in 1974, near the Nepalese border. The freedom fighters were severely outnumbered, and the fight was more of a massacre. This was the final blow for the organized guerilla warfare known as the VFF. The Khampas and Amdowas were out of options.

It was interesting to view how each source examined for this paper differed slightly in the facts it chose to include and exclude, thereby making its point more poignant. For example Gompo Tashi Andrugtsang's memoirs do not provide even a hint of the CIA's or America's help, while Dunham's book clearly identifies Andrugtsang as one of those involved in cooperation with the CIA operatives. This could be because the memoir was published in 1973, when the guerillas were still active in Tibet and the relationship between the CIA and the VFF could not be disclosed. The archival primary sources were particularly helpful in showing that the U.S. was well aware of the situation in Tibet but the State Department was complacent to help politically because of its official ties to China.

Melvyn Goldstein's work was particularly helpful, because of its objectivity regarding both parties' claims. It is important to remember that although many among the ranks of the Tibetan rebels were monastically educated and could read and write Tibetan, there are very few records that can be obtained from the rebels themselves.

Most of the planning and negotiations were done verbally through informal tribal and monastic networks and thus very few primary sources could be obtained. This definitely presented a problem with studying the rebellion from the point of view of the guerillas themselves.

It was an extremely lucky and helpful that Gompo Tashi Andrugtsang's memoirs were published and translated into English. As mentioned in the introduction, this topic is not yet widely researched, although there are many books of general Sino-Tibetan history which include a few chapters on this important event. There are also several works on the Sino-American relations over the issue of Tibet, however it is this paper's aim to focus on the history of the rebellion itself.

REACTIONS IN INDIA TO THE CHINESE INVASION

Consequent upon the entry of 40,000 troops from Eastern Tibet's provincial capital of Chamdo from eight directions, the smashing of the small Tibetan resistance force resulting in the death of some 4000 Tibetans and the capture of Ngapo Ngawang Jigme, the regional Tibetan Governor, India's Ministry of External Affairs sent a note to the Government of the People's Republic of China on October 26, 1950 which *Inter alia* stated as follows:

- "Now that the invasion of Tibet has been ordered by Chinese Government, peaceful negotiations can hardly be synchronised with it and there naturally will be fear on the part of Tibetans that negotiations will be under duress. In the present context of world events, invasion by Chinese troops of Tibet cannot but be regarded as deplorable and in the considered judgement of the Government of India, not in the interest of China on peace".

In India's view, thus, the entry of Chinese forces into Tibet was an act of invasion. Clearly India did not regard that as an internal matter of China. Sardar Patel reacted to the situation very sharply in a letter to Prime Minister

Nehru less than two weeks later on 7th November, 1950. In the letter he not only charged the Chinese of perfidy but analysed the strategic implications of the Chinese invasion of Tibet with a great deal of foresight and clairvoyance.

Inter alia, the then Deputy Prime Minister made the following points:

- 'The Chinese Government has tried to delude us by professions of peaceful intention'.
- 'The final action of the Chinese, in my judgement is little short of perfidy. The tragedy of it is that the Tibetans put faith in us; they chose to be guided by us; and we have been unable to get them out of the meshes of Chinese diplomacy or Chinese malevolence'.
- 'Even though we regard ourselves as friends of China, the Chinese do not regard us as their friends'.
- 'We have to consider what new situation now faces us as a result of the disappearance of Tibet, as we knew it, and the expansion of China almost upto our gates'.
- 'We can therefore, safely assume that very soon they will disown all the stipulations which Tibet had entered into with us in the past'.
- 'That throws into a melting pot all frontier and commercial settlements with Tibet on which we have been functioning and acting during the last half a century'.
- 'While our Western and North-Western threat to security is still as prominent as before, a new threat has developed from the North and the North-East. Thus, for the first time, after centuries, India's defence has to concentrate itself on two fronts simultaneously'.

Sardar Patel could not have been more clinically precise and more right. Quite by coincidence, the same day as Sardar Patel wrote to Prime Minister Nehru on Tibet, the Tibetan Government appealed to the United Nations for its intervention through a letter to the Secretary General on November 7, 1950 as follows:

- "Though there is a little hope that a national dedicated to peace will be able to resist the brutal effort of men trained to war, we understand that the United Nations has decided to stop aggression wherever it happens".

However, ten days later when El Salvador formally asked the General Assembly to include the Chinese aggression against Tibet on its agenda, the matter was not taken up by the august body for discussion at the suggestion of the Indian delegation. The Indian delegation asserted that a peaceful solution which is mutually advantageous to Tibet, India and China could be reached between the parties concerned. In the outcome Tibetan officials signed on Agreement with China on May 23, 1951 under duress and without the authority of the Tibetan Government in Lhasa on 'Measures for the Peaceful Liberation of Tibet'.

Known as the 17-Point Agreement between the Chinese Peoples Government and the local Government of Tibet, it was, quite contrary to Indian assurances, neither advantageous to Tibet nor to India. The latter was simply ignored. The peaceful Liberation of Tibet was achieved by 23000 Chinese troops entering Lhasa on 9th September, 1951 from all sides! The 17-point Agreement was not an Agreement but a dictate. The Dalai Lama and his Government came to know of it four days after it was 'signed' when Radio Beijing broadcast it on 27th May, 1951. They did not even know its contents until then. A shocked and stunned Tibet 'heard' the news.

The Agreement empowered the Chinese Government to enter its forces into Tibet and to handle its external affairs. Tibet was deprived of the symbols of its Sovereignty in one assault. The occupation of Lhasa in September that year was followed by the occupation of other principal cities of Tibet as far as Rudok and Gartok in the far west and Gyantse and Shigatse in Central Tibet. Then Tibet was cut into pieces and parts of it incorporated in China's neighbouring provinces. A large part of Tibet's Kham province was incorporated into China's Sichuan province and its another portion into Yunnan. A new Chinese province called Qinghai was also created with the bulk of Tibet's Amdo province and part of Kham.

The remaining part of Amdo was incorporated into the Gansu Province. With only a little part of Kham and the Central Province of U-Tsang left, Tibet was reduced to a shadow of its former self. The People's Liberation Army had come to liberate Tibet of its serfdom. It reduced it to servitude. As early as on 6th April, 1952, MaoTse Tung himself admitted in the "Directive of the Central Committee of CPC on the Policies For Our Work in Tibet":-

- "Not only the two Silons (Prime Ministers) but also the Dalai and most of his clique were reluctant to accept the Agreement and are unwilling to carry it out — And yet we do not have a material base for fully implementing the agreement, nor do we have a base for this purpose in terms of support among the masses or in the upper stratum".

While that was the situation on the ground, India sanctified the Chinese military occupation of Tibet by accepting it as a region of China in the 1954 Sino-Indian Agreement on trade with Tibet. As that Agreement enunciated the principles of Peaceful Co-existence, the panchashila, Dr. Bhimrao Ambedkar, said the following in the Rajya Sabha: "Our Prime Minister is depending on the Panchsheel which has been adopted by Comrade Mao and the Panchsheel which is one of the clauses in the No-Aggression treaty on Tibet. I am indeed surprised that our Hon'ble Prime Minister is taking this Panchsheel seriously. Hon'ble Members of the House, you must be knowing that Panchsheel is one of the significant parts of the Buddha Dharma. If Shri Mao had even an iota of faith in Panchsheel, he would have treated the Buddhists in his country in a different manner". Dr. Ambedkar then warned the Prime Minister in no uncertain terms:

- ".... Prime Minister will realise the truth in my words when the situation matures further. I don't really what is going to happen. By letting China take control over Lhasa (Tibetan Capital) the Prime Minister has in a way helped the Chinese to bring their armies on the Indian borders. Any victor who annexes Kashmir can directly reach Pathankot, and I know it for sure that he can reach the Prime Minister's House also".

Eight years later the Chinese annexed Aksai Chin in North eastern Kashmir. Prime Minister Nehru had his share of warnings but apart from his genuine desire to have close and friendly relations with China, he knew it was not possible for the Indian Armed forces to take on both Pakistan and China, a spectre to which Sardar Patel had drawn his attention.

Nehru's effort was to avoid a direct military confrontation with the Chinese throughout the fifties. He had no power to halt the Chinese avalanche through Tibet. In December, 1950 he had stated that the last voice in regard to Tibet should be the voice of the people of Tibet and of no one else. The Chinese guns had effectively silenced that voice and the men behind them crossed the Himalaya into India equally effectively in the late fifties and early 60s. Our armies could not stop them even at our frontier. Reacting to the Chinese betrayal and belligerence, Dr. Rajendra Prasad said at the Gandhi Maidan in Patna on October 24, 1962:

- "Freedom is the most sacred boon. It has to be protected by all means — violent or non-violent. Therefore Tibet has to be liberated, from the iron grip of China and handed over to Tibetans".

Even before the Chinese invasion of India, there had been voices galore in India to protect Tibet's freedom and the Tibetan right to self-determination. Acharya Kriplani who in the Lok Sabha debate in 1954 had openly charged China of having committed an act of aggression and in 1958 had talked about Panchshila having been born in sin because it was enunciated to put the seal of our approval upon the destruction of an ancient nation associated with us spiritually and culturally, said of Tibet in the Lok Sabha on May 8, 1959L:

- "It was a nation which wanted to live its own life and it sought to have been allowed to live it own life. A good government is no substitute for self-government".

The same year at the all India convention on Tibet on 30 May, 1959, Lok Nayak Jaya Prakash Narayan, in his Presidential address, pleaded for a United World opinion to be created 'against Chinese aggression and for Tibet's independence'. He emphatically called it a fight for the Rights of Man'. He, however, predicted that Tibet was not lost forever. 'Tibet will not die' he said, because there is no death for the human spirit. Jaya Prakash Narayan concluded:

- "Tyrannies have come and gone and Caesars and Czars and dictators. But the spirit of man goes on forever. Tibet will be resurrected".

It is a tribute to Nehru's character as an ardent lover of peace and international harmony that even after the Chinese branded India as running dogs of imperialism, nay even after they launched their pincer movement against India in 1962 a concerted attack in all the three sectors of the Indo-Tibetan border in the Himalayas, and inflicted a crushing defeat on the Indian Armed forces, he stuck to his advocacy of PRC's entry into the U.N. A large section of India's public opinion failed to interpret India's Tibet policy in terms of the Prime Minister's lofty idealism or the constraints on him in terms of India's actual military capabilities, faced as it was now with aggression from two quarters.

It was seen throughout the fifties as a policy of yielding too much ground to the Chinese in regard to Tibet. Said Acharya Kriplani in the Lok Sabha repeatedly: (1954, 1958, 1959). 'In international politics when a buffer state is destroyed by a powerful nation, that nation is considered to have committed aggression against its neighbours'. 'England went to war with Germany not because Germany had invaded England, but because it had invaded Poland and Belgium'. 'I do not say that because China conquered Tibet we should have gone to war with it. But this does not mean that we should recognise the claim of China on Tibet.

We must know that it is an act of aggression against a foreign nation'. 'A small buffer state on our borders was deprived of its freedom. When we made a protest, we were told we were the stooges of western powers (If I remember it right, we were called running dogs of imperialism)". The criticism in the Indian Press, that watchdog of the people, in regard to India's Tibet policy was even more blatant and gallic. After the Peoples Liberation Army crushed the Peoples rebellion in Tibet, the Indian Express wrote in an editorial entitled "India and Tibet" on March 20, 1959:

- 'The Government of India's silence in the face of this situation is difficult to decipher and even more difficult to condone. Discretion and restraint are too often alibis for moral and political poverty'.

Above all, the Tibetans as a brutally oppressed people are entitled, as fellow human beings, to the goodwill of the civilized world, not least of India which in its long history has also known bondage and suffering'. On March 30, The Times of India in its editorial on Repression in Tibet commented: 'The news from Peking has killed the last lingering hope that, faced with a popular revolt in Tibet, the Chinese would try to come to terms with the people rather than seek to coerce them into surrender' 'All the levers of power are in fact in the hands of the commanders of the Chinese forces in the region'.

'But the military victory of the Chinese is in fact a political defeat'. 'The Chinese, determined to exploit the rich mineral wealth of the region, will now do everything they can to quicken the pace of change, break the power of monasteries, settle large number of their own people in the region and integrate it completely with the rest of China'. 'In the face of a military fait accompli, the Indian government can do little to restore Tibetan autonomy, but even so there is no reason for it to stretch the concept of non-interference to the point where it has to maintain an uneasy silence in the matter'. In its editorial 'The Rape of Tibet', the Hindustan Times said the same day: (March 30, 1959):

- 'Let us hold our heads low to-day. A small country on our border has paid the ultimate penalty for its temerity to aspire for independence. Tibet is dead'.
- 'Tibet was dying a long time before death came. It was eight years ago that the Chinese communist moved in to assert a theoretical suzerainty over a people with a long history as a distinct entity, geographical, ethical, linguistic, cultural and religious'.
- 'But if the Chinese did at times establish effective rule over Tibet, let it also be remembered by those who are now willing enough to help Peking rewrite history that there was a Tibetan king who once extracted tribute from the celestial empire'.
- 'Tibet is dead. Much else could die with Tibet if we do not even now heed the warning'.

The Indian Press was adequately voicing the mood of the people of India and India's leadership had to pay heed. Prime Minister Nehru broke his silence on the troubling question of Tibet in the Parliament of India on March 30, 1959, the same day as the above editorials appeared. He spoke of the relationship of India with Tibet being something deeper than the changing political scene, that he wanted to have friendly relations with the people of Tibet and he wanted them to progress in freedom. At the same time, it was important, he said, for us to have friendly relations with China. The next morning, the Indian Express retorted that he could not equate the aggressor with the aggressed and reminded him of his own statements in 1949 to the US House of Representatives:

- 'Where freedom is menaced or justice threatened, or where aggression takes place India would not be neutral'.

Meanwhile, things moved in Tibet at a dramatic speed — faster than anticipated. The Dalai lama had gone back to Tibet in 1956 at the instance of Nehru after participating in the 2500th Buddha Jayanti Celebrations. Chou-en- Lai had assured Nehru at that time that 'Tibet was not China but an autonomous region which had been part of the Chinese state'. In his March 30, 1959 statement to the Lok Sabha, Nehru quoted Chou-en-Lai as having said that 'China practice the Chinese intensified the socialist purges against Tibetans, parcelled out its territories to become part of Chinese provinces, considerably reinforced the Chinese army, denied the Tibetan monasteries of their spiritual and material wealth, and wee making plans, so the Tibetans believed, for abducting the Dalai Lama to Peking. Their worst suspicions were confirmed when their religious and temporal head was invited to come to a theatrical show at the Chinese military barracks on March 10, 1959 without any bodyguards. In a massive demonstration of their will to protect their leader, the people of Lhasa surrounded Norbulingka, Dalai lama's Summer Palace, to prevent him from attending the Chinese show. Within days the episode turned into a national uprising touching every part of Tibet. Open fighting broke out in Lhasa and several places outside the capital with Tibetan blood littered everywhere as a consequence of Chinese repression. With no help available from any quarter, the Dalai Lama left his hearth and home and his kingdom to seek refuge in India and appealed for international help from outside. On 28th March, Chou-en-Lai 'dissolved' the Government of Tibet by an order of the State Council. Even the fiction of Tibetan autonomy was scrapped. Prime Minister Nehru interpreted the gory march of events in Tibet to the Parliament of India on March 30, 1959 how the Khampa region of Tibet was incorporated into China and how their reforms had brought the Chinese into trouble with the Khampas whom he described as 'mountain people, rather tough people, not liking anybody ruling them; how this conflict had 'come out into the monasteries and valued manuscripts.

Right when as the Prime Minister was telling the Parliament, 'our sympathies go out very much to the Tibetans', the ruler of Tibet, the Dalai Lama was already at the portals of India. He actually crossed into our territory on the evening of March 31, 1959, after seeking political refuge two days earlier before entering India. As he walked into freedom, he denounced the 17-Point Agreement with China and declared it null and void. On 5th April in his Press Conference in Delhi, Prime Minister Nehru agreed that the 1951 Agreement between China and Tibet had broken down and confessed that there was no autonomy in Tibet. He said that rather emphatically:

- 'Now what has happened in Tibet is related to the Agreement between China and the authorities in Tibet, in 1950, I think. You will see that on both sides there, it is stated that agreement has ended or broken up. There is no doubt about it, and events also indicate that. Now, that is an important fact that it has broken down,'. The agreement was based on two factors — (I) on the recognition of the suzerainty of China over Tibet and (ii) the autonomy of Tibet. These are two major factors. The breakdown of the Sino-Tibetan agreement, which in any case had been a one-way affair and hardly an agreement, meant that both major factors comprising it, *i.e.* (I) the recognition of the Chinese suzerainty over Tibet by the people and the government of Tibet and (ii) the autonomy of Tibet had collapsed. Tibet was without a Tibetan government, even it and it was a land with millions of Tibetan people under the occupation of an alien force exercising rights which it did not have under any law temporal or moral. Tibet, which in Nehru's own view expressed at the Press Conference on April 5, 1959, culturally speaking, was "an offshoot of India" had been shamelessly annexed by China and swallowed up.

At his Press Conference India's Prime Minister admitted: 'it is obvious that at present, since this uprising, there is no autonomy in Tibet'. The Indian Press and leading public figures in India, therefore, grilled Nehru on his Tibet policy even further. On April 8, 1959, in a forceful editorial titled "Second Thoughts", the Leader commented:

- 'When the World allowed Japan to work her will upon Manchuria, it did not promote the cause of peace... When Britain and France committed aggression in Egypt, President Eisenhower did not uphold their action even though the United States is more akin ideologically to Britain and France than India is to China....... Pt. Nehru can do no better than emulate the example of President Eisenhower and ask China to retrace here steps."

"THOUGHT" reminded Nehru in a pungent editorial on April 11, 1959, of what he knew already, that the 1951 Agreement stood on the twin pillars of Tibet's autonomy and China's suzerainty. Without the first the latter would be a grotesque imposition. On April 20, 1959, the Times of India seriously questioned Prime Minister Nehru's conviction that 'Tibet's autonomy and Chinese suzerainty' could coexist. There was thus a strong demand that since the situation on the ground in Tibet had changed materially, India too alter the course of its policy in the matter.

Prime Minister Nehru however continued to explain that India's policy kept three factors in view, "the major factor being, of course our own security;

the second factor, 'our desire to have and continue to have friendly relations with China' and the third factor, our strong feelings about developments in Tibet". Prime Minister Nehru was soon in for rude shocks. While he continued in his quest for continued friendly relations with China, the Chinese openly charged India of keeping the Dalai Lama in India under duress. Nehru met the charge by declaring in the Indian Parliament on April 27, 1959 that the Dalai Lama was free to go anywhere he chose and anyone including the Chinese Ambassador was fee to meet him. Moreover, while the Chinese were fuming and fretting at their embarrassment to see 'the Dalai Lama and his clique' successfully cross into India despite their attempts by air and on the ground to track him down before he did so, they shamelessly called India expansionist — inheritor of the British tradition of imperialism and expansion. That was typical of the behaviour of the Chinese government of the time.

Before the world could call them imperialist and expansionist, for what they had done in Tibet and to Tibet, they started levying these charges against India which had done nothing but acquiesce in their colonial occupation of Tibet and was hoping to sustain a friendly relationship with them despite the loss of Tibet as a buffer. Nehru called the Chinese charges strange and use of the cold war language. He told the Lok Sabha on April 27, 1959. "It would be a tragedy if the two great countries of Asia, India and China, which have been peaceful neighbours for ages past, should develop feelings of hostility against each other. We for our part will follow this policy, but we hope that China also will do likewise and that nothing will be said or done which endangers the friendly relations of the two countries which are so important from the wider point of view of the peace of Asia and the world. The Five Principles have laid down, *Inter alia,* mutual respect for each other. Such mutual respect is gravely impaired if unfounded charges are made and the language of cold war used". However, these pleas made no sense to China's rulers. Their plans to complete their work in Tibet went apace and as they consolidated their hold, they moved further South. Peace in Asia and the world must come under their own terms. Meanwhile their territorial claims stemming from their own imperial borders must be made a reality, by peace if possible, by war if necessary. When India saw the writing on the wall and placed a few pickets on the border, ill manned, ill equipped and ill connected, they came down like a hurricane in one clean sweep destroyed them.

And in their defence, they charged India of a forward policy which invited quite naturally their wrath, while a full scale military occupation of Tibet in the decade of the 50s was no part of a 'forward Policy' to which India had any right to react. The 19th century was one of colonial expansion. The first half of the twentieth century was marked by two world wars as a legacy of those colonial powers. In the second half of our century, mankind has taken pride in liquidating much of the abominable legacy of the colonial and the imperial times. Even the Soviet empire has collapsed. But the torch of colonialism is still burning strong in Tibet. All his life Nehru had fought and fought successfully against the forces of colonialism and imperialism and fascism.

He could not have been oblivious to what the Chinese were doing in Tibet but he had been hoping that the Chinese would heed the verdict of history against such forces, listen to reason and fulfil their own promises about respecting the autonomy of Tibet. By the year 1962 this great statesman of Asia and the world was a thoroughly disillusioned person. All the pillars of his Tibetan policy and policy towards China had fallen one by one. The Chinese had successfully breached the sovereignty and the territorial integrity of India. Tibet's autonomy was a matter of the past which India had bartered for the independence that country had enjoyed till 1950 and the friendship with China had turned into a nightmare of bitter hostility. The Sino-Indian Agreement of 1954 enshrining Panchshila now lay in shreds. It died a natural death in 1962 with neither side willing to revive it and China stood as the undisputed monarch of all it surveyed in Tibet and beyond upto the territories of India now under its occupation. In the wake of their mastery over the Roof of the World, the Chinese turned Nehru's dream of Sino-Indian friendship, so elegantly proclaimed in the slogan Hindi-China Bhai Bhai, into a nightmare that ultimately sapped life out of that most precious jewel of India.

CHINA'S TIBET POLICY

China's Tibet policy has not been consistent as it was influenced either by hardliners or moderates at different times during over last fifty years. The domestic policies of China and external environment equally impacted on its Tibet policy. In the early 50s, China did not face much international hostility in the matter of occupation of Tibet when the PLA marched into Tibet as the USA was deeply involved in Korean War and the Taiwan Strait crisis and the world was re-grouping in the frame of Cold War at that time.

There are five discernible phases of different approaches in China's Tibet policy:

- *Phase-I (1951-1959):* The 1951 agreement, if we look back, grants full autonomy to Tibet in the matters of governance, religion, language and culture and preserving the traditional religious and administrative institutions like the institutions of the Dalai Lama and Panchen Lama with in the geographical boundaries of (greater) Tibet and vesting the foreign and defence matters with the Chinese central government. However, as a young communist nation, they were in great hurry to introduce communist reforms in Tibet. It was a sudden and painful experience for Tibetans who had been leading an almost isolated different system for several centuries, away from external interference. Tibet was a neutral during the World War II. This alienated the Tibetan people and their leadership. As a result riots and rebellion broke out in Tibet many times between 1952 and 1957, with certain external support. Mao in Feb 1957 had said that conditions in Tibet were not ripe for reforms and that the implementation of reforms be postponed till 1962. He also offered to reduce the Han cadres in Tibet. The Dalai Lama had dismissed two Prime Ministers who insulted the Chinese in early 1950s. Mao's policy of moderation and gradualism also had the support of the Dalai Lama and the Tibetan elite but it was not implemented in practice4. The exodus of the Dalai Lama and his supporters to India in 1959 marks the end this phase.

- *Phase-II (1959-1976):* This is the critical period of Chinese handling of Tibet issue. It was dominated by the hard line policies and internal power struggle in China. The 'Great Leap Forward' and 'Great Proletarian Cultural Revolution' brought unparallel turmoil with in China. The excesses by the CPC members in Tibet like attack on religious institutions, culture and language and increasingly strained relationship with India only further alienated the Tibetans. China reorganized Tibet by making U-tsang as Tibet Autonomous Region and merging Kham and Amdo regions with Yunnan, Sichuan, Gansu and Qinghai provinces.
- *Phase-III (1978-1986):* This is the period when Deng Xiaoping adopted soft policy to handle Tibet issue and for the first time proposed talks with the Dalai Lama. This policy also ended in failure but a communication line was set up for the first time between the Dalai Lama and the Chinese leadership.
- *Phase-IV (1987-2001):* The failure of Deng's soft policy emboldened the hands of the hawks in the CPC and China adopted a different approach to solve Tibet issue through economic development instead of focusing on political solution alone. This model has met with partial success as the Dalai Lama diluted his demand from independence to autonomy, yet the Chinese leadership did not show much interest in carrying any negotiations with the Tibetan leadership.
- *Phase-V (2002- —):* This period is marked by realistic handling of Tibetan issue, which combines winning the people of Tibet through economic development and conducting dialogue with the Tibetan leadership in exile.

INDIA'S POLICY ON TIBET

India's policy towards Tibet has always been consistent and principled. The first formulation regarding Tibet was made in the 1954 "Agreement between the government of the Republic of India and the government of the People's Republic of China on trade and inter-course between Tibet region of China and India". Here, Tibet is referred to as the region of China, which means Government of India recognizes Tibet region as a part of the People's Republic of China. In 1988, the India-China Joint Press Communiqué stated "Tibet is an autonomous region of China and that anti-China political activities by Tibetan elements are not permitted on Indian soil".

India's position was further stated in the Declaration on Principles for Relations and Comprehensive Cooperation between India and China signed in 2003 during the visit of the Prime Minister of India to Beijing. It says 'the Indian side recognizes that the Tibet Autonomous Region is part of the territory of the People's Republic of China and reiterates that it does not allow Tibetans to engage in anti-China political activities in India.' The latest joint statement issued during the visit of the Chinese Premier, Wen Jiabao to India in April 2005, states 'the Indian side reiterated that it recognized the Tibet autonomous Region as part of the territory of the People's Republic of China and that it did not allow Tibetans to engage in anti-Chinese political activities in India.'

India welcomes and encourages the talks between the Dalai Lama and the Chinese government. The Dalai Lama has appreciated India's position on Tibet.

NEHRU'S NOTE ON TIBET POLICY

Nehru did not respond directly to Sardar Patel's letter, but a few days later, he dictated a Note that would become the corner stone of India's Tibet Policy until the Prime Minister's death, and in a way, till today. We shall look at this Note to try to understand Nehru's fears and motivations.

In November 1950, Nehru had already accepted that the frontier between India and Tibet had de facto become the border between India and China. It was a surprising statement because at that time, the Chinese troops had not marched further than Chamdo, still several weeks away from Lhasa, and several months from the McMahon Line.

Nehru says: "I think it may be taken for granted that China will take possession, in a political sense at least, of the whole of Tibet." He further admits that for the Tibetan people the "autonomy can obviously not be anything like the autonomy, verging on independence, which Tibet has enjoyed during the last forty years or so."

It is beyond comprehension how Nehru, who wanted to be the hero of the oppressed nations, could at the same time accept that a nation 'verging on independence', should lose its independence before his eyes, and he could so easily accept it as a fait accompli. Another point made by Nehru is that "it is exceedingly unlikely that we may have to face any real military invasion [of India] from the Chinese side, whether in peace or in war, in the foreseeable future."

It is not clear what was meant by 'real' invasion, however Nehru came to the conclusion that China would not take the risk to have too many new enemies; for that would weaken China. He was proved wrong. Nehru's Note concludes: "We cannot save Tibet".

Regarding the Tibetan Appeal to the UN, Nehru finally decided to do as little as possible: "It will not take us or Tibet very far. It will only hasten the downfall of Tibet." The facts showed that Tibet was an independent nation, it was clear that China, as the aggressor, was in the wrong and that it was India's moral duty to defend this position, but under the pretext that it would not 'take us very far', the moral stand was dropped and Tibet abandoned to its fate.

All this shows that India had no Tibet Policy.

What should a Tibet Policy be today?

Does Delhi have a Tibet Policy today? If it does not have one, what shape should a Tibet Policy take? To answer this, it is important to have a look at what are India's present interests in Tibet?

They are, of course, of different nature; first and foremost are the strategic interests flowing from the long common (and disputed) border with China. But they are also diplomatic (visa issue), economic (border trade), cultural and civilisational. The presence of the Dalai Lama and more than a lakh of his countrymen and women is an important factor to be taken into account. After defining these interests, a formal (or informal) policy should accordingly be drafted.

The Strategic Interests

Let us have a look at strategic interests as many other issues flow from this core subject. There is currently an argument in India that the country is not prepared for a war. This is an undisputable fact. A few months back a Weekly magazine published a cover story arguing: "Fifty years after its only defeat, the Indian Army is still unprepared for a battle with its scheming adversary, China. Low on equipment and lacking in infrastructure, the bloated war machine is in urgent need of an overhaul."

Though Defence Minister A.K. Antony affirmed that no infiltration takes place across the LAC in Arunachal Pradesh, he recently admitted: "there have been instances of a few Tibetan herb collectors inadvertently crossing over into Indian territory in the last two years." It is common knowledge that the Chinese are masters at testing the ground by sending herders or herb collectors to scout areas that they 'perceive' as theirs.

Behind this new Tibet Policy should be that fact that it is not necessary for India to always be in denial mode. It does not help to engage China.

Does it Mean that 1962 can Repeat Itself?

Take the roads for example: in January 2008, during a visit to Itanagar and Tawang, the Prime Minister announced a Rs 24,000 crores package for the State. The priority was given to the roads (in particular, the construction of a Trans-Arunachal Highway). With the road being enlarged between the plains of Assam and Tawang (en route to the Tibet border), one finds today the messiest imaginable road site; it has become the favorite topic of local jokes. There are however differences between 1962 and 2012: the Indian leadership did not then dare to use the Air Force; it will not be the case today. A full squadron of Sukhoi-30 aircraft have now been deployed at Tezpur air base in Assam (another squadron has been brought to Chabua in Upper Assam). Further, the IAF is planning to open six Advanced Landing Grounds, as well as several helipads in areas close to the border. This may take some time, but the process has started.

Were India attacked today, it will not remain a localized conflict like in 1962; any Chinese misadventure would trigger an 'all-out' conflict, and India would certainly not hesitate to attack the PLA infrastructure in the Nyingchi Prefecture, north of the McMahon line and elsewhere in Tibet. It has been in the public domain that two new infantry divisions are being raised and that the Government is looking for a place in the Northeast to set up the headquarters of a Mountain Strike Corps.

This should be one more deterrent factor for China. Another crucial issue is the support of the local population in Arunachal and Ladakh. In 1962, some villages fully supported the invading Chinese troops. How else could the PLA have built a road from Bumla, the border pass, to Tawang in 18 days? It is not difficult to imagine the staggering amount of accurate intelligence required for this feat.

An important question is "what will China gain from a misadventure on India's territoory, apart from a hypothetical Asian supremacy?" It is clear that China cannot militarily 'take back' Tawang. The PLA could at the most occupy a few 'disputed pockets' like Samdorong Chu valley, north of Tawang or

Demchok in Ladakh, but in the process, Beijing would lose India's present goodwill and the international respect it earns with its 'peaceful rise' policy as well as its integration into the world scene as a responsible State.

Further, it should not be difficult for India to get logistic support from inside Tibet and eventually support a military rebellion; at least a civil disobedience could be organized. Let us not forget that an alien PLA has already to deal with a resentful local population on the Tibetan plateau. The recent immolations of monks and nuns in Eastern Tibet are a proof of this. The launch of the Agni-V long range missile also adds to the deterrence. It has already made Chinese policy makers ponder. The People's Daily stated that it reflects India's "intention of seeking regional balance of power".

If Beijing wants again to 'teach a lesson' to India, it will indeed be a Himalayan task, and what will Beijing gain in the bargain? China can nevertheless use some asymmetric types of warfare, cyber-warfare is one of them.

Traditionally, the Himalayan frontier has been a frontier between India and Tibet; the 1914 border agreement (i.e. the McMahon Line) delineates the frontier in the North-East. This is not acceptable to Beijing which denies the existence of the McMahon Line. It is the main reason why the border talks have today come to a standstill. Presuming that the next generation of Chinese leaders would attempt a 1962-like adventure against India, the Tibet factor would become crucial. The Indian Government could for example immediately recognize the Central Tibetan Administration in Dharamsala as the legitimate exiled government of Tibet.

A Tibet Policy should be based on deterrence, as India can't match today with China in terms of infrastructure and armed forces. Some of the developments mentioned above should be part of this policy of deterrence.

Diplomatic Contacts between Dharamsala and Delhi

A few years ago, the diplomatic contacts between Dharamsala and Delhi were enhanced when the post of the Dalai Lama's Liaison Officer (an officer of the Indian Ministry of External Affairs) was upgraded to the rank of Director and a post of Deputy Liaison Officer was created. In the recent years, successive Foreign Secretaries have visited Dharamsala and called not only on the Dalai Lama, but also on the Kalon Tripa (Prime Minister), the elected head of the Central Tibetan Administration.

However, there is still a feeling that "we should not upset the Chinese" and often ministers are 'shy' to meet the Dalai Lama and the Kalon Tripa. Officials contacts should be upgraded at the ministerial, if not prime-ministerial levels. It could be explained to the Chinese ambassador that it is nothing against the People's Republic of China, but the mere fact that the Dalai Lama is an 'honoured guest' and one and half lakh of his countrymen/women live in India, requires some coordination meetings from time to time.

Further, India should continue to insist to reopen its Consulate General in Lhasa. It would be an important step to restore the traditional relations. But when the question came to open a Consulate in Lhasa, some Chinese India experts objected. Zhao Gancheng, director of South Asia Studies at the Shanghai Institute for International Studies criticized India's proposal saying that the move was motivated by political, rather than economic interests: "The Indian government hopes to closely watch, observe, and infiltrate the Tibetan area after the opening of a Lhasa consulate,... The issue regarding Tibet is an internal affair and we won't tolerate any external forces imposing a negative impact on the situation in Tibet."

In this case, why to have a Nepali Consulate in Lhasa? Has (and had) Nepal closer contacts with Tibet than India? Zhao Gancheng, who, by the way is often invited by Indian think-tanks, seems unaware of the traditional bonds between Tibet and India. The Indian presence on the Roof of the World is older than the British 'imperialist' (for the Chinese) inroads in Tibet.

One of the best proofs is the collections of thousands of 700-year old Sanskrit manuscripts found in Tibetan monasteries by the scholar Mahapandit Rahul Sankrityayan when he visited Tibet in the 1930's. Such examples could be multiplied.

If the Indian Government had wanted "to watch, observe, and infiltrate" Tibet, they could have done it long ago, with or without a Consulate General in Lhasa. Regarding the visa issue, if China continues to issue visas on stapled paper for the residents of J&K or Arunachal Pradesh, India should simply reciprocate for Tibetans, Uyghurs and Mongols from Inner Mongolia.

Trade between India and Tibet

Trade has, for centuries, been a traditional link between Tibet and India. Even when the Government of India decided to 'bury' Tibet as a de facto Independent nation in 1954, an agreement on 'Trade and Intercourse' between Tibet and India was signed (it is remembered as the Panchsheel Agreement). Inter alia, it says:

The High Contracting Parties mutually agree to establish Trade Agencies:

(1) The Government of India agrees that the Government of China may establish Trade Agencies at New Delhi, Calcutta and Kalimpong.

(2) The Government of China agrees that the Government of India may establish Trade Agencies at Yatung, Gyantse and Gartok.

The Trade Agencies of both Parties shall be accorded the same status and same treatment. Indians and Chinese traders were allowed to use the following places, (1) Yatung, (2) Gyantse and (3) Phari as trademarts. Further the Government of India agreed that trade may be carried on in India, in places like (1) Kalimpong, (2) Siliguri and (3) Calcutta.

The Chinese Government of China specified (1) Gartok, (2) Taklakot, (3) Gyanima-Khargo, (4) Gyaniina-Chaltra, (5) Ramura, (6) Dongbra, (7) Puling-Sumdo, (8) Nabra, (9) Shangtse and (10) Tashigong as markets for Indian traders in Tibet.

Traders and pilgrims were allowed to use the following passes and routes: (1) Shipki pass (Himachal), (2) Mana pass (Uttarakhand), (3) Niti pass (Uttarakhand), (4) Kungri Bingri pass, (5) Darma pass (Uttarakhand), and (6) Lipulekh pass (Uttarakhand)

Unfortunately, after the 1962 conflict, all these trade marts and passes were closed. Since then, a series of border trade agreements were signed to reopen Lipulekh-la in Uttarakhand (1991), Shipki-la in Himachal Pradesh (1991).

In 2003 a Memorandum on Expanding Border Trade was signed between India and China; it was agreed to reopen Nathu-la as a border pass. Article II says: "The two sides agree to use Nathu-la as the pass for entry and exit of persons, means of transport and commodities engaged in border trade. Each side shall establish checkpoints at appropriate locations to monitor and manage their entry and exit through the Nathu-la Pass."

A recent report of the Institute of Peace and Conflict Studies explains: "Border trade markets [are] scheduled to be opened from Monday to Thursday every week. A permit fee of Rs. 50 each would be levied for every vehicle entering Sikkim side from China. Similarly, a fee of 5 Yuan (Rs. 25 approximately) would be levied for every vehicle crossing over to the Chinese side up to the trade mart point at Renqinggang.

Unfortunately, business is not flourishing as yet. On April 21, 2011, iSikkim reported: "The fifth edition of Indo-China trade through the Nathu-la border in 2010 recorded absolute zero import. In 2009 also the Nathu-la border trade closed for the season recording zero import. As per the official record, [year] 2010 saw exports worth a little over Rs 4 crore."

The Sikkimese publication quoted Kesang Diki, the Tibetan Autonomous Region's in-charge, affirming that the reason for zero import was the non-feasible list of items. She requested the Indian Government to expand the trade list and cater to today's market demands. Many feel that most of the items listed in the schedule are obsolete and do not have a commercial value;

interestingly both the Tibetan and the Sikkimese traders agree on this. It is worth noticing that a few hundred kilometers westwards the trade is with Nepal is blooming.

The website China Tibet Online affirms that the "total volume of cross-border petty trade between Tibet and Nepal has increased remarkably in the first quarter of 2011". Like for India, Europe and the United States, the trade is heavily tilting in China's favour, but the Nepalis do not seem to mind too much.

A new Tibet Policy should take into account this important traditional bilateral activity and if there is a political will, the situation could greatly improve, with both side benefiting from it. Further, new traditional land ports such as between Walong-Rima in the Lohit Valley, Bumla in the Tawang district or Demchok in Ladakh could be opened, once the security concerns are taken care of. The softening of the borders would be one of the measures to bring more understanding on both sides of the frontier.

Pilgrimage

The Panchsheel Agreement mentions that as both India and China were "desirous of promoting trade and cultural intercourse between Tibet Region of China and India", (1) pilgrims from India of Lamaist, Hindu and Buddhists faiths may visit the Kailash and Manasarovar lake while pilgrims from Tibet may visit Banaras, Sarnath, Gaya and Sanchi. Today the immediate need is to open a new route for the Kailash-Manasarovar yatra. Demchok should be easier than the present one through Uttarakhand. Unfortunately, the Chinese side seems overcautious about the project.

In a longer term, if the security risks can be sorted out, the old Tsari pilgrimage around the Dakpa Sheri, the Pure Crystal Mountain in Tsari region of Southern Tibet could be reopened for the Buddhist populations of Arunachal Pradesh. It would, of course, raise the problem of visas as the Chinese authorities still claim the Indian State as part of 'Southern Tibet'. A special agreement would be required for this pilgrimage which occurs every 12 years, as part of it is located south of the McMahon Line. However, if allowed, the sacred yatra could greatly help to 'soften' the border. Year 2016, is the next date for the Tsari pilgrimage.

Buddhist Studies

As part of a global Tibet Policy, India should take the lead in promoting Buddhism and Buddhist studies. In this context, the Global Buddhist Congregation (GBC), organized by the Ashoka Mission in November 2011 was a good exercise. Some 900 monks and nuns from over 40 countries attended the event in Delhi. China, as usual, objected to the function. Beijing was particularly incensed by the invitation sent to the Dalai Lama to address the valedictory function. China even threatened to call off the 15th round of border talks between the Special Representatives if India refused to yield and cancel the Conference. Beijing also objected to the Prime Minister and the President of India attending the opening ceremony of the Congregation.

Eventually, India partially backed out with the Prime Minister and the President suddenly becoming 'busy', but the program with the Dalai Lama was reconfirmed. The External Affairs ministry issued a bland statement "We are looking forward to the 15th round of Special Representatives' talks in the near future and the two sides remain in touch to find convenient dates for the meeting."

The Ministry explained to China that the Congregation was of a religious nature and not a political event; further it had no power to cancel it. The Conference came at a time when Beijing had been trying to take on the leadership of the Buddhist world movement through its involvement in projects as in Lumbini and Nalanda and later a Buddhist Conference in Honk Kong.

One could think that the atheist regime in Beijing does not believe in Buddhism, but on the contrary, Beijing recently seems to embrace the philosophy taught by the Great Gautama, for political purposes at least.

The Economist reported that China plans to invest $3 billion in Lumbini, the birthplace of the Buddha. The magazine explains: "After Prachanda, the leader of Nepal's Maoists, stepped down as Prime Minister in 2009, he met representatives of the Asia Pacific Exchange and Cooperation Foundation (APECF) several times. In July, the Chinese media reported that the Hong Kong-based foundation which is widely thought to have China's backing had signed an agreement with UNIDO, the UN's industrial development organization, to invest $3 billion in Lumbini."

The objective is to make Lumbini a 'Mecca for Buddhists' (under China's sponsorship). Unfortunately for Beijing, the dynamic 82-year old Lama Lobzang from Ladakah and his colleagues from the Himalayan belt decided to celebrate the 2600th anniversary of the Enlightenment of the Buddha and to do it in India.

The Global Buddhist Conference eventually resolved to "preserve and conserve sacred sites and holy relics worldwide, particularly those that are historically connected to the life and times of Buddha such as Lumbini in Nepal, and Bodhgaya, Sarnath and Kushinagar in India". It was stated that Buddhism can help the human civilization which "today faces many challenges such as conflict, violence, extremism, discrimination, injustice, inequality, materialism, environmental degradation, natural disasters" and that solutions "to these issues of global concern can be found within the principles and values contained in Buddha's teachings."

India should certainly have a say in most of these issues whereas Buddhist ethics cannot flourish in China where the individual liberties are still very restricted under an authoritarian regime. India should give a lead to the Buddhist world in which Tibet and the Dalai Lama (representing the true Nalanda tradition) have a significant role to play. Once again, Indian leaders should not be shy to attend these types of religious functions.

Tibetan Studies

Tibetan studies is also a field where India has traditionally been present as most of the Tibetan literature originated from India. Unfortunately, here also it is China which invests in this field. Traditionally, scholars, pundits, lamas from India and Tibet have criss-crossed the Himalayas. For centuries, vast amounts of knowledge have freely been exchanged between the subcontinent and the Land of Snows over the Himalayan passes.

Today the situation has changed. From August 1 to 4, 2012, the 5th Beijing International Seminar on Tibetan Studies was held in the Chinese capital under the auspices of the China Tibetology Research Center. It is said it attracted 246 scholars from 21 countries and regions including Mongolia, India, Japan, France, Australia and the United States.

According to the organizers, the Seminar on Tibetan Studies was aimed at 'preserving culture and serving society'. The topics of discussion focused on social development in Tibet. The China Daily quoted Lhagpa Phuntshoks, the Director-General of the China Tibetology Research Center who stated during his opening speech: "Tibetan studies are expanding in China, with the government investing heavily in the protection of traditional heritage, printing of historic texts in the Tibetan language and the cultivation of young researchers". Sitar, the Vice-president of the China Association for Preservation and Development of Tibetan Culture declared that "China has been steadily endeavoring to preserve the Tibetan language, cultural relics, folk arts such as the Epic of King Gesar, and the religious practice. It is for this purpose that we organized a panel on Development, Sustainability and Livelihood Security in Tibetan-inhabited Areas."

The question is why should China have the monopoly of Tibet studies? Delhi, with the help and support of institutions in the Himalayan regions as well as Dharamsala, should revive Tibetan studies in a big way.

Further, why not open Chairs on Tibetan history, culture and politics in some of the main Indian Universities; particularly in J&K, Himachal Pradesh,

Uttarakhand, Sikkim and Arunachal Pradesh? The age-old intellectual, spiritual and also environmental relations between India (particularly the Himalayan belt) and Tibet should flourish again. The People's Republic of China can keep the monopoly on Tibetan studies. A new Tibet Policy should promote the traditional links and help reestablish them through regular conferences/ seminars and exchanges.

THE INFLUENCE OF INDIA'S SECURITY CONCEPT ON ITS CHINA POLICY

Earlier sections of this book explain changes in India's post-Cold War security concept and adjustments to its China policy. In the process of this discussion, we have distinguished two phases of adjustment to both the post-Cold War India security concept and China policy, and established that these changes were more or less simultaneous. We have also found that India's China policy reflects its security concept; in other words that adjustments to the content of India's China policy correspond to continuities and discontinuities in India's security concept. It may be said that this consistency demonstrates the important influence India's security concept has had on its China policy.

Policy-making, in any event, is the linking of concepts and policy; in other words, concepts, through government policy-making, crystallize into policy. Exploring the evolution of the Indian policy-making class and mechanisms, therefore, also benefits understanding of the manner in which security concepts of different eras and phases have influenced India's China policy.

India's foreign policy behaviour during the Cold War was largely determined by a few predominant personalities, both its foreign and security policies having long been dominated by Nehru and Indira Gandhi. The two leader's views on China had decisive influence on India's China policy. When considering India's defeat in the 1962 Sino–Indian Border Conflict and the open wound it represented to both the Nehru family and the INC, their adoption of an unyielding tack toward China was the sole political means of saving face. Sino–Indian relations consequently remained in stalemate for nearly 30 years. When Rajiv Gandhi replaced his mother in 1985, he seemed at first to follow her line on foreign policy. The rapidly changing international situation, however, forced him to veer from it, and specific improvements in Sino–Soviet relations compelled his adjustments to India's China policy. Soviet leader Mikhail Gorbachev urged Rajiv Gandhi during a visit to India in 1986 to improve relations with China, saying it would suit Soviet interests, and hinting at a press conference that the USSR would no longer be willing to provide support to India in the event of Sino–Indian conflict. In this situation, Rajiv Gandhi considered that India on its own would be powerless against a threat on two fronts. He was hence forced to change his preparations for a two-front war, as it was apparent that dispelling tensions along the eastern front through reconciliation with China would allow him to concentrate India's energies on the western front with Pakistan.

The Nehru family's stately bearing was absent after the Cold War, and the INC's power had declined. The insularity that had characterized India's foreign policy-making process since independence, however, did not change. The nation's foreign and security policy stayed in the hands of the prime minister and cabinet from 1991 to 1996, during which time the views of Prime Minister Rao and leaders of the INC government on security and foreign policy matters were decisive, and the influence of parliament, think tanks and academic institutions was negligible. It is notable, however, that Rao's background as home minister, defence minister and external affairs minister throughout the 1980s, as well as his status as the Congress Party's elder statesman, signified that he was a loyal adherent of Nehruvianism, and unrepresentative of any new type of thinking. The transformation of India's security concept during the Rao administration, therefore, can be understood as entirely the result of external forces.

The changes in the international and domestic situation compelled Rao to change his understanding of national strength. He began emphasizing the strategic influence of economic strength and promoting restoration of the economy as a matter of urgency in withstanding security threats in the aftermath of the Cold War. This passive reaction to a complex situation gave the impression of India's overall foreign policy as passive and defensive. India adopted a focused approach to diplomacy during this period, directing its energies towards restoring the economy but maintaining a low profile in international affairs, as expressed in its China policy. Rao continued and furthered Rajiv Gandhi's adjustments by focusing on stabilization of Sino–Indian political relations and establishing tranquil borders as means to ensuring the recovery of India's domestic economy.

Two major changes occurred in India's foreign policy-making process during 1998. The first was the BJP's assumption of office that ended the long-standing INC power monopoly, and established foundations for a clean break with the traditional security concept. Although the BJP's domestic policies had a relatively ideological slant and promoted a Hinduist revival, the party was pragmatic as regards foreign policy. In contrast to the Congress Party, it dared to confront history, criticise India's previous foreign policy and introduce new thinking. Jaswant Singh, successively the Vajpayee government's External Affairs Minister and Finance Minister, published early in 1999 a book entitled *Defending India* in which he systematically describes his new security concept.

Various views were thereafter expressed in government-issued articles. The BJP was obviously preparing to move on from the passive security concept of the Rao era. The second major change was India's refinement of its foreign policy-making mechanism. The November 1998 establishment of the National Security Council symbolized India's casting off of the influence and control of personality-based policy-making in favour of scientific research, inquiry and decision-making, and comprehensive long-term planning. The introduction by National Security Advisory Board subordinated to the National Security Council of scholarly authorities, reporters and former government and military officials demonstrated how much more open India's foreign policy-making process had become.

The BJP differed in its approach to China policy from both that of the Cold War era Nehru family, with its 1962 complex, and the early 1990s Rao government, which had been wearied and bound hand and foot by domestic and international pressure. The BJP's seizing of this historic opportunity confirmed India's rise as the nation's long-term strategic goal and placed its relationship with China on the strategic level. In other words, the BJP saw the Sino–Indian relationship as an important influence on India's rise. Although the two nations would be dealing with historically significant problems, they could be seen as a starting point.

The gradual opening of India's foreign policy-making process, moreover, made way for a vibrant exchange of ideas regarding China policy, which fell roughly into three groups: the first held that Sino–Indian cooperation suits both sides' interests and that post-Cold War China has no intention of making an enemy of India, desiring instead friendly relations and strategic partnership; the second that China is a long-term strategic threat to India because China's strategic objectives lie in establishing hegemony over Asia, which necessitates India's containment and, therefore, limitation of Indian influence. India, therefore, should adopt diametrically opposed policies; and the third group, situated between the two, held that the two nations could simultaneously rise to become main Asian powers and that competition and cooperation could coexist. Discussions on how to evaluate and understand China by Indian scholars and strategic circles are ongoing. After frequent debates among Indian National Security Council groups, the third, middle-ground viewpoint seems to be gaining acceptance.

When the INC regained power in 2004, a variety of factors led the new government to carry on with the previous administration's security concept. The new INC government's China policy was its predecessor's legacy, because the rise of India's international status during the BJP coalition government left the INC powerless to dispute the success of the previous government's foreign policy. The INC's democratized and more youthful leadership team was also willing to jettison historical baggage and look to the future. Although the Nehru family's leadership role within the Congress Party remained uncontested, the influence of Prime Minister Manmohan Singh and Foreign Minister Mukherjee on foreign and security policy could not be disregarded. Moreover, the liberalization of India's foreign policy-making process was superimposed against a long-standing civil service system which ensured continuity of policy. In other words, many masterminds of BJP foreign policy still active in the external affairs ministry, defence ministry and other relevant functional departments under the INC, as well as in consultative committees, the media, think tanks and other non-functional departments, continued to exert influence.

Substantial changes occurred in India's China policy after the end of the Cold War whereby the nation's long-standing (1962–1988) antagonistic approach became one of reconciliation and engagement. These adjustments originated to a great extent in changes in the sub-continent's post-Cold War security concept, manifest in two major shifts which effected two major phases of adjustment in India's China policy. The new post-Cold War China policy nonetheless retained traces of the former, programme, imbuing it with a duality that reflected the overlap of India's old and new security concepts.

A change in India's security concept first became apparent during the period from the end of the Cold War to 1998. The first phase of adjustments this change triggered in India's China policy was evident in the sub-continent's extended concept of military might as national strength to one encompassing economic factors, and acknowledgement of the strategic value of economic strength in countering what it perceived as the looming threat of marginalization within the international community. Restoration of the domestic economy hence became a main measure through which to resist security threats in the post-Cold War era. Having made this shift in foreign policy objectives towards economic recovery, India set about creating a favourable environment within which to achieve this goal. Overall implementation of a China policy of preserving stable Sino–Indian relations by guaranteeing border tranquillity was vital to achieving this strategic objective. India consequently focused on the feasibility of reconciliation and, in view of China's reflective, inward-looking mood, no longer viewed China as an enemy. As regards India's specific policies, while focusing on the establishment of a progressive means to guaranteeing tranquil borders, thereby stabilizing Sino–Indian relations, India at the same time sought communication and cooperation in other areas. To avoid provoking China, the Indian government made tactical adjustments to its approach to Tibet from that of exploiting the issue and causing uproar to handling the matter in a low-key manner. The new developments apparent in India's security concept in 1999 brought with it the second phase of adjustments to India's China policy.

Indian leaders considered that the nation's security environment had improved to the extent that it constituted a strategic opportunity for India to rise to global-power status. This change in thinking and understanding caused the second shift of objective in India's foreign policy from that of improving the economy to the grand goal of global-power status. It corresponded to India's acknowledgement of the crucial nature of the Sino–Indian relationship and change of focus from border tranquillity and stable political relations to comprehensive considerations of how the two nations' relationship would strategically affect India's; rise. These insights compelled a shift of objective in India's China policy towards making China a positive factor in the subcontinent's rise; also recognition that this objective could be accomplished only by maintaining a stable basis for Sino–Indian relations. Official introduction during this phase of a comprehensive security concept signalled India's adoption of a more pragmatic, comprehensive handling of its relations with China. The specific steps it adopted were: increasing economic cooperation with China, thus benefiting India's economic development and stabilizing bilateral political relations; strengthening military communication and security dialogue, thus deepening understanding of China's strategic intentions towards India, increasing mutual trust, minimizing misunderstandings and avoiding conflict; and seeking Chinese support in its quest for a permanent seat on the UN Security Council, which would expand India's political power and international prestige.

In the course of research, however, it became apparent to the author that India's security concept did not undergo a thoroughgoing change after the Cold War ended, as elements of the Cold War approach remained in place.

Although India's security concept extended after 1988 to include both military and economic security, the ultimate purpose of national defence as regards a fundamental guarantee of security nonetheless remained that of increased military strength to safeguard national unity and territorial integrity. India abandoned its strategy of pursuing security through alliances, yet still viewed parity and the principle of checks and balances as hallmarks of its national defence.

Influenced as it was by traditional concepts, post-Cold War India's China policy was imbued with vigilance. Even though India did not perceive China as a threat in the short term, it was nevertheless concerned that the swing in balance of power between the two was not in its favour, and that China constituted a potential obstacle to India's rise. Indian leaders consequently embarked on a race against China to expand comprehensive national strength, particularly military force, including India's nuclear capability, as the means to a balance of power. India at the same time sought to offset Chinese influence both regionally and globally through development of strategic relationships with the United States, Japan and other nations. The sub-continent also remained vigilant in the long-standing issues of border disputes and Sino–Pakistani relations, and maintained pressure on China in this regard.

Changes in post-Cold War India's security concept were thus the result of both domestic and foreign factors. The first change during the early post-Cold War period was triggered by passive reactions to transformations in the nation's domestic and international situation that, in turn, prompted a passive transformation of thinking and understanding, manifest in passive defensiveness of India's foreign policy, specifically its China policy. The security concept that appeared during the late 1990s was comparatively proactive. The expanded strength of India's domestic economy and improvement of its external environment compelled a new understanding of security issues, as expressed in the proactive change in its security concept. This assertiveness was manifest in strategy and in an active, enterprising foreign policy. Seizing the historic opportunity to realize India's rise had become the common security objective of both major Indian political parties. Decentralization of political power and expanded openness of the foreign policy-making process, however, caused India's old and new security concepts to bind into one, and the resultant duality of India's hybrid security concept since the Cold War's end is reflected in its China policy. As India's dual security concept will continue into the foreseeable future, the duality of its China policy will be difficult to change.

INDIA SHOULD REVISIT ITS TIBET POLICY

The Indian government's response to the protests in Tibet has been to merely state its "distress" about the situation and reaffirm its position that Tibet is an "internal" affair of China. New Delhi had assured Beijing that its position on the Tibet issue is "clear and consistent" and that this "would not change in the future." The Indian position is based on its traditional opposition to separatist movements and to foreign intervention in support of such movements. Also, given the present dynamics of India-China relations with greater synergy as the goal, New Delhi does not favour supporting the Tibetan cause. However, protests by Tibetans have implications for India as the Tibet issue is entangled with the India-China border dispute.

The Tibet issue is rooted in the histories of the three countries – India, China and Tibet. Tibet has existed throughout history as a distinct civilization with rich culture, language, religion, polity and identity. Through the centuries

India and Tibet have maintained strong religious and trade ties, and have shared a peaceful border. But the advent of British power in the Indian sub-continent altered the nature of this relationship.

The British Raj's policy towards Tibet was shaped by the Great Game and the need to prevent Russia from posing a threat to India. It was against this backdrop that the Raj called for the tripartite Simla conference in October 1913, which was attended by representatives from British India (Henry McMahon), Republican China (Chen Yifan) and Tibet (Lonchen Shatra). The goal was to settle the boundary between British India and Tibet on the one hand and between Tibet and China on the other. The result was the Simla Agreement of 1914, which the Chinese representative initialled but only under British pressure. The Agreement divided Tibet into Inner and Outer Tibet. China was given sovereignty over Inner Tibet but only suzerain control over Outer Tibet. And the boundary between India and Tibet was demarcated, with the Raj retaining trading and extra-territorial rights in Outer Tibet.

Independent India inherited this arrangement, which boiled down to sustaining Tibet as a buffer zone with de facto independent status under Chinese suzerainty. In the post-1949 period, when the People's Republic of China came into being, India urged China to let Tibet continue as an autonomous region in line with its historical status, religious, cultural and political identity. However, the entry of 20,000 PLA troops in 1950-51 into Tibet ended its independent status and eventually brought to the fore the India-China border issue.

During his 1954 visit to China, Jawaharlal Nehru had raised the issue of inaccurate border alignment as depicted in some Chinese maps. Premier Zhou Enlai responded that these maps were reproductions of old Kuomintang maps and that his government has had no time to revise them. However, Nehru's December 14, 1958 letter, in which he had once again raised the issue of Chinese maps depicting the border alignment inaccurately, elicited a different response from Zhou. The Chinese Premier wrote back on January 23, 1959 stating that the Sino-Indian border was never delimited and that China has never recognised the McMahon Line.

After the 1962 India-China war, China began to claim some 90,000 square kilometres of Indian territory in the eastern sector and 38,000 square kilometres in the Aksai Chin area. These claims flow directly from China's control over Tibet and its felt need to consolidate its rule over this rebellious territory.

Between 1947 and 1954, India's position on Tibet was based on recognising it as an independent nation. Tibet represented itself as an independent country at the Asian Relations Conference held in New Delhi in March-April 1947. But India subsequently gave up this position on April 29, 1954, when it signed an agreement with China on trade and intercourse between India and Tibet. Under the terms of the agreement, India gave up all extra-territorial rights and privileges that it had inherited from the British Raj and recognised Tibet as part of China. This, in effect, was a unilateral concession without the Indian government gaining anything in return. In subsequent decades, New Delhi has repeatedly reiterated that Tibet is a part of China, in spite of the latter's encroachment into and extravagant claims over Indian territory, the border war it imposed on India in 1962, and the unresolved border dispute at the centre of which lies Tibet. In effect, such reiteration has meant the dilution of a bargaining card in the border negotiations. In 2003, the Vajpayee government went further than any other government before by stating that the "Tibetan Autonomous Region of China is part of the territory of China." This has two critical implications for Indian security. First, it excluded Inner Tibet (present day Sichuan, Yunnan and Qinghai provinces) from the geographical notion of Tibet, thus recognising Inner Tibet as Chinese land. Second, it provided China a greater opening to advance its claims on Arunachal Pradesh. For, Outer Tibet or the Tibetan Autonomous Region (TAR), according to the Chinese definition, includes Arunachal Pradesh, which it refers to as its 'southern state'.

India has consistently failed to understand nuances in Chinese diplomatic practice and negotiating tactics. China is tackling the Tibet problem at two levels. One, it is involving the Dalai Lama's representatives in fruitless talks, while also disparaging him as a 'splittist' who aims to disintegrate China. Two, it is arm-twisting India by repeatedly claiming that Arunachal Pradesh is part of China. Here, it is worth noting that at the sixth round of talks with Tibetan representatives Chinese negotiators had conveyed that the Dalai Lama should accept Arunachal Pradesh as part of China, which the Dalai Lama has refused to accept. China is not seriously considering a resolution to the Tibet issue or the border dispute with India. It is simply buying time till the Dalai Lama passes away, after which, it hopes, the Tibetan movement would fizzle out. This would also further weaken India's bargaining position on the border negotiations while at the same time gaining for itself greater manoeuvrability.

The presence of the Dalai Lama in India along with 120,000 Tibetan refugees spread across 35 settlements is leverage for India. But India has so far steadfastly avoided using the Tibetan card. Given the intricate linkage between the Tibet issue and the border dispute, India needs to revise its policy on Tibet. Its present policy of appeasement and unilateral concessions has not stopped China from claiming Indian territory. Chinese maps continue to show Arunachal Pradesh as part of China, and Jammu and Kashmir as falling outside India. Some Chinese maps still do not represent Beijing's revised position on Sikkim. The latest unrest among Tibetans provides an opportunity for India to revisit and revise its Tibet policy. First, India should make it clear to the Chinese government that developments in Tibet are a concern for India and that it cannot remain unaffected by developments there. Second, on the border issue, instead of merely restating that all of Arunachal Pradesh is an integral part of its territory, India should make it very clear that these are non-negotiable. Third, upholding its democratic principles as well as its cultural affinity with the Tibetans, India should impress upon the Chinese that while it does not support political activity by Tibetans in its soil, it also cannot suppress peaceful demonstrations by them. Fourth, India should move away from its 'over-cautious' and diffident policy on Tibet and adopt a more independent stand that takes into account its national interests.

CENTRAL GOVERNMENT'S POLICY AND DALAI LAMA

Starting from the point of maintaining the unification of the motherland and national unity, the central government adopted an attitude of patient waiting towards the Dalai Lama after he fled abroad. His position as a vice-chairman of the NPC Standing Committee was preserved until 1964. However, surrounded by foreign anti-China forces and Tibetan separatists, the Dalai Lama completely renounced the patriotic stand which he once expressed and engaged in numerous activities to split the motherland.

Publicly advocating that "Tibet is an independent state." In June 1959, the Dalai Lama issued a statement in Mussoorie, India which read "Tibet had actually been independent." In March 1991, during his visit to Britain, the Dalai Lama told the press that Tibet "is the biggest occupied country in the world today." He proclaimed on many occasions that "the task of realizing the independence of Tibet has fallen upon all Tibetans in and outside Tibet."

Setting up the "government in exile." In the early 1960s, the Dalai clique convened the "people's congress of Tibet" in Dharamsala, India, which established the so-called "Tibetan government in exile." A so-called "constitution" was promulgated, which states that "the Dalai Lama is the head of state," "the ministers shall be appointed by the Dalai Lama" and "all work of the government shall not be approved without the consent of the Dalai Lama." The 1991 revised "constitution" of the Dalai clique still stipulates that the Dalai is "the head of the state." The Dalai Lama and his so-called "government in exile" kept levying an "independence tax" on Tibetans residing abroad, established "offices" in some countries, published magazines and books advocating "Tibetan independence" and engaged in political activities for "Tibetan independence."

Reorganizing the armed rebel forces. In September 1960, the Dalai clique re-organized the "religion guards of the four rivers and six ranges" in Mustang, Nepal, which carried on military harassment activities along the Chinese border for ten years.

Its first commander-in-chief Anzhugcang Goinbo Zhaxi wrote in his memoirs *Four Rivers and Six Ranges* that "a series of attacks were organized on Chinese outposts" and "sometimes, 100 or 200 Tibetan guerrillas went as far as 100 miles into the area occupied by the Chinese." The Dalai Lama wrote articles praising Goinbo Zhaxi.

Spreading rumors and calumnies and plotting riots. Ignoring facts, the Dalai Lama fabricated numerous lies to sow dissension among the various nationalities and incite the Tibetan people to oppose the central government during his 30-year self-exile abroad. He said that "the 17-Article Agreement was imposed on Tibet under armed force"; "the Hans have massacred 1.2 million Tibetans"; "owing to Han immigration, the Tibetans have become a minority in Tibet"; "the Communists in Tibet force women to practice birth control and abortion"; the government opposes religious freedom and persecutes religious people; traditional Tibetan culture and art are in danger of extinction; the natural resources in Tibet have been seriously depleted; there is severe environmental pollution in Tibet, etc. The riots in Lhasa from September 1987 to March 1989 were incited by the Dalai clique and plotted by rebels who were sent back to Tibet. The riots incurred severe losses to the lives and property of Tibetans.

The Dalai's words and deeds have showed that he is no longer only a religious leader as he claims. On the contrary, he has become the political leader engaged in long-term divisive activities abroad.

CHINA'S CLAIM TO TIBET IS FACTOR IN BORDER DISPUTE

This is perhaps the most militarized Buddhist enclave in the world. Perched above 10,000 feet in the icy reaches of the eastern Himalayas, the town of Tawang is not only home to one of Tibetan Buddhism's most sacred monasteries but also the site of a massive Indian military buildup. Convoys of army trucks haul howitzers along rutted mountain roads. Soldiers drill in muddy fields. Military bases appear every half-mile in the countryside, with watchtowers rising behind concertina wire.

A road sign on the northern edge of town helps explain the reason for all the fear and the fury: The border with China is just 23 miles away; Lhasa, the Tibetan capital, 316 miles; and Beijing 2,676 miles. "The Chinese army has a big deployment at the border, at Bumla," said Madan Singh, a junior commissioned officer who sat with a half-dozen soldiers one afternoon sipping tea beside a fog-cloaked road. "That's why we're here." Though little known to the outside world, Tawang is a flashpoint in relations between the world's two most populous nations. It is the focus of China's most delicate land-border dispute, a conflict rooted in Chinese claims of sovereignty over all of historical Tibet.

In recent months, both countries have stepped up efforts to secure their rights over this rugged patch of land. China tried to block a $2.9 billion loan to India from the Asian Development Bank on the grounds that part of the loan was slated for water projects in Arunachal Pradesh, the state that includes Tawang. It was the first time China had sought to influence the territorial dispute through a multilateral institution. Then an Indian general announced that the Indian military was deploying extra troops and fighter jets in the area. The growing belligerence has soured relations between the two Asian giants and has prompted one Indian military leader to declare that China has replaced Pakistan as India's biggest threat.

Economic progress might be expected to bring the countries closer. China and India did $52 billion of trade last year, a 34 percent increase over 2007. But businesspeople say that border tensions have infused official deliberations over business deals, dampening the willingness of Chinese and Indian companies to invest in each other's countries. "Officials start taking more time, scrutinizing things more carefully, and all that means more delays and ultimately more denials," said Ravi Bhoothalingam, a former president of the Oberoi Group, the luxury hotel chain, and a member of the Institute of Chinese Studies in New Delhi. "That's not good for business."

The roots of the conflict go back to China's territorial claims to Tibet. Not only does the Dalai Lama, the exiled spiritual leader of the Tibetans, live in the foothills of the western Himalayas with the blessing of the Indian government, but China insists that this swath of northeast India has historically been part of Tibet, and thus should be part of China. Tawang is a thickly forested area of white stupas and steep, terraced hillsides that is home to the ethnic Monpa people, who practice Tibetan Buddhism, speak a language similar to Tibetan and once paid tribute to rulers in Lhasa. The 6th Dalai Lama was born here in the 17th century.

The Chinese army occupied Tawang briefly in 1962, during a war with India fought over this and other territories along the 2,521-mile border. More than 3,100 Indian soldiers and 700 Chinese soldiers were killed and thousands wounded in the border war. War memorials highlighting China's aggressions in Tawang here are big draws for Indian tourists. "The entire border is disputed," said Ma Jiali, an India scholar at the China Institutes of Contemporary International Relations, a government-supported think tank in

Beijing. "This problem hasn't been solved, and it's a huge barrier to China-India relations."

In some ways, Tawang has become a proxy battleground, too, between China and the Dalai Lama, who passed through this valley when he fled into exile in 1959. From his home in the distant hill town of Dharamsala, he wields enormous influence over Tawang. He appoints the abbot of the powerful monastery and gives financial support to institutions throughout the area. Last year, the Dalai Lama announced for the first time that Tawang is a part of India, bolstering the Indian government's territorial claims and infuriating China.

Traditional Tibetan culture runs strong in Tawang. At the Tawang monastery, an important centre of Tibetan learning, monks express apprehension about China's rule over Tibet, which the Chinese army seized in 1951. "I hate the Chinese government," said Gombu Tsering, 70, a senior monk who watches over the monastery's museum. "Tibet wasn't even a part of China. Lhasa wasn't a part of China." Few expect China to try to forcefully annex Tawang, but military skirmishes are a real danger, analysts say. The Indian military recorded 270 border violations and nearly 2,300 instances of "aggressive border patrolling" by Chinese soldiers last year, said Brahma Chellaney, a professor of strategic studies at the Centre for Policy Research, a research organization in New Delhi. Mr. Chellaney has advised the Indian government's National Security Council.

"The India-China frontier has become more 'hot' than the India-Pakistan border," he said in an e-mail. China has grown increasingly hostile to the Dalai Lama after a severe outbreak of ethnic unrest in Tibet. This year, it turned its diplomatic guns on India. China moved in March to block a $2.9 billion loan to India from the Asian Development Bank, a multi-nation group based in Manila that has China on its board, because $60 million of the loan had been earmarked for flood-control projects in Arunachal Pradesh, the state that includes Tawang. The loan was approved in mid-June over China's heated objections.

Weeks after China first tried to block the loan, the chief of the Indian air force, now retired, told a prominent Indian newspaper that China posed a greater threat than Pakistan. Another official, J.J. Singh, the governor of Arunachal Pradesh and retired chief of the Indian army, said the next month that the Indian military was adding two divisions of troops, totalling 50,000 to 60,000 soldiers, to the border region over the next several years. Four Sukhoi fighter jets were immediately deployed to a nearby air base. Since 2005, when Chinese Prime Minister Wen Jiabao visited India, the two countries have gone through 13 rounds of bilateral negotiations over the issue. A last round was just held last month, with no results. Though China has actually resolved many of its border disputes in recent years, India remains a glaring exception.

The Government of Tibet in Exile

From July 20 to 23, 1994, Beijing staged the Third Forum on Work in Tibet which recommended the total destruction of an entire civilization flourishing on the Tibetan Plateau for thousands of years. This cultural "empire" once encompassed far-flung areas like Buryatia, Tuva and Kalmykia in Russia; Mongolia; Laddakh, Lahaul-Spiti, Sikkim, and Arunachal Pradesh in India; Mustang, Dolpo and Solo Khumbu in Nepal; Bhutan and parts of western China.

The policy formulated in 1994 in Beijing-and these days pursued with Cultural Revolutionary zeal in Tibet-will mean the annihilation of the spiritual homeland of this shared culture. Implementation of the Third Work Forum is thus having a crippling impact on the traditional culture of millions of non-Tibetans as the well-spring of their cultural inspiration is forcibly drained and there is nothing to replenish the continuous growth and development of this distinct and highly evolved civilization.

Losing Hearts and Minds

The decisions made at the Third Forum rest on two fundamental conclusions which Beijing drew. It realized it was losing out in two vital fields-ideology and propaganda. For a state whose existence is justified by its ideological superiority and the power of its propaganda to shape the thinking of the masses, the implications of this for the future was at best uncertain, at worst dangerous. Beijing concluded it was losing the ideological war because, despite the unrelenting assault on Tibetan Buddhism, Tibetans were as devoted to their traditional beliefs as ever. Beijing has succeeded in physically enslaving the country but it has not won over the hearts, minds and loyalty of the Tibetan populace.

Communist ideology, enforced by the military might of China, had failed to dent the heart of Buddhism. Added to this was the communist authorities' total bafflement at the non-violent policy underpinning the Middle Way Approach advocated by His Holiness the Dalai Lama to resolve the issue of Tibet's future status. For a regime which is based on Mao's dictum that political power grows out of the barrel of a gun, this supposedly eccentric philosophy which says victory lies in capturing the hearts and minds of people by the power of ideas rather than killing by the power of the gun comes as a bolt from the blue. Much of Beijing's knee-jerk reaction to, and its bafflement at, His Holiness the Dalai Lama's new policy of rapprochement lies at the heart of its new hardline policy.

Beijing considered it was losing the propaganda war because, for one reason or the other, the world's media and its pop culture considered-at least for the moment-Tibet and Tibetan Buddhism their very own cuddly pandas. Despite its financial might China found it extremely difficult to exterminate this image of Tibet and get its voice heard on the Tibetan issue in the court of the international media. In order to address these weaknesses the Third Forum concentrated on two issues. One was to focus on Tibet's economic development in the hope that this would keep Tibetan demonstrations off the streets. This was tantamount to bribing the Tibetans with promises of riches to come if they toed the party line. The other concern was to win the coming and new generations of Tibetans over to the Chinese viewpoint.

Beijing has given up on the present generation of Tibetans as a lost cause. If the coming generations of Tibetans were also lost to the 'Dalai Clique' this, the Chinese concluded, would have dangerous consequences for Chinese rule in Tibet. The 15-year-old Gyalwa Karmapa's dramatic escape from Tibet in January 2000 was a warning to the Beijing authorities of the erosion of loyalty to China. The Karmapa's flight, and the earlier escape of Agya Rinpoche, the abbot of Kumbum Monastery, came as a huge embarrassment for China, because retaining these high lamas gave China a degree of legitimacy for its rule in Tibet. This is the reason why Beijing is enforcing with greater strictness its 1993 instruction of recalling young Tibetans studying in schools and monasteries run by Dharmasala in India. This is also the rationale for Beijing closing down schools in Tibet which are privately run by Tibetans.

For these reasons Tibet today is in the throes of a second Cultural Revolution as the Chinese authorities step up their long-term strategy to exterminate Tibet's distinct cultural and ethnic identity. The authorities are pursuing a four-pronged strategy to achieve their final objective. They have stepped up repression while employing their huge propaganda machine to paint a rosy picture of Tibet. They have quickened the pace of economic development to dampen Tibetan nationalism and are simultaneously moving more Chinese settlers onto the Tibetan Plateau to change Tibet's demographic composition and to ease social unrest because of mounting unemployment back in China.

The Third Work Forum on Tibet was convened by the top Chinese leadership and was presided over by President Jiang Zemin. The authorities have now enshrined this Work Forum as the most "important strategic policy to rejuvenate Tibet" and have hailed its directives as the new manifesto for party work on the plateau. The significance of the Third Work Forum lies in the fact that it overturned the more liberal policies laid out for Tibet's "development" by the First and Second Work Forums held in 1980 and 1984.

The first two work forums were initiated by the late Hu Yaobang, then Secretary General of the Chinese Communist Party.

This liberal and somewhat maverick leader is credited with masterminding a series of measures to improve the social, economic and political conditions in Tibet. The brief spell of liberalization markedly improved the living conditions of the majority of Tibetans and contributed to a more relaxed intellectual and social climate.

The Third Work Forum reversed these policies and reinstated hardline measures under which Tibet is still reeling today. The Tibetans in Tibet perceive the current repressive policies as a second Cultural Revolution. The question is why did China choose to jettison its earlier more liberal policies and adopt a manifesto which is leading to the systematic destruction of Tibet's distinct culture. The answer lies in domestic and international events which forced China to formulate a series of hardline policies on Tibet which eventually crystallized into the Third Work Forum for Tibet. The world which confronted China in the late 1980s and early 1990s was a frightening one.

Starting from 1987, Tibet was rocked by a string of protest demonstrations, which called for Tibetan independence. One of the largest demonstrations which erupted on March 5, 1989 in Lhasa, forced the authorities to impose martial law on the city. These demonstrations are now seen to have been an inspiration behind the outburst of Chinese students' pro-democracy uprisings. The authorities saw the series of Tiananmen Square demonstrations as a sign of their Central Government losing control, and in an attempt to regain supremacy, the authorities slaughtered-perhaps hundreds if not thousands of students on June 4, 1989. These demonstrations were a chilling replay to the authorities of the May 4, 1919 student demonstrations in Beijing which signalled a political and cultural awakening across the erstwhile Middle Kingdom.

Bejing's fears of losing control were exacerbated by external events which saw the unraveling of the communist world. The Solidarity Movement in Poland, the fall of the Berlin Wall, and the implosion of the Soviet Union fed Beijing's paranoia over threats to the Chinese Communist Party hold on power. Official China's fears were further inflamed by the rapidly changing attitude of the broad masses as they turned back from communism to traditional beliefs like Confucionism, Buddhism, Islam, Christianity and indigenous folk cults. In the eyes of ordinary citizens communism was becoming totally discredited and this, more than anything else, was the biggest nightmare for China's leadership. The leadership's justification for staying in power was being disavowed by the masses. For a one-party dictatorship this historically indicates the first step along the slippery road to dissolution and removal of power.

For these reasons the Chinese leadership then reverted to its earlier view that traditional beliefs were its real enemy. In competing with Buddhism, Confucionism, Islam, Christianity and other isms, communism was losing out in terms of its ability to retain the loyalty and allegiance of the masses. The leadership revived the old aphorisms once served up to the Tibetan people to justify their policies to destroy Tibetan Buddhism during the Cultural Revolution. Bewildered Tibetans were then told that just as there cannot be two suns in the sky, so there cannot be both Buddhism and socialism in Tibet. Inevitably Buddhism then had to give way to socialism. And again, today, religion is being blatantly sublimated to Chinese state power.

These were the fears of the Chinese leaders when they met in Beijing in 1994 to hammer out their new Tibet initiatives. For the Chinese authorities Tibet is an especially sensitive issue because of their conviction that hostile Western forces are using the issue of Tibet to "westernize" China and to lead to its territorial fragmentation. The third generation Chinese leaders came to the conclusion that stability in Tibet was vital to the stability of China as a whole. Earlier, Tibet was merely of peripheral concern to the vital interests of China's sprawling communist empire. Now, with the Third Work Forum, the authorities were saying, "We must clearly understand that we must do our work in Tibet not only for the sake our of own region's stability and development, not only for the interests of our people, but also for the sake of the whole nation's stability and development."

In Tibet, China faced peculiar problems because of the inherent strength of Tibetan Buddhism and the depth of devotion of the populace to His Holiness the Dalai Lama. The sustained burst of religious revival that followed in the wake of the brief spell of liberalization in Tibet confirmed the leadership's worst fears that decades of concerted assault on Tibetan culture and religion had not extinguished the people's traditional beliefs and values. From merely nuisance value, the Chinese leadership now viewed Tibetan Buddhism as a very real and imminent threat to the stability of Chinese rule in Tibet.

At the same time the Chinese leadership's attitude towards His Holiness the Dalai Lama changed. From being an uncertain ally in the peace process in Tibet, the current Chinese leadership now saw him as a full-blown "enemy". A top-level conclave held in Beijing on March 10, 1993 concluded that, "There are different factions within the Dalai Clique; they are, however, unanimous in their political nature and position. They differ from each other in ideological viewpoints and ways of expressing them. Different strategies must be adopted to use their differences, to deal with them differently in order to divide and destroy them."

Repeated statements by high-level officials describe the struggle against "splittism", the official term for Tibetan independence, as a "life-and-death struggle". At the 1994 annual meeting of the "TAR" Communist Party Committee to brief members on the policy thrust of the Third Work Forum on Tibet, Raidi, deputy Secretary of the Committee said, "Up to now, his (the Dalai Lama's) standpoint on Tibet's independence has never changed, and we must reveal his double-faced true colour. The focal point in our region in the struggle against splittism is to oppose the Dalai Clique. As the saying goes, to kill a serpent, one must first cut off its head."

In short, the Third Work Forum decided that Beijing was in a position to solve the Tibet issue without the Dalai Lama's involvement. It abandoned the earlier liberal policy of including His Holiness the Dalai Lama in any future settlement of Tibet's status. His Holiness the Dalai Lama was clearly singled out as the cause of China's "Tibet problem".

The Third Work Forum also abandoned the policy of granting concessions to Tibet because of the plateau's "special characteristics". This policy had been the cornerstone of recommendations made by the First and Second Tibet Work Forums.

To carry out its new hardline policies in Tibet, Beijing appointed Chen Kuiyuan as the "TAR" Party Secretary in 1992. Chen Kuiyuan's appointment is significant because he had a track record for being a tough and ruthless administrator. He had already served as the First Secretary of the Chinese Communist Party in Inner Mongolia and is credited with repressing the rebellious Mongols, many of whom refer to him as "the butcher". Chen Kuiyuan was especially recommended to the post by Hu Jintao, the current Vice-President of China, who was then the First Secretary of the Chinese Communist Party in Tibet.

Tackling Tibetan Nationalism

The Third Work Forum policies chalked out for Tibet contained four key elements. China stepped up the scale of repression in Tibet. External propaganda work was escalated. The pace of economic development in Tibet- and its corollary of encouraging more Chinese settlers and businessmen to take advantage of the economic boom on the "roof of the world"-was also increased. In short, Beijing had decided to tackle Tibetan nationalism head-on and observers are still assessing the consequences on both Chinese rule in Tibet and on the populace.

Beijing remains convinced that these key components of its current policy will stabilize Chinese rule over Tibet and solve once and for all, the vexed problem of its negative image over the way Tibet has been handled. One main target of the current policy of repression is Tibetan Buddhism. Chinese leaders are increasingly alarmed by the proliferation of monasteries and temples which the period of liberalization spawned throughout Tibet: they are seen as the bastions of Tibetan nationalism. The authorities have set up "Democratic Management Committees" to control monasteries and nunneries and created "Work Inspection Teams" to supervise the "education" of monks and nuns.

A major thrust is underway to break the bond of loyalty between the clergy in Tibet and His Holiness the Dalai Lama in India. Campaigns like "Strike Hard" and "Patriotic Re-education", unleashed in 1996, are aimed at crippling the rise of Tibetan Buddhism which the authorities suspect is weaning the loyalty of the Tibetan people away from the communist party and towards His Holiness the Dalai Lama. One salient feature of the "Strike Hard" campaign is how differently it is interpreted in China and Tibet. China's "Strike Hard" campaign was started to weed out corruption. Tibet's version is used as a political tool to eliminate those whom the authorities label "splittists". In Tibet, rather than striking at corruption, the authorities turn a blind eye to this social disease in the hope that it will erode the traditional morality of Tibetans and undermine Tibetan Buddhism.

In fact, at a secret meeting held in December 1999 in Chengdu, capital of Sichuan province, Chen Kuiyuan, the hardline Party Secretary of "TAR" recommended to the Central Chinese Government that an all-out effort must be made to eradicate Tibetan Buddhism and culture from the face of the earth so that no memory of them will be left in the minds of coming generations of Tibetans-except as museum pieces.

Chen Kuiyuan stated that the main cause of instability is the existence of the Dalai Lama and his Government-in-Exile in Dharamsala and these must be "uprooted". He recommended that Tibet, Tibetan people and Tibetan Buddhism-in other words the very name of Tibet-must be destroyed and the "Tibet Autonomous Region" be merged with provinces like Sichuan. While treating Tibetans to boot-heel subjugation at home, internationally China was on an overdrive propaganda blitz. At a brainstorming conclave held on March 10, 1993, Zeng Jian-hui, Vice-Minister of the Propaganda Ministry, told participants, "The propaganda work on the question of Tibet is one of the focal points of the entire external propaganda work...With regard to attacks by the West and the Dalai Clique and their frequent activities, our external propaganda should launch offensive. We should expand our spheres of influence; in particular, we should infiltrate our propaganda into the mainstream life of the West.

"Firstly we should continue to send Tibetan scholars and Tibetan singing and dancing troupes abroad to lecture and perform. Secondly, relevant embassies and consulates should aim at the public opinion and the activities of the Dalai Clique in the countries where they are stationed and utilize speeches, picture exhibitions, special articles and other forms to carry out propaganda work, so as to win over officials and people of those countries... We should reinforce the work of utilizing the power of foreign propaganda. A few years ago, in the light of the situation of that time, we made arrangements for foreign journalists to visit Tibet."

The September 3, 2000 edition of *People's Daily* carried a story headlined "Tibet Welcomes Foreign Journalists for Objective Reporting". It stated that "A senior Tibetan official said Sunday that Tibet welcomes foreign journalists to come for objective and just reporting, but not those who take distorted views. Raidi, Deputy Secretary of the Tibet Autonomous Regional Committee of the Communist Party of China and Chairman of the Standing Committee of the Tibetan Autonomous Regional People's Congress, made the remarks at a meeting here with a press delegation of Thailand." In this context, it is interesting to note that N. Ram, the editor of India's *Frontline* magazine, devoted 36 pages of the September 15, 2000 issue to promote the Chinese line and recommended that the Indian Government expel the Central Tibetan Administration from Indian soil for being the main stumbling block to normal relations between India and China. It is difficult to assess to what extent the views contained in his stupendous reporting marathon are his own.

These editorial outbursts are in line with policy decisions outlined in the early nineties. During a two-day secret conclave in March 1993 in Chengdu, Vice-Minister Zeng Jian-hui, told participants, "All foreigners that we entertain and send to Tibet must have a relatively objective opinion of Tibet. We should use people from abroad to carry out the propaganda on Tibet for us, which is more powerful than if we do it."

Along with its external public relations strategy, China is presently carrying out a potentially much more dangerous policy of speeding up the pace of Tibet's economic development and its related drive to bring more Chinese settlers onto the Tibetan Plateau. Beijing's Western China Development Programme, which incorporates Tibet in its ambit, is devised to shift the focus of China's economic activities from Coastal China to the interior-both to narrow the imbalance in the level of economic development between the two regions and to ease population pressure on the coastal areas which attract millions of migrant workers. The focus of Beijing's Western China Economic Development Programme in Tibet is to exploit the plateau's still untapped minerals and other natural resources and to upgrade Tibet's infrastructure-like roads and telecommunications-to facilitate transportation of these resources to China. The other purpose of the heightened level of economic activity is to divert the Tibetans' attention from their political fate to focus on their livelihood-thus undermining Tibetan nationalism. The Chinese authorities aim to manipulate the situation in Tibet still further by bringing in more Chinese settlers who would then demographically cement Chinese rule once and for all. These current hardline policies and their implementation in Tibet are impacting the stalled Sino-Tibetan Dialogue and will vitally affect the ability of Tibetans to survive as a distinct people and culture.

Beijing's Flawed Perceptions

The basic flaws in China's new policy in its search to resolve the problem of Tibet is thinking the solution can exclude the involvement of His Holiness the Dalai Lama. The other is in attempting to solve the problem over the heads of Tibet's citizens.

These two fundamental mistakes will exacerbate China's Tibet problem, not solve it. The reason lies in the history of Tibet and in the sentiments of the people. The institution of the Dalai Lamas of Tibet is more than 600 years old, if we start from the birth of the first Dalai Lama in 1391. In the course of its growth and development, the very institution itself came to symbolize fundamental beliefs and the political destiny of the nation. The bond between the Dalai Lamas and the Tibetan people is fundamental and unbreakable; any attempt, however sustained, will never succeed in driving a wedge between the two.

Consequently, China's current policy of forcing Tibetans-especially monks and nuns-to denounce His Holiness the Dalai Lama and pledge loyalty to the Chinese Communist Party will prove counterproductive.

In view of this the Third Work Forum's basic assumption that in the case of Tibet time is on the side of China, and that Beijing can stall the problem of Tibet till the demise of the present Dalai Lama whereupon the issue of Tibet will solve itself, is fatally flawed-based as it is on a mistaken perception of the role played by the institution of the Dalai Lamas in the development of Tibetan history.

This assumption, if not reviewed, revised and abandoned, will prove catastrophic for the Chinese leadership and for those who chose to turn their whimsical personal analysis into state policy. The reason is simple. The Chinese Communist Party was founded in the 1920s and came to power in 1949. Within this short span of time the masses have lost faith in communist ideology, and members of the party these days pay mere lip service to the ideological justifications of the party. Conversely, the institution of the Dalai Lamas as a political force is more than 300 years old. These days the Dalai Lama is recognized by Tibetans throughout the world as the heart of Tibetan nationalism. How can a party which has lost its soul outlast an institution which symbolizes the very soul of a people? For these reasons it is imperative for China to review and re-assess its current hardline stance towards Tibet. China must re-start its stalled peace process over Tibet and consider His Holiness the Dalai Lama as a vital and active partner in the procedures. If China does this it will have won a powerful ally and companion along the road to peace, stability and continued prosperity.

CHINA'S CREEPING AGGRESSION AGAINST INDIA 1950 ONWARDS

China was not satisfied with its military occupation of Tibet and adhering to Tibet's traditional boundaries with India. China's military occupation of Tibet and India's supine, submissive and strategically oblivious policies under Nehru from 1950 onwards emboldened China to make demands on India for redrawing and realignment of India's erstwhile borders with Tibet. China forcibly incorporated a major portion of Aksai-chin, an area equal to that of Switzerland, under her control to link Tibet with Xingjian. Nehru's reaction was to keep the Parliament and the Indian nation ignorant about Chinese aggression for over 5.6 years.

The Indian military establishment starved of defence budget allocation commensurate with the needs to meet the Chinese threat, was emasculated and became the victim of Chinese military humiliation in 1962 due to the incompetence of India's political rulers. An Indian spurt of military build-up in reaction of Chinese aggression of 1962 petered out by 1967 or so. Virtual inertness followed till about 1986-87 when Rajiv Gandhi as PM listening to the advice of Indian military hierarchy made funds available for a forward military build-up in Arunachal Pradesh stemming China's aggression in Sumdorong. China stopped in its tracks. The lesson for India was exercise of firmness of purpose when confronting China.

This military up gradation was brought to a virtual halt by 1991-1993 when India's then Finance Minister now Prime Minister effected cuts in India's defence budgets for nearly a decade. Defence preparedness and upgradation of defence infrastructure against China especially in the North East came to a virtual stop India's spasmodic spurts to improve India's defensive postures along the India-Tibet border therefore did not impose a sustained restraint to China's creeping rhetorical and physical aggression against India. Today, China is now terming Arunachal Pradesh as Southern Tibet and therefore a legitimate target for a future Chinese military action, intruding across in the international border in Sikkim, and upping the ante in the Aksai-chin Sector in Laddakh.

China's Revived Upsurge in Military Intransigence: The Contextual Factors

The major contextual factors prompting China's revived military intransigence along the India-Tibet border can be listed as follows:

- Tibet uprisings and insurgency in Xingjian prompting China's strategic nervousness over its hold on its peripheries.
- India's growing strategic proximity to the United States upsetting the power-balance.
- Upgradation of India's military postures in Aksai-chin sector and Arunachal Pradesh which could be a deterrence to Chinese military adventurisms
- Opening of the Golmud-Lhasa railway facilitating speedy Chinese military buildup in Tibet.

China probably perceives that now maybe the opportune time for China to "teach India a military lesson" before India enhances her global political profile and before India narrows her military differential with China along the India-Tibet border. Current border provocations by China along the India-Tibet Border need to be viewed in this light.

China's Reluctance to Reach Border Settlement with India

China's reluctance to reach border settlement with India on the India-Tibet border arises from:

- Chin's intention to keep alive this issue as a constant strategic pressure-point against India
- Border settlement of the India-Tibet Border would involve physical demarcation by boundary markers, identified and authenticated by both sides.
- Above would rob China the strategic propensity to keep coming up with revised claims on the alignment of the border/LAC.

It is high time India recognizes the futility of continued boundary settlement talks with China. It lulls the Indian establishment into complacency.

Territorial Adjustments with China by Indian Government

The biggest problem which India faces in facing China squarely is the multiplicity of voices within India pleading that India could swap Aksai-chin with Tawang or carry out adjustments in Tawang to accommodate China. Such voices and views remind one of Munich and Chamberlain. India needs a Winston Churchill to meet the China threat. India's political leaders, policy establishment and strategic analysis should desist from such advocacy as it not only belittles them but more importantly belittles India.

The Indian public will never accept any territorial adjustments with China by any Indian Government. The Indian public will oppose tooth and nail any such misadventure by any Indian Government. Nehru as India's tallest political leader was never forgiven by the Indian public for his misplaced trust in China's peace rhetoric and China then stabbing India in the back. It led to his untimely demise. Other Indian Prime Ministers too should desist from stepping over the similar crevice.

Strong and Assertive Military Preparedness

It is encouraging to note that plans do exist now for an augmented Indian military profile along the India-Tibet border to meat China's large-scale military build-up in Occupied Tibet. The Prime Minister needs a personal over-watch on defence preparedness along the India-Tibet Border. However such an augmentation needs to be done on a fast track basis and not left to the vagaries of India lethargic civil bureaucracy.

India does not have to be apologetic about its legitimate defence preparations along the India-Tibet border. Strong defence preparedness along India's borders is the sovereign right and an inescapable duty of the Indian Government. India's Prime Minister made a bold attempt to visit Arunachal Pradesh some time back, but why did be back-out of visiting Tawang which would been symbolically more assertive. India's Prime Minister failed to send the appropriate message to China. When is the Indian Prime Minister going to visit Leh and Indian territory at Chushul and Pangong Lake? Nehru belatedly did so in 1959 or so to raise the morale of Indian troops guarding India's borders.

China's military intransigence along the India-Tibet border arises from strategic and military Chinese arrogance fortified by India's appeasement and supine polices more resembling those of vassal states of China in the past. It is unwarranted on the part of India's political leaders, policy establishment and strategic analysts to term increased media focus on China's military misdemeanors along the India-Tibet border as amounting to generation of "war hysteria" India's strategic image as emerging global power is seriously damaged when responsible Indians start advocating swaps of Indian territory or adjustments in Tawang to accommodate China.

China is "India's Enemy Number One" in Indian strategic perceptions. This is based on China's demonstrated policies of strategic encirclement of India intended to keep India strategically off-balance. China has used India's other arch-enemy Pakistan as a proxy for her designs and strategy against India. China, if serious in altering this Indian perception has to re-cast her South Asian strategy, desist from redefining the boundary alignments along the India -Tibet Border and maintain peace and tranquillity on India's borders.

6

Aksai Chin : The Sino-Indian Boundary Partition

The western portion of the Sino-Indian boundary originated in 1834, with the Sikh Confederacy's conquest of Ladakh. In 1842, the Sikh Confederacy, which at the time ruled over much of Northern India (including the frontier regions of Jammu and Kashmir), signed a treaty which guaranteed the integrity of its existing borders with its neighbours. The British defeat of the Sikhs in 1846 resulted in transfer of sovereignty over Ladakh, part of the Jammu and Kashmir region, to the British, and British commissioners contacted Chinese officials to negotiate the border. The boundaries at its two extremities, Pangong Lake and Karakoram Pass, were well defined, but the Aksai Chin area in between lay undefined.

W. H. Johnson, a civil servant with the Survey of India, proposed the "Johnson Line" in 1865, which put Aksai Chin in Kashmir. Johnson presented this line to the Maharaja of Kashmir, who then claimed the 18,000 square kilometres contained within. Johnson's work was severely criticized as inaccurate. His boundary line was described as "patently absurd", and extending further north than the Indian claim. Johnson was reprimanded by the British Government for crossing into Khotan without permission and resigned from the Survey. According to Francis Younghusband, who explored the region in the late 1880s, there was only an abandoned fort and not one inhabited house at Shahidulla when he was there - it was just a convenient staging post for the nomadic Kirghiz. The abandoned fort had apparently been built a few years earlier by the Kashmiris. In 1878 the Chinese had reconquered Xinjiang, and by 1890 they already had Shahidulla before the issue was decided. By 1892, China had erected boundary markers at Karakoram

Pass. In 1893, Hung Ta-chen, a senior Chinese official at Kashgar, handed a map of the boundary proposed by China to George Macartney, the British consul-general at Kashgar. This boundary placed the Lingzi Tang plains, which are south of the Laktsang range, in India, and Aksai Chin proper, which is north of the Laktsang range, in China. Macartney agreed with the proposal and forwarded it to the British Indian government. The British presented this line, known as the Macartney-MacDonald line, to the Chinese in 1899 in a note by Sir Claude MacDonald. In 1911 the Xinhai Revolution resulted in power shifts in China, and by the end of World War I, the British officially used the Johnson Line. However they took no steps to establish outposts or assert actual control on the ground. According to Neville Maxwell, the British had used as many as 11 different boundary lines in the region, as their claims shifted with the political situation. From 1917 to 1933, the "Postal Atlas of China", published by the Government of China in Peking had shown the boundary in Aksai Chin as per the Johnson line, which runs along the Kunlun mountains. Upon independence in 1947, the government of India used the Johnson Line as the basis for its official boundary in the west, which included the Aksai Chin.

On 1 July 1954, India's first Prime Minister Jawaharlal Nehru definitively stated the Indian position, claiming that Aksai Chin had been part of the Indian Ladakh region for centuries, and that the border (as defined by the Johnson Line) was non-negotiable. According to George N. Patterson, when the Indian government finally produced a report detailing the alleged proof of India's claims to the disputed area, "the quality of the Indian evidence was very poor, including some very dubious sources indeed". The traditional and customary basis for the border was also presented by the Indian side in the meetings between officials of the governments in 1960.

In 1956–57, China constructed a road through Aksai Chin, connecting Xinjiang and Tibet, which ran south of the Johnson Line in many places. Aksai Chin was easily accessible to the Chinese, but access from India, which meant negotiating the Karakoram mountains, was much more difficult. The road came on Chinese maps published in 1958.

THE PUZZLE OF AKSAI CHIN

In the western sector of the China-India border, the dispute has centred on the Aksai Chin area. The British left Aksai Chin area as "undefined" at the time of their transfer of power in 1947.nehru himself once stated that " it is a matter of argument as to what art of it (Aksai Chin) belongs to us and what part of it belongs to somebody else.... The point is, there has never been any delimitation there in that area and it has been a challenged area." Before the British left India, the British-Indian government had shown no boundary at all in that area on its official maps. In Volume XII of Aichison'd Treaties published in 1931, it was stated that"The northern as well as the eastern boundary of the Kashmir state is still undefined." The Survey of India maps published in the 1900s and 1930s did not indicate any boundary alignment or show any colour difference in this are, and wide spaces between Kashmir and Xinjiang and between Kashmir and Tibet were shown blank. Louis Dane, Indian Foreign Secretary, stated clearly in a letter to the Indian office that Aksai Chin was I Chinese Xinjiag. The neighbourhood of the Lanak Pass at the head of the Changchenmo valley was supposed to be the most northerly boundary point on the Kashmir-Tibet border.

In 1945, guided by Olaf Caroe, then foreign secretary of India, on new Survey of India maps the Aksai Chin area began to be shown by a colour-wash with the words "Boundary Undefined" marked on it. In 1947, the Indian Army in its "top secret" m submitted to the British Cabinet Mission accepted the Karakoram range as the northern boundary of India in the western sector.

However, after the signing of the trade agreement concerning Tibet in 1954, following Nehru's instructions, new Survey of India maps began to show an international boundary in the western sector running along the crest of the Kunlun range, which for the first time placed the whole Aksai Chin area within the Indian territory. According to Sir H.A.F. Rumbold, an official in the Indian Office, the Simon Commission wished to include a map of India in Volume I of their report in 1929. Rumbold found nothing in the India office to justify the line on the Kunlun range shown on some maps. The Commission accordingly adopted a line roughly along the crest of the Karakoram range, excluding the Aksai Chin area. Nehru, even on August 28, 1959, stated in the Lok Sabha that "This was the boundary of the old Kashmir state with Tibet and Chinese Turkestan. Nobody had marked it."

On the other hand, Chinese maps have shown the Karakoram range as its boundary in the western sector at least since the 1920s. There was no evidence that the British-Indian authorities ever disputed this with the Chinese government before they left India in 1947. The widely accepted modern concept of boundary marking involes three steps: delimitation, delineation and demarcation. Delimitation involves defining the boundary in written terms through treaties and agreements. Delineation involves sketching the boundary in maps through joint boundary surveys. Demarcation involves marking the boundary line on the ground through pillars, chains and other markers.

Reviewing the historic facts for the entire China-India border, such a China-India boundary has never existed, though each side has made its own territorial claims. Historical facts have also showed that, in the old days, wide desolate tracts in the remote high mountains between the two countries were physically inaccessible. Therefore, the China-India border dispute has been the dispute on the "zone" rather than the " line" in the eastern and western sectors. Mutual understanding and recognition of such historical evolution of the China-India border should become the starting point for the future border deliberations.

INDIA-CHINA (AKSAI CHIN AND ARUNACHAL PRADESH)

In the 1962 Sino-Indian War, China seized a Switzerland-sized area, Aksai Chin (Aksayqin), and overran Arunachal Pradesh (an Indian state the size of Austria). There are also other, smaller pockets of disputed area. The PRC withdrew from virtually all of Arunachal Pradesh to the Line of Actual Control (LAC), which approximates the McMahon Line that is found in a 1914 agreement initialed by British, Tibetan, and Chinese representatives. Chinese and Indian forces clashed in the Sumdorong Chu valley of Arunachal Pradesh in 1986-87. Relations began to thaw in 1988.

On 7 September 1993, China and India signed an accord to reduce tensions along their border and to respect the LAC. During November 1996, China and India agreed to delimit the LAC and institute confidence-building measures (CBMs) along the frontier. The agreement pledged nonaggression, prior notification of large troop movements, a 10-km no-fly zone for combat aircraft, and exchange of maps to resolve disagreements about the precise location of the LAC. In August 1997 the sides ratified the CBM agreement. There seems to have been little substantive progress, except for a series of high-level visits. The most recent, on 27 April, was the first visit by a PRC Chief of Staff to India. However, two weeks before the visit the new Indian Defence Minister, George Fernandes, accused the PRC of repeated violations of Indian territory, including the construction of a helipad on "Indian" territory in the disputed zone, and of aiding Pakistan's nuclear and missile programs. On 3 May he publicly labelled China as India's number one threat and alleged that the PRC was stockpiling nuclear weapons in Tibet, expanding naval activity off the Burmese coast, and conducting surveillance against India from Burma's Coco Islands. After the visit of General Fu Quanyou and PRC protests, Fernandes said that his characterization of China as India's principal threat was a personal view, but he went on to pledge that the number of Indian troops along the frontier with China would not be reduced. Such a statement calls into question part of the agreed CBMs. (To view a map of this area click here.) China and India have yet to address their fundamental and very large land boundary disputes. Moreover, their bilateral relations are complicated by the issues of

Tibet (Xizang), Sikkim, and Kashmir. India plays host to the Dalai Lama and a large number of Tibetan refugees. They present an implicit threat to Chinese control of Tibet, which it invaded in 1950. On its maps, the PRC continues to portray Sikkim, which was absorbed by India in 1974, as an independent country. In addition to the Aksai Chin, China and India dispute another section of Kashmir (the area west of Aksai Chin).

INDIA-CHINA BORDER AGREEMENT: MUCH ADO ABOUT NOTHING

Beijing successfully engineered signing a border defense cooperation agreement (BDCA) with India on October 23, 2013, in what seems to be a Chinese plot to subvert the debate surrounding its recent strategic offensive behavior. While the agreement seems to have set a positive tone to future talks between New Delhi and Beijing, it does not translate into any substantial shift in the Chinese policy. The latest mechanism is a mere token agreement that has not resulted in tangible progress on the ground.

India and China display a peculiar case of "constrained cooperation," in which the convergence of their economic interests tends to mask their prevailing strategic differences. Yet these divergences, of which the territorial and boundary dispute is foremost, still hold the potential of upstaging ties at any point.

This was demonstrated in April 2013, when a platoon-strength contingent of the Chinese People's Liberation Army (PLA) intruded deep inside the Depsang Plateau in eastern Ladakh, a region of Jammu and Kashmir that shares a border with China. The troops pitched tents in Indian-claimed territory, violating earlier confidence-building measures and pushing India into a diplomatic and military tizzy.

What perhaps is most distressing is that China's Depsang offensive happened despite numerous meetings of the India-China Joint Working Group and four confidence-building agreements, signed in 1993, 1996, 2005, and 2012. In addition to the Depsang occurrence, border guards of the PLA have repeatedly intruded into the eastern sector of Arunachal Pradesh, a state in northeast India, and the northern Ladakh sector.

The writing on the wall following the Depsang incident was clear. China holds the political and military will and capability to covertly notch up tensions in the Himalayas with India, at any time and place of its choosing.

Given that China and India have not mutually agreed upon a Line of Actual Control (LAC), sporadic incidents of border transgressions increasingly appear to be becoming a covert Chinese strategy of asserting its claims in

India's western sector, especially in northeastern Ladakh and in Arunachal Pradesh in the eastern sector. The LAC is not physically demarcated on the ground or in military maps, and there is continuing reluctance and official refusals by China to show its version of the LAC to India-thus pointing towards a larger ploy of progressively building up a case for its claims in eastern Ladakh and Arunachal Pradesh.

China and India reiterated in the latest BDCA that neither side would use its military capability against the other. But in the event of China launching another underhanded operation in Arunachal Pradesh or the Ladakh sector, what picture would emerge?

Following the Depsang incident, India announced that both sides would pull back troops to their earlier positions along the LAC. But China haggled with India, agreeing to withdraw its troops from Indian territory provided that New Delhi tear down a line of defensive fortification in an area called Chumar. China also managed to get India to restrict its forward patrols in the area and unflinchingly negotiated for a BDCA. At this stage, India cannot afford to give in to further Chinese demands, such as suspending infrastructure development in its own territory near the LAC. Has China ever offered an explanation for the blizzard ininfrastructure construction it is carrying out in the Tibet Autonomous Region adjoining India?

China's cross-frontier incursions undermine the spirit of every confidence-building measure relating to the border areas New Delhi and Beijing have undertaken. The Depsang incident of 2013 casts an ominous shadow on Chinese intentions with respect to the border issue and sweeps away the spirit of the prior border-peace arrangements. In terms of making tangible progress toward a breakthrough on the larger question of border resolution, India and China have failed abjectly.

A Toothless Agreement

It appears that China has successfully managed to call the shots in the drafting of the BDCA by skirting the primary issue of resolving the boundary dispute. There are no lucid answers as to how exactly the BDCA stands apart from the other confidence-building measures that India already shares with China vis-à-vis the border question. And in many respects, the BDCA is loaded in China's favor.

For example, the BDCA's Article II stipulates that the two countries should share strategic information, but it does not elaborate on what specifically constitutes "information about military exercises, aircraft, demolition operations and unmarked mines." It is doubtful that China will be transparent enough to provide information about its military and cargo flights to forward landing strips near the borders. Article II also appears to be drafted so as to provide a cover for the Chinese Air Force in "locating aerial vehicles that may have crossed or are possibly in the process of crossing the line of actual control" in the border areas - suggesting China may be upping the ante and securing the possibility of launching an air offensive in these areas.

Overall, the BDCA remains a commitment-deficient agreement. It contains no binding assurance that the Indian and Chinese military headquarters will set up a hotline, stating that the two sides "may consider" the move. Article VI states that there would be "no tailing" of each other's patrols in disputed forward areas. However, Indian border guards placed to check and prevent such incursions have been met with an antagonistic Chinese PLA.

Article III elaborates the process through which the BDCA shall be implemented through meetings between border personnel, military officers, and other departments and groups. There is nothing novel in these announcements; they have been in place for many years.

A Problem "Left over from History"

The banality of the text of the latest border defense cooperation agreement is proof that India is losing to China in terms of strategic leverage. With recent confidence-building measures only seeking to "consult" and "coordinate" border affairs, the ability of these mechanisms to achieve any sort of breakthrough to the interminable territorial and boundary dispute between China and India appears increasingly doubtful.

Instead, China has chosen to use the BDCA as a platform which provides it official cover to bide its time and strike when the Chinese political and military leadership see a window of vulnerability. Chinese politico-military history contains many references to dealing with obdurate problems "left over from history" by patiently waiting to resolve them "once conditions are ripe," in the words of the China's first premier, Zhou Enlai. Sun Tzu, the ancient Chinese military strategist, famously stated, "Engage people with what they expect... It settles them into predictable patterns of response, while you wait for the extraordinary moment — that which they cannot anticipate."

Demonstrating politico-military belligerence and stealth on various fronts appears to have become a defining feature of Chinese strategy, be it the protracted standoffs with India over the border, with Japan over the Senkaku Islands, or with the Philippines over the Scarborough Shoal. China's creation of the East China Sea Air Defense Identification Zone byon November 23 is testament to Chinese attempts at force projection that provides a stage for the long-term Chinese strategy of chipping away at contested claims with India. Beijing appears intent at keeping the border dispute alive as a tactical pressure point against India. China seems to be awaiting an opportune moment in which the existing military asymmetry with India will widen and Beijing will be positioned to bring the dispute to a close on its own terms.

ARUNACHAL PRADESH'S BORDER ROADS

The state of Arunachal Pradesh in India's northeastern frontier has been appearing quite regularly in the Indian national security and strategic imagination for some years now. Strident Chinese territorial claims, particularly over the Tawang hill tract, have managed to unsettle New Delhi and the Indian strategic community. Against this backdrop and given that Arunachal is the largest state in India's northeastern region in terms of territory, it becomes important to assess the border roads infrastructure and connectivity in this strategically-crucial frontier state.

The state was a theatre in the 1962 Sino-Indian war, in which India had faced major losses and had to fight in extremely unprepared conditions, with almost no road connectivity. While Indian forces did manage to resist strongly at several border points the fall of Tawang and Bomdi La towns were without resistance as there was no proper supply and road infrastructure to maintain Indian army positions. Air dropped supplies sometimes, fell into the hands of the Chinese who had occupied Tawang. This was 50 years ago but the road infrastructure and connectivity in Arunachal Pradesh still leaves a lot to be desired in terms of strategic preparedness for the Indian Army and for the general economic development of the state.

The need to construct proper roads in Arunachal Pradesh dawned on the Indian government only after it suffered in the war against the Chinese, and a skeletal network of roads was built subsequently in this difficult terrain mostly aimed at maintaining military posts and supplies in various strategic parts of the state.

This was the first layer of work done on roads in the state, and only fed specific sectors such as Bhalukpung-Bomdi-La-Tawang, Itanagar-Ziro-Along-Mechuka, and the eastern sector which included a maze of roads with no inter-connectivity. The Assam government has four-laned the Stilwell Road in its territory but on the Arunachal side, the Road remains perennially under construction.

Internal connectivity within Arunachal Pradesh remains one of the pressing problems which need urgent attention-to travel to five different towns in Arunachal Pradesh, one has to cross back into Assam as many times. Air dropping of essential civil and military supplies in remote areas of Arunachal Pradesh is the prevailing norm and a number of AN-32 transport aircraft are used on a daily basis from the Guwahati, Jorhat and Dibrugarh supply bases in Assam. The road that leads to the central part of Arunachal Pradesh, particularly to its capital Itanagar, falls mostly in Assam and has been over the years ill-maintained and is prone to annual floods. The Border Roads Organisation which is in charge of maintaining these crucial roads have done a decent job, keeping in mind the difficult terrain, high rainfall and frequent landslides which sometimes sweep entire stretches of roads away, but overall, the effort is woefully inadequate..

The Trans-Arunachal Highway project which was announced by Prime Minister Manmohan Singh in 2008, has failed to pick up pace with preliminary feasibility studies still being conducted in many parts of the state. The Highway project comes very late, as the pressure on the existing road infrastructure has already increased manifold given the burden of civil supplies as also the massive convoys of army supplies and movement which has become necessary due to the current policy of trying to match Chinese army mobilization across the border.

The need for a second network of border roads in Arunachal Pradesh is almost 10-15 years late, and will certainly take another 10-15 years, if not more, to come to fruition.

It has been noted that in many parts of Northeast India, the second layer of road connectivity and infrastructure development has begun only when the pressure on the current infrastructure has become enormously high, often compounding implementation woes; the consistent and painful delays in project implementation, can be attributed to a clear policy planning failure on the part of both the central and state governments.

Similarly, the Bogibeel project for a bridge over the river Brahmaputra in Dibrugarh in Assam, was mooted more than a decade back, but saw work begin only just some years ago, and is now estimated to be completed only in the year 2030. This bridge has the potential to connect the middle and eastern parts of Arunachal Pradesh and save on traveling time, as these areas are now dependent on the Kaliabhoomoora Bridge across the Brahmaputra in Tezpur.

The central government still seems to be sleeping on major bottlenecks in terms of road infrastructure and connectivity as is evident in various parts of Northeast India.

Major road expansion work is overdue in critical stretches such as Numaligarh-Kohima-Imphal and Guwahati-Shillong-Silchar-Aizawl, which has resulted in clogging the streets of major state capitals like Kohima, Shillong and Aizawl. The Trans-Asian Highway too, has made little progress. There needs to be greater urgency in policy implementation in order to serve the needs of not just Arunachal but the Northeast and the nation as a whole in terms of economic development and strategic military preparedness.

China's claims on Arunachal absurd: Chief minister Dorjee Khandu

The Chief Minister of Arunachal Pradesh Dorjee Khandu, termed China's claims to Arunachal Pradesh as its territory as "simply absurd". "I have been telling repeatedly that Arunachal Pradesh is an integral part of India and that Chinese claims are simply absurd.

"We are the only state in the northeast where Hindi is the link language among various tribes who speak different dialects," Khandu said after his swearing in. "Now, we are all set to welcome the Dalai Lama who is visiting the state from November 8."

He also said his government's topmost priority would be to work for the overall economic uplift of the state, especially focusing on developing infrastructure and boosting education and health sectors. "Now, after the people have given us a thumping victory in the elections, we need to work even harder to achieve accelerated pace of development and growth in the state," Khandu said.

"Social sectors, health, education, roads and infrastructure are the areas that we are going to give maximum thrust and focus to this time."

PM, Wen talk Peace, not Dalai

PM Manmohan Singh discussed the border issue with his Chinese counterpart Wen Jiabao in Thailand's resort town of Hua Hin, with both leaders stressing the need to narrow differences and preserve the peace. Both Prime Ministers refrained from specific discussion of the discord over Arunachal Pradesh and the Dalai Lama' visit to the state, both of which recently caused tension in ties. But they agreed it was imperative maintain peace along the disputed border area.

Officials accompanying the Prime Minister told the media that the two sides agreed to build further "trust and understanding". During the meeting, Wen insisted China wanted a ''steady and healthy'' relationship with India. New Delhi maintained that both leaders agreed not to allow differences to impede ''functional cooperation''.

Both leaders had a ''productive meeting'' that lasted nearly an hour on the sidelines of the ASEAN and East Asia summit. "We want to have a healthy and steady relationship with India. I hope we can use this opportunity to exchange our views on all related issues,'' said Wen. However, the contentious issue of the Dalai Lama's proposed visit to Arunachal Pradesh remains unaddressed, prompting analysts in India to predict the Wen-Singh meeting will not mean a softening of Beijing's tough stance toward New Delhi.

"In June, for example, no sooner than Hu Jintao and Manmohan Singh had appeared hand-in-hand at the first-ever BRIC summit, hosted by Russia, than the Chinese state-controlled media ran fresh vituperative attacks against India," said strategic affairs analyst Brahma Chellaney. "India, in this decade, had hyped the outcome of every bilateral summit meeting with China to such an extent that today it is staring at the costs of such ritualized happy talk. In that light, a cautious appraisal of the Wen-Singh meeting is warranted," Chellaney added. Foreign ministry officials said Wen recalled the countries jointly establishing the Strategic and Cooperative Partnership for Peace and Prosperity in 2005.

Day before PM-Wen meet, Rao says no Curbs on Dalai

A day before the crucial meeting between PM Manmohan Singh and his Chinese counterpart Wen Jiabao in Thailand, India said it shares a "complex relationship" with China marked by outstanding issues, all of which are likely to figure in the discussion between the two leaders on Saturday. Singh is expected to meet Wen on the sidelines of the ongoing East Asia and ASEAN summit. The meeting was hurriedly arranged after Wen expressed his intention to meet Singh last week.

"It is a relationship which has developed in many areas. It is also a complex relationship and there are outstanding issues between the two. The meeting provides an opportunity to address all such issues," said foreign secretary Nirupama Rao. Tibetan leader Dalai Lama's scheduled visit to Arunachal Pradesh has led to angry exchanges between the two countries, but Rao on Friday again reiterated that Dalai Lama was free to visit any part of the country. "We are against any political activity by Tibetans in our country. We regard Dalai Lama as a respected, spiritual figure and, as we have said earlier, he is free to visit any place in the country," said Rao. She admitted that Dalai Lama had expressed an interest in visiting the state which China claims as its own even though she added that she wasn't aware of it anymore.

Despite Rao's earlier statement to that effect, the Chinese foreign ministry on Tuesday had again issued a statement saying that it was firmly opposed to the Tibetan leader's visit to "so-called Arunachal Pradesh". The two sides, however, will have another opportunity to calm things down when their foreign ministers, S M Krishna and Yang Jiechi, meet next week in Bangalore during the ninth trilateral meeting of foreign ministers from India, China and Russia. Meanwhile, Singh said before his departure to Thailand that he would discuss with ASEAN leaders new initiatives to accelerate the process of engagement in areas such as greater economic integration, people-to-people contacts, agriculture, human resource development, education, science and technology and information and communications technology.

PM Snubs China, says Dalai Lama will visit Arunachal Pradesh

Despite China's strong objections, India has not shown any inclination to block the proposed visit of Dalai Lama to Tawang in Arunachal Pradesh. The Prime Minister, Dr Manmohan Singh, on Sunday also described the border dispute between the two countries as "complex." Dr Singh, during the gala dinner on Saturday night, reiterated the country's position that the exiled spiritual leader, "Dalai Lama is an honoured guest of India and a religious leader." Though Dr Singh and his Chinese counterpart, Mr ven Jiabao, apparently did not discuss the Dalai Lama's travel plans, sources disclosed that it was clearly indicated that the New Delhi adhered to the stand that the Tibetan leader was free to travel wherever he wished to. Despite the simmering differences, both the Prime Ministers agreed to strengthen efforts to build "political trust and understanding."

Asked whether Mr Wen sought to know specifically about the Dalai Lama's plans, the Prime Minister said that he reminded that the Dalai Lama was an honoured guest and "we do not allow him to indulge in political activities." The Prime Minister also reminded his Chinese counterpart that at the time of the Beijing Olympics last year, India took "resolute action against the Tibetan refugees, when there were reports that some of them disrupt the process." Asked whether the Dalai Lama was visiting Tawang on November 8, the Prime Minister replied: "I am not aware of the Dalai Lama's plan. But I have explained our position." Much to the chagrin of China, the Dalai Lama plans to make a week-long visit to Arunachal Pradesh in the first week of November.

If the bilateral meet between the two premiers veered around soft words and congratulations, it was at the last night's dinner, the contentious issues became part of their menu. Territorial disputes, Chinese incursions, trans-border river disputes and other differences, which" cannot be wished away" were all discussed across the table. "We had a frank exchange of views during the gala dinner. We discussed all the issues and agreed that a mechanism for bilateral cooperation should be resolved amicably in the spirit of strategic and cooperative partnership." On a significant note, the Prime Minister observed, "we both agreed that there is the complex boundary question, which cannot be wished away."

Reiterating that boundary question "is a complex question, " the Prime Minister said that "pending the resolution of the boundary question, we both have an obligation to maintain peace and tranquillity along the border." Both India and China agreed that views on all the relevant issues would be exchanged during the Chinese foreign minister's visit to India on October 27. The other contentious issue of Beijing building a dam on the Brahmaputra was also raised, as the two premiers sat side by side. "I did raise this issue with Premier Wen Jiabao yesterday," the Prime Minister said. "I conveyed to him that cooperation in the area of trans-border rivers is of mutual benefit." Dr Singh then informed that Premier Wen said that "keeping in view the overall friendly relations and humanitarian aspects, the Chinese side has been providing hydrological data during the flood season." The Chinese premier also said that relevant "discussions on transborder river issues could be held through the expert level mechanism that we have constituted."

China's Ambassador to India Zhang Yang met officials of the Ministry of External Affairs (MEA) shortly after his government expressed "strong" dissastisfaction over Prime Minister Manmohan Singh's visit to Arunachal Pradesh during electioneering. There was no word about what Yang had discussed with the MEA officials. Earlier, Chinese Foreign Ministry spokesman Ma Zhaoxu had said: "We demand the Indian side address China's serious concerns and not trigger disturbance in the disputed region so as to facilitate the healthy development of China-India relations."

"China is strongly dissatisfied with the visit to the disputed region by the Indian leader disregarding China's serious concerns," Mas added in a statement posted on the ministry's website. He noted that China and India had "never officially settled" demarcation of their border, and China's stance on the eastern section of the China-India border was "consistent and clear-cut". The Indian Government has all along indicated that Arunachal Pradesh is an integral part of India and that the people of that state have a democratic right to elect a government of their choice.

Singh had toured and addressed an election rally in Arunachal Pradesh on October 3. Recently, China had blocked a part of a loan to India from the Asian Development Bank (ADB) for developmental projects in Arunachal Pradesh. China also protested a visit to the state last month by exiled Tibetan leader the Dalai Lama. India says China is illegally occupying 43,180 sq kms of Jammu and Kashmir. On the other hand, China accuses India of possessing some 90,000 sq km of Chinese territory, mostly in Arunachal Pradesh.

Singh had earlier visited Arunachal Pradesh on January 31 and February 1 and had then referred to it as "Our land of the rising sun" at a public rally, which was objected to by China. China apparently saw it as India's assertion of its claim on Arunachal, which it claims is a "disputed territory".

India Rejects China's Protest against PM's Arunachal Visit

India rejected China's protest against Prime Minister Manmohan Singh's visit to Arunachal Pradesh, whose ownership is disputed by Beijing, with Finance Minister Pranab Mukherjee describing it as "nothing new" and the government expressing "disappointment". "It is nothing new. China had objected earlier to my visit to Tawang when I was the foreign minister," Mukherjee told reporters on the sidelines of an India-Bangladesh dialogue in New Delhi.

Earlier in the day, external affairs ministry spokesman Vishnu Prakash said: "We express our disappointment and concern over the statement made by the Chinese ministry of foreign affairs since this does not help the process of ongoing negotiations on the boundary question." He said Arunachal Pradesh, which borders Tibet, was an "integral and inalienable part of India" and its people are "proud participants in the mainstream of India's vibrant democracy". He said China was "well aware of this position" of the Indian government. External Affairs Minister S M Krishna added: "I have said it in parliament that Arunachal Pradesh is an integral part of India. We rest it at that."

Their comments followed a Chinese foreign ministry statement that Beijing "is strongly dissatisfied with the visit to the disputed region by the Indian leader disregarding China's serious concerns". "We demand the Indian side address China's serious concerns and not trigger disturbance in the disputed region so as to facilitate the healthy development of China-India relations," spokesman Ma Zhaoxu said in Beijing. Ma said China and India had never officially settled the demarcation of their border, and China's stance on the eastern section of the China-India border was consistent and clear-cut. Beijing in 2003 gave up its territorial claim over India's Sikkim state but maintains that nearly all of Arunachal Pradesh belongs to it. The mountainous state of Arunachal shares a 1,030 km unfenced border with China.

Also Tuesday, China's ambassador to India, Zhang Yan, called on the Indian foreign ministry to convey his government's stand on the prime minister's visit to Arunachal Pradesh. The Chinese statement, however, made no reference by name to Manmohan Singh, who visited Arunachal Pradesh October 3 to campaign for the Congress in assembly elections that took place in the state Tuesday.

At the same time, Prakash said that India was "committed to resolving outstanding differences with China in a fair, reasonable and mutually acceptable manner, while ensuring that such differences are not allowed to affect the positive development of bilateral relations". "We hope that the Chinese side will similarly abide by this understanding." An Indian lawmaker also slammed

Beijing for criticizing Manmohan Singh's visit to Arunachal Pradesh. "It is simply blasphemous on the part of China to oppose or express dissatisfaction over the visit of our prime minister to Arunachal Pradesh," Takam Sanjay, a ruling Congress MP in the Lok Sabha from Arunachal Pradesh said.

China 'Strongly' Protests PM's Visit to Arunachal!

Ten days after the event, China expressed "strong" dissatisfaction over Prime Minister Manmohan Singh's visit to Arunachal Pradesh during electioneering. "We demand the Indian side address China's serious concerns and not trigger disturbance in the disputed region so as to facilitate the healthy development of China-India relations," Chinese Foreign Ministry spokesman Ma Zhaoxu said.

"China is strongly dissatisfied with the visit to the disputed region by the Indian leader disregarding China's serious concerns," Mas said in a statement posted on the ministry's website. He noted that China and India had "never officially settled" demarcation of their border, and China's stance on the eastern section of the China-India border was "consistent and clear-cut". Singh had toured and addressed an election rally in Arunachal Pradesh on October 3. Recently, China had blocked part of a loan to India from the Asian Development Bank (ADB) for developmental projects in Arunachal Pradesh. China also protested a visit to the state last month by exiled Tibetan leader the Dalai Lama.

India says China is illegally occupying 43,180 sq kms of Jammu and Kashmir. On the other hand, China accuses India of possessing some 90,000 sq km of Chinese territory, mostly in Arunachal Pradesh. "Arunachal Pradesh is an integral part of India. We rest at that. Regardless of what others have to say, it is Government of India's position that Arunachal Pradesh is an integral part of India. Period," Krishna said. The External Affairs Ministry also issued a statement expressing disappointment and concern over Chinese objection to Manmohan Singh's visit to Arunachal Pradesh.

Beijing Queers Pitch ahead of Singh-Jiabao Meet

India's attempts to discern its way through the complexities of China's apparent carrot-and-stick diplomacy is not bearing fruit. While on one hand, as official sources revealed, the two sides worked together to arrange a meeting between PM Manmohan Singh and his Chinese counterpart Wen Jiabao during the upcoming East Asia Summit in Bangkok, Beijing queered the pitch for such a meeting by stating again that it was "firmly opposed" to Tibetan leader Dalai Lama's visit to Arunachal Pradesh.

Wen Jiabao had himself expressed a desire to meet Singh during the East Asia Summit starting later this week when he recently met petroleum minister

Murli Deora during an SCO meet in China. Immediately after this, India worked hard to schedule a meeting between the two leaders along the sidelines of the summit and, as things stand now, the meeting seems a certainty. Wen Jiabao offered to meet Singh immediately after Beijing lodged a protest against Singh's visit to Arunachal. Perhaps under the impression that he made the offer in a genuinely damage-control mode, the Indian side worked overtime with the Chinese to ensure the meeting did take place. However, China's seemingly recalcitrant stand on "so-called Arunachal Pradesh" continues to mar any attempt to build more confidence between the two nations. "China's position on so-called Arunachal Pradesh is consistent and clear and we firmly oppose the Dalai Lama's visit to the region. We believe that this further exposes the Dalai Lama clique's anti-China and separatist nature," Chinese foreign ministry spokesman Ma Zhaoxu said, adding that China's stance on Arunachal Pradesh was consistent. For India, the remark is a real dampner also because it shows scant regard for the fact that foreign secretary Nirupama Rao had categorically stated that India looked upon Dalai Lama as a religious leader and that he was free to go anywhere in the country. MEA sources reacted on Tuesday by stating that the latest Chinese outburst on Arunachal was totally uncalled for as India has already made its position clear. "India has made its position amply clear. The only restriction from our side is that no Tibetan should carry out any anti-China activity from Indian soil. As far as Dalai Lama is concerned, there is no restriction on him visiting any part of the country".

China Accuses India of Provocation

As the time approaches for the proposed visit of His Holiness the Dalai Lama to Tawang in Arunachal Pradesh next month to declare open a hospital built with contributions from the Tibetan exile community, China has stepped up its rhetoric against India. The recent visit of Prime Minister Manmohan Singh to Arunachal Pradesh to canvass for the candidates of his party in the just concluded elections to the State Assembly of Arunachal Pradesh on October 12 has been used as a pretext for the renewed criticism of the Indian policy on Arunachal Pradesh. Dr. Manmohan Singh's visit to Arunachal Pradesh has been projected as his visit to the so-called Southern Tibet.

China never fails to bring on record its protests and concerns over the visits of Indian leaders to Arunachal Pradesh for whatever purpose. The fact that it has done so after the recent electoral visit of Dr. Manmohan Singh should not, therefore, have been a matter of surprise and undue concern. What is disturbing is the kind of language used by a spokesperson of the Chinese Foreign Office in commenting on the visit and the even stronger language used by the "Global Times", in an editorial on the subject on October 14, 2009. The "Global Times" is a sister publication of the Party-controlled "People's Daily".

The fresh campaign against India on the subject was triggered off by the comments of a spokesperson of the Chinese Foreign Ministry. Ma Zhaoxu, the spokesperson, was quoted by the "Global Times" as saying on October 13 that China was "seriously dissatisfied" by the visit of the Indian Prime Minister, who was accused of "ignoring China's concerns by visiting southern Tibet". The "Global Times" quoted the spokesperson as saying further as follows: "China and India have not reached any formal agreement on the border issue. We demand that the Indian side pay attention to the serious and just concerns of the Chinese side and not provoke incidents in the disputed region, in order to facilitate the healthy development of China-Indian relations."

There has been a difference in the translation into English of the spokesperson's remarks by the BBC and the "Global Times". While the BBC quoted the spokesperson as telling India "not to trigger disturbances in the disputed region", the "Global Times" spoke of the spokesperson telling India "not to not provoke incidents in the disputed region."

The editorial of the "Global Times" titled "Indian PM's visit a provocative move" described the Indian Prime Minister's visit as a "provocative and dangerous move" and alleged that the visit was designed to put the area under India's de facto administration. It accuses India of encouraging the "immigration of more than one million Indians to the region" and warns: "India, however, will make a fatal error if it mistakes China's approach for weakness. The Chinese government and public regard territorial integrity as a core national interest, one that must be defended with every means......The disputed border area is of strategic importance, and hence, India's recent moves – including Singh's trip and approving past visits to the region by the Dalai Lama – send the wrong signal. That could have dangerous consequences."

The text of the editorial is annexed. The conventional wisdom is that since any military confrontation could affect China's economic development and its aspirations of rising as a major power on par with the US, Beijing will restrict itself to angry rhetoric and will not indulge in any ground action in the Arunachal Pradesh area. This wisdom has some validity, but overlooks the fact that China is feeling increasingly insecure in its peripheral areas because of the recent violent uprisings by the Tibetans last year and the Uighurs this year. Its increasing nervousness and feelings of insecurity in its border areas could lead to irrational and unpredictable reflexes vis-a-vis the Arunachal Pradesh issue.

We should avoid countering China's renewed rhetoric with our own rhetoric. While maintaining our cool, we should press ahead with the construction of the infrastructure in the Arunachal Pradesh area and strengthening our defensive capabilities there without talking about them from the roof-top. We should not advise His Holiness not to visit Tawang. When he visits Tawang, we should pay close attention to his personal security. The period before and after the visit of His Holiness to Tawang should call for extra vigilance from our side. China may not indulge in any ground action till the visit of President Barack Obama to China next month is over. What it might do after Obama's visit is a matter which needs close monitoring.

ARUNACHAL PRADESH TERRITORIAL DISPUTE BETWEEN INDIA AND CHINA

International law never supports a country or a state which attempts to plunder the territory from other countries or states by threatening or warfare. Article 2 of The UN Charter clearly defines that "all Members shall refrain in their international relations from the threat or use of force against the territorial integrity or political independence of any state" (Reynolds 2004.) It is so-called a territorial dispute, which is "a disagreement over the possession or control of land between two or more countries" ("Territorial Dispute.") What leads the territorial dispute is not only relevant to the possession or control of natural resources such as oil, coals, fertile land or rivers, but also culture and religion. In addition, it has been said that "in many cases territorial disputes result from vague and unclear language in a treaty that set up the original boundary" ("Territorial Dispute".) Consequently, many territorial disputes possibly generate some conflicts between countries, and even worse, they can become a primary cause of wars and/or terrorism.

A long time ago, before the territorial dispute between China and India emerged in Arunachal Pradesh, the first ancestors of the tribal groups migrated from Tibet during pre-historic period. Even though ancestors were there, little is known about the history of Arunachal Pradesh. Recorded history is only available in the Ahom chronicles from the sixteenth century: the British Christened, originally known as northeast Frontiers Agency (NEFA,) took administrative control of Arunachal Pradesh and it remained under this rule until 1948. Arunachal Pradesh is northeast India's largest and remotest state, as it has railways and air services connecting only three of its town. Natives in Arunachal Pradesh used to eat "their food in uncooked condition ignorant about the discovery of fire" (WebDigitech.) They were really isolated and not aware of the development and revolution which was occurring in this globalized world. The major cause of China-India territorial dispute, which deprived peace from Arunachal Pradesh, is from immediately after Chinese Revolution in 1911. At that time, Qing Dynasty, the last Chinese Dynasty, fell and the Emperor of Qing Dynasty resigned. As a result, China, Tibet and Mongolia became equal and separate countries. In these three countries, Tibet and Mongol tried to be approved internationally as independent states, and undertook to international society. However, on the other hand, Han Chinese Republicans started small war to subjugate reins of government of Tibet and Mongol. Therefore, they could not be independent states at that time.

In 1912-13, the British Raj made agreements with tribal leaders that defined the area that was known as NEFA. British rule could have very small impact on the isolated, self-sufficient in terms of economy and militarily uncontrollable tribal peoples. In order to arrange this conflict, in 1913 and 1914, the British administrator, Sir Henry McMahon, drew up the 550-mile McMahon Line as the border between India and China in Shimla, during a conference which also discussed the Tibetan and Chinese borders ("McMahon Line.") This conference is called Shimla Conference. Regardless of this reconciliation, the McMahon Line was rejected by the Chinese government in 1947 ("Arunachal Pradesh.")

Following this dispute, the Chinese troops crossed the McMahon Line on the August 26th, 1959 ("Arunachal Pradesh.") They abandoned this in 1961, but in October 1962 crossed the line once again with force ("McMahon Line.") As a result, Sino-Indian War broke out. The Chinese extended their frontier as they intruded deeper and deeper. However, this war did not go on for a long time. In 1963, the Chinese agreed to withdraw back to the McMahon Line, and also returned Indian prisoners of this war at that time.

Environment Aspects

By losing Arunachal Pradesh located on the northeastern tip of India, bordering Bhutan on the west, China on the north, Myanmar on the east and the states of Assam on the south, either China or India would receive some damage in terms of economy. Both China and India are able to run good business because Arunachal Pradesh is a very good place for tourists from all over the world to visit. Evergreen forest, which covers more than 60 percent of the state area, certainly makes people feel comfortable to stay there.

From this fact, Arunachal Pradesh is known for its forest resources. Forest products and industries are considered as a lifeline in Arunachal Pradesh. In fact, 75 percent of its total workforce is engaged in agriculture (mainly shifting cultivation.) Therefore, if either China or India could obtain Arunachal Pradesh, it would be able to improve its economy by taking advantage of agriculture and tourism.

In addition to it, there are many fairs and festivals there such as Losar, the New Year's Celebration of the Monpas. Another famous festival there is called Reh, which is associated with the Idu Mishmis, the six-day celebrations' special attraction is the Priest dance. Fairs or festivals are held every month, thus tourists can visit there any time for sightseeing.

Conflict Aspects

In 1962, the Chinese had a claim on what India deemed its own territory called Arunachal Pradesh. China sent many well-trained and well-armed troops to the disputed region. On the other hand, India had only ill-equipped troops there, which made them more difficult to beat Chinese troops.

The Sino-Indian (Indo-China) War was started by China on October 16, 1962 on account of the territorial dispute against India. Chinese attacked India on October 20, 1962 because it was unable to reach political accommodation on disputed territory along the 3,225-kilometer-long Himalayan border. The Chinese did not invade farther, and on November 21, 1962 declared a unilateral cease-fire. They had accomplished all of their territorial objectives, and any attempt to press farther into the plains of Assam would have stretched their logistical capabilities and their lines of communication to a breaking point. Finally, the Chinese defeated India in 1962, which as a result led to the retreat of Indian Army in terms of doctrine, training, organization and equipment from the disputed area.

Environment and Conflict Overlap

Arunachal Pradesh dispute was classified as a territorial dispute, but both China and India had big enough territories on their own. Thus, this dispute was not really caused by a decline of resources (territory.) Therefore, the dispute is direct more likely than not even it has been argued for about one century long. China and India had a direct conflict over the fertile land which certainly supports their economy by agriculture. Major crops in the area are, for example, rice, maize, ginger and potato. These major crops yielded 134,807, 48,346, 34,890 and 32,434 in hectare respectively (Gov't of Arunachal Pradesh.)

Because Sir Henry McMahon, the British administrator, clearly established the McMahon Line as the border, which could establish buffer zones around its colony in South Asia, between British India and Tibet in 1913-14, the British have also something to do with Arunachal Pradesh dispute in terms of strategic interest. China is also relevant to the territorial dispute. On account of various disagreements with the British, China refused to accept the terms imposed by Britain. As a result, China did not recognize the validity of the McMahon

Line. China probably was mostly concerned about the loss of their essential resources such as land from losing Arunachal Pradesh. Therefore, British India and China were major countries in this territorial dispute with respect to strategic interest.

Even though both India and China found a peaceful solution to the border dispute in late 1980s, officials from two countries have met more than 15 times to argue the Arunachal Pradesh.

Chinese Foreign Ministry spokesman Kong Quan said that "As far as the incident mentioned, after investigations, we have found that the Indian side crossed the eastern sector of the Line of Actual Control (LAC). At the request of the Chinese side, the Indian people who crossed the LAC, returned to the Indian side of the LAC" (Joseph 2003.) Thus, China still claims that "90,000 square kilometers of land in Arunachal Pradesh and does not recognize the northeastern state as part of Indian Territory" (Joseph 2003.)

Outcome of Dispute: Compromise

Arunachal Pradesh was part of the state of Assam until 1987 and was previously called NEFA. However, Arunachal Pradesh finally could gain statehood status on Feb. 20th, 1987 after making allowances for the security consideration in the east and Sino-Indian tensions ("Arunachal Pradesh.") India was satisfied with this outcome of dispute while China still does not admit the result.

Smoothening the India-China Border Wrinkles

The 17th round of India-China border talks (Feb. 10-11) in New Delhi passed off without any "free and frank" exchanges, that is, there was no disagreement. The first meeting was at the joint secretary level with military experts on both sides. The situation on the border was reviewed and apparently was found satisfactory. The meeting it appears, was constructed by both sides to ensure no negative vibration emerged.

The main meeting, the 17th round of talks between the Special Representatives (SRs) of the two sides was much wider in scale because matters outside the border issue were discussed. The Indian Ministry of External Affairs (MEA) statement said the talks were held in a "candid, friendly and constructive atmosphere". Mr. Shivshankar Menon, the Indian SR and Mr. Yang Jiechi, the Chinese SR are veterans in the foreign policy game and India-China relations. On the Chinese side they know the stakes they are playing with. They have in their pocket "something to give" on the border issue if need be. But no one can say for sure what that is. It must be kept in mind that the old Chinese position "if India makes concessions in the east" has not become irrelevant. In China's foreign policy dealings, nothing once stated becomes irrelevant unless it is stated so officially.

The three-step process agreed to by both sides to resolve the boundary question was reiterated. The process has arrived at step-2 to reach a framework for a resolution of this question. This will be based on the Agreement on the Political Parameters and Guiding Principles for the settlement of the India-China Boundary Question. The SRs discussed possible additional Confidence Building Measures (CBM).

Other issues discussed, according to the MEA release included areas of mutual interest including cooperation in the East Asia Summit process as well as developments in West Asia and Afghanistan. Pakistan should have figured in the discussions, but it appears that the Chinese do not want it to be seriously included in the "India-China strategic partnership and co-operation". It is too sensitive a subject.

China made its general position on the border clear when reacting to Indian President Pranab Mukherjee's visit to Arunachal Pradesh in November last year. Chinese foreign ministry spokesman Qin Gang urged *(Xinhua, Nov.30 2013)* India not to indulge in acts that complicate the boundary issue and work with China to create conditions for talks and preserve peace and tranquility on the border.

The *Xinhua* commentary went on to say "The so-called Arunachal Pradesh was established largely on three areas of China's Tibet-Monyul, Loyul and Lower Tsayul currently under Indian illegal occupation. These three areas, located between the illegal MacMahon Line and the traditional customary boundary between China and India, have always been Chinese territory." The commentary added that in February 1987, Indian authorities declared the founding of the so-called Arunachal Pradesh. Before further meetings on the border issue the Chinese side drew the lines. That is, the basic Chinese position that the border lay along the northern banks of the river Bramhaputra; India set up Arunachal Pradesh illegally; and if India did not work with China and on its directions, China could revert to a hard-line position. This is China's position on the eastern sector of the India-China border. It is, therefore, not surprising that even Chinese incursion into India's Depsung area in the western sector last year was generally kept outside the main agenda.

The focus is now testing out the Border Defense cooperation agreement signed during Prime Minister Manmohan Singh's visit to China last October. With national elections in India barely two months away and opinion surveys emphatically suggesting that UPA government led by the Congress has little or no hope to return to power for the third time in a row, it was only right for Prime Minister Singh and National Security Advisor (NSA) Menon to take no new initiatives on the border and analyze the efficacy of Border Defence Agreement signed between the two countries last October.

The new hierarchy in New Delhi will be well advised to consider relations with China on a much bigger canvas. While getting played by China on the boundary question, New Delhi must not lose sight of other strategic interests regionally and globally.

The Chinese leadership including the People's Liberation Army (PLA) are full of hubris as the next global super power. On the India-China border, the Chinese attained confidence of military superiority, and would continue to play mind games. The Border Defence Agreement was proposed by China, and India agreed to it only after some critical amendments. China went through with it but was not satisfied. The agreement could not put the Indian forces and border development in a strait jacket. It is going to come up with more CBMs on the border in due course. This is something Indian experts must look out for. There was some speculation that because of support to Uighur separatists from extremist elements in Pakistan, China-Pakistan relations was becoming weaker. True, the Chinese were furious with Pakistan especially during the 2008 Beijing Olympics. But weak relationship? Emphatically no. Beijing is determined to crush the Uighur separatists as evidenced by the hard crackdown in Xinjiang.

Pakistan is of immense importance to China. It concerns Chinese interests in the Gulf and the Middle East with Pakistan being a Muslim nation. Afghanistan now looms on the horizon, but it is a tricky issue. Certainly, China is discussing Afghanistan with India but all its cards on the burning issue remain hidden. China's support to Pakistan on Pakistan's issues with India continues to be as strong as ever. On Kashmir, there has been no change in position though statements are deliberately muted. It has done nothing and said nothing on Pakistan sponsored and Pakistani based terrorism against India. Yet it high profiles the so-called "three evils" terrorism, separatism and religious extremism. China's cooperation against terrorism and extremism across the world remains a hollow trumpet till date.

A new worrisome development has taken place. The BBC reported recently that Pakistan had manufactured nuclear weapons exclusively for Saudi Arabia. There were denials but not convincing enough. It is well known that China had supplied Saudi Arabia CSS-2 nuclear capable missiles in the 1980s. Obviously, these were meant for regional use. But nuclear capable missiles without nuclear warheads is an incongruous military doctrine. China has been modernizing Pakistan's nuclear weapons capability and fissile material production facilities. The three countries tie up very nicely as the Saudis remain the mainstay not only of Pakistan's economy but of its military modernization. After all Pakistan, a Sunni majority country like Saudi Arabia, owns the "Islamic bomb"! The above scenario is not an idle thought. The world is aware of the Pakistani nuclear scientist Dr. A. Q. Khan's nuclear trade network leading to major proliferation. China was a self-effasive but root player in this. The west let both China and Pakistan off lightly for their own geostrategic reasons. After Saudi Arabia and the US differed on the approach to the Syrian crisis the Saudis are moving back to engage China and Pakistan with more resolve. The Saudi crown prince was in Pakistan recently and his agenda included defence cooperation.

On the other end of the Indian Ocean is the issue of freedom of navigation in the South China Sea. China is increasingly trying to force control of the international maritime route through which around 50 percent of global trade passes. Using vague historical evidence mainly manipulated, China claims sovereignty of the Spratly group of Islands in the South China Sea. It is using the naval flag march here to intimidate other claimants. India is likely to get into conflict with China on its oil exploration with Vietnam in Vietnam's waters claimed by China. There are a whole range of issues that are likely to come up in India-China interface in the next five years. The new dispensation in New Delhi will have to deal with them.

How these issues are dealt with is another question. Prime Minister Manmohan Singh made non-conflict and warm relations with China and Pakistan his top priorities. He failed because such a relationship does not exist in the minds of either of these two countries. In the course of his policies, Dr. Singh bent over too much.

The foregoing are only illustrative examples of issues that India will come to face. It is not suggested that India should adopt aggressive postures against China. But at the same time, India should get out of the habit of rolling over to achieve what is not achievable. Firmness on issues of national and strategic importance is imperative. Prime Minister Singh did this in the case of the nuclear deal with the US at the Nuclear Suppliers Group (NSG) despite China's opposition till the last moment. Unfortunately, the Chinese official criticism on President Pranab Mukherjee's visit to Arunanchal Pradesh did not elicit a suitable demarche from India.

DISPUTED TERRITORY BETWEEN CHINA AND INDIA

Arunachal Pradesh

Both countries retain their strong claims to the disputed territory, however, fueled by national pride and national security interests. China's "Go West" development policy and July 2006 opening of the Qinghai-Tibet railway have received mixed responses from Indian policymakers; those who favour expanded trade and people-to-people contacts have regarded the developments as positive, but some within the national security establishment have raised concerns that they will allow Beijing to extend its military power projection into Tibet and beyond into South and Central Asia.

Three rivers running through India—the Indus/Sengge Chu, Sutlej/ Langqen Tsangbo, and Brahmaputra/Sang Po—originate in Tibet, a fact that has spurred Indian fears that China could use upstream dams and barrages to control the flow of water into India. India, for instance, has blamed a series of flash floods along the Sutlej River in its state of Himachal Pradesh to China's reluctance to supply hydrological data to India in a timely manner or allow Indian scientists to conduct surveys of melting glaciers on Chinese soil. The absence of any water-sharing treaty between both states as a result of the disputed status of their borders contributes to these water tensions.

Regional Affairs

Regionally, Sino-Indian cooperation has been the exception rather than the rule. Beijing watches closely New Delhi's increasing engagement of East Asia, including relations with nations that have historically had particularly difficult interactions with Beijing, such as Japan, Vietnam, and Indonesia. At the same time, Indian strategists have expressed quiet concern over China's growing influence in the subcontinent, not only its maintenance of a robust political and military relationship with India's rival Pakistan, but also its extensive political, economic, and security relationship with Burma, growing relations with Bangladesh and Nepal, and increasing naval presence in the Indian Ocean. China's admission as an observer to the South Asian Association for Regional Cooperation (SAARC) in November 2005, with New Delhi's reluctant acquiescence, has been cited as further evidence of China's emergence as a player in India's backyard and the desire of India's smaller neighbours to draw China into the region as leverage.

India has viewed growing Chinese influence in Burma, which is strategically located along the eastern end of the Indian Ocean, with great suspicion. In the mid-1990s, India had been one of the most vocal and ardent supporters of Burma's democracy movement, led by Aung San Suu Kyi. However, the combination of India's aim to forge closer links with Southeast Asia as part of its "Look East" policy, its need for Burma's support in countering insurgent groups in India's northeast, its desire for access to Burma's natural resources, including energy (often in competition with China), and its alarm over China's growing military ties to the Burmese junta led India to adopt a more conciliatory engagement policy with the Burmese leadership by the late 1990s to counterbalance Chinese influence.

Most notably, the presence of Chinese radar technicians in Burma's Coco Islands, which border India's Andaman and Nicobar Islands, has fueled concern in New Delhi (and Washington) that Beijing is monitoring naval activities in the region. Furthermore, China's efforts to develop alternative overland routes to transport oil and gas imports through port facilities at Gwadar in Pakistan's Baluchistan province, which is at the entrance of the Strait of Hormuz, as well as through Bangladesh and Burma, have been viewed by India as part of a Chinese "string of pearls" strategy of economic and military encroachment into South and Central Asia. Indeed, China's senior-most leaders have openly declared Beijing's attention to placing priority focus on naval modernization, including greater power-projection capability. Indian policymakers fear that China's moves could undermine India's regional preeminence.

At the same time, India's joint naval exercises in the South China Sea—with Vietnam in 2000 and Singapore in 2005, joint patrols with Indonesia in the Andaman Sea beginning in 2002, and exercises off the Japanese coast with the U.S. and Japanese navies in April 2007, have sparked concerns in Beijing. The Indian Navy, the world's fifth-largest, has also set up a Far Eastern Naval Command (FENC) off Port Blair on the Andaman Islands to increase its presence in the Strait of Malacca and potentially monitor Chinese naval activities in the region. Such mutual suspicions could result in China-Indian naval rivalry in and around the Indian Ocean over time. For their part, East Asian nations have increasingly looked to India as a potential partner in economic and regional security affairs, with some, such as Japan, apparently considering India as a potential element in a hedging strategy against China. South Asian countries have likewise begun to play the "China card" in order to counterbalance India's influence in their affairs or gain policy concessions from India and the West. For instance, as relations have soured between New Delhi and Dhaka in recent years, China has become Bangladesh's largest supplier of military hardware and has replaced India as Bangladesh's overall largest trading partner. In Nepal, China defied international suspension of military aid and other support to King

Gyanendra's regime after the monarch suspended democracy from February 2005 to April 2006, calling the situation Nepal's "internal affair." King Gyanendra reciprocated by shutting down the office of the Dalai Lama's representative in Nepal as well as the Tibetan Refugee Welfare Office.

In the end, China and India each recognize the inexorable reality of the other's increasing involvement in its neighborhood. In response, the two nations are quietly balancing the prospects for cooperation and competition in their relationship without letting any residual suspicions, tensions, or mistrust derail their mutual desire to test the possibilities of political rapprochement, economic engagement, and confidence-building in the years ahead.

People-to-People Contacts

People-to-people contacts between China and India have increased in recent years, albeit from a low base. Regular direct flights were established in 2002, when China's tourism authorities designated India as an "authorized destination." More than 5,000 Indian students are currently studying in Chinese universities. In India, enthusiasm for Chinese popular culture is growing, and Indians tend to respect, if not envy, China's economic and political rise, which they would like to have their own country mirror. India dubbed 2006 the "Year of Friendship with China," and China declared 2007 the "Year of China-India Friendship through Tourism."

Nonetheless, while official interaction is on the rise and public opinion polls suggest that a majority of citizens and businessmen in both states hold favorable views of each other overall, popular interaction remains relatively minimal, restricted by the language barrier, cultural differences, and other factors. Chinese and Indian observers alike will note that the Chinese have more natural affinity with countries in East and Southeast Asia, while Indians are more comfortable in dealing with English-speaking countries and other South Asian states. Mutual mistrust persists, particularly within India's older generation, whose memories of the Sino-Indian border conflict lead it to view China with suspicion. India's media and educational system have also nurtured the notion that China "stabbed India in the back" in 1962 and is sitting on Indian land. India's visa policy, in fact, is very restrictive and suspicious of the entry of citizens from China (among other nations, including the United States), further constraining popular contact.

For their part, the Chinese have expressed difficulty in understanding India's cultural and interpersonal style and have tended to be snobbish in their view of India and its state of development relative to China. While Indians may be focusing increasingly on China, relatively little Chinese popular attention is directed toward India. Few Chinese students study in India, for instance. Even at the official level, a similar lack of symmetry in the level of attention paid by China and India toward each other appears to prevail.

Negotiating Strategies

One repeated emerging criticisms of India's negotiating strategy is that "unilateral concessions" have been made too often by India, without similar concessions being made by China. When PRC military forces started moving into Tibet in 1950, the Republic of India quickly moved to (a) give up the Forward Rights inherited from the days of British India, which stemmed from the Simla Convention and Anglo-Tibetan Agreement of 1904; and (b) instead recognise Chinese control over Tibet in stronger terms than the hitherto used term "suzerainty".

In effect, a "Tibet Card" was there to be played at a time of PRC uncertainties. A robust Indian intervention might have maintained Tibet as an effective buffer between India and China, or at least enabled concessions to be won by India on the Himalayan—Karakoram borders. This is the reverse logic behind recent Indian comments that "China has failed to appreciate that if Arunachal is claimed to be the southern part of Tibet Autonomous Region (TAR), India cannot accept Tibet to be within China. India's formal position on Tibet articulated in 1954 and 2003 is therefore a tentative and unilateral diplomatic offer that can only be sustained and the circle completed once China recognizes Arunachal as part of India". Reinvoking such a "Tibet Card" has been floated in some Indian circles in the past few years.

Having lost that opportunity, the next criticism of Indian negotiating strategy is that, faced with an immediate PRC military presence in Tibet and renewed Chinese claims over Aksai China and Arunachal Pradesh, Nehru ignored the chance of a trade-off seemingly offered by China in 1960; whereby Aksai China would have gone to China and Arunachal Pradesh would have gone to India. Instead, India refused to engage in sovereignty negotiations in the 1950s, maintained its claims to the fullest, neglected to build up its own military forces, yet still engaged in adventurist forward probing movements in the late 1950s. At the time, Nehru rejected the idea of territorial trade-off; India "will not concede one piece of territory in return for another in the same manner as a similar dispute between China and Burma was settled this year"; for "there is no question of barter in these matters ... facts are facts".

His formal position was, in the formal *Indian Note* of June 16 1962; quite simply that "this boundary is well known and well recognized and has been so for centuries and cannot be the subject of any negotiations". The trouble was the precise boundaries were not well known, were not well recognized, and had not been in shape for centuries. The irony is that the territorial agreement reached between Burma and China in 1960 involved China following the MacMahon Line alongside other mutual concessions and swapping of territory; as did the 1963 Agreement between China and Pakistan with regard to mutual concessions over claims and territory in the Karakoram reaches.

Nehru might have said "facts are facts" but the fact of the matter is that China's military superiority and continuing occupation of Aksai Chin created a very different subsequent set of facts in the wake of India's military defeat at the hands of China in 1962. The problem for consideration of negotiated resolution of the territorial dispute is that demands and offers have shifted. From the outside, an obvious trade off would be between the *Western* Sector and the *Eastern Sector*; which is where Noorani argued that "there is no territorial dispute which has been, and still is, more susceptible to a solution than India's boundary dispute with China. Each side has its non-negotiable vital interest securely under its control. India has the McMahon Line; China has Aksai Chin" In other words, China's *de facto* control of Aksai Chin could be reflected in agreed *de jure* sovereignty for China, and India's *de facto* control of Arunachal Pradesh could in turn be reflected in agreed *de jure* sovereignty for India. This had been Zhou Enlai's seeming suggestion in 1960, and was the "Package Plan" floated by Deng Xiaoping during 1980. The problem is that the Indian government has never taken up such trade-off offers, with Chinese comments made about the weakness of the Indian governments in taking any compromise deal to the Indian public. The separate *sector-by-sector* approach advocated by India when discussions resumed in the 1980s, rather than *overall package* trade-off deals suggested by China, has not worked, it has merely led the PRC to maintain its particular claims in all Sectors.

Another possible example of unilateral concessions was Rajiv Gandhi's visit to Beijing in 1988. Various concessions were made by him. He agreed that the settlement of the border dispute no longer was necessary as a precondition for improvement of bilateral relations, secondly he agreed that some members of the Tibetan community in India were engaged in anti-China activities, and thirdly he agreed that Tibet was an internal affair for China. Ganguly considered the results were "clearly asymmetric" as no support on the Kashmir issue was received from China, which "underscored the stark debility of India's negotiating capabilities vis-à-vis China". On the other hand, the earlier unequivocal support for Pakistan's case in Kashmir was moderated by a more neutral position by the 1990s, the PRC eventually announcing it was "not taking sides on Kashmir".

A final example of "unilateral concessions" came in the 2003 *Declaration on Principles for Relations and Comprehensive Cooperation between India and China*, in which India explicitly recognised the sovereignty of China over Tibet. A careful look at the text shows one-way agreement, one-way obligations, one-way concessions. On the one hand, it stated that "The Indian side recognizes that the Tibet Autonomous Region is part of the territory of the People's Republic of China and reiterates that it does not allow Tibetans to engage in anti-China political activities in India"; before going on to immediately say, on the other hand, "The Chinese side expresses its appreciation for the Indian position and reiterates that it is firmly opposed to any attempt and action aimed at splitting China and bringing about "independence of Tibet". As can be seen, there was no recognition of Indian territory (Arunachal Pradesh?) by China; not even return recognition by China of India's sovereignty claims over Sikkim, the Princely State reincorporated into the Republic of India in 1975, an incorporation which China had refused to recognise. Indian commentators may have read the accompanying *Trade Memorandum* designating Natu La as a border trade post as recognition by China of India's sovereignty over Sikkim, but that was implied rather than explicit, *de facto* rather than *de jure*.

Meanwhile, New Delhi has refused to lay out its formal position, other than the reiteration of its full claims of the Indian Parliament in November 1962, a unanimous vote to get China to vacate all Indian-claimed territories that China occupied. Specific territorial negotiations involving sensitive political climb downs or concessions might well be conducted in private out of the public gaze, yet there seems no indications of this either. India could then indicate some sort of territorial trade-off, short of this maximalist reiteration of its full claims which China is unlikely to accept. Of course, India indicating a territorial trade-off would not necessarily meet with Chinese acceptance, given Indian suspicions that China is happy enough to avoid definitive frontier settlement; but at least it would clarify the issue, and in such an eventuality enable India to more straightforwardly strengthen her own presence and power towards China along the border. In IR terms, if *engagement* proved unsuccessful in leading to territorial settlement, then India could go for a degree of *internal balancing* through building up its military presence and power in Arunachal Pradesh and Ladakh. Some Indian commentators have suggested that "when the Agni-III is finally ready for deployment, it is likely that the Chinese will come down to the table for negotiations and there is likely to be further progress on the border dispute". It could also go for a degree of *external balancing* with others vis-à-vis China but that is a much wider issue. It could try adjusting its bigger policy on Tibet, in effect playing a "Tibet Card" to engineer geopolitical shifts in the future; though would be a much more high risk strategy immediately bringing it up against China's perceived "core interest" of averting internal fragmentation.

If India's strategy over the disputed territories has been hesitant, this has been exacerbated by the very opaqueness, the "Chinese whispers" coming from Beijing. What exactly does China really want, what is its bottom line? For example, are PRC reiterations of claims over the whole of Arunachal Pradesh, re-invoked with greater vigour since the 1990s, just a maximalist initial tactic to end up with the Tawang pocket, thereby strengthening its control over Tibet, a line of argument by Chinese commentators like Ma Jiali and others. Are some suggestions in PRC circles of a different trade-off, Aksai Chin to India and Arunachal Pradesh to China, serious? Did China's acceptance in 2003 of Nathu La as an official border trade post between India and China represent full and definitive acceptance by China of Sikkim's incorporation into India; and what is the significance of rising "incursion" incidents into Sikkim during 2008 by Chinese troops; uncertainties that undermine Wen Jiabao's assertions in 2005 that "Sikkim is no longer the problem between China and India?" Is talk in the PRC that "China won't make any compromises in its border disputes with India" a tactical ploy by China to get India to make compromises? If it is, then a trade-off deal is likely at some point. If it is not, then indefinite deadline/stand off is likely, unless one or the other disputant state attempts to decide it on the military battlefield.

One emerging line from the PRC, with implications for India, is PRC emphasis and definition of a "core interests" diplomacy, reflecting the rise of China; "as the country becomes stronger, China is now on the trajectory to develop its own doctrine of diplomacy". This has been a development in the last couple of years, overlapping with rising friction along the disputed Himalayan reaches; generally what the PRC calls "the recalibration of its strategic focus in diplomacy to 'core interests'", over which it is taking a more obstructive/assertive line. This sense of "core interest" can be primarily seen at stake for the PRC in Taiwan and also Xinjiang. It can also be seen with PRC statements with regard to Tibet, whereby "Tibet related issues remain a core interest of China that refers to state sovereignty and territorial integrity. This is neither a religious issue nor a human right issue". The question is how far China's "core interest" framework may be "expanding". If such a "core interest" linkage is also invoked for Arunachal Pradesh (or in PRC eyes *Zang Nan* "Southern Tibet") as "Tibet-related issues", then one would have less expectations of territorial agreements being reached between India and China, and more likelihood of armed resolution in the future. Such trends were the spur for Barat Verma at the *India Defence Review* to warn that for the PRC "the most attractive option is to attack a soft target like India and forcibly occupy its territory in the Northeast...Beijing's cleverly raising the hackles on its fabricated dispute in Arunachal Pradesh to an alarming level, is the preparatory groundwork for imposing such a conflict on India"; a scenario dismissed in China as a "provocative and inflammatory illusion". Nevertheless, IR security dilemma dynamics may indeed lead to increasing military tension as both sides reinforce their military positions, and "war talk" about the disputed territories increases.

Concerned voices are easy to find as "tensions over a boundary dispute between the two sides are escalating". One reason for Indian concerns is the increasing number of "incursion" incidents along the border, though denied by China. The official India leadership downplays such trends, India's Foreign Secretary Niripuma Rao thus asserting in September 2009 that "there has been no significant increase in intrusions across all Sectors of the Line of Actual Control (LAC)", but that such India-perceived incursions were "because there is no mutually agreed or delineated border". This ignores the earlier increase the previous year, whereby the number of India-perceived "incursions" by the PRC has increased from 140 in 2007 to 280 in 2008, with a similar number in 2009. Such incursion incidents involved not just the *Eastern Sector* around Arunachal Pradesh but now also the *Western Sector* around Aksai Chin/Ladakh; a particular widening development that Indian commentators like Bhaskar Roy have found "sinister" and which Kanwal sees as "aggressive tactical posturing" on the part of China. Admittedly, such border incursions, reflecting different perceptions of where the LAC actually is, have often been trivial in themselves; for example Chinese troops painting rocks in red paint or cross-LAC sheep grazing. Chinese troop movements near and around the narrow Siliguri corridor "chicken's neck" linking north-east India to the rest of India do though cause immediate geopolitical concerns to India.

Certainly, a substantive military build up along the Aksai Chin and Arunachal Pradesh borderlines has also been evident. Partly this has been an infrastructure race, in which India has been belatedly trying to catch up and match China's better established road, and now railway, infrastructure in these disputed borderlands. It has also involved increasing military deployment, again by India to match China's already established forces in places like Linzi airbase. This is reflected in India increasing its ground forces in the border regions facing China. In the *Eastern Sector*, this has also involved the Indian Air Force (IAF) deploying advanced long range Sukhoi Su-30 warplanes to Tezpur for potential cross-LAC operation; complemented by six surface-to-air Akash missile squadrons. In the *Western Sector*, this has also involved the Indian Air Force reactivating disused high altitude airstrips like Daulat Beg Oldi and Fukche. Such reinforcements have been picked up in the PRC, and denounced as "unwise military moves".

Meanwhile, Brahma Chellaney asked the question in 2006 "will India—China border talks ever end"? He argued that "after a quarter century of unrewarding negotiations with Beijing, India ought to face up to the reality that it is being taken round and round the mulberry bush by an adversarial state that has little stake in an early border resolution"; in which "the more the talks have dragged on, the less Beijing has appeared interested in resolving the border disputes other than on its terms". His prognosis was simple, "it is time for it to draw the line, at least in the negotiations" and "to re-evaluate the very utility of staying absorbed in a never-ending process". Three years later, in the wake of the 2009 talks, his sense was the same, "the latest round of the unending and fruitless India—China talks on territorial disputes was a fresh reminder of the eroding utility of this process". The PRC may indeed wish to keep the issue open as a way of distracting and threatening India; but other dynamics may be leading the PRC to postpone decisive border negotiations. The PRC may well consider tightening its hold on Tibet itself as a greater priority, shaken during the disturbances that swept across Tibet and Tibetan areas in the spring of 2008? The PRC may also want to delay decisive border territorial resolution with India until it has resolved the Taiwan issue first? Garver also has wondered how far Beijing's apparent slowdown and readiness to avoid territorial resolution with India, is because of "understanding between Pakistan and China that neither will settle their territorial disputes with India independently of the other". Such a consideration point to the wider Pakistan—China—India triangle interplay around the disputed territories that stretch along the Himalayas from Arunachal Pradesh in the east to Aksai Chin and Kashmir in the west, which overlap with basic power balancing by the China—Pakistan "nexus" against India. The overlaps between the varied territorial disputes was shown in 2009 when China gave visas for the entry of Kashmiri separatists to visit China, in the wake of India giving permission to the Dalai Lama to visit Arunachal Pradesh.

What is certain is that any quick decisive territorial resolution between India and China is unlikely. Following rising border frictions, the PRC media reported "China—India border dispute turns sour", with hard hitting nationalist blogs being noticeable in the Chinese official and state controlled media in the autumn of 2009. Admittedly, the Indian and Chinese leadership did again reaffirm dialogue in autumn 2009. However, this reaffirmation was in cautious terms "to gradually narrow differences on border issues between the two countries ... to continue talks, with the aim of incrementally removing the barriers to a solution that was fair and acceptable to both sides". Despite the euphemistic headline from the official Chinese media that the two countries had reached "concensus on narrowing border differences"; in reality this merely indicated the existence of a gap without showing how and when it would be resolved. Talk of "gradually" and "incrementally removing" barriers to a solution flags up the slowness of any likely process, whilst offering nothing on what solutions could then emerge once such barriers have been, incrementally, removed.

What of solutions? Could outside arbitration be one way forward? Nehru himself had offered such a route in the immediate aftermath of war in the shape of the International Court of Justice (ICJ) at The Hague.

However this was badly received in Parliament and Nehru then backed away immediately from this. In reality the ICJ seems ill equipped to deal with direct large scale territorial disputes between major powers, whilst China's reluctance to have outside bodies disposing of sovereignty issues is higher even than India's.

One bilateral solution which we can return to, involves a *logic of geography*, the "watershed/crestline" line along the Himalayas/Karakoram. It has a degree of clearness, "the advantage of having a border on such a prominent line as the high watershed of the Himalaya is that it is easily identifiable, historically traditional and politically neutral".

It may also be sellable to both parties. Thus, "as far as the Indian public is concerned, they have been brought up to believe that the Himalaya is the traditional boundary and they will be willing to concede any territory that lies beyond it without demur"; whilst "such a boundary should also be acceptable to China as it is based on the same watershed principle which they have accepted in defining their boundaries with Myanmar, Sikkim and Nepal.

This watershed principle was an angle suggested by Zhou Enlai in the abortive 1960 discussions. In effect, applying the watershed principle would leave Aksai Chin to China and almost all Arunachal Pradesh with India.

Admittedly, Tawang remains problematic. The Tawang District's 2,085 square kilometres is around 2.5% of Arunachal Pradesh's entire 82,743 area, and its population of 38,924 is around 3.6% of Arunachal Pradesh's 1,091,120 inhabitants (2001 figures), relatively small shares on paper. Neutralization of the entire Tawang subdivision pocket might be an option. Within the Tawang District, given that the Tawang Subdistrict and the District capital Tawang (27°34'47"N) itself lies north of the Se la Pass and the Ka crest line (27°32'26"N), whereas the Lumla and Jang Subdistricts lie on the southerly India-facing slopes of that crest line; could a division of Tawang District be carried out, with the Tawang Subdistrict allocated to China and the Lumla and Jang Subdistricts allocated to India? However, local opinion at the District capital Tawang, population c. 20,000, would probably vote in favour of staying in 'India' rather than going into the 'PRC', though an independent 'Tibet' option would provide an interesting third option.

Having Tawang subdivision inhabitants relocate further south if they wished might be another solution, though ugly in political and human terms. Meanwhile, if the Dalai Lama's death was followed by any proclaimed rebirth at Tawang, a not impossible scenario, the situation would be still more complicated with the PRC.

Failing dramatic regime change scenarios of regime collapse/democratization in the PRC, and re-establishment of a genuinely autonomous or independent Tibet, and Tawang notwithstanding; some sort of trade off involving Aksai Chin and Arunachal Pradesh seems the most likely way forward. In using relatively clear cut neutral geographic principles, the deadlocked politics and unclear history could perhaps be sidelined?

Such a trade off would give neither side too much geopolitical advantage, but also ensure a degree of security for each? A *logic of geography* for the future for the national leaderships that would enable these two neighbours to get past the inconclusive divisive *logic of history* between them, and would provide a mutually satisfactory *logic of power* in terms of geopolitical equilibrium outcomes. Failing resolution of their territorial issues, the grinding tectonic plates along the Himalayas will continue to have their geopolitical counterpart as the two Asian giants look at each other across these disputed areas.

7

Line of Actual Control

The Line of Actual Control (LAC) is a demarcation line that separates Indian-ruled lands from Chinese-held territory. It is the effective border between India and the People's Republic of China (PRC). The LAC is 4,056-km long and traverses four Indian states: Jammu and Kashmir, Uttarakhand, Himachal, and Sikkim. On the Chinese side, the line traverses the Tibet Autonomous Region. The demarcation existed as the informal cease-fire line between India and China after the 1962 conflict until 1993, when its existence was officially accepted as the 'Line of Actual Control' in a bilateral agreement. However, Chinese scholars claim that the Chinese Prime Minister Zhou Enlai first used the phrase in a letter addressed to Indian Prime Minister Jawaharlal Nehru dated 24 October 1959.

Although no official boundary had ever been negotiated between China and India, Indian government even today claims that the Johnson Line of 1865 is the effective border between China and India while the PRC government considers the Macartney-MacDonald Line of 1899 the accepted boundary.

In a letter dated 7 November 1959, Zhou told Nehru that the LAC consisted of "the so-called McMahon Line in the east and the line up to which each side exercises actual control in the west".

During the Sino-Indian War (1962), Nehru refused to recognise the line of control: "There is no sense or meaning in the Chinese offer to withdraw twenty kilometers from what they call 'line of actual control'. What is this 'line of control'? Is this the line they have created by aggression since the beginning of September? Advancing forty or sixty kilometers by blatant military aggression and offering to withdraw twenty kilometers provided both sides do this is a deceptive device which can fool nobody."

Zhou responded that the LAC was "basically still the line of actual control as existed between the Chinese and Indian sides on 7 November 1959. To put it concretely, in the eastern sector it coincides in the main with the so-called McMahon Line, and in the western and middle sectors it coincides in the main with the traditional customary line which has consistently been pointed out by China."

The term "LAC" gained legal recognition in Sino-Indian agreements signed in 1993 and 1996. The 1996 agreement states, "No activities of either side shall overstep the line of actual control." The Indian government claims that Chinese troops continue to illegally enter the area hundreds of times every year.

In 2013, there was a three-week standoff between Indian and Chinese troops 30 km southeast of Daulat Beg Oldi. It was resolved and both Chinese and Indian troops withdrew in exchange for an Indian agreement to destroy some military structures over 250 km to the south near Chumar that the Chinese perceived as threatening. Later the same year, the BBC reported that Indian forces mistook planets for Chinese spy drones for six months. They recorded 155 such intrusions. Later the planets were identified by the Indian Institute of Astrophysics as Venus and Jupiter. In October 2013, India and China signed a border defence cooperation agreement to ensure that patrolling along the LAC does not escalate into armed conflict.

Neville Maxwell

Neville Maxwell (born 1926 in London) is a retired Australian-British journalist and author of the 1970 book *India's China War*, which is considered an authoritative analysis of the 1962 Sino-Indian War. However, he has been criticised for his pessimistic views on Indian democracy.

In March 2014, Maxwell leaked the Henderson Brooks–Bhagat Report, which was written by two Indian army officers in 1963 to examine India's defeat in the Sino-Indian War and had been kept top-secret by the Indian government for over 50 years.

India's China War

An Australian born in London, Maxwell was educated at McGill University in Canada and the University of Cambridge in England. He joined *The Times* as a foreign correspondent in 1955 and spent three years in the Washington bureau. In 1959 he was posted to New Delhi as the South Asia correspondent. In the next eight years he travelled from Kabul to East Pakistan and Kathmandu to Ceylon, reporting in detail the end of the Nehru era in India and the post-Nehru developments. During the 1962 Sino-Indian War, Maxwell wrote for

The Times from New Delhi, and was the only reporter there who did not uncritically accept the official Indian account of events. This eventually led to his "virtual expulsion" from India.

In 1967 Maxwell joined the School of Oriental and African Studies in London a senior fellow to write his book *India's China War*. He was with the Institute of Commonwealth Studies at Oxford University at the time when the book was published in 1970. The book was widely praised across a diverse range of opinions, including British historian A. J. P. Taylor, Chinese premier Zhou Enlai, and US Secretary of State Henry Kissinger. On the other hand, Singaporean leader Lee Kuan Yew considered it "revisionist, pro-China history".

In India, Maxwell is perceived as hostile to the Indian narrative of victimhood and received ferocious personal attacks. The Indian government charged him with breach of Official Secrets Act, forcing him to stay out of India to avoid arrest, until the charges were annulled by Prime Minister Morarji Desai eight years later. Maxwell is recognised as the authority on the Sino-Indian War. His conclusion, which is also reached by American scholar Allen S. Whiting, that India's Forward Policy provoked China to decide for war, is now regarded as the orthodox scholarly view on the cause of the war. US President Richard Nixon and Secretary of State Henry Kissinger both read his *India's China War*, which influenced their decision to seek rapprochement with China.

INDIA'S CHINESE POLICY CHALLENGES UNDER CONGRESS GOVERNMENT

India's new government led by the Congress Party, has until now focused entirely on its relations with Pakistan. The reason for this could be that most of the foreign policy hands in the current policy establishment have been former High Commissioners in Pakistan and therefore at more professional ease to deal with it. However, India's most significant foreign policy challenge is China and not Pakistan. Pakistan despite its nuclear weapons arsenal is not our "strategic competitor"; it is only a, regional 'spoiler state'. But in India's aspirations to rise to an effective regional power status, China is a "strategic competitor" both in the South Asia context and also in the Asian security context.

India's policy making establishment and especially within the Congress Party, with its hangovers of 'Panch Sheel' and non-aligned mindsets, has short memories when it comes to China's policies of strategic destabilization of India. They are still under way. Similarly, the Indian media suffers from a total amnesia of China's perfidious policies in South Asia to the strategic detriment of India. China has adroitly exploited both these vulnerabilities of India. China in its approaches to South Asia in the last fifty-five years, with particular reference to India has relied heavily on "power politics", creation of 'spoiler states' on India's periphery and upsetting the natural balance of power in the Indian sub-continent. The new Indian Government policy establishment may like to consider the following observations when formulating its policy stances towards China:

* Only when countries have accepted the existence of conflict and sought to manage it through a balance of power have enduring periods of general peace resulted" -Former US President Nixon.
* "It can be a fundamental and analytically mischievous error to confuse peace with tranquillity, certainty or predictability." "To achieve peace, people do not necessarily have to become admirable or gentle." -Prof John Mueller.
* "Peace therefore cannot be aimed at directly; it is the expression of certain conditions and power relationships. It is to these relationships –not to peace-that diplomacy must address itself" -Former US Secretary of State, Henry Kissinger.

So while India must pursue peace and conflict-avoidance in its relationship with China, the new Indian Government should recognize that the route to peace lies through power relationships and power politics. But first, a look at the Congress Party's "China Baggage". The Congress Party Needs to Jettison its "China Baggage":

Contemporary Congress Party articulations give an impression that its perspectives remain time-frozen in the Nehruvian-era China politics. Current international strategic realities dictate that the following main planks of Congress Party's China perspectives are no longer relevant:

* Non-alignment is dead. The concept could operate in a bi-polar world only. Further, both the superpowers gave no credence to this concept. If India was given importance then, it was not because of Nehru and nor for its non-alignment policies. India was given importance for its intrinsic potential as a power in the making.
* 'Panch Sheel' (five principles of peaceful co-existence) enunciated by Chou-en-lai and Nehru stood negated when China sneakingly occupied Aksai-Chin in the 1950s and later the Sino-Indian War of 1962.
* "Panch Sheel" concept stood further negated in the following years when China in its policies of strategic de-stabilisation of India built-up Pakistan's nuclear weapons arsenal, attempted to make Myanmar a military client state and entered into a Mutual Defence Agreement with Bangladesh.

* Multipolar world as espoused by China and currently being seconded by the Congress Party Government is an unworkable proposition in today's international strategic realities. Neither China nor France has been able to win concrete support for multi-polarity.

The Congress Government would be well advised to jettison its above baggage and formulate its approaches to China on the basis of power-politics and in consonance with existing global power relationships. Hans J Morgenthau, the most noted foreign affairs authority has remarked that: " A nation can only take a rational view of its national interests after it has parted company with the crusading spirit of a political creed." The Congress Party Government needs to jettison the crusading missions of the Nehruvian era. It only brought more conflict and contentiousness for India.

Power-Relationship Approaches of India to China

India's national security interests imperatives dictate that any long range formulation of its China policy should deliver the following end-aims:

- China's assistance to Pakistan in terms of WMD Proliferation is curtailed, if not ended.
- China's intrusive influence in the Indian sub-continent in the form of creation of regional 'spoiler states' acting as its proxies is curtailed.
- China's attempt to build a naval presence in the Indian Ocean through Pakistan, Bangladesh or Myanmar is impeded.
- China's unobtrusive influence in India's politics through the Communist Parties, a strategically unwise Indian media and India's pseudo-liberal establishment is rendered ineffective.
- China's strategic nexus with Pakistan and Bangladesh is neutralized.

A quick glance at the above would reveal that except for the last point, India on its own, cannot tackle these challenges. India would have to co-opt or be co-opted in existing global power relationships that are working to constrain China's power politics in their respective regions. To arrive at the answer, a brief look is required at the existing strategic realities and global power equations and these are:

- United States global predominance is estimated to continue well into the major portion of the 21st century.
- United States is the only superpower existent today with the strategic, political and economic might to enforce its will globally.
- Russia is unlikely under existing circumstances to emerge in a resurgent mode for another three to four decades. Its strategic power potential stands shrunk decisively.

- China's massive military modernization and expansion of her strategic assets are nowhere near to challenging US supremacy.
- China is a revisionist power. It challenges the status-quo and in the process generates strategic uneasiness in global strategic equations of its intentions and motives.
- China today stands strategically hemmed-in by the United States on its Western and Eastern flanks.

India therefore has no choice but to be co-opted in the United States scheme of things to protect her national security interests vis-à-vis China. The United States too is not engaged in 'Containment' of China; but only in 'Constrainment' so that its policies do not create strategic turbulence in contiguous areas.

In terms of South Asia alone, India's national security interests dictate that Pakistan needs to be cut to size and accept its asymmetric equation in the Indian sub-continent. India cannot hope that China will assist her in this direction. China is a major part of the problem of Pakistan's intransigence and military adventurism against India.

Here again the United States enters into the picture in multiple ways: (1) To control Pakistan directly and coerce it into strategic compliance from desisting from military adventurism. (2) To neutralize China-Pakistan strategic nexus by building strategic counter-pressures against China. (3) United States global naval supremacy is unquestionable and in relation to India's Indian Ocean strategic interests, major convergence exists between India and USA.

Here again, in the South Asian context, the answer is clear, that in relation to China, the national security interests of India are best served by entering the power-relationships of the United States in terms of Asian security. Until India builds up her military and strategic power to levels commensurate with those of China, it has no options in her China policy but to get co-opted with the China policies of the United States.

Buildingup of her Strategic Assets by India as Part of its China Policy

In this connection two points need to be addressed, namely:

* China's attitudes towards India changed after the BJP Government's nuclear weapons tests in 1998. After the rabid Chinese reactions for a year or so, China realised that it had to adapt to the new strategic reality, that India had arrived to claim some strategic space in the "power-politics" scene. Hence the flurry of Chinese high level official visits thereafter and the stupendous growth of two way trade. An

argument can therefore be made in terms of China relations that India's power politics has stimulated trade exponentially.

* China's attitudes towards India changed as it dawned on Chinese leaders that India was getting drawn into an increasing strategic partnership with the United States and increasing military-to-military contacts also.

A major deduction from the above is that an essential component of India's policies towards China should also be the building up of her own independent strategies assets to add power to her diplomacy in the form of:

* SLBMs (Sea Launched Ballistic Missiles). The third leg of India's nuclear arsenal triad is overdue.
* ICBMs (Inter Continental Ballistic Missiles). At present Indian missiles do not have a reach upto Bijing.
* Cruise Missiles. With multimode launch capabilities.
* Nuclear Submarines. The project is over 15 years old. It needs to be resuscitated and put on priority.
* Strategic Bombers. These are an essential element of the nuclear triad.

China's missile arsenal is predominantly deployed in Tibet, Sichzuan and Yunnan— all targeted against India and with an inherent element of political coercion. Development of India's strategic assets as given above would make India's foreign policy approaches towards China more strategically equitable and in the process generating equitable responses from China.

The new Congress Government has come into power, seemingly obsessed with the conviction that the policies of the previous BJP Government must be changed at all costs. It needs to note that India's foreign and defence policies need to be bi-partisan in character and content. The previous Government adopted the "power politics" approach to China as evident from the nuclear weapons tests and also evolving a strategic partnership with the United States. Both these had an effect on China and its policies towards India and South Asia in general. One could also attribute the Chinese neutrality during the Kargil War 1999 to this approach

The Congress Governments in the past followed ill-conceived and ill-advised policies towards China based on mistaken beliefs. This led to India's national humiliation in 1962. The new Congress Government in power today should jettison its " China baggage" of the past and adhere to the "power politics" approach towards China. It is not to suggest that India enter into confrontationist stances with China; it is to suggest that while peace must be the quest in India-China relations it does not distract India from the parallel track of foreign policy i.e. To adopt power relationships and build strategic assets so necessary to maintain "real peace". India's new policy establishment needs to be reminded what one Chinese author has observed on China's perspectives on international relations: " Power is the cornerstone of Chinese politics. Chinese politicians and diplomats are often recognized as masters of power politics having inherited a well-spring of experience of power play over the millennium".

STATE OF THE INDIAN ARMY PRIOR TO 1962

When the IA was ordered into NEFA in closing stages of 1959, it was faced with a deployment without adequate regional roads and infrastructure in this, one of the highest battlefields in the world. Almost all the posts in the forward and even some in the rear were supported by airlifts. Nearly everything had to be air dropped, right down to the daily rations, but due to the severe terrain, it was later estimated that only thirty percent of supplies dropped were recovered.

The rations provided to the troops had a calorific value suited for warfare on the plains rather then the high-calorie diet that is required for mountain warfare. Lentils, which are the staple food of the Indian "Jawan" soldier, could not be cooked at high altitudes. Pressure cookers, though requested were unavailable due to "administrative delays". Oil cookers, essential for keeping warm and cooking, were also in short supply.

Since the troops were widely dispersed without connecting roads, medical facilities were poor. Even the helicopters used for airlifts, recently purchased from Russia, were inadequate for high-altitude operations, and there was a marked shortage of spare parts. Winter clothing, and sometimes even basic clothing, was unavailable. New recruits rarely had the full list of items that were supposed to be issued to them. The army had no means of carrying heavy loads in the mountains and hence its mobility and firepower was severely reduced. Its main means of transport in the era of jets were mules and human porters.

The state of weapons and the training of the "jawans" (soldiers) were inadequate for the terrain they were on and the foes they faced. Almost all the equipment and weapons were of 1950s vintage. For instance, the standard infantry rifle issued was the Lee Enfield.303, dating back to W.W.II. Also, when the 4th Indian Division was deployed, it was not trained nor acclimatized for high altitude warfare. Most of its heavy equipment had to be left in the plains because of the lack of transportation. Thus they had precious little firepower they could call on if need be.

The already grave situation was made worse by a personal feud between the then Finance Minister Morarji Desai and the Defense Minister Krishna

Menon. This had resulted in an obstructive finance ministry that did not allow the release of essential foreign exchange to buy what little equipment that had been sanctioned. Consequently, the Army's equipment was allowed to become obsolete. Desai claimed that supplies were deliberately withheld from Indian troops in the affected areas. There was considerable unhappiness about this in the Army, both at this and against Menon in general. Because of the playing off of different sections of the military as a result of political manovering and infighting, along with the supply crisis, morale was very low. Menon went to Ladakh personally in 1960 to appease dissent.

Think tanks at the time were at a general consensus that, to counter the Chinese threat, India should do three things:

1. Increase the number of, infrastructure supporting and supplies given to troops,
2. Station of sufficient mobile armoured troops at strategic points on the plain to check any potential Chinese advance, whilst keeping an eye on Pakistan.
3. Train and arm sufficient numbers of Tibetan and other ethnic guerrilla groups to tie down significant numbers of Chinese troops behind the front lines, hampering transfer of troop, communication, and material. It was said that "the principal problem seems to be lack of interest on the part of the present Indian Government" to enact these suggestions.

The combination of ill-supply, ill-preparedness, numerical and technological inferiority and the heavy-handed decisions taken by a government with little care for ground realities of the impending conflict coalesced to certain the failure of the Indian Army against the Chinese. The training and professionalism of the Indian Jawan could not make up for the tremendous odds stacked against them.

Conflict Begins

The establishment of posts in the forward areas without adequate military support had created a situation that was ripe for a military disaster. On 8 September 1962, Brig. Dalvi, Commander, 7th Brigade received a message from his adjutant that around 8 am, about 600 Chinese soldiers had crossed Thagla Ridge and had surrounded the Dhola post. The post commander had requested immediate reinforcements. The Chinese had chosen the spot and the timing well: Thagla Ridge, which overlooked the key Chinese garrison at Leh, was an exceedingly remote area with terrain that was not conducive for troop movement. In addition, it was a Saturday and it would take a long time for the information to reach Delhi along the chain of command. India's chain of command was further drawn out and complicated by Nehru's

Meanwhile, a conference was held with GoC, 4th Division Gen. Niranjan Prasad presiding and it was decided that:

1. The Dhola post commander would be ordered to stay put, without withdrawal. The Assam Rifles wing at Lumla, which was two days march away, would be ordered to establish contact with Dhola.
2. The detachments of 9 Punjab at Shakti and Lumpu would move to Dhola while the ones at Towang would move to Lumpu. Dalvi knew that Towang, along with Tsangdhar and Hathungla, were vital positions that had to be defended at all costs. Any diversion of 9 Punjab to Dhola would leave Towang defenseless.

There were no plans to cater for a major clash at Towang if one should occur. Also, the route from Towang to Thagla was fit only for man pack columns, making troop movement difficult. A sound move would have been to abandon Thagla Ridge and concentrate on defending Towang. However, under political pressure from Brigadier General Staff at XXXIII Corps HQ, 9 Punjab was ordered to depart for Lumpu. Thus began Operation Leghorn with the limited aim of persuading the Chinese to leave Indian territory. The haphazard manner in which 9 Punjab was dispatched exposed the sad fact that Army HQ had no strategic plan in place to deal with a major Chinese response to the Forward Posts policy. Had Nehru not specifically ordered the military to not construct responses to this scenario, again, disaster may have been averted. On 12th September, a meeting was held between Gen. L. P. Sen (Commander, Eastern theater), Gen. Umrao Singh and Gen. Niranjan Prasad. at Tezpur. Gen. Sen reiterated New Delhi's decision to "expel" the Chinese from Indian territory. Unfortunately, this was far removed from the ground situation. Gen. Umrao Singh correctly pointed out that the Chinese could quickly build up to Divisional strength and easily outbid any Indian reinforcements in the Thagla area.

Furthermore, all Indian supply trips to areas around Dhola would have to be by airdrops, while the Chinese roadhead was a few miles behind Thagla Ridge. Umrao Singh suggested that Dhola post should be withdrawn 3 miles to the south to the original map marked boundary, and that, moreover, sending 7 Brigade to Thagla would expose Towang and make defense of Nagaland and Manipur more onerous. Unfortunately, Army HQ ignored this sound military advice, due to political, rather than strategic, pressure. This would contribute to the tragic events leading it the defeat of 26th October - purely due to political expediency of pandering Indian security for long-winded, and, in retrospect, empty, Chinese claims of good faith.

The Chinese resorted to their previous methods adopted in Longju and Khenzemane. The Namka Chu, a fast moving riverlet with 4 bridges crossing it, had now become the de-facto military boundary, and later, the front. All 9 Punjab could do at this point was to dig in opposite the Chinese to prevent further incursion into Indian territory. 9 Punjab was pinned down opposite to Chinese posts and could not mount an attack due to the Chinese being on higher ground with clear lines of fire. In addition, any attack by 9 Punjab without proper bridging equipment, which they did not have, would have been suicidal due to constant Chinese monitoring.

9 Punjab finally managed to reach Dhola on the morning of 15th September and found Chinese troops on both sides of the Namka Chu river. The Chinese had control of the whole of the Thagla Ridge area, and when challenged, demanded that the Indians withdraw as the PRC decided to demarcate it "sacred Chinese land." The Chinese troops met were not mere Frontier guards, as was expected, but well armed troops with automatic weapons - the warmaking divisions of the PRC.

On 17th September, COAS HQ ordered 9 Punjab to "capture" Thagla Ridge. Brigadier Dalvi, the only senior commander in the area, refused to execute the order given the ground situation and asked for it to be countermanded. Meanwhile, in New Delhi the public was being assured that "the Army has been told to drive away the Chinese from our territory in NEFA", a task to which the IA was in no position to do. Dalvi realized that the Dhola had

On 20th September, a Chinese sentry near Bridge II on Namka Chu threw a grenade on the Indian position whereupon both sides opened fire. In the resultant shoot-out, 4 Chinese sentries were killed while there were 5 Indian casualties. The situation thus had escalated to a full-fledged shooting match. Meanwhile Eastern Command HQ and XXIII Corps finally managed to supply reinforcements and shore up 7 Brigade by rushing 1/9 Gorkhas and 2 Rajputs by 26th September. Stocking of supplies for 9 Punjab and the other regiments began belatedly but efforts were hampered due to severe lack of available portage. On the on the opening day of the war, October 20, 1962, 513 soldiers, 282 Jawans and officers died.

CROSSING THE LINE

Chinese-Indian border incursions are nothing new: according to the Indian government, 334 "encroachments" have already happened in 2014 (with 411, 426 and 213 incidents in 2013, 2012 and 2011, respectively). Disputed since China annexed all of Tibet in 1950, the border still eludes clarification. India claims about 15,000 square miles of Chinese-controlled territory in Aksai Chin, while China claims Indian Arunachal Pradesh (about 34,000 square miles) as "Southern Tibet".

The failure to clearly demarcate the China-India border has led to overlapping perceptions of where the so-called Line of Actual Control (LAC) lies, guaranteeing that rival border patrols will run into each other and force the issue.

It's possible that troops stationed high up in the Himalayas are just horribly out of touch with international politics. Alternatively, the People's Liberation Army could be airing its own foreign policy views in opposition to the civilian leadership.

Then again, this could also be a co-ordinated strategy on the part of the Chinese: talking peace and dangling economic incentives while implementing hard-nosed security policies, just as Beijing is doing in the East and South China Seas.

But whatever is behind the latest dial-up in tensions, it has taken emotions to a height unseen in years.

Making a scene

Territorial issues haunt Indian-Chinese relations even at the best of times – and so it went during Xi's visit. India had mixed success keeping Tibetan protests out of the Chinese president's path: to safeguard the atmosphere before his arrival in Ahmedabad, 52 Tibetan students were pre-emptively detained, and north-east Indian staff in Xi's hotel were banned from their workplace. But still, Tibetan girls descended onto Hyderabad House, site of the Delhi meeting, shouting anti-Chinese slogans. Other activists scaled scaffolding outside Xi's hotel and unfurled pro-Tibetan banners.

Some Indians speculated that the authorities deliberately allowed the protesters to reach Hyderabad House in retaliation for the border incursion. If true, beating up the protesters and bundling them away within minutes is a strange and feckless way to send a message to China.

In any case, ahead of Xi's arrival, it had been predicted that he would pressure New Delhi to help curtail the Dalai Lama's activities and shut down the Tibetan "government-in-exile". New Delhi reportedly rejected these demands – but in a signal that the incursions had introduced a *froideur* into proceedings, it also refused to resurrect its expression of support for "One China Principle" in the customary joint declaration. All this might sound like it calls for a reasonable sort of detente – but the problem is, New Delhi and Beijing need far more from each other than that.

Forced co-operation

The economic case for co-operation is obvious. China and India are currently trading only at the volume of US$66.4 billion, although India suffers a trade deficit of around US$35 billion. The 16 deals signed during Xi's visit will bequeath a Chinese investment of US$20 billion in Indian power equipment, automobiles, infrastructure development and airlines.

For India, securing foreign investment is a crucial priority. China has plenty of capital to invest, and if Modi is serious about co-operating in global institutions with the other BRICS, he will have to defrost New Delhi's relations with Beijing.

But for China, embroiled in various sharp territorial disputes with neighbours on its eastern Pacific front, improving relations with India is a point of paramount security importance.

With Modi headed to the US with an imperative to repair relations with Washington, this just weeks after he implicitly decried Chinese "expansionism" in Tokyo, hopes that the world's two largest countries will manage to improve their relationship may be premature at best.

Dalai Lama Visit Ignites Sino-Indian Border Dispute

In early November, the Dalai Lama is going to visit the majestic Tawang Monastery, perched atop a ridge in the Indian province of Arunachal Pradesh. Surrounded by thick clouds and perennial mist, the monastery sometimes seems almost to be suspended from heaven.

It is also at the very centre of thousands of square kilometres of terrain claimed by both China and India, although India currently possesses it. It now risks becoming a proxy battleground on which both India and China seek to proclaim their sovereignty. The religious leader's visit can be seen as a card played by both India and the Tibetan exile community to keep pressure on China.

Home to one of the most sacred Buddhist monasteries, Tawang is the birthplace of the sixth Dalai Lama, Tsayang Gyatso, in the 17th century. The current Dalai Lama passed through this region when he fled into exile in 1959. Chhime Chhoekyapa, the exiled Tibetan spiritual leader's aide, told the media that the Dalai Lama is "going there for teaching. This has nothing to do with politics, there is nothing political about it." In Chinese eyes, however, and perhaps Indian eyes as well, everything the Dalai Lama does has something to do with politics. And this is a region that Beijing calls "Southern Tibet."

When asked about the Dalai Lama's upcoming visit, Beijing officials have fumed. "China expresses strong concern about this information," said Jiang Yu, the spokeswoman for China's Foreign Ministry. "The visit further reveals the Dalai clique's anti-China and separatist essence. China's stance on the so-called Arunachal Pradesh is consistent. We firmly oppose Dalai visiting the so-called Arunachal Pradesh." Tension has slowly been ratcheting up between the two Asian giants, with media commentators fanning the flames. "Is China itching to wage war on India?" asked Professor Brahma Chellaney in the September issue of the Far Eastern Economic Review. Reports have appeared in Chinese state media alleging that India was moving troops and fighter aircraft to the northeast, specifically into Sikkim and Arunachal Pradesh.

India, however, is acutely aware of its shortcomings in the territory it controls. The Chinese, with their extensive roads and railways, can actually come up to the Line of Actual Control, take a stroll and walk back. Two years ago, Chinese soldiers demolished a Buddhist statue that Indians had erected at Bumla, the main border pass above Tawang, according to a member of the Indian Parliament, Nabam Rebia. It takes several days for India's troops to get to the border. But slowly India is finding its voice as it struggles to speed up its own preparedness.

China claims around 90,000 square kilometres of territory, roughly the size of Arunachal Pradesh, regarding the area as "disputed." China lays claim to Tawang on behalf of the Tibetans. But in the exile community in Dharamsala, where the Dalai Lama and thousands of Tibetan refugees live, the community is not impressed.

They do not claim Tawang as Tibetan, let alone Chinese territory. The Dalai Lama's travel plans were announced a week after his recent visit to Taiwan to visit victims of tropical storm Morakot. China denounced the Taiwan trip, although its complaints were remarkably muted. The visit to Arunachal Pradesh has now drawn further attention to China's treatment of Tibetan activists and the Dalai Lama's calls for cultural and religious freedom and autonomy.

Tawang became part of modern India when Tibetan leaders signed a treaty with British officials in 1914 that established the McMahon Line between Tibet and British-run India. Tawang fell south of the line. The treaty, the Simla Convention, is not recognized by China. "We recognize it because we agreed to it," said Samdhong Rinpoche, prime minister of the Tibetan government-in-exile. "If China agreed to it now, it would be a recognition of the power of the Tibetan government at that time."

Tawang's native population is almost entirely Buddhist. Its origin is obscure. It was a part of the kingdom of Tibet in medieval times although local tribal rulers have governed it from time to time. The British declared the area off-limits in 1873. India's independence from Britain severed it from Tibet. In 1962 Chinese troops conquered Tawang during the invasion of Tibet and for six months it was controlled by the Chinese. After their retreat, Tawang again came under Indian control.

India denied the Dalai Lama permission to visit Tawang the last time he requested to do so. This time it is playing the Dalai Lama card to the full. Officials in India's Ministry of External Affairs insist that "things are changing" and that India is getting more assertive. On Sept. 16, India's foreign minister, S.M. Krishna, rejected China's opposition to the visit.

In an interview on IBN7, the sister channel of India's CNN-IBN, Krishna said China's objections had no merit. While the government has not explicitly said the visit will be permitted, Krishna said: "Arunachal Pradesh is a part of India and the Dalai Lama is free to go anywhere in India. The only question is that he is not expected to comment on political developments." Analysts say the Tibetan leader's visit will reassert Arunachal's status as an Indian territory. "The timing of his trip [to Arunachal Pradesh] is significant. It comes while the debate over his visit to Taiwan is still hot," said Bhaskar Roy, a New Delhi-based China analyst. "Tibetans are as good at playing these games as the Chinese. They know such a visit will keep up the pressure on China."

In Dharamsala, Samdhong Rinpoche, Tibet's prime minister in exile, called Beijing's objections to the visit "absurd," adding that "Arunachal Pradesh and the Tawang region are an integral part of India. If the Dalai Lama, who has stayed in India for the last 50 years, is visiting any part of the country why does this bother China?

If the Dalai Lama goes to Chinese territories it can raise objections but in this case has no business to interfere." The Arunachal Pradesh government is urging New Delhi to ignore the Chinese opposition. "Chinese claims over Arunachal Pradesh are simply baseless and not correct. Arunachal Pradesh is an integral part of India and would continue to be so," said Chief Minister Dorjee Khandu. "They [the Chinese] are opposed to everything that His Holiness does," said a spokesman for the Dalai Lama's private office in Dharamsala.

Tawang's strategic importance cannot be ruled out. The place provides the shortest route from Tibet into India. The Dalai Lama himself took this route to escape into India in 1959. Indian defence officials have already raised alarms declaring China and not Pakistan to be India's biggest threat. They believe that control over Sikkim and Arunachal Pradesh would enable Chinese forces to overrun the entire northeast border region. Chinese troops repeatedly have attempted to gain control of Sikkim's evocatively named Finger Area, a tiny but key strategic location where Beijing does not dispute the frontier.

In June this year, General J J Singh, governor of Arunachal Pradesh and former chief of army staff, announced the deployment of two army divisions of around 25,000 to 30,000 soldiers each along the Arunachal Pradesh border with China. The strength of India's Sukhoi fighter jet fleet in the Northeast is being increased. It remains to be seen if the Dalai Lama's visit will be the trigger that causes them to be used.

THE MACARTNEY-MACDONALD LINE

In 1893, Hung Ta-chen, a senior Chinese official at Kashgar, handed a map of the boundary proposed by China to George Macartney, the British consul-general at Kashgar. This boundary placed the Lingzi Tang plains, which are south of the Laktsang range, in India, and Aksai Chin proper, which is north of the Laktsang range, in China. Macartney agreed with the proposal and forwarded it to the British Indian government. This border, along the Karakoram Mountains, was proposed and supported by British officials for a number of reasons.

The Karakoram Mountains formed a natural boundary, which would set the British borders up to the Indus River watershed while leaving the Tarim River watershed in Chinese control, and Chinese control of this tract would present a further obstacle to Russian advance in Central Asia. The British presented this line, known as the Macartney-MacDonald Line, to the Chinese in 1899 in a note by Sir Claude MacDonald. The Qing government did not respond to the note, and the British took that as Chinese acquiescence. Although no official boundary had ever been negotiated, China believed that this had been the accepted boundary.

1899 to 1947

Both the Johnson-Ardagh and the Macartney-MacDonald lines were used on British maps of India. Until at least 1908, the British took the Macdonald line to be the boundary, but in 1911, the Xinhai Revolution resulted in the collapse of central power in China, and by the end of World War I, the British officially used the Johnson Line. However they took no steps to establish outposts or assert actual control on the ground. In 1927, the line was adjusted again as the government of British India abandoned the Johnson line in favour of a line along the Karakoram range further south. However, the maps were not updated and still showed the Johnson Line.

From 1917 to 1933, the "Postal Atlas of China", published by the Government of China in Peking had shown the boundary in Aksai Chin as per the Johnson line, which runs along the Kunlun mountains. The "Peking University Atlas", published in 1925, also put the Aksai Chin in India.

When British officials learned of Soviet officials surveying the Aksai Chin for Sheng Shicai, warlord of Xinjiang in 1940–1941, they again advocated the Johnson Line. At this point the British had still made no attempts to establish outposts or control over the Aksai Chin, nor was the issue ever discussed with the governments of China or Tibet, and the boundary remained undemarcated at India's independence.

Since 1947

Upon independence in 1947, the government of India used the Johnson Line as the basis for its official boundary in the west, encompassing Aksai Chin. However, India did not claim the northern areas near Shahidulla and Khotan, for including which in Indian territory, among other things, Johnson had been criticised. From the Karakoram Pass (which is not under dispute), the Indian claim line extends northeast of the Karakoram Mountains north of the salt flats of the Aksai Chin, to set a boundary at the Kunlun Mountains, and incorporating part of the Karakash River and Yarkand River watersheds. From there, it runs east along the Kunlun Mountains, before turning southwest through the Aksai Chin salt flats, through the Karakoram Mountains, and then to Pangong Lake.

On 1 July 1954 Prime Minister Nehru wrote a memo directing that the maps of India be revised to show definite boundaries on all frontiers. Up to this point, the boundary in the Aksai Chin sector, based on the Johnson Line, had been described as "undemarcated."

During the 1950s, the People's Republic of China built a 1,200 kilometres (750 mi) road connecting Xinjiang and western Tibet, of which 179 kilometres (111 mi) ran south of the Johnson Line through the Aksai Chin region claimed by India. Aksai Chin was easily accessible from China, but was more difficult for the Indians on the other side of the Karakorams to reach. The Indians did not learn of the existence of the road until 1957, which was confirmed when the road was shown in Chinese maps published in 1958.

The Indian position, as stated by prime minister Jawaharlal Nehru, was that the Aksai Chin was "part of the Ladakh region of India for centuries" and that this northern border was a "firm and definite one which was not open to discussion with anybody".

The Chinese minister, Zhou Enlai argued that the western border had never been delimited, that the Macartney-MacDonald Line, which left the Aksai Chin within Chinese borders was the only line ever proposed to a Chinese government, and that the Aksai Chin was already under Chinese jurisdiction, and that negotiations should take into account the status quo.

In April 2013 India claimed, referencing their own perception of the Line of Actual Control (LAC) location, that Chinese troops had established a camp in the Daulat Beg Oldi sector, 10 km on their side of the Line of Actual Control. This figure was later revised to a 19 km claim. According to Indian media, the incursion included Chinese military helicopters entering Indian airspace to drop supplies to the troops. However, Chinese officials denied any trespassing having taken place. Soldiers from both countries briefly set up camps on the ill-defined frontier facing each other, but the tension was defused when both sides pulled back soldiers in early May. In September 2014, India and China had a standoff at the LAC, when Indian workers began constructing a canal in the border village of Demchok, and Chinese civilians protested with the army's support. It ended after about three weeks, when both sides agreed to withdraw troops.

Trans Karakoram Tract

The Johnson Line is not used west of the Karakoram Pass, where China adjoins Pakistan-administered Gilgit–Baltistan. On 13 October 1962, China and Pakistan began negotiations over the boundary west of the Karakoram Pass. In 1963, the two countries settled their boundaries largely on the basis of the Macartney-MacDonald Line, which left the Trans Karakoram Tract in China, although the agreement provided for renegotiation in the event of a settlement of the Kashmir dispute. India does not recognise that Pakistan and China have a common border, and claims the tract as part of the domains of the pre-1947 state of Kashmir and Jammu. However, India's claim line in that area does not extend as far north of the Karakoram Mountains as the Johnson Line.

8

Facts Behind China-India Border Dispute and McMahon Line

If a general of the Chinese imperial government representing the Manchu dynasty had, by force of arms, pillage and plunder, succeeded in subjugating the North American continent and on that basis had artificially created a border line between the United States and Canada called, let us say, The Manchu Line, would a sovereign U.S. government abide by thus border line?

Let us suppose further that the boundary line demarcated by this general included, for the Canadian side, parts of Buffalo, Detroit, Seattle and Duluth. Let us suppose again that the treaty between Canada and the U.S. dictated by this general had never been accepted by any government of the United States, and that in truth the people of the U.S. regarded this treaty and its boundary line as illegal, null and void, and as the imposition of a foreign power at a time when the U.S. was weak, divided and under the domination of a foreign imperialist power.

All we have to do with this analogy is to just change the name — Canada to India, United States to China and China to Great Britain — and the picture becomes immeasurably clearer than it is represented in the U.S. press.

THE MCMAHON LINE

It is the position of the Chinese People's Republic that the so-called McMahon Line — named after the British General McMahon — is illegal, null and void, and the result of a predatory, imperialist imposition of the British government in the year 1914.

No Chinese government ever accepted the McMahon Line. Neither did the Imperial Government of China in 1914, nor the Chiang Kai-Shek government ever agree to it. The very fact that even the Chiang Kai-Shek clique, which is nothing but a tool of U.S. imperialism, has not dared to dispute the Chinese People's Republic's position of the China-India border dispute, it in itself the most eloquent testimony to the correctness of the Chinese position.

Nevertheless, the Chinese People's Republic has made every effort to achieve a reasonable and just settlement of the territory in dispute. It has consistently shunned the use of arms.

Proposals For Negotiations

Although the border dispute is almost three years old now, and the Chinese have made innumerable other approaches to the Indian government to settle it on some amicable and acceptable basis the Nehru government has invariably turned them down. In the past two months alone the Chinese government made several proposals for negotiations. It made a notable effort on August 4, and another one on September 13. In neither of these proposals did the Chinese government lay down any preconditions for the negotiations. Nor did the Chinese government resort to the type of language which could in any way be construed as a threat to India.

On the contrary, the diplomatic notes directed to the Indian government were couched in the most conciliatory language, and were calculated to effectuate a reasonable settlement which would safeguard the territorial integrity of China as well as India. As a matter of fact, the London Times, certainly no friend of the Chinese revolutionary government, had to publicly admit on October 8 that if military operations were resumed on the Sino-Indian border, "onlookers will have to note that it was New Dehli.. , that declined to embark upon them (talks)..."

The position of the London Times is of exceptional importance because it has always sided with India as against China. The London Times was obliged to make the above statement only after the Indian paper, Tribune, had reported that at a cabinet meeting the Indian government had decided to use armed force to deal with China.

Nehru's "Limited Offensive"

It was also reported in the world press on October 8, that Nehru had authorized India's new commander-in chief of the eastern border area to "fight a limited offensive operation." These are the incontrovertible facts. As to what lies behind the aggressive attitude of the Nehru government, it must be borne in mind first of all that the imperialist world, particularly the U.S. would like nothing better than to see the two principal Asiatic powers, the two powers which hold the greatest revolutionary promise for mankind in the east, locked in military combat, shedding the blood of thousands, absorbing the resources and energies of millions of people, which should be used to construct a revolutionary way of life.

The efforts of the U.S. government, it must be noted, have been directed, insofar as India is concerned, not only to make it economically and financially dependent upon U.S. monopoly interests, but also to inflame the Indian bourgeoisie, particularly its right-wing extremist elements, against the Chinese People's Republic.

Four Billion U.S. Aid

According to The New York Times of October 22(1969), the U.S. has poured into India more than four billion dollars. A substantial section of this money has gone to line the pockets of Indian businessmen, government officials, and especially the extremist elements who are interested in diverting the mass discontent of the Indian peasants and workers into other channels. U.S. diplomats, State Department planners, and military figures in the Pentagon have for a long time felt that the biggest diversionary tactic that imperialism could employ to disrupt the revolutionary anti-imperialist front was to continually stir up, bribe and corrupt as many of the representatives of the Indian bourgeoisie as it could to fan the flames of an India-China war.

Nehru himself was subjected to unremitting pressure when he was in the U.S. More U.S. aid was used as bait to lure Nehru into the trap of a protracted India-China war, which can only result in further detriment to India, China and the cause of all oppressed people.

Since Nehru's Visit

Since the Indian Prime Minister left the shores of the U.S. there have been only rare intervals in which there has been a let up in the war fever fanned by the Indian bourgeoisie and its agent Nehru. For a long time Nehru played the role of moderator between left and right in the Indian-China border dispute, cautioning the extremist elements of the bourgeoisie in Parliament, and repudiating suggestions for offensive operations by his military advisers. But his October 4 decision, taken after a cabinet meeting, made it clear beyond any shadow of a doubt that he had completely capitulated to the right wing on this issue and was kowtowing to U.S. imperialist interests. The present military efforts of the Chinese are merely a response to the offensive action taken after the Indian cabinet session.

A Defensive Battle

The Chinese government is fighting a defensive battle. It is only too well aware that U.S. imperialism is ready at all times to take advantage of any preoccupation that China may have with India to open another front against China wherever and whenever it finds it feasible, whether it be in the Pescadores, the Taiwan strait or new harassments over the air space of China. There are those who say China should give in — give up what belongs to China in the interest of peace. These are the people who are always ready to give, especially things that do not belong to them. When to give — or whether to give — is a question which only the Chinese can decide, as it as *their* territory. Surely the Chinese, who have gone through hell and fire in the course of 22 years of civil war, in which they have had to trade many times — space for time — and in fact have endured many retreats, need no reminders on this score.

Solidarity Of Asian People

The workers of the world and the progressive anti-imperialist countries in particular, are most deeply concerned in a speedy, reasonable and honorable settlement on the part of China and India. Such a settlement can only be arrived at if the ruling group in New Delhi accepts China's offer for the resumption of talks on a high level between the two governments without any pre conditions. A border settlement would remove a tremendous obstacle to the solidarity of the Asian people who are struggling for a new life, and would be a tremendous rebuff to imperialism and its servants and underlings.

INDIA-CHINA RIVALRY EXPOSED IN ONGOING BORDER DISPUTES

As a consequence, the 4,056-kilometer (2,520 miles) frontier between India and China, one of the longest inter-state borders in the world, remains the only one of China's land borders not defined, let alone demarcated, on maps or delineated on the ground. While Indians doubt China's sincerity in border negotiations, Chinese question India's leaders' will and capacity to settle the dispute in a "give-and-take" spirit. Up until 2005, there was a great deal of optimism about a possible breakthrough. Evidence of this came during Prime Minister Vajpayee's China visit in June 2003 when New Delhi's readiness to address Chinese concerns on Tibet was matched by Beijing's willingness to resolve the Sikkim issue by recognizing the trade route through the Nathu La Pass on the China-Sikkim frontier with India and later showing Sikkim as part of India in its maps.

For its fraction, New Delhi reiterated its stance on the Tibetan Autonomous Region as part of China. This visit also paved the way for border talks to be held through special representatives of the leaders to find an early "political solution" to the boundary question, rather than going only by the legal and historical claims of the two sides. India indicated its willingness to settle for the territorial status quo by giving up claims to the Aksai Chin in Ladakh and hoped China would give up its claims to Arunachal Pradesh in the eastern sector and recognize the McMahon Line just as Beijing had accepted Tibet's British-drawn boundaries with Afghanistan and Myanmar (formerly known as Burma).

In order to give a new thrust to the ongoing border negotiations, an "Agreement on the Political Parameters and Guiding Principles for the Settlement of the Boundary Question" was signed during Chinese Prime Minister Wen Jiabao's visit to India in April 2005. The joint statement issued at the end of the visit talked of a "Strategic and Cooperative Partnership" between India and China.

No Group

Since then, though, Beijing has upped the ante by demanding major territorial concessions in populated areas of Arunachal Pradesh on terms that many in New Delhi see as "humiliating and non-negotiable." Tawang, in particular, has emerged as a sticking point since the Chinese claim it to be central to Tibetan Buddhism given that the sixth Dalai Lama was born there. Ties between China and India were strained even further in May 2007 when the Chinese government refused a visa to an Indian official from disputed Arunachal Pradesh to visit China, and the Indian government's invitation soon thereafter to Taiwan's opposition Kuomintang (K.M.T.) party presidential candidate, Ma Ying-jeou, to visit India in June 2007 to hold talks with senior Indian officials. China voiced its opposition to Ma's visit and called on India to abide by the "One China policy."

Thereafter came media reports of the People's Liberation Army (P.L.A.) encroachments across the Line of Actual Control (L.A.C.) and Chinese small arms supplies to insurgents in India's volatile northeast via Bangladesh and Myanmar. Then, in August 2007, Beijing demanded the removal of two old Indian Army bunkers near the tri-junction of Sikkim, Bhutan and Tibet, claiming that these were located on their territory. This move raised questions about China's declared policy of treating Sikkim as part of Indian territory. Not surprisingly, China's increasing assertiveness over the disputed borders has led to a rapid meltdown in the Sino-Indian border talks and a "mini-Cold War" has quietly taken hold at the diplomatic level during the past two years, despite public protestations of amity.

Some observers argue that Hu Jintao's desire to control the choice of the next Dalai Lama has led to pressuring India to concede access to the Tawang Monastery, which is crucial to this choice. The deterioration in Sino-Indian relations under Hu, however, should not have come as a surprise given his reputation as a hardliner over Tibet. (After all, Deng Xiaoping had groomed him for the Chinese Communist Party leadership because of his prominent role in the successful suppression of the Tibetan revolt in 1988.) In this context, the rapid pace development of road, rail and military infrastructure in Tibet close to its borders with India and Nepal is seen as preempting any possible destabilization of Tibet post-Dalai Lama.

Others, however, do not see any sinister designs in western China's development. Instead, they attribute the recent downturn in Sino-Indian relations more to domestic power struggles within the Chinese Communist Party (C.C.P.) than to the Dalai Lama succession issue or to Chinese concerns about India's growing tilt toward the United States. While there may be an element of truth in all these arguments, there are other more fundamental reasons behind the recent chill in Sino-Indian relations. Apparently, the strategic consequences of India's economic resurgence coupled with U.S. Secretary of State Condoleezza Rice's offer in March 2005 to "help make India a major world power in the 21st century" have greatly bothered the Chinese. This offer, and the long-term India-U.S. defense cooperation framework and the July 2005 U.S.-India nuclear energy deal that followed soon after, have been compared by Chinese strategic analysts to "the strategic tilt" toward China executed by former U.S. President Richard Nixon in 1971 to contain the common Soviet threat. Claiming that these developments have "destabilizing" and "negative implications" for their country's future, China's India-watchers have started warning their government that Beijing "should not take India lightly any longer."

Chinese leaders be led to believe that China's growing economic and military might would eventually enable Beijing to re-establish the Sino-centric hierarchy of Asia's past as the U.S. saps its energies in fighting small wars in the Islamic world, Japan shrinks economically and demographically while India remains subdued by virtue of Beijing's "special relationships" with its South Asian neighbours. However, a number of "negative developments," from Beijing's perspective, since early 2005 — the Indian and Japanese bids for permanent seats on the U.N. Security Council, the formation of the East Asia Summit that includes India, Australia and New Zealand, the Indo-U.S. nuclear deal, India's ability to sustain a high economic growth rate of eight to nine percent and the strategic implications of India's "Look East" policy — have apparently upset Chinese calculations.

Therefore, after a hiatus of a few years, Chinese media commentaries have resumed their criticism of Washington's "hegemonic ideas" and for drawing "India in as a tool for its global strategic pattern." Some Chinese analysts express serious reservations about U.S. efforts to draw "India in as a tool for its global strategic pattern," arguing that "India's DNA doesn't allow itself to become an ally subordinate to the U.S., like Japan or Britain." Nonetheless, most see India as a "future strategic competitor" that would be an active member of an anti-China grouping due to the structural power shifts in the international system and advocate putting together a comprehensive "contain India" strategy based on both economic tools (aid, trade, infrastructural development) and enhanced military cooperation with "pro-China" countries.

COOPERATION OR RIVALRY

Both China and India are feeling the pressure of diminishing oil discoveries and flat-lined oil production at a time when expansion of their domestic economies is rapidly increasing demand for energy. They have made energy the focal point of their diplomatic overtures to states far and wide. More significantly, faced with a market in which politics has an equal, if not greater, influence on price as economics, the two have also decided to coordinate their efforts to secure energy resources overseas.

In essence, China and India plan to work together to secure energy resources without unnecessarily bidding up the price of those resources, thereby agreeing to a consumer's cartel representing 2.3 billion potential consumers. Together, their combined markets and purchasing power offers an extremely attractive partner to energyproducing states, especially the ones that face Western pressure over their human rights records or the nature of their political institutions.

It has been argued by many that cooperation between China and India on energy issues is the only way ahead if both states want to gain economies of scale and negotiation muscle. In many ways, both states face similar constraints in achieving energy security and a coordinated approach would benefit them both. Competition only ends up driving up the costs of acquisition, thereby diminishing future returns. And there has been recognition of this at the highest levels of the government in both states. China and India signed a range of memoranda on energy cooperation that covers a full scope of areas, including upstream exploration and production, the refining and marketing of petroleum products and petrochemicals, the laying of national and transnational oil and gas pipelines, frontier and cutting-edge research and development, and the promotion of environmentfriendly fuels. The two states have agreed to strengthen the exchange of information when bidding for oil resources in a third party country in order to realise mutual benefit. China has pledged to promote cooperation with India in civil nuclear energy and to view this cooperation in the context of climate change and increasing non-polluting sources in the energy mix. The former Indian petroleum minister, Mani Shankar Aiyar, made it clear that he thought that India and China joining hands to bid jointly for oil and gas assets under a "monopsonistic" arrangement was much better than the two states competing in their quest for energy resources. He had even floated the idea of an Asian energy grid that might follow the trajectory of the European Coal and Steel Community, which grew into the EU. According to Aiyar, "India and China don't have to go through fratricide in order to arrive at the conclusion that it is better to cooperate on energy security."

Two of the most talked-about ventures exemplifying Sino-Indian cooperation in this area have been investments by China and India in the exploration of hydrocarbon fields in Iran and Sudan. China and India hold a 50 per cent and 20 per cent stake respectively in the development and exploration of the Yadavaran field in Iran, while China's share is 40 per cent and India's 25 per cent in Sudan's Greater Nile Oil project. The proposal for a single transportation route for natural gas imports from Iran has also been floating around, with the promise of extending the India-Iran gas pipeline via Pakistan to China. In a first alliance of its kind between the Chinese and Indian state energy companies, a successful joint offer was made to buy Petro Canada's 38 per cent stake in Al Furat Production Company, Syria's largest oil producer, which is operated and majority owned by Royal Dutch Shell.

This was followed by India's largest gas distributor, Gas Authority of India (GAIL), setting up a joint venture with Beijing Gas Group Company to distribute compressed natural gas (CNG) in Beijing. It has also signed a memorandum of understanding with the China National Offshore Oil Corporation (CNOOC) to develop offshore oil and gas projects in Indonesia and Australia. India and China had also come together to jointly bid for stakes in oil ventures in Colombia and Kazakhstan. China has sought close cooperation with India in its offshore and deep-sea oil exploration projects.

While such attempts at cooperation have engendered a lot of enthusiasm in some quarters, these developments form a small part of a much broader China-India energy relationship, which remains largely competitive, if not conflictual. It is the structural realities of global politics that make it highly likely that China and India will compete for energy resources in the coming years. They are two rising powers in Asia, and each is trying to expand its reach and influence.

The border dispute between the two states remains unresolved, and suspicion of each other's motives remains high. India views Chinese attempts to support Pakistan and improve its relations with its other neighbours as an attempt to limit India's reach and influence. China, however, is concerned about recent Indian moves to get close to the United States and views this as part of the U.S. strategy to contain China. The security dilemma between China and India remains as potent as ever, and despite some positive developments in recent years, it is unlikely to subside anytime soon. This will also shape the energy relationship between the two states in the coming years. In many ways, this competition is already under way under various guises.

Chinese Overtures in India's Neighbourhood

China's interest in oil exploration in the Indian Ocean is a matter of strategic concern for India. Concerns have been expressed in India about what has come to be known as China's "string of pearls" strategy of bases and diplomatic ties stretching from the Middle East to southern China that includes Gwadar port in Pakistan, Chittagong in Bangladesh, and Hambantota in Sri Lanka. While Bangladesh has granted China exploration rights for developing natural gas fields of its own, friction in India-Bangladesh ties has precluded cooperation between India and Bangladesh on the issue of energy. China's activities near the Kenyan port of Mombasa will make India further wary of Chinese long-term plans vis-à-vis India.

After India realised that one of its closest neighbours and a major source of natural gas, Myanmar, is drifting towards China, it reversed its decades-old policy of isolating the Burmese junta and has now begun to deal with it directly. New Delhi not only assured investment in developing the Sittwe Port and extended a $20 million credit for renovation of the Thanlyin Refinery, but it also supported Myanmar against the U.S. censure motion in an attempt to lure the junta to grant preferential treatment to India in the supply of natural gas. But the Chinese firms were the ones that got preferential treatment in the award of blocks and gas, apparently in recognition of China's steady opposition to the United States moves against Myanmar's junta in the UN. This failure has further galvanised India into wooing Yangon even more aggressively.

Apart from India's existing infrastructure projects in Myanmar, which include the 160-kilometer India-Myanmar friendship road built by India's Border Roads Organisation in 2001, India is looking into the possibility of embarking on a second road project and investing in a deep-sea project (Sagar Samridhi) to explore oil and gas in the Bay of Bengal as well as the Shwe gas pipeline project in western Myanmar. Even as the Burmese military junta was readying for a violent crackdown on monks and democracy activists, the Indian petroleum minister was in Yangon signing a production deal for three deep-water exploration blocks off the Rakhine coast. While India did support the United Nations Human Rights Council resolution against Myanmar, it tried to tone it down to little effect as it tried to balance its democratic credentials with its desire to retain its influence with the Burmese military government. India has found it difficult to counter Chinese influence in Myanmar, with China selling everything from weapons to food grains to Myanmar.

Emerging Competition in Central Asia

As the geopolitical importance of Central Asia has increased in recent years, all the major powers have been keen to expand their influence in the region, and India is no exception. It shares many of the interests of other major powers such as the United States, Russia, and China vis-à-vis Central Asia, including access to Central Asian energy resources, controlling the spread of radical Islam, ensuring political stability, and strengthening of regional economies. But unlike China and Russia, its interests converge with that of the United States in Central Asia and some have even suggested that it is in U.S. interests to have a greater Indian presence in Central Asia to counter growing Chinese or Russian involvement. Central Asia is crucial for India not only because of its oil and gas reserves that India wishes to tap for its energy security but also because other major powers such as the United States, Russia, and China have already started competing for influence in the region. India's concern about rising Chinese influence in Central Asia was also reflected in India's desire to become a member of the Shanghai Cooperation Organisation (SCO). While ostensibly the SCO is aimed at tackling the security concerns in Central Asia, including extremism and separatism, it also serves as an important instrument in keeping control of the region and limiting U.S. influence there.

India has been granted an observer status, but China made sure that Pakistan was also invited, thereby diminishing India's influence. China has a major geopolitical advantage in Central Asian oil politics.

Oil resources in the region are of vital importance to China's future oil security and will become an important basis for China's future military strategy. In the event of an unexpected military crisis, China would have to rely heavily on oil resources in mid-Asia to sustain military operations. The extension of the pan-Asian global energy bridge from Central Asia to Iran would link China to the Middle East.

This lifeline from the Caspian Sea to China, incorporating the Middle East, would most benefit China's long-term strategic energy security policy. It would leave China in a much less vulnerable position with respect to both oil reserve depletion and transportation risks. By drastically shifting the most important and busiest global energy artery from the Strait of Malacca to a line across mainland China, the creation of new geopolitical tendencies inside Asia would be inevitable. China would undoubtedly benefit from such a pivotal geostrategic position, particularly as its coastal regions would serve as the refining link between Middle Eastern and Central Asian crude oil—and the Asian-Pacific market. Chinese aspirations as an "energy bridge" in Central Asia are long term and will require massive international investment in pipeline infrastructure and coastal refineries. The Chinese National Petroleum Company (CNPC) has an oil-swap agreement with Iran. Oil purchased by China from the Uzen oil field in Kazakhstan is pumped to a refinery near Tehran, with China receiving an equivalent amount of Iranian crude exported from Iran's Gulf coast. China's other deal with Kazakhstan includes a commitment to build a 3,000-kilometer pipeline from the oil fields to the Xinjiang province of China, and a 250-kilometer pipeline to the border of Iran (via Turkmenistan). Indian and Chinese state-owned oil companies were engaged in a bidding war to acquire a Canadian company with oil fields in Kazakhstan.

China's National Petroleum Corporation won the bid against India's ONGC after offering a higher sum for Petro Kazakhstan. The Caspian Sea region in Central Asia is another region that is going to see major powers, including China and India, jostling for influence, given its new-found importance as a still-growing source of oil and gas. The area is distant from world markets, generating uncertainty whether Caspian oil will increasingly be sent east or will continue to flow west through Russia or Turkey. In all probability, China is likely to emerge as a new energy hub for Caspian oil and more pipelines will be built to western China, even as India is yet to make any significant headway in exploiting the region's resources.

Courting of Russia

India's ONGC has a 20 per cent stake in exploration and development of the Sakhalin-I oil and gas fields in Russia and has been keen to import natural gas from Sakhalin. But China outmaneuvered India by offering a $6 billion loan offer to the Russian Oil company, Rosneft, which then asked India to outbid China if it wanted to be considered for the exports. India's OVL also lost out to China in the acquisition of BP's oil assets in Russia. In one of the first big-ticket oil asset acquisitions by China in Russia, TNK-BP, which controls the OAO Udmurtneft fields in Russia, decided to opt for China's Sinopec in the place of OVL. Though India has expressed its desire to buy nearly a quarter of its annual oil imports in the next decade from Russia, and Russia plans to increase the share of its energy exports to Asia from the current 5 per cent to around 25 per cent, India will have to compete with other Asian nations, most significantly China, which are as eager to court Russia.

While the Chinese have a natural advantage of having a common border with Russia, their diplomacy also seems to be more proactive. Energy issues are driving China and Russia into the arms of each other politically, leading to the mobilisation of the Shanghai Cooperation Council to focus on energy issues, with the possibility of it evolving into a military alliance to rival NATO.

Sino-Russian ties have improved considerably following a plethora of agreements and declarations on energy security cooperation. Russia could become an important supplier of oil to China in the coming years. The two states have performed a feasibility study on a $1.6 billion, 2, 200-kilometer oil pipeline project to bring Serbian oil to northeast China which the Chinese government views as one way for alleviating its dependence on the Middle East oil supplies. Russia is a world-class gas producer, which fits well into the Chinese strategy to diversify its energy requirements and thus alleviate its dependence on oil. For such a venture to be economically viable, however, significant international confidence and cooperation is required at a multinational level; investment and demand by Japan and Korea is required to realise such a scheme. Russia is also investing in nuclear power reactors in China.

China, India, and the West

A key area of friction and a barrier to engagement between the democratic West and autocratic Beijing is China's relationship with energy-rich "rogue states." Chinese companies, backed by political intent and government finances, are willing to invest in countries with high political risk. With competition for scarce energy resources intense, China has pursued deals with international pariah states that are off limits to Western companies because of sanctions, security concerns, or ethical policy and the threat of international condemnation. China's relation with state sponsors of terrorism provides a great deal of money, allowing these countries to continue to harbour terrorists and to maintain a policy of oppression and exploitation of their people. This highlights the ideological affinity between China and other authoritarian regimes that are also anxious for market transition while maintaining singleparty rule—Myanmar, Vietnam, Cambodia, Laos, Iran, Sudan, and North Korea. China remains unconcerned as to the source of vital energy, whether Iranian, Kazakh, Sudanese, or Angolan. China considers anyone who helps with its oil security problem to be a friend of Beijing. China's unconditional assistance and opaque commercial transactions, which do little to encourage these rogue States to improve their governance systems, is viewed in Beijing as necessary in order to guarantee its own continued economic growth.

India, conversely, seems to be aligning itself with the West and is investing significantly in trying to evolve a strategic partnership with the United States. The desire of the George W. Bush administration to achieve full civil nuclear energy cooperation with India as part of its broader goals of promoting nuclear power and achieving nuclear security has marked a new phase in the rather unstable bilateral relationship between the world's oldest and the world's largest democracies.

The nuclear agreement creates a major exception to the U.S. prohibition against nuclear assistance to any country that doesn't accept international monitoring of all its nuclear facilities. India, with sixteen nuclear plants, plans to build seven more and has been promised U.S. help to triple its collection by 2020. China remains the only major power that has taken an ambivalent stand of the nuclear deal. While it has indicated that it is willing to promote bilateral cooperation with India in civil nuclear energy, it has also hinted that it might step up its nuclear cooperation with Pakistan.

Given the strained relationship between Iran and the United States, India's traditionally close ties with Iran have emerged as a major factor that is influencing how certain sections of U.S. policymakers are evaluating the Indo-U.S. partnership. Though India has tried to carefully balance its relations with Iran and the United States, because of intense U.S. pressure, especially after the signing of the nuclear deal, India has moved closer to the United States on the issue of the Iranian nuclear programme.

The United States, preoccupied with the global war on terrorism, is becoming increasingly concerned with Chinese diplomatic activity, particularly in Asia and the Middle East, where its own presence in these regions could be marginalised. China's record of arms sales and support to energy-rich Middle Eastern countries and state sponsors of terrorism in the Gulf region continues to agitate Washington. Asia's oil imports from the Middle East are set to increase rapidly, primarily because of rising demand in China and India and Japan's continuing requirement to import all of its oil requirements. Ensuring reliable and stable flows from the Gulf region will be Asia's biggest challenge. This may result in the political and economic dependence of many Middle East states shifting from the West towards Asia. As it is America's dependence on Middle East is much less than that of other major global economies as only 17 per cent of its oil imports flow from the region. In fact, it is China that will be importing almost 70 per cent of its oil from the Middle East by 2015. Unless new sources of oil production are exploited, Middle East reserves as a percentage of global stocks will be proportionally greater by 2025, as other key production areas see their resources dwindle. Middle East producers accounted for 31 per cent of the world's oil supply in 2000, and this figure could grow to 70 per cent by 2025. The Middle East will therefore continue to be the most significant region for oil-energy production.

China will continue to maintain a strong interest in oil production in both Iraq and Iran. These two energy partners are an insurance measure against reduced production from Central Asian oil fields. Iran has explicitly stated its desire for China to replace Japan as the country's largest energy trading partner. China is also considering to revive a $1.2 billion deal that it signed with Iraq during Saddam Hussein's regime in 1997 to develop the Iraqi oil field of al-Ahdab. Energy also remains the backbone of the Sino-Saudi relationship.

Until 1993 China was a net oil exporter, but it has since become the secondgreatest oil consumer after the United States. More than half of Chinese oil imports originate in the Persian Gulf, with 15 per cent in Saudi Arabia. Total Saudi-Chinese trade grew 59 per cent in 2005 to $14 billion and may reach $40 billion in the next four to five years. By 2010 the Middle East might account for 95 per cent of China's imported oil. Saudi Arabia has also emerged as a major investor in Chinese refineries. In 1999 Saudi Arabia's Aramco Overseas Company provided a $750 million investment—25 per cent of the total project—in a petrochemical complex in Fujian capable of processing eight million tons of Saudi crude oil per annum. Saudi Arabia, in cooperation with several members of OPEC, intends to build a new refinery in Guangzhou involving a total investment of $8 billion. China is assiduously attempting to enlarge its sphere of influence throughout the Persian Gulf, and its relationship with Saudi Arabia is a key component of this strategy.

The move in 2005 by the Chinese state-owned CNOOC to take control of the California-based oil exploration and production company Unocal Corporation in a $19 billion bid sent shock waves through the U.S. Congress. Although the Chinese maintain that their interest in Unocal was purely commercial in accessing substantial oil and gas reserves in Southeast Asia, the United States feared a broader Chinese strategy to secure global energy resources. China remains concerned over U.S. aspirations to dominate the Persian Gulf in order to secure its own energy requirements while simultaneously containing China's expansion in the region. Some in Beijing, therefore, consider the United States as a major threat to China's future energy security and remain reluctant to rely on the United States for the security of China's seaborne oil imports, thereby resulting in a focus on developing a blue-water navy to protect its sea lanes of communication. The Iraq war and its aftermath also seem to have reinforced China's fears that it is locked in a zero-sum contest for energy with the United States and added urgency to its mission to lessen dependence on Middle East oil supplies. However, if the American predominance of the Middle East weakens and China's global profile rises in region, India, along with several other regional states, will consider that a threat to its energy security with the distinct possibility of military conflict over the region's valuable resources.

CHINA AND INDIA'S RIVALRY EXTENDS TO THE ARCTIC

While the recent troop standoff in a remote Himalayan desert spotlights a long-running border dispute between China and India, the two emerging giants are engaged in a rivalry for global influence that spreads much farther afield.

From Africa to the Arctic, the world's two most populous countries are bumping up against each other in their search for resources and new markets. Their rivalry is spilling over into global diplomacy and international institutions where Beijing and Delhi have elbow-jabbed over development loans and a seat for India on the U.N. Security Council.

It is visible in the building of infrastructure in nations like Ghana, which is rich in gold, cocoa and timber and is a new oil producer. Ghana's government moved into a presidential palace financed by India in February. A month later, China handed over a new foreign ministry building.

An outright clash between the two remains unlikely. But bickering on the global stage could make bodies such as the World Bank and the United Nations less efficient, and send ripples through institutions that are increasingly important in guiding global trade, commerce and diplomacy and influence policies that affect people around the world.

"They have their tentacles throughout this global infrastructure," said Ashwin Kaja, an American lawyer leading an initiative to establish a China-India institute at Beijing's Renmin University and Jindal University in Sonipat, India. "If they start fighting, the threat becomes bigger and bigger as their influence grows. They are one third of humanity; it's not a small figure. They are not just countries."

Though the two nations once celebrated a shared vision as leaders of developing nations in the 1950s, that amity was shredded by a 1962 border war that still clouds relations. The recent crisis began April 15 when about 50 Chinese soldiers pitched tents on territory that both countries claim and set off finger-pointing about territorial grabs.

On Monday, Beijing and New Delhi announced an end to the three-week standoff, agreeing for troops on both sides to pull back before the fracas threatened several high-level meetings.

The two governments are publicly trying to put the best face on relations, accentuating the positive benefits of trade and diplomatic cooperation. The Indian foreign minister travels to Beijing on Thursday to prepare for a visit to Delhi later this month by Li Keqiang, his first overseas trip since becoming Chinese premier in March.

Neither country wants to threaten booming business ties. China became India's biggest trading partner in 2011 when two-way trade hit nearly $75 billion, up from $5 billion in 2002.

It declined slightly last year because of the global economic downturn, and it is also heavily skewed in China's favour. Next month, China will host its first South Asian trade expo, designed to lure companies from India and elsewhere in the region.

But distrust runs high. China is a longtime ally and weapons supplier to Pakistan, India's bitter rival, and has been building strong ties with Nepal, Bangladesh and Sri Lanka, feeding Indian fears of encirclement. China is wary of India's growing ties with the United States.

Chinese dam-building on the upper reaches of the Brahmaputra River has raised fears in India that Beijing might one day reduce or turn off critical water supplies.

A dispute over territorial claims in Arunachal Pradesh led to Beijing in 2009 trying to block part of a loan to India from the Asian Development Bank earmarked for a flood control project there.

China was upset in 2011 when India's state oil company, Oil and Natural Gas Corp., accepted an invitation from Vietnam to explore for oil and gas in the disputed South China Sea, bringing New Delhi into a festering territorial spat on China's doorstep.

"You can never avoid flash points," Kaja said. "The U.S. and China have lots of flash points but the difference I think is that between the U.S. and China, there is a lot more dialogue... and those are the kinds of channels that need to be created."

Their competition extends far beyond their immediate neighborhoods.

Both are pushing to gain a foothold in the Arctic, where melting ice is opening passages for shipping and could create a boom in the extraction of fossil fuels and minerals. Both China and India, along with other Asian nations and the European Union, have applied for observer status at the obscure Arctic Council.

"Neither China or India have any basis to claim to be Arctic nations, but because of the rush for minerals and resources there is a fear that we will be left behind if we don't also stake our claims in these distant parts," said

Sreeram Chaulia, dean of Jindal's School of International Affairs. Both countries are building up their navies to project influence, and the Chinese presence in the Indian Ocean is expected to grow. David Shinn, a former U.S. ambassador in Africa, expects China's navy to make more frequent visits to port cities across the Indian Ocean — in South Asia, the southern Middle East and on the east coast of Africa — within the next 10 years and to expand its reach to North African ports on the Mediterranean Sea.

"India will be concerned by a growing Chinese naval presence in the western Indian Ocean, which it has always considered its preserve.

It has tolerated a significant U.S. presence there, but it has never considered the U.S. an enemy," said Shinn, who now teaches international affairs at George Washington University.

This more permanent Chinese presence "will push India to ensure good military, particularly naval relations, with all the countries in the western Indian Ocean and along the east African coast," he said.

In the recent border standoff, neither side engaged in much more than posturing.

"They were just staring at each other. So I guess that in a way is a metaphor for the relationship," Chaulia said. "There is no way that India and China can be comrades or brothers and sisters. I don't think we can be that rosy-eyed. But certainly we can manage the problems."

RECENT DEVELOPMENT HISTORY

India became a free country through peaceful transition of sovereignty in 1947. China had a proletarian revolution in 1949 led by Mao Zedong. Both democratic India and Communist China embarked upon ambitious science, technology, and economic development programs through centralized planning. Both emphasized self-reliance through local initiatives, restricting the flow of foreign capital and technology for nearly three decades.

During this time, the Peoples Republic of China (PRC) controlled its economy and protected it from outside influences far more than India did. For at least 10-15 years since the revolution in 1949, the only source of foreign capital and technology for China was its ideological partner, the Soviet Union. That relationship began to crack in 1962 because of the USSR's reluctance to transfer nuclear technology to the Peoples Republic. China continued its isolation and suffered serious stagnation for 20 or so more years, until after Mao's death in 1976.

During this period, India too strictly regulated its economy, allowing only partial and highly restricted entry of foreign capital and technology. The

Indian economy began to open its door a bit more widely by the middle of the 1980s, at about the same time as China.

By this time, the global economy had already taken hold of the national economies in North America, Europe, and the Pacific Rim. Post-Independence era regulations proved a mixed blessing for India. It missed 20 years of the information technology revolution that was sweeping the world and driving the global economy – remember how the IBM was kicked out of India in the middle of 1970s. The private sector stagnated under those regulations. The protected government sector thrived despite its magnificent mismanagement. India's industrial development suffered. While these negative trends were the legacy of regulations, government policy of self-reliance helped built a robust infrastructure of techno-economic institutions and personnel that were ready to march forward when the global economy did finally reach India. Through regulations India was also able to protect its local industries and markets from unbridled speculation and exploitation by multinational corporations. Let me return to China for a minute.

Deng Xiaoping took command of China in 1979, three years after Mao's death. With a massive shift of public policy, Deng gave 190 degree turn to the Chinese economy by opening it to foreign capital, technology, and competition. The scene that I witnessed in China when I went there for the first time in 1980 was a totally different scene than what is going on there today. Despite the open door policy, economic modernization remained laggard through the entire decade of the 1980s. Things began to change rapidly in the next decade. Since then, the Chinese economy has been growing at about 9-10% per year, surpassing any other country for a sustained growth at such a high rate. In terms of GDP per capita, it is the world's 4th largest economy, and is likely to overtake Japan within the next five years. It is one of the world's largest exporters of consumer items through retailers like Wal-Mart, Carrefour, Target, and Tesco. Even garlic in the United States is being imported from China. The American Wal-Mart is probably the biggest buyer of consumer goods made in China. "It bought $19 billion worth of Chinese goods in 2004, amounting to some 15% of China's total exports to America in that year. (The Economist, September 23rd, p. 43)

Since 2000, China's contribution to global GDP growth (in purchasing-power-parity terms) has been bigger than America's, and more than half as big again as the combined contribution of India, Brazil and Russia, the three next largest emerging economies. China's massive build-up of American Treasury bonds affects American interest rates and thus Americans' willingness to spend. Its low-priced manufactures give western consumers more buying power. Its thirst for energy has helped push oil prices to record highs. Its entry to the World Trade Organization in 2001 has speeded up the opening of the world's biggest market. (A Survey of China, The Economist, March 25th, 2006, p. 3)

India has finally left behind its "Hindu growth rate" of 3% to hit an annual growth rate of 8+%. Its technological capability is strong. It is the most preferred destination of IT outsourcing, now moving away from being the world's call center to being a vital feeder to the global knowledge industry. India's economic base is vast – 4th largest in the world in terms of purchasing power parity and 12th largest in terms of GDP. It is projected to become one of the five largest economies in the world by 2050 along with China and Brazil. But per capita incomes remain low ($3000.00, approx.) in international comparisons. Income disparities are wide. Nonetheless, the markets are huge, with the current consumer class estimated to be around 350 million, about the size of the entire European Community.

The combined economies of India and China are already bigger than that of the EU countries put together. At the present rate of growth, the combined consumer class in the two countries will reach about a billion people within the next 5-10 years. These developments have far-reaching implications for the two countries themselves and the world at large in the 21st century.

CHALLENGES AND IMPLICATIONS FOR DOMESTIC POLICY REFORM

The challenges facing China and India for sustaining rapid economic growth and meeting the MDGs are similar in nature. First there is the matter of continuing to reduce poverty and hunger and maintain food security. Two other serious issues concern the widening rural-urban income gap and the degradation of the environment. Also of concern is the need to restructure agriculture and markets to meet more diversified consumer and export market food demand, and the need to adopt policies that enable both countries to maintain comparative advantage in commodity production. How these challenges are addressed will determine to a large degree the success in meeting the MDGs, the ability to sustain growth and the role that these economies will play in world markets.

Food Security and Poverty

Two important questions related to achieving the MDGs of poverty and hunger reduction need to be answered. How does the growth in agriculture and in the non-agricultural economy affect poverty alleviation? What can we learn from the experience of China and India? Ravallion and Chen (2004) for China and Ravallion and Datt (1996) for India conclude that there is a strong link between poverty reduction and increased agricultural productivity. However, Besley *et al.* (2004) argues on the basis of an enormously rich data set and very sophisticated econometrics that agriculture has played a minimal role at best in India's reduction of poverty (Timmer 2005). The China case study provides several interesting results on key factors that have determined the changes in rural poverty in China. Overall economic growth has been a key primary source of rural poverty reduction. But while economic growth is an essential and necessary condition for nationwide poverty reduction, it is not a sufficient condition. As incomes have grown the impact and effectiveness of general economic growth on poverty reduction has weakened. Fan *et al.* (2002) for China and Fan *et al.* for India (2002) examine the poverty impact of various agricultural investments and subsidies. Their work suggests that there are important multipliers at work and that the impact of these multipliers changes over time. In addressing the question of poverty impact of agriculture *per se* we need to look at the links between the agricultural and non-agricultural economy including rural non-farm employment.

Taking the aforesaid views into consideration, we observe in China that the TVEs provided a strong link between agricultural and non-agricultural economy which undoubtedly accounted for the sharp drop in poverty. Also fostering poverty alleviation has been the egalitarian nature of the reforms under the HRS. By contrast, the links between the agricultural and non-agricultural economy have been less strong in India and have been hampered by a host of regulations which have slowed the development of both agriculture and industry. Overall growth in the GDP is increasing in India while growth in agricultural GDP has been declining which does not speak well for reducing rural poverty.

Based on projections using the GTAP model both country studies conclude that they can meet domestic cereal grain demands without reliance on significant imports. Since the food shortages of the mid-1960s, foodgrain self-sufficiency has been a dominant feature of Indian agricultural policy. China also sets a high priority on foodgrain self-sufficiency. However, maintaining self-sufficiency in wheat production will almost certainly require improved management of water resources in the Punjab and neighbouring states and in the North China Plain.

Foodgrain self-sufficiency at the national level does not ensure food security at the regional or household level. It is a paradox that with more than 260 million people below the official poverty line in 1999-2000, India is one of the leading exporters of rice. Poverty incidence is expected to continue to fall in India from 26.1 percent in 1999-2000, reaching 8 percent in 2015 well beyond the MDG. But achieving this goal would appear to depend on the success of the reforms which target the growth in agriculture to rise from the sluggish 1.5 percent to 4 percent*per annum.*

From the experience of both China and India, the policy implications seem clear. Attention must be given to raising agricultural productivity and incomes in those areas that have thus far not benefited from new technologies or trade liberalization. At the same time emphasis should be on creating jobs in the non-farm sector, whether rural or urban based. For China this will require continuing reform of state-owned enterprises (SOEs) and encouragement of labour-intensive private industry. India's continuing reforms should foster growth in employment in both the manufacturing and service sectors.

The Widening Income Gap

In addition to the rural-urban income gap, especially that between agriculture and new, dynamic industries, there are regional disparities such as between the coastal and the central and western provinces in China or between the Punjab and Haryana and the states of Eastern India. Further within regions there is the disparity between those that have become commercialized, for example through contract farming and those that follow traditional practices. Disparity in India exists between the more commercialized farmers in the Punjab and Haryana as opposed to those in Bihar and Orissa. The issue here is not necessarily absolute poverty, but what Hayami (2005) describes as relative poverty. The less favourable areas need better education and health services and equal access to social services. Gulati *et al.* (2005) argue to this end that China and India should accelerate growth, improve efficiency and at the same time ensure that growth is both equitable and sustainable. To improve efficiency, India should phase out subsidies and efforts should be focused on developing infrastructure and new technologies. However, for many the path out of poverty lies not in agriculture but in non-farm opportunities. Both countries are experiencing rapid migration from rural to urban areas. But too little attention is paid to facilitating migration of rural workers to urban jobs where investments in the rural economy have a low payoff.

Both China and India are committed to addressing the income gap, but the approaches will be very different. China recently approved a 15 percent increase in the money earmarked for agricultural development, and rural services. Also China has initiated the "Five Balanced Development Strategies: balanced development between rural and urban, between economic growth and social progress, among regions, between human intervention and environmental conservation, and between internal and external economies."

The proposed strategies and reforms are bold but there are many barriers to achieving the lofty goals of the programme.

The UPA Government came to power in India in May 2004 and the National Common Minimum Programme forms the bedrock of economic policy with the highest priority for agriculture and a holistic approach to agriculture and rural development.

But India faces a different set of policy and institutional constraints. Rationalizing subsidies and extending reforms that liberalized industry to agriculture through the removal of regulations and restrictions to trade seem to be crucial. India also must address the problem of a high variability in income and livelihood among regions and states.

Environmental Issues

Rapid economic development challenges the ability of China and India to manage resources, sustain agricultural growth rates and meet food security and poverty reduction objectives. In both countries, economic development has taken precedence over protection of the environment. The environmental issues can be summarized under five main headings: air, water, soil, habitat destruction and biodiversity losses. Of particular concern to sustainability of agricultural growth and to food security are problems relating to misuse of land and water resources.

Soil problems — erosion, fertility losses, salinization and desertification are reducing the land area suitable for cultivation. Overuse of fertilizer (China's use of nitrogen is three times the world average) is resulting in both environmental problems and problems related to food and water safety. For example, the high levels of nitrates found in the drinking water in many cities in north China pose a threat to the health of infants. Of immediate concern to both China and India is the growing scarcity and competition for water and declining water quality. The overexploitation of groundwater has contributed to the slowing of growth in grain production in two of Asia's breadbaskets, Northwest India and the North China Plain. This has important implications in particular for the long-term growth in wheat production in these regions.

The Indian National Common Minimum Programme, a politico-economic agenda that guides new government policy decisions, lists among its reform priorities stopping the misuse of water and the unsustainable use of land. In China and India major schemes are underway both to conserve water and to reallocate water between basins — for example from the Yangtze (north). These are long-range projects. Meanwhile, institutional changes are being tested and implemented with mixed success to improve the efficiency of water use and provide equitable allocation of water among competing uses and users.

This includes programmes and projects designed to transfer operation and management responsibilities to local user groups — known as irrigation management transfer. Managing the common property resource, groundwater, to avoid overexploitation presents the biggest challenge.

The Restructuring of Agriculture

A conceptual framework plotting the transformation of agriculture against the degree of diversification. As incomes rise, food consumption moves at first toward less diversification. Households give up consumption of inferior sources (maize and root crops) for preferred cereal grains (rice and wheat). This is followed by diversification into horticultural crops and livestock products (including fisheries).

This transformation set off by a rise in incomes began in China in the early reform period (1978-1984) and occurred in India largely as a result of the 1991 reforms. The result of these non-agricultural reforms in India was to improve the terms of trade for agriculture and bring forth private investments in horticultural and livestock products. Farms may become more specialized, but agriculture as a whole becomes more diversified to meet changing consumer demands and the potential for exports. Finally, as suggested above, farm household incomes are likely to become more diversified. Countries, regions of countries, and farm households may, of course, be at different stages in this transformation process. The challenge is to provide as wide a scope as possible for participation in the transformation process at the farm level.

Farms in Asia are small (2 ha or less) and in many instances are getting smaller. There is currently a sharp debate among academics as to whether small-scale agriculture can continue to play its historic role. In short, how will agriculture be commercialized? Can small farms have productive cultivation let alone provide the minimum output required to earn a livelihood? Does commercialization of agriculture imply larger farms?

Increasing commercial orientation, vertical integration and coordination of the farming sector with large-scale food processors, wholesalers and retailers who have private standards of food quality and safety could affect the viability of small farms.

Evidence from China and India and elsewhere in Asia suggest that small-scale farms will continue to have a role to play. But restructuring of agriculture implies a change in the farm household unit to accommodate changes in domestic and export marketing. While there are economies of scale in distribution and marketing, there are few, if any, economies of scale in the production process. In fact, as demonstrated in China with both family plots under collective agriculture and with smallholdings under the household responsibility system, small-scale farming can be more efficient than large-scale enterprises. At the same time the high degree of fragmentation in farm holdings, particularly in China where the farm may be divided into five or more scattered plots, presents an obstacle to efficient management. Furthermore, there are advantages for farms to work together or to form groups to share services such as extension or tractor provision or for contracting with private sector marketing firms.

The farm size issue has important policy ramifications. The skewed land tenure situation in India suggests that large farms are likely to be more commercially oriented. In China and other parts of Asia there is often a restriction on farm size to maintain an egalitarian policy.

Maintaining Competitive Agriculture

A traditional response to the widening rural-urban income gap has been to subsidize agriculture. Countries have taxed agriculture in the early stages of development and then subsidized agriculture. The transition from tax to subsidy tends to occur when agriculture declines to 15 percent of the GDP.

The experience of India shows that continuing the current pattern of subsidies can be costly. They absorb funds that could be more effectively used for measures to enhance agricultural productivity — rural infrastructure and agricultural research. Furthermore, WTO and FTA agreements are putting pressure on developing countries to reduce protection. China has looked upon this as an opportunity to promote trade liberalization and decrease the highly protected state-owned industries. Trade liberalization has brought about a sharp shift in trade of goods in a manner consistent with comparative advantage.

The export of less labour-intensive bulk commodities such as grains has declined while the export of labour-intensive higher valued commodities such as horticultural crops and animal products has risen. In India there has been trade liberalization since the 1990s. Contingent on domestic reforms, the India study argues that present high levels of bound tariff for agricultural commodities can be further reduced, barring certain sectors identified as sensitive (notably edible oils and dairy products), as India is cost competitive in agricultural products.

The India country study refers to the "spaghetti bowl" of trade agreements that India has with trading partners and the same would hold true for China. Multilateral trade agreements are preferable to discretionary regional agreements although progress in negotiating the latter has been slow.

This fact notwithstanding, it is clear that Asia is moving toward a more liberalized trading environment. This stands in sharp contrast to the developed countries who continue to protect their farm economies. Subsidies to farmers in these countries are extremely large despite promises made in the Uruguay Round to reduce them significantly.

PROSPECTS OF RESOLVING CHINA-INDIA BORDER DISPUTE

Today, some security experts such as Mr. Bharat Verma, the editor of *Indian Defence Review*, in this world are still talking about China's military attacks on India before 2012, or even within 6 months. However, such noises cannot halt the historic wheels of Chindia partnership from rolling forward. As the two new emerging powers, their leaders know clearly that each is not a threat to the other.

China has been called the world workshop whileIndia the world office. In the course of their rise, the challenges they will face are the same or similar. They need more policy coordination and more functional cooperation in the world dominated by the developed nations in the global platforms such as G20, BRIC, BASIC, and China-Russia- India Trilateral Dialogue. Chinaand India joined hands last year during the United Nations Climate Change Conference in Copenhagen, effectively presenting the stance of emerging economies and developing countries on climate change.

For the past 10 years, the two governments have made joint efforts to cement and strengthen their bilateral relations. In 2003, Indian Prime Minister Atal Vajpayee visited China and signed Declaration on Principles for Relations and Comprehensive Cooperation between China and India. Both sides reaffirmed that they would promote a long-term constructive and cooperative partnership.

They emphasized that their common interests outweigh their differences. The two countries are not a threat to each other. Neither side shall use or threaten to use force against the other.

They are committed to qualitatively enhance the bilateral relationship at all levels and in all areas while addressing differences through peaceful means in a fair, reasonable and mutually acceptable manner. They emphasized that the differences should not be allowed to affect the overall development of bilateral relations.

On the border question, they reiterate their determination to seek a fair, reasonable, and mutually acceptable solution through consultations on an equal footing. They agreed that pending an ultimate solution, they should work together to maintain peace and tranquility in the border areas, continue implementation of h agreements signed for this purpose, including the clarification of the line of actual control. The two governments decided to appoint special representatives to promote the process of the border negotiations.

As one of the sensitive issues in the China-India relations, India recognizes that the Tibet Autonomous Region is part of the territory of the People's Republic of China and India does not allow Tibetans to engage in anti-China political activities in India.

In recent years, the trade relationship between the two countries has been seen in both countries as a crucial driver of overall bilateral relations, amid persisting political strains over the long-running border dispute.China became India's largest trading partner in 2008, with bilateral trade reaching $52 billion.

Trade fell to $43 billion on account of the financial crisis, but has rebounded in the first two months of this year with Indian exports, mainly driven by iron ore, rising 75 per cent. It is predictable that rapid development of trade relations will certainly affect bilateral political relations in a positive manner.

Fast growing trade relations have come under increasing strain with India's trade deficit continuing to widen.India filed a record number of anti-dumping investigations against China at the World Trade Organization in 2009.

India's recent restrictions on the import of Chinese telecom equipment, in light of security concerns, have added to the list of strains.

The telecom issue, however, was not raised by China during the President's ongoing visit. With the bilateral trade rapidly growing, these differences or disputes are normal.

We believe that all these problems can be resolved by bilateral consultations. Describing trade and economic cooperation as a pillar of bilateral ties, Indian president Patil said India and China should work together to realize trade target of US$ 60 billion in 2010 that had been set.

In 2006 Presiden Hu Jintao visited India and the two sides agreed on a 10-pronged strategy to expand and intensify bilaterlal strategic and cooperative partnership.

In 2008, during the Indian Prime Minister Manmohan Singh visit to China, the two countries concluded a " Shared Vision for the 21st century", which forms the basis for bilateral cooperation on global issues.

China and India have agreed to enhance political, economic ties and bolster people-to-people contact during a meeting between Indian President Pratibha Patil and Chinese Premier Wen Jiabao here on May 27, 2010. President

Hu Jintao held talks with her. President Patil said India-China relations were of global and strategic significance, and all political parties in India were supportive of further advancing such relations.

President Hu said that China and India should work more closely to address global issues such as economic downturn, climate change, energy security and food security. The two countries should maintain close communication and coordination within multilateral mechanisms such as China-Russia-India, BRIC, BASIC, and G20, in a bid to increase the voice of developing countries.

China and India do not pose as threat to each other and their common interests far outweigh their differences. The two countries should understand and respect each other's core national interests and major concerns, properly handle their differences, and seek common development and a win-win situation.

A good China-India relationship makes both winners while a confrontational one makes both losers.

FUTURE SCENARIOS FOR CHINA AND INDIA AND THEIR IMPLICATIONS

In the country studies for China and India, analysis was undertaken using the Global Trade Analysis Project (GTAP) model and projections of future growth were made to the year 2020. Through this exercise the implications of rapid growth for production and consumption of agricultural products and trading opportunities for other countries in the region and the world have been assessed, based on certain assumptions.

Prospects for Growth and Domestic Implications

The analysis conducted in the China case study projects average annual growth in GDP of 8 percent in 2006 to 2010 gradually slowing to 6-7 percent in the following decade. Several factors favour this strong growth performance, including macroeconomic stability, high domestic savings, increased spending on research and development, continued high levels of FDI, improved market environment and trade liberalization, and the commitment to greater equity — granting higher purchasing power to lower income groups. Also noted are obstacles that will tend to reduce growth particularly in the long run — a decline in the domestic savings rate, an ageing population and pressures on the natural resource base for sustained agricultural production.

While China's growth rate is projected to decline somewhat in the near future, the India study suggests that GDP growth could be rising from the current levels of 6-7 percent to 7-8 percent. It should be noted that these growth projections apply to two economies of considerably different size. Nevertheless, how does one explain the divergence? Part of the explanation is related to the incremental capital output ratio (ICOR). In India it is currently about 4 and expected to decline.

In China while the ICOR was 4 in the early 1980s it has steadily risen since then and in 2002 was 5.4. In short, despite reforms in state-owned industries in China, India uses capital more efficiently.

Also favouring India is the demographic dividend, with the percentage of the population in the 15 to 59 age group increasing from 59 percent in 2001 to over 63 percent in 2011 which could add 1 percent to GDP growth. In China, by contrast, the ageing population and sharp decline in population growth due to the one child policy will eventually slow overall economic growth.

The picture for agriculture is somewhat mixed. The land area used in crop production is gradually shrinking due to urbanization and in some instances environmental degradation. Thus for staple crops, production growth depends on an increase in yields. China has already achieved high yields in staple crops, and further gains will depend on technological breakthroughs.

Indian crop yields are low by comparison with China and other countries. This is attributed in part to the neglect of investments in research and extension beyond the early Green Revolution years. In both China and India the yields for the principal Green Revolution crops, rice and wheat, have plateaued, due in part to falling groundwater tables and environmental degradation. However, if priority can be given to investment in research and development and infrastructure, there appears to be ample scope, particularly in India, for increasing yields and agricultural productivity.

As a result of continued rapid economic growth and increase in income per capita, demand for high income elasticity products, like milk, livestock and horticultural products will continue to grow. China and India are committed to maintaining cereal grain self-sufficiency. The projections for both economies indicate that food security can be maintained at a national level without resorting to significant imports. The baseline scenario presented in the China study, for example, indicates that in 2020 China will maintain or surpass self-sufficiency in rice, horticulture, pork and poultry, fish and processed foods, and come close to self-sufficiency in wheat, fibre and beef and mutton. In the case of India, despite low current growth rates of output for many crops, the expectation is that self-sufficiency can be maintained in rice, wheat, coarse grains, sugar, cattle and meat, fish and other foods.

The country should also come close to self-sufficiency in other crops (although the model predicts significant decline in both production and consumption of these crops) and milk. However, both countries will need to adopt policies that ensure food security at a regional and household level where hunger and poverty still persist.

China's agricultural production structure is expected to shift more towards labour-intensive products such as vegetables, fruit, fish and processed foods, while self-sufficiency in land-intensive products such as oilseed, fibres and coarse grains is predicted to fall further from current levels. The largest increases in Indian agricultural production are predicted for oilseed, sugar, fibres, milk, fish, other agricultural products and other foods, while negative or low growth rates are expected in cattle and meat, rice, wheat, coarse grains and other crops. Nevertheless, for some of the high growth products India will continue to require significant imports, especially of oilseed, fibres and other agricultural products.

The dollar-a-day-poverty index had fallen to 16 percent in China in 2002 while it was 34 percent in India. Poverty is projected to continue to decline in India. With a GDP growth rate of 8 percent or more the poverty rate should fall from 26 percent in 1999-2000 to 14 percent in 2010 and then to 8 percent in 2015. There appears to be an implicit assumption in these figures that the reduction in poverty will come largely from growth in employment in the non-farm sector. The analysis of the Chinese experience suggests that the impact of rapid economic growth on poverty reduction tends to slacken eventually if the rural sector does not grow hand in hand. As incomes have grown, the impact and effectiveness of general economic growth on poverty reduction have weakened.

Implications for Asia and the Greater Pacific Region

Trade liberalization, globalization, and pressures to meet WTO and FTA agreements are generating a substantial growth in trade. China will have the largest impact on Asia and the Pacific region because China's economy is two-and-a-half times larger than that of India, it is growing faster and it is more integrated with the rest of the world.

For example, China received some US$60 billion of FDI last year while India received only US$5 billion. FDI and multinational investments are a means of importing technology and entrepreneurial and management skills. By 2020 China is projected to be the world's second largest importer and exporter.

At the level of the overall economy, both China and India will be major importers of energy and minerals principally from Australia, the Russian

Federation and the Middle East. China is projected to drop from 92 percent self-sufficiency in energy in 2001 to 67 percent in 2020. Recognizing this as a potential constraint to growth, China is taking steps to improve efficiency in the use of energy.

The high total factor productivity (TFP) growth projection in the China country report indicates that reliance on energy imports can be reduced by as much as 60 percent and minerals by 50 percent. Aided by FDI and information technologies, China and India along with other developing countries are finding it increasingly easy to transfer technology from developed countries to exercise their comparative advantage in manufacturing. However, both countries have historically made low use of external resources, relative to their economic size, and national initiatives will continue to play an important role in determining their growth paths.

As noted previously, both China and India are projected to be self-sufficient in cereal grains and do not provide a serious threat to global food security. India is projected to continue its current role as a major net exporter of rice.

Both China and India will be major importers of oilseed, plant-based fibre and forestry products. Soybean meal, for example, will come from destinations as distant as Brazil.

In China there is already a trend in trade away from land-intensive crops such as food and feedgrains and sugar, and towards export of labour-intensive, high value commodities — horticultural crops, livestock, and aquaculture products. The predictions of the two country reports with regard to net exports and imports in 2020.

The use of different scenarios in the China report indicates that China presents considerable opportunities for other agricultural exporters under the baseline and high GDP growth scenarios, but these opportunities are significantly reduced under the high TFP growth scenario. The Indian data, on the other hand, under-represent opportunities for catching up in productivity via technological change.

The China report examines changes in the patterns of agriculture and food trade that are likely to emerge by 2020. Interestingly, Chinese exports to India are predicted to increase by 1 179 percent over their 2001 level, while Indian exports to China are predicted to grow by only 79 percent.

The Indian study did not undertake a comparable analysis, but the figures presented in the China report tend to reflect the relatively narrow range of India's net agricultural exports at present — mainly rice, followed by wheat and sugar.

The major diversification in China's exports is predicted to take place in Southeast Asia and "other" Asia, while exports to Japan, Republic of Korea, Hong Kong Special Administrative Region, China, and Taiwan Province of China are predicted to remain fairly stable. Less important growth areas for China include the Russian Federation, Australia and New Zealand, and Central and South America.

On the import side, however, major growth in agricultural trade should come from the more developed Asian countries as well as most other parts of the world excepting Southeast and other Asian countries. For the developing countries in Asia, China is emerging as a significant competitor in agricultural products. In particular the current trade surplus in agricultural products that the Southeast Asian region enjoys with China is predicted to turn negative. Meanwhile many Asian countries will find it difficult to compete with non-agricultural exports from India and China such as textiles, given the comparatively low wages in these two economies.

Bibliography

Allen Carlson, *Unifying China, Integrating with the World: Securing Chinese Sovereignty in the Reform Era,* Stanford: Stanford University Press, 2005.

Amitabh Sikdar: *India and China : Strategic Energy Management and Security,* Manas, Delhi, 2009.

Anderson, J.: *Transnational Democracy: Political Spaces and Border Crossings,* Routledge: London and New York, 2002.

Anil, K.C.: *Military and Democracy in South Asia : Challenges, Politics and Power,* Sumit Enterprises, Delhi, 2009.

Barber B.R.: *Strong Democracy. Participatory Politics for a New Age.* Berkeley, University of California Press, 1984.

Barsoux, J.L. : *Transnational Management: Text, Cases and Readings in Cross-Border Management,* Boston: Irwin/McGraw-Hill, 2000.

Baviera, A. S. P.: *China's Relations with Southeast Asia: Political Security and Economic Interests,* Philippine APEC Study Center Network, 1999.

Bhat, T.P. : *India and China : Trade Complementarities and Competitiveness,* Bookwell, Delhi, 2008.

Chandra, R.: *Judicial System in Mechanical Warfare,* Lucknow, Print House (India), 1992.

Coakley, J.: *The Territorial Management of Ethnic Conflict,* 2nd edn London: Frank Cass, 2003.

Cole, Alan : *Mothers and Sons in Chinese Buddhism,* Stanford, CA: Stanford University Press, 1998.

Count De Lesdain: *From Pekin to Sikkim: Through the Ordos, the Gobi Desert, and Tibet,* A.E.S., 1995.

Cunningham, Fiona and Rory Metcalf: *The Dangers of Denial: Nuclear Weapons in China-India Relations,* The Lowy Institute, Sydney, 2011.

Deepak, B R : *India and China : 1904-2004 : A Century of Peace and Conflict,* Manak, Delhi, 2005.

Diener, Alexander C., and Joshua Hagen. *Borders: A Very Short Introduction.* New York: Oxford University Press, 2012.

Digumarti Bhaskara Rao: *Military Conversion : Impact on Science and Technology,* Discovery, Delhi, 2003.

Dixit, A.K. : *Military Wars and Rescue Techniques*, Cyber Tech Pub, Delhi, 2010.

Dixit, J.N. : *India and Regional Developments : Through the Prism of Indo-Pak Relations*, Gyan, Delhi, 2004.

Donnan, H. and Wilson, T. M.: *Borders: Frontiers of Identity, Nation and State*, Oxford: Berg, 1999.

Ehrenberg, John : *Civil Society: The Critical History of an Idea*, New York, New York University Press, 1998.

Evelyn Goh, *Meeting the China Challenge: The U.S. in Southeast Asian Regional Security Strategies*, DC: East-West Center, 2005.

Fisher, Richard: *China's Military Modernization*, Praeger Security International, Westport, 2008.

Frankel, Francine and Harry Harding: *The China – India Relationship: What the United States*

Gabriele Rabkin: *Far Away From Home: Tibetan Refugee Children Write And Paint Their Stories*, Paljor Pub, 2006.

Gao, Mobo: *The Battle for China's Past: Mao and the Cultural Revolution*, London, Pluto Press, 2008.

Gaur, Mahendra : *Indian Policy of Neighbour*, Delhi, Kalpaz Pub., 2006.

Gautam Das: *China Tibet India: The 1962 War And The Strategic Military Future*, Har-anand Publications, 2009.

George Mathew: *Grass Roots Democracy in India and China : The Right to Participate*, Sage, Delhi, 2007.

Goldstein, Avery: *Rising to the Challenge: China's Grand Strategy and International Security*, Stanford University Press, Stanford, 2005.

Gupta, Asha: *Military Rule and Democratization : Changing Perspectives*, Deep & Deep, Delhi, 2003.

Gupta, S.: *Disrupted Borders: An Intervention in Definitions of Boundaries*, London: River Oram Press, 1993.

Hamilton Bower: *Diary of a Journey Across Tibet (From Leh, Ladakh, to Peking, China in 1891 and 1892)*, Himal books. 2003.

Huntington, S.P.: *The China Modernisation Military and the State*, N.Y., Vintage Books, 1964.

Ian Storey: *ASEAN and the South China Sea: Movement in Lieu of Progress*, Washington, D.C., Jamestown Foundation,2012.

Ikram, S. M.: *Indian Muslims and Partition of India*. Delhi: Atlantic, 1995.

Imtiaz, A.: *State and Foreign Policy: India's Role in South Asia*, New Delhi, Vikas, 1993.

Isabella L. Bishop: *Among the Tibetans*, AES, 1996.

Jagannath P. Panda: *China's Path to Power : Party, Military and the Politics of State Transition*, Pentagon, Delhi, 2010.

James R Blaker: *Transforming Military Force : The Legacy of Arthur Cebrowski and Network Centric Warfare*, Pentagon Press, Delhi, 2008.

Jha, Prem Shankar : *India and China : The Battle Between Soft and Hard Power*, Penguin Books India, Delhi, 2010.

Joon Ahn: *The Rise of China and the Future of East Asian Integration*, Asia-Pacific Review, London, Carfax Publishing Company, 2004.

Juvale, R.P. : *Military Strategy and Diplomacy*, Cyber Tech Publications, Delhi, 2010.
Kapur, C.K. : *Chinese Military Modernisation*, Manas, Delhi, 2003.
Karubaki Datta: *Essays on Tibetan Cultural Heritage*, Serials Publications, 2008.
Keane J.: *Democracy and Civil Liberty*, London, Verso, 1988.
Kelly, John B.: *Indian Military and Pakistan War*, Oxford, Clarendon Press, 1968.
Kudaisya, Gyanesh: *The Aftermath of Partition in South Asia*. London: Routledge, 2000.
Kunju, N. : *Indo-Pak : Nuclear Cold War*, Reliance, Delhi, 2002.
Lamrimpa, Gen : *Calming the Mind: Tibetan Buddhist Teachings on Cultivating Meditative Quiescence,* Ithaca, NY: Snow Lion, 1995.
Laquer, Walter, *The New Terrorism: Fanaticism and the Arms of Mass Destruction*, Oxford: Oxford University Press, 1999.
Lohia, Ram Manohar: *Guilty Men of India's Partition*. Allahabad: Navahind, 1960.
Mary, W.: *Military Space Force: the Cultural Dimensions of Authority,* Cambridge, Belknap Press, 1985.
Moran: *Buddhism Observed: Travelers, Exiles and Tibetan Dharma in Kathmandu*, Cambridge Univ Press, Paperback, 2006.
Murray, W. and A. Millet: *Military Effectiveness: The First World War,* Cambridge University Press, Cambridge, 2010.
Naomi C. Rose: *Escape to Freedom: The Dangerous Trek of Tibetan Youth*, Paljor Publications, 2010.
Nayyar, K K : *National Security : Military Aspects*, Rupa, Delhi, 2003.
Nevile, P.: *Lahore: A Sentimental Journey*. New Delhi: Penguin, 1993.
Peter Van Der Veer: *Patterns of Middle Class Consumption in India and China*, Sage, Delhi, 2008.
Phuskele, Preeti : *India and China : Emerging Superpowers*, ICFAI University, Delhi, 2009.
Posen, B.R.: *The Sources of Indian Military Doctrine*, Ithaca, 1984, Cornell Univ. Press.
Prabir De: *India and China in an Era of Globalisation : Essays on Economic Cooperation*, Bookwell, Delhi, 2005.
Prabla, Dixit: *Communalism: A Struggle for Power*, New Delhi, Orient Longman, 1981.
Raj Kumar: *Weapons and Military Technology*, Sumit Enterprises, Delhi, 2009.
Raza, Hashim S.: *Mountbatten and the Partition of India*. New Delhi: Atlantic, 1989.
Robert M Cassidy: *Counterinsurgency and the Global War on Terror : Military Culture and Irregular War*, Pentagon Press, Delhi, 2008.
Rosen, P.: *Societies and Military Power: India and its Armies*, Ithaca, Cornell University Press, 1996.
Salim, Ahmad: *Lahore 1947*. New Delhi: India Research Press, 2001.
Samuel P. Huntington: *The Soldier and the State : The Theory and Politics of Civil-Military Relations*, Natraj Pub, Delhi, 2005.
Sarat Chandra Das: *A Journey To Lhasa And Central Tibet*, Rupa Pubilcations, 2007.
Scobell, Andrew: *Cult of Defense and Great Power Dreams: The Influence of Strategic Culture on China's Reltionship with India*, Strategic Studies Institute, Carlisle, 2002.

Seibert Hummel: *Eurasian Mythology in the Tibetan Epic of Ge-Sar*, Library of Tibetan Works and Archives, 2004.

Seshagiri, K. L. : *Mahatma Gandhi and Comparative Religion*, Motilal Banarsidass, New Delhi, 1978.

Simon, D. : *Public Administration and Policy of Indian Military*, New York, Knopf, 1950.

Som, A.: *Lahore: Portrait of a Lost City*. Lahore: Vanguard Books, 1998.

Spector, Leonard S., *Going Nuclear*, Cambridge, MA: Ballinger Publishing Company, 1987.

Stuart R. Schram: *The Political Thought of Mao Tse-Tung*. New York: Praeger, 1969.

Takeuchi Yoshinori: *Buddhist Spirituality: Vol. 1: Indian, Southeast Asian, Tibetan and Early Chinese*, Motilal Banarsidass, 1995.

Thampi, Madhavi : *India and China in the Colonial World*, Social Science Press, Delhi, 2010.

Toni Huber: *Amdo Tibetans in Transition: Society and Culture in the Post-Mao Era*, Vajra Publications, 2011.

Tsepak Rigzin: *Festivals of Tibet*, Library of Tibetan Works and Archives Publication,2004.

Tsering Wangmo Dhompa: *A Home in Tibet*, Hamish Hamilton, 2013.

Velez-Ibanez, Carlos: *Border Visions and Management*. University of Arizona Press, 1996.

Wakamiya Yoshibumi, *The Postwar Conservative View of Asia,* Tokyo: LTCB International Library Foundation, 1999.

Wapner, Paul : *Environmental Activism and World Civic Politics,* Albany, SUNY Press, 1996.

Wilson, T. M.: *New Borders for a Changing: Cross-border Cooperation and Governance,* London: Frank Cass, 2003.

Wolf Charles: *China and India, 2025: A Comparative Assessment*, RAND Corporation, Santa Monica, 2011.

Wolfgang Bertsch: *A Study of Tibetan Paper Money: With a Critical Bibliography,* Library of Tibetan Works and Archives, 1997.

Wolpert, Stanley: *Shameful Flight: The Last Years of the British Empire in India*. Oxford and New York: Oxford University Press, 2006.

Zaman, M.: *Students' Role in the Pakistan Movement*. Karachi, Quaid-iAzam Academy, 1978.

Zenath, L.: *Indian Foreign Policy in a Unipolar World*, MacMillan, New York, 2009.

Index

A

Agreement, 48.

Aksai Chin, 1, 4, 5, 6, 7, 8, 9, 14, 21, 22, 31, 32, 33, 34, 38, 40, 41, 43, 44, 46, 49, 52, 53, 57, 59, 60, 62, 65, 67, 70, 71, 72, 77, 78, 79, 80, 83, 84, 87, 88, 90, 91, 92, 112, 113, 147, 170, 187, 188, 189, 190, 191, 214, 215, 217, 218, 219, 220, 221, 232, 237, 238, 244.

Armed Conflict, 110.

B

Bilateral Relationship, 101, 107, 121, 122, 252, 264.

Border Argument, 43.

Border Dispute, 220.

Border Negotiations, 31, 38, 41, 110, 120, 171, 219, 243, 251, 270.

Border Roads, 194, 195, 248.

Border Settlement, 67, 71, 185, 243.

Border War, 4, 9, 57, 60, 78, 87, 89, 90, 91, 92.

Boundary Dispute, 27, 44, 48, 100, 103, 117, 191, 195, 196, 217, 220.

C

China Dispute Boundary, 27.

China Policy, 14, 30, 106, 164, 165, 166, 167, 168, 169, 226, 227, 244.

China War, 112, 223, 224.

Chinese Invasion, 53, 135, 145, 147.

Collision of the Sino-Indian War, 51.

Conflict Aspects, 206.

Conflict Avoidance Measures, 115.

D

Dalai Lama, 18, 25, 32, 44, 52, 66, 67, 69, 79, 94, 98, 99, 114, 125, 128, 129, 131, 132, 133, 134, 135, 136, 137, 138, 139, 141, 143, 146, 150, 152, 153, 154, 155, 156, 158, 159, 162, 163, 171, 172, 173, 174, 175, 176, 179, 180, 181, 183, 184, 191, 196, 197, 198, 199, 201, 202, 203, 219, 234, 235, 236, 244, 245.

Defensive Battle, 242.

Diplomatic Contacts, 158.

Dispute Boundary, 27.

Domestic Policy, 258.

Drawing the Line, 25.

E

Emerging Competition, 249.
Environment Aspects, 205.
Environmental Issues, 261.

F

Formidable Challenge, 103.

G

Government of Tibet in Exile, 176.

I

India and China Dispute Boundary, 27.
India-China Divide, 14.
India-China Rivalry, 243.
Infrastructure Structure, 45.
International Relations, 217.

L

Line of Actual Control, 25, 42, 54, 55, 67, 86, 93, 102, 112, 118, 119, 125, 190, 191, 207, 218, 222, 233, 235, 238, 244.

M

MacDonald Line, 60, 79, 222, 237, 238, 239.
McMahon Line Border, 24.
Military Intransigence, 185.
Military Intransigence, 185, 186.
Mystery of the McMahan Line, 17.

N

Negotiating Strategies, 213.
Neville Maxwell, 1, 22, 71, 72, 75, 82, 112, 188, 223.

P

Peace-Building Measures, 116.
Policy on Tibet, 79, 155, 171, 172, 216.

R

Resolving the Boundary Dispute, 48.
Responsible for War, 78.

S

Sino-Indian Border Dispute, 93, 234.
Sino-Indian Relations, 42, 47, 53, 54, 96, 98, 99, 100, 101, 106, 107, 108, 111, 117, 122, 244, 245.
Sino-Indian War, 25, 28, 51, 52, 85, 190, 205, 215, 222, 223, 224, 225.
Strategic Interests, 14, 94, 156, 209, 227.
Symbiotic Relationship, 93.
Systems Theory, 108.

T

Territorial Disputes, 48, 49, 50.
Tibet in Exile, 176.
Tibet Policy, 127, 165, 166, 168, 170, 171, 173, 179.
Tibetan Nationalism, 177, 180, 181, 183.
Tibetan Resistance, 130, 141, 143, 144.
Toothless Agreement, 192.
Trans Karakoram Tract, 239.

❑❑❑